# ENVIRONMENTAL LAW

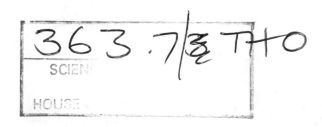

AUSTRALIA
LBC Information Services Ltd
Sydney


CANADA and USA
Carswell
Toronto


NEW ZEALAND
Brooker's
Auckland


SINGAPORE and MALAYSIA
Thomson Information (S.E. Asia)
Singapore

# ENVIRONMENTAL LAW

*Sweet & Maxwell's Textbook Series*

**Justine Thornton, M.A. (Cantab.)**
*Barrister*
**and**
**Silas Beckwith, LL.B. (Lond.)**
*Barrister, Lecturer in Law, London Guildhall University*

LONDON
SWEET & MAXWELL
1997

Published in 1997 by
Sweet & Maxwell Limited of
100 Avenue Road, London NW3 3PF
(http://www.smlawpub.co.uk)
Typeset by LBJ Enterprises Ltd,
Aldermaston and Chilcompton
Printed in Great Britain by
Clays Ltd, St. Ives plc.

No natural forests were destroyed to make this product;
only farmed timber was used and replanted.

A C.I.P. catalogue
record for this book
is available from
the British Library.

ISBN 0–421–571–500

# FOREWORD

Hardly anybody would disagree with the statement that the environment needs protection; this basic rule of the game in our society seems well recognised today. Opinions only differ on the question of how much protection the environment needs, how this protection should be organised and to what part of the society the rule of the game should apply: to England, to Northern Ireland, to Gibraltar, to the European Union, to the Falklands or to the whole planet?

We are at the beginnings of our discovery of environmental law, as it is and as it should be effectively to ensure protection. We try to find appropriate rules to prevent deterioration of this planet and to leave *urbem et orbem* in a better state than they were when we took over from our fathers.

The environmental law which is presented in this book focusses on the United Kingdom: indeed, the reader cannot hope to understand European Community or international environmental law, if he does not first know and understand the provisions which affect his own neighbourhood. Of course, provisions which preserve, protect and improve the quality of the environment are technical and sometimes difficult to understand. But the authors have taken particular care to make this a transparent and readable text.

Most of the law which is presented in this book is of a very recent date, and most of it is statute law. This is not surprising: environmental problems are first and foremost problems of the affluent society, which is very complex and complicated. And the number of environmental standards is increasing, simply by the fact that the emission of pollutants into the air, the water or the soil can no longer be seen as an activity which can take place uncontrolled: pollution becomes simply too expensive for this planet. Before anybody raises concern about too many environmental standards, he should first have a look into the number of technical standards, which BSI and other national and international standardisation bodies produce annually. In the European Community, we have more than fifty thousand standards!

This book is constructed in a way that enables the reader easily to find his way through the numerous and interdependent provisions which the authors so carefully and lucidly describe and I hope that he enjoys this reading. For me, it was sometimes a pure pleasure to go through the text and rediscover the structure of the law that tries to protect the environment. I cannot but hope that the success of this book encourages the authors to write more on environmental issues.

Ludwig Kramer
European Commission
Brussels

# PREFACE

This book is designed principally for law students, although we hope that it may be useful to those of other disciplines. It considers environmental law from domestic, European Community and international perspectives. Environmental law is a rapidly developing and often complex subject, which we have tried to present in an accessible form without sacrificing detail. We have endeavoured to state law and policy on the basis of materials available to us up to May 1, 1997. References to the U.K. government are therefore references to the Conservative government which held office prior to the 1997 general election.

Many people have helped us to write this book by providing inspiration, support and advice. The following people deserve particular thanks: John Bates; Malcolm Grant; Richard Ground (for his assistance with the Planning Law chapter); Hugo Jolliffe (for his assistance with the chapters dealing with E.C. and International Law), and Alex Mehta (for his assistance with Integrated Pollution Control).

Our primary debts of gratitude, however, are owed to one another. The book has been a joint effort from start to finish. As the task of writing the book has been shared equally between us, so too must be the responsibility for errors and for infelicities of style.

Justine Thornton and Silas Beckwith
June, 1997

# TABLE OF CONTENTS

# TABLE OF CASES

# Table of Statutes

# TABLE OF STATUTORY INSTRUMENTS

# TABLE OF E.C. LEGISLATION

# TABLE OF CONVENTIONS

# Chapter 1

## THE NATURE OF ENVIRONMENTAL LAW

*"The protection and preservation of the environment is now perceived as being of crucial importance to the future of mankind."*[1]

### Introduction

Over the course of this century, the relationship between human beings and the planet on which they live has changed fundamentally. At the beginning of the century, it was not possible for mankind and the technology upon which he relied to alter the environment radically. As the century draws to a close, however, huge increases both in population and in scientific knowledge have given us the power to make irrevocable changes to our planet.[2]

Each year, six million hectares of productive dryland turns into worthless desert. In 11 years, this will amount to an area the size of Saudi Arabia. Acid rain is destroying forests and lakes, and is damaging the cultural heritage of nations. By early next century, the effect of "greenhouse" gases may have increased average global temperatures enough to raise sea levels so that coastal cities are flooded. Other industrial gases threaten to deplete the planet's protective ozone shield, leading to a sharp rise in the number of human and animal cancers.

To appreciate the scale of what is taking place, it is instructive to consider things in this way: imagine that the hundreds of millions of years of our planet's history, during which natural resources have slowly been accumulating, is a period of one year. In other words, imagine that the world began on January 1st, and that it is now midnight, on December 31st. On this scale, the oldest known rocks appeared on February 25th, but the first plants did not begin growing until November 1st. Humans did not appear until December 29th. The industrial revolution, which has been responsible for most of mankind's exploitation of natural resources, took place only two seconds ago.[3]

The environment is the source of the energy and materials which mankind transforms into goods and services to meet his needs. It also acts as a vast sink for the wastes and polluting substances he generates. It provides a number of basic conditions

---

[1] *Cambridge Water Co. v. Eastern Counties Leather plc* [1994] 1 All E.R. 53, *per* Lord Goff.
[2] *Europe's Environment: The Dobris Assessment* (eds David Stanners and Philippe Bourdeau) (1996), The European Environment Agency.
[3] *ibid.*

1

needed for the existence of a successful economy — a stable climate, for example. Environmental resources form the basis of, and therefore set limits to, economic development. Many environmental problems are rooted in an increased demand for natural resources and in the increased pollution and waste associated with current patterns of economic development.

How much human-induced change can the world's environment sustain? Our understanding of environmental systems is still too limited to provide any conclusive answers. A number of warning signs, however, suggest that human activities have already irreparably damaged the environment in the name of economic development. This book examines one response to the challenge of reconciling environmental protection with economic growth — that of environmental law.

## Definition of "Environmental Law"

What is, or is not, properly the province of "environmental law" will depend very much on the definition of "environment" which we adopt. Perhaps the simplest and most memorable definition of "environment" is that given by Albert Einstein, who once said: "The environment is everything that isn't me".

If we adopt Einstein's definition, of course, there will be very little activity which does not have an "environmental" impact — the activities of prostitutes or muggers, for example, have a direct impact on our surroundings — yet laws which control these activities would not normally be regarded by lawyers as "environmental" law. In practical terms, what lawyers mean when they speak of "environmental law" is relatively clear: it is simply that body of law to which the label "environmental" has, to date, been attached. This body of law is concerned with protecting the natural resources of land, air and water (the three "environmental media") and the flora and fauna which inhabit them. However, whilst this labelling of certain human concerns as "environmental" and of others, by implication, as "non-environmental", can help to identify and clarify the issues, it can sometimes conceal the important fact that there is scarcely any area of human activity which does not impinge on the protection of environmental resources.

Like many legal terms, the term "environmental law" may be seen as having a central "core of meaning" surrounded by what may be called a "penumbra of uncertainty".[4] Within the core are to be found those laws relating to the protection of natural resources and people's enjoyment of them. Just outside the "core" are laws designed to protect the quality of life of particular groups of people — laws, for example, relating to sanitation in dwellings, or to the health and safety of employees. Such laws are more usually categorised by lawyers as "environmental health law". Further still outside the "core", but within the "penumbra", lie laws which protect society generally, such as laws relating to road traffic or vandalism. At the very edge of the "penumbra" are laws designed to protect and enhance people's commercial activities, such as the laws relating to consumer credit or to the carriage of goods by road, rail and sea. The latter, although not generally thought of in any sense as "environmental law", can have a profound impact on the protection and enjoyment of

[4] See Hart, *The Concept of Law* (1961).

natural resources because they affect people's perception of what is, or is not, an appropriate lifestyle, and this in turn has implications for the ways in which natural resources are managed.

## The Legal Definition of "Environment"

The uncertainty surrounding the proper scope of environmental law is reflected by the existence of various different legal definitions of "environment". For the purposes of U.K. law, the most relevant definition is to be found in the Environmental Protection Act 1990, which defines the "environment" as consisting of: ". . . all, or any, of the following media, namely the air, water and land . . ."

The International Convention on Civil Liability for Environmental Damage,[5] however, includes in its definition of "environment" natural resources both "biotic" and "abiotic", thus covering not only the natural environment but also the man-made environment, including man-made landscapes, buildings and objects which form part of man's cultural heritage. The definition also makes specific mention of the *interaction between* various elements of the environment. Thus, the "environment" includes the ways in which the environmental media interact with one another, and the ways in which they interact with the man-made environment and with the fauna and flora which inhabit them.

## Definition of "Pollution"

The legal regime in the U.K., which this book examines, is primarily concerned with the control of *pollution*. The term "pollution" is not directly defined in any of the major environmental statutes. One academic, however, has provided a useful definition as follows:

" . . . the introduction by man into the environment of substances or energy liable to cause hazards to human health, harm to living resources and ecological systems, damage to structures or amenity, or interference with legitimate use of the environment."[6]

This definition accords with that adopted by the E.C. in the Directive on Integrated Pollution Prevention and Control, which defines "pollution of the environment" as:

" . . . the direct or indirect introduction as a result of human activity, of substances, vibrations, heat or noise into the air, water or land which may be harmful to human health or the quality of the environment, result in damage to material, property, or impair or interfere with amenities and other legitimate uses of the environment."[7]

[5] Convention on Civil Liability for Damage Resulting from Activities Dangerous to the Environment, June 21, 1993, Lugano. 32 I.L.M. 1228 (1993).
[6] M. W. Holdgate, *A Perspective on Environmental Pollution* (1979).
[7] E.C. Council Directive 96/61, September 24, 1996, Art. 2(2) [1996] O.J. L257/26.

## Definition of "Harm"

It can be seen, then, that the concepts of "harm" and "damage" play a central rôle in defining pollution. Because of the subtle ways in which environmental factors interrelate, however, these concepts are not as simple as they may at first appear. Take as an example the deposit on land of toxic alkaline wastes by chemical manufacturers in Lancashire in the nineteenth century. Today, this would be regarded as a clear example of environmental harm. Nearby streams were rendered lifeless. The land on which the waste had been deposited could no longer support plant life. Gradually, however, rain and atmospheric carbon dioxide caused the calcium hydroxide on the surface of the land to disappear. This left an extremely limey soil containing few nutrients, in which a colony of beautiful orchids flourished, free from the competition of other plant life. These sites are now protected as the most important sites in the U.K. for orchids.[8]

The definition of "harm" in U.K. legislation is used as a mechanism to limit the extent of environmental regulation in given contexts. Thus, in the Environmental Protection Act 1990, the statutory regime relating to integrated pollution control (IPC) uses a wider definition of "harm" than does the regime which regulates contaminated land. For the purposes of the IPC regime, the Act states that "harm" means:

> " . . . harm to the health of living organisms or other interference with the ecological systems of which they form part and, in the case of man, includes offence caused to any of his senses or harm to his property; and 'harmless' has a corresponding meaning."[9]

A similar definition is employed for the purposes of the waste management regime.[10] Under the contaminated land regime, however, the reference to offence to the senses of man is omitted from the definition of "harm". Thus, certain matters, such as ruined views and unpleasant smells caused by contaminated land, are placed beyond the scope of regulation.[11]

## THE STRUCTURE OF THIS BOOK

Following this introductory chapter, the book begins with a chapter on international environmental law. Arguably the biggest environmental crises facing us at present (climate change, depletion of the ozone layer) are global in form. Any effective response to these problems must be an international one. The chapter starts by outlining the general nature of international law and then examines the history and development of international environmental law. It then offers an analysis of some of

---

[8] Mellanby, *Waste and Pollution — The Problem for Britain* (1992).
[9] EPA 1990, s.1(4).
[10] EPA 1990, s.29(5).
[11] EPA 1990, s.78A(4).

the principles which have emerged within the international environmental protection regime, in particular the concept of "sustainable development", which now finds expression in the U.K.'s own domestic pollution control regime. The third chapter outlines the principles of European Community environmental law and policy, and examines its effect on environmental law in the U.K. As we shall see, the influence of the E.C. on U.K. environmental law is great. It is not to be thought, however, that the flow of ideas is always one way. The U.K. Integrated Pollution Control regime, for example, has been "exported" to Europe and has been responsible for shaping E.C. policy.

The chapters which follow are concerned with the U.K. environmental protection regime. The bulk of environmental regulation in the U.K. is derived from statute. Historically, however, the common law has sometimes functioned to combat environmental problems, particularly through the tort of nuisance and through actions under the rule in *Rylands v. Fletcher*, both of which are examined in Chapter 4. Chapter 5 examines the contribution made by planning law to environmental protection. The U.K. planning regime is amongst the most sophisticated in the world, and, because environmental protection and land development are inextricably linked, an understanding of how the planning system works is vital to an appreciation of the specific environmental controls which it supplements.

The remaining chapters consider the specifics of the U.K. statutory regime in relation to the three environmental media. Chapter 6 examines the integrated pollution control regime, which was introduced by the Environmental Protection Act 1990. The notable feature of this regime is that it attempts to tackle the effects of polluting substances in all three media together. An integrated and holistic approach to environmental problems is increasingly becoming a dominant feature of modern environmental policy. This has been reflected in the U.K. by the recent centralisation of the many regulatory agencies involved in environmental protection by the creation of the Environment Agency (see below). The idea of an integrated approach, however, is not yet so developed as to remove the need for media-specific environmental controls. These are examined in Chapters 7, 8, 9 and 10, whilst Chapters 11 and 12 deal, respectively, with the problems of noise pollution and of nature conservation, both of which have in recent years been the subject of much passionate debate.

## THE HISTORY AND DEVELOPMENT OF ENVIRONMENTAL REGULATION IN THE U.K.

Laws to protect mankind from the environmental effects of his activities can be traced to medieval times. In 1273, Edward I, in order to protect the health of his subjects, issued a decree prohibiting the burning of sea coal. Another proclamation forbidding the use of coal (at times when Parliament was sitting) was later issued by Elizabeth I, who caused one offender to be executed. It was not until after the Industrial Revolution, however, in the latter half of the nineteenth century, that any significant body of environmental law developed.

The unpleasant social conditions created by pollution, overcrowding and disease provided the stimulus for legal regulation. The tort of nuisance, which had existed since medieval times, was the first legal response. Its focus on the protection of individual property rights, however, made it an inefficient and inappropriate solution for the wide-ranging social consequences of industrialisation. The need for more effective controls prompted the intervention of Parliament. In 1863, Britain established a nation-wide system of air pollution control. The Alkali Act 1863 created the Alkali Inspectorate, which was the world's first pollution control agency. Water pollution was regulated by a statute of 1861, and by more comprehensive legislation in 1876. Legislation to deal with nuisances, such as the deposit of waste, was introduced in the late 1840s and was consolidated in the Public Health Act 1875 and subsequently in the Public Health Act 1936.

Early environmental legislation was the product of *ad hoc* reactions to specific environmental problems as they occurred, and reflected little by way of preventive policy. With the exception of the Alkali Inspectorate, control over pollution was exercised at a local level by municipal authorities. Legislation was not, as it is today, motivated partly by a desire to protect the environment for its own sake and to preserve it for the future of mankind. Rather, it grew out of the immediate and pressing need to do something about the insanitary living conditions of an industrialising nation. Moreover, in the nineteenth century, the dominant philosophy was one of mankind's triumph over nature by science and technology. The relatively small population, and the limits of industrial technology, meant that depletion of natural resources was not seen as a problem. Natural resources were there to be exploited. During the latter half of the century, however, a very gradual change in this attitude started to take place, reflecting an awareness that man was merely one constituent part of a global ecosystem. It is only in the latter half of the twentieth century, however, that the idea that this ecosystem might place significant limits on the activities of mankind has been fully recognised.

Environmental law in the U.K. may be said to have come of age in the 1970s. Hitherto, legislation relevant to the environment had largely been directed towards public health and the safety of employees. In 1972, however, an international conference on the environment, held in Stockholm, promoted the idea that the environment was to be seen as an entity in itself which required protection, and since that date protection of the natural environment has become one of the central objectives of the international legal system.[12] 1972 was also the year in which the U.K. joined the European Community. The E.C.'s programme of action on the environment has been one of its most successful ventures and has stimulated the U.K.'s legal response to environmental problems. Modern environmental legislation, then, is characterised by a move away from the protection of individuals to the prevention of environmental pollution generally. Recent environmental statutes demonstrate a more coherent and integrated response to environmental degradation than did their predecessors, in particular because they address the problem of balancing the need for environmental protection against the need for economic growth.

---

[12] Michael Bowman, "Environmental Litigation and the International Legal System", (1995) *Environmental Liability*.

# THE PATTERN OF MODERN ENVIRONMENTAL REGULATION

## Sources of Environmental Law

### Legislation

As has been said, the principal source of environmental law in the U.K. is legislation. The common law fulfils only a minor and residual rôle in environmental protection. The Environmental Protection Act 1990 regulates industrial emissions, waste management, nuisances, litter and genetically modified organisms. The Water Resources Act 1991 regulates the pollution of water and the management of water resources, whilst the Water Industry Act 1991 is concerned with the supply of water and the handling of sewage. The Town and Country Planning Act 1990 contains most of the legislation relating to land development, whilst the conservation of nature is regulated principally by the Wildlife and Countryside Act 1981. The Environment Act 1995 establishes a statutory regime for dealing with contaminated land and provides the basis for national strategies on air quality and waste management. It also establishes the Environment Agency as the unified administrative body for environmental matters in England and Wales.

Much of the legislation referred to above may be thought of as "framework" legislation. That is to say, there is a tendency for the statutes in question to set out general broad principles and then to leave the everyday rules needed for the implementation of those principles to be published as delegated legislation in the form of statutory instruments, or (as is the case with the contaminated land regime) in the form of government guidance drawn up by the Secretary of State and approved by Parliament. Byelaws — for example those made by the Countryside Commission with respect to rights of way over its land — are another frequently used form of delegated legislation.

Unlike the validity of statutes, the validity of delegated legislation may, on an application for judicial review, be challenged in the courts on the basis that it is *ultra vires* (in other words that the statute under which the delegated legislation has been made does not allow for the making of a particular rule). The marked dependence of modern environmental statutes on delegated legislation has meant that judicial review, which is considered more fully below, has played a key rôle in the development of U.K. environmental law.

The advantage of delegated legislation for environmental law is that it can be made quickly by the Secretary of State, without the need for lengthy Parliamentary procedures, in order to respond to new environmental problems — for example, the discovery that a substance hitherto thought to be safe is causing environmental problems. Such flexibility is vital to the rapid development of environmental law, which requires continual modification in the light of scientific knowledge. The disadvantage of secondary legislation, however, is that it reduces democratic accountability because, although statutory instruments may be scrutinised and overturned by the courts, they are made without the line-by-line scrutiny of Parliament which characterises the passing of a statute.

## *Other rules*

Other rules on the environment are to be found in Circulars, Codes of Practice and Policy Guidance Notes. Compliance with the rules contained in these "quasi-legal" or "informal" documents is not directly enforceable by criminal or civil proceedings and the precise legal status of them depends upon the statutory provisions that give rise to the rules which they contain and upon judicial interpretation of those statutory provisions.[13] This will vary from case to case. A common statutory requirement, however, is for a regulatory body to "have regard to" certain matters contained in these documents. It may be said, broadly speaking, that where an administrative body makes a decision without having regard to those matters, an action for judicial review will lie to compel that body to reconsider its decision.

## Sources of Environmental Policy

Command papers, and reports by the Royal Commission on Environmental Pollution, are important sources of environmental policy. Command papers are documents prepared by the government, outlining policy on matters of general interest to Parliament and to the public. Royal Commissions perform an investigative rôle for the government. They undertake a serious and lengthy analysis of problems which Parliament does not have the time fully to consider. They aim to provide an expertise and an impartiality, unaffected by transient political considerations, which can be lacking in Parliamentary debates.[14]

## THE BODIES RESPONSIBLE FOR ENVIRONMENTAL REGULATION

### The Department of the Environment

The Department of the Environment has primary responsibility for environmental matters, although other government departments, in particular the Department of Transport and the Ministry of Agriculture, Fisheries and Food, are required as a matter of policy, and sometimes by statute (for example, if and when they give directions to the Environment Agency[15]) to take account of environmental considerations in formulating policy. The Department of the Environment is concerned not only with originating environmental policy, but with clarifying and ensuring the proper implementation of existing legislation, for example by issuing Circulars and Planning Policy Guidance Notes (PPGs). The Department is headed by the Secretary of State for the Environment.

---

[13] See generally the observations of R.E. Megarry in (1949) L.Q.R. Vol. 60, p. 125.
[14] See Clokie and Robinson, *Royal Commissions of Inquiry* (1937).
[15] EA 1995, s.7.

## The Secretary of State

As has been said, the Secretary of State is responsible for issuing environmental regulations in the form of statutory instruments under powers granted to him by the various environmental statutes. In addition, his function may be seen as that of enforcing the statutory duties of those responsible for taking environmental decisions and of ensuring that those decisions are properly taken. He has a general power to direct the Environment Agency in the exercise of its functions,[16] together with a number of more specific supervisory powers. Thus, for example, under the Integrated Pollution Control regime, the Secretary of State may give the Environment Agency directions as to whether or not to grant particular authorisations for the carrying on of certain activities.[17] He also has power to "call in" applications for authorisations and to decide them for himself (a task he usually delegates to an inspector) or to cause a local inquiry to be held.[18] He has a similar power in relation to applications for planning permission[19] and can revoke or modify planning permission in certain circumstances.[20] He also has the power to make Nature Conservation Orders which impose restrictions on the rights of landowners. Under the statutes, the Secretary of State is also responsible for determining appeals by persons who are aggrieved by decisions made by the Environment Agency or by other bodies responsible for environmental decision-making.

## The Environment Agency

The creation of the Environment Agency, which came into being in April 1996, reflects a growing trend towards the centralisation of environmental control and may be seen as a recognition of the fact that the integrated nature of environmental problems means that they cannot be effectively resolved at a local level. In announcing the creation of the Agency at the *Sunday Times* Environment Exhibition in London in July 1991, the Prime Minister said: "It is right the integrity and indivisibility of the environment should be reflected in a unified agency."

The Agency represents an amalgam of three bodies which had previously been responsible for environmental regulation: the National Rivers Authority (previously responsible for regulating pollution of watercourses); Her Majesty's Inspectorate of Pollution (which was responsible for administering the integrated pollution control regime), and the Waste Regulation Authorities (which, operating at a local level, administered the waste management regime). The Agency, however, does not have a monopoly in the field of environmental regulation. Other bodies, such as local authorities, Waste Collection Authorities, the Countryside Commission and the Nature Conservancy Councils, continue to fulfil important rôles.

---

[16] EA 1995, s.40.
[17] EPA 1990, s.6(5).
[18] EPA 1990, Sched. 1, para. 3.
[19] TCPA 1990, s.77.
[20] TCPA 1990, s.100.

## Functions of the Agency

The Environment Agency has a number of different functions:

- It grants licences to deal with waste;

- It gives "discharge consents" to discharge substances into waterways;

- It grants "authorisations" to operate industrial processes regulated by the integrated pollution control regime;

- It supervises the operation of these licensed activities;

- It maintains a body of inspectors who investigate alleged breaches of the environmental licensing regime and decide whether or not to prosecute offenders.

The Agency, then, is mainly concerned with pollution control. Its functions in this regard are exercisable for the purpose of: " . . . preventing or minimising, or remedying or mitigating the effects of, pollution of the environment."[21] Although pollution control is the Agency's primary function, it also has some responsibility for nature conservation.

In formulating proposals which relate to the Agency's *pollution control* functions, Ministers and the Agency merely have a duty to "have regard to the desirability of" conserving and enhancing natural beauty and the conservation of flora, fauna and geological or physiographical features of special interest.[22]

In formulating any proposals which relate to any functions of the Agency *other than the exercise of its pollution control functions*, however, the Ministers and the Agency have a *duty* to: " . . . further the conservation and enhancement of natural beauty and the conservation of flora and fauna . . . [etc.]"[23]

The reason for this difference, as Viscount Ullswater explained during the passage of the legislation, is that: "To further conservation in every case would be inconsistent with the Agency's rôle in issuing environmental licences."[24]

The government was worried that a positive duty to further conservation in the exercise of its pollution control functions might cause problems for the Agency, in particular by providing the basis for its licensing decisions to be challenged by way of judicial review. As Sir Kenneth Carlisle M.P. explained in committee in the House of Commons:

> "For example, the Environment Agency might licence a new process, which pollutes less than the existing technology that it will replace. As pollution of any sort cannot further nature conservation, the Agency might have to turn the application down even though the new process would lead to less pollution."[25]

---

[21] EA 1995, s.5(1).
[22] EA 1995, s.7(1)(b).
[23] EA 1995, s.7(1)(a).
[24] *Hansard*, H.L., March 2, 1995, col. 1659.
[25] *Hansard*, H.C., May 11, 1995, col. 193.

## The Agency's Principal Aim

The Environmental Protection Act 1995 provides:

> "It shall be the principal aim of the Agency . . . so to protect and enhance the environment, taken as a whole, as to make . . . [a] . . . contribution towards attaining the objective of sustainable development . . . "[26]

The way in which this aim is to be achieved is qualified in two important respects:

(a) It is to be fulfilled "subject to the provisions of this Act or any other enactment". This means that where legislation requires the Agency to deviate from its duty to protect and enhance the environment, the requirements of the legislation will prevail;

(b) In exercising its functions, the Agency must take into account any likely costs.

The Environment Act 1995 provides that in exercising its statutory powers, or in deciding on the manner in which those powers are to be exercised, the Agency is required to: " . . . take into account the likely costs and benefits of the exercise or non-exercise of the power or its exercise in the manner in question."[27]

During the passage of the Environment Act, concern was expressed that if the duty to consider costs were to apply to all of the Agency's activities, it might prove to be an obstacle to environmental protection because it would allow for the judicial review of almost any decision which the Agency made on the basis that a full and detailed cost-benefit analysis had not been undertaken. This view, however, was not shared by the government. As Viscount Ullswater explained, the government was: " . . . not seeking to impose on the Agency a requirement to undertake a full cost-benefit analysis before it acts in any case or to follow slavishly the results of such analysis."[28]

His Lordship expressed the view that because it is not always possible precisely to quantify costs and benefits in relation to environmental protection, the legislation would not mean that the Agency could act only where it could demonstrate an excess of benefit over cost. Rather, the legislation meant that the Agency would be required to take some account of costs in exercising its functions, but that this must not interfere with its ability to ensure effective environmental protection, management and enhancement.

## Local Authorities

Local authorities continue to have important functions in relation to the environment. In particular, they are responsible for administering the air pollution regime in Part I of the Environmental Protection Act 1990, which applies to industrial processes which

---

[26] EA 1995, s.4(1).
[27] EA 1995, s.39.
[28] *Hansard*, H.L., 1995, Vol. 561, col. 1384.

have not been prescribed for integrated pollution control. In addition, they are responsible for administering the statutory nuisance regime and for making planning decisions within their areas. They also have important and complex functions in relation to contaminated land.

## A COHERENT LEGAL REGIME

As has been noted, environmental law originated as a collection of rules that grew up sporadically as a haphazard and piecemeal response to environmental problems. Over the last 25 years, however, environmental law has begun to develop the coherence associated with more sophisticated legal regimes. Coherence in a legal regime may be said to come from the fact that the everyday rules of the regime are underpinned by a set of principles, and that these principles are in turn underpinned by an ethical philosophy.[29]

## Diagram 1: "A Coherent Legal Regime"

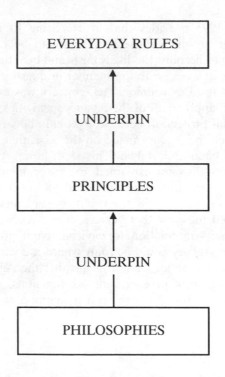

Each of the three tiers of this model is examined in turn below.

### (1) The "everyday rules"

An analysis of the rules used to protect the environment reveals that two distinct approaches are adopted: the *preventive* and the *remedial* approach.

[29] Hughes, "The Status of the 'Precautionary Principle' in Law", (1995) J.E.L. Vol. 7(2).

Preventive rules aim to stop pollution before it happens, for example by setting limits on the concentrations of particular pollutants which are permitted to enter the environment, or by curtailing certain industrial activities and uses of land which have the potential to cause pollution. The operation of the planning system is an example of the preventive approach. The E.C.'s Environmental Impact Assessment Directive requires Member States to adopt measures to ensure that, before consent is given, projects likely to have significant environmental effects by virtue of their nature, size, or location are subjected to a formal assessment of those effects. The U.K. government has chosen to implement this Directive through the planning system.

Remedial rules, on the other hand, are aimed at cleaning up pollution after it has occurred, punishing the polluter, ensuring that he pays the costs of clean-up and compensating people who have suffered as a result of pollution. The use of the criminal law to protect the environment is an example of a remedial control, with its emphasis on punishing the polluter. The operation of the common law is also primarily remedial. All remedial controls, however, are of course preventive in so far as they serve as a deterrent to potential polluters.

The various statutes which control pollution make use of both preventive and remedial controls. They are preventive, for example, because they require licences to be granted before substances can be released into the environment. They are remedial because they make use of the criminal law to punish an offender and to compel him to clean up his pollution. The statutes also provide for the granting of injunctions. The injunction is hybrid in character in that, by restricting an activity which is giving rise to a pollution problem and at the same time preventing its recurrence, it contains an element of both prevention and cure.

The "everyday rules" of environmental law derive from a number of different sources, namely the common law, planning legislation (primary and delegated), specific environmental legislation (primary and delegated) and explanatory guidance. Whilst it is possible to classify the rules according to their source, it is also possible to classify them in terms of the *branch of the law which is used to enforce them*. Thus, the environmental protection regime is enforced through the law of tort, through the criminal law, and through the operation of administrative law. The use of the law of tort for environmental protection is considered in Chapter 4. The remaining branches of law are considered briefly below.

## *The Criminal Law*

The criminal law is widely used to enforce the U.K. pollution control regime. Its use symbolises society's moral condemnation of environmentally harmful activities, but is not without its problems. Concern is growing that existing mechanisms for enforcing the criminal law may not be entirely appropriate in environmental matters. For example, in prosecutions in which it is alleged that a company has failed to use the "best available techniques not entailing excessive cost"[30] in order to reduce pollution, jurors or lay magistrates, inevitably inexperienced in such matters, are asked to adjudicate on the merits of various competing industrial technologies. The evidence will often be highly technical and the decision will involve a consideration of the

---

[30] EPA 1990, s.23.

appropriate balance to be struck between economic and environmental factors. It has been suggested that in such circumstances, decision-making may be neither consistent nor of a high standard.[31] Upon this decision, however, may rest not only the commercial reputation of the techniques involved, but ultimately the liberty of the company's managers and directors.

It may also be questioned whether the criminal law is appropriate for dealing with cases of "historic pollution" in which the accused, at the time when he set in motion the train of events which have now led to his prosecution, was acting in accordance with the law as it then stood. This type of criminal liability, which can arise under the contaminated land regime (discussed in Chapter 7), would seem to offend against the constitutional principle that the limits of the criminal law should be known in advance.

## Administrative Law

Administrative law is emerging as a vital element of the regulatory framework of environmental law. Environmental legislation, like planning legislation, grants a formidable array of powers to the Secretary of State and to other regulatory bodies. Judicial review provides the primary mechanism by which decisions by these bodies can be challenged by individuals and pressure groups. As has been noted, the heavy reliance of modern environmental law on "framework" legislation, fleshed out by guidance, regulations and the decisions of the enforcing authorities, means that a great many of the everyday rules for environmental protection are made without the scrutiny of Parliament. Scrutiny of these rules must therefore be undertaken by the courts, which ensure, through the mechanism of judicial review, that the authorities properly perform their duties and do not exceed or abuse their powers, or in other words, that they act in accordance with the principles of administrative law.

The courts have developed a number of such principles. They will review an exercise of power to ensure that a public body has not misinterpreted the law, that it has considered all factors relevant to its decision, that it has not taken into account any irrelevant factors, that it has acted for a purpose expressly or impliedly authorised by statute, and that it has not acted in a way that is so unreasonable that no reasonable body would so have acted. In addition, the court will ensure that the authority has observed the procedural requirements set out in the statute, that the decision taken by the authority is proportional to the problem it is trying to solve, and that the principles of fairness or natural justice have been observed.[32]

Recent developments in the law have increased the usefulness of judicial review as a mechanism for environmental protection. In order to have *locus standi* to bring an action for judicial review, the applicant must demonstrate that he has a "sufficient interest" in the matter to which the application relates. Prior to 1994, the courts, in applying this test, were reluctant to grant *locus standi* to environmental pressure groups to bring judicial review proceedings, for fear that this might open the floodgates to a multiplicity of claims which would place a burden on the courts. Thus, in *R. v. Secretary of State, ex p. Rose Theatre Trust Co.*,[33] an interest group specifically

---

[31] See Harris, "The Environmental Protection Act 1990: Penalising the Polluter" [1992] J.P.E.L. 515.
[32] See Clive Lewis, *Judicial Remedies in Public Law* (1992).
[33] [1990] 1 Q.B. 504.

formed to defend the remains of an Elizabethan theatre was refused standing on the basis that, as individuals, none of the group had any special interest in the matter above and beyond the general interest of the public. In 1994, however, the rules of *locus standi* were relaxed. In *R v. Pollution Inspectorate, ex p. Greenpeace (No. 2)*,[34] Otton J. was prepared to allow Greenpeace standing to challenge a government decision to grant permission for the handling of nuclear waste. He held that Greenpeace had a sufficient interest in the matter because it was a well-established and responsible body, acknowledged as such by international agencies, and because its members included many people living in the area of the proposed activities who would be affected by them. Otton J. took the view that Greenpeace could assist the court by providing expertise, and noted that if Greenpeace were refused standing, there might be no other way in which the issues in question could be brought to the attention of a court.

Judicial review, however, is limited in what it can achieve. The rôle of the court is confined to ensuring that public authorities perform their functions properly. The court cannot substitute its own views on the merits of a decision for the views of a public authority. This point was emphasised by Smith J. in *R v. Secretary of State for Trade and Industry, ex p. Duddridge*.[35] The case concerned an application for judicial review brought on behalf of three children whose parents were concerned that electric cables laid as part of the national grid would emit non-ionising radiation which would enter their homes and schools and expose them to the risk of developing leukaemia. Smith J. stated:

> "It is important to make clear at the outset that it is not the function of this court to decide whether there is in fact an increased risk of leukaemia . . . The Court appreciates that the parents of these children are deeply concerned about these issues and it is not through any lack of sympathy with that concern that the court must decline to decide them. The only issue before the court is whether the Secretary of State acted unlawfully."

The courts, however, are not necessarily well suited to assume a rôle other than the one which they have at present. In legislating and in making decisions, the Secretary of State or other regulatory agency will rely on information from a variety of sources such as industry, academics, environmental groups and consumer protection groups. The objectivity of each group's viewpoint must be assessed. It is likely that a number of technical questions will need to be considered. The costs of enforcement must be taken into account, as must the effects of the legislation or decision on market competition. The final decision, then, will inevitably represent a compromise between the viewpoints held by a number of relevant groups.

The institutional constraints on the courts mean that they cannot hope to have the same information available to them. Although a court has access to the sources of the law, in factual matters it is often limited to consideration of a record created by those over whom it has no control. Moreover, it has only a limited amount of time in which to get to grips with technical facts. In the light of these factors, then, and quite apart

---

[34] [1994] 1 W.L.R. 570.
[35] (1995) J.E.L. Vol. 7(2) 224.

from the constitutional doctrine of the "separation of the powers", it is perhaps right that the court's rôle should be confined merely to asking whether the public authority's actions are consistent with the principles of administrative law.[36]

## (2) The principles on which environmental regulation is based

U.K. environmental law, influenced by the E.C, is beginning to develop a set of principles which underpin its rules. All of these principles were initially developed outside the U.K. and are therefore explored more fully in the chapters on International and European Community law. The importance of the principles was acknowledged by the U.K. government in its first comprehensive White Paper on the environment, entitled "This Common Inheritance: Britain's Environmental Strategy",[37] which was published in 1990. The principles may be stated as follows:

- "Sustainable development";
- The "preventive principle";
- The "polluter pays principle";
- The "precautionary principle".

Although there is widespread agreement that these words do indeed constitute principles of environmental law, there is much less agreement on what, precisely, the words mean.

### The Precautionary Principle

An examination of the "precautionary principle" serves to illustrate the uncertainty which surrounds all of the principles. The government has interpreted the principle as follows:[38]

"Where there are significant risks of damage to the environment, the government will be prepared to take precautionary action to limit the use of potentially dangerous materials or the spread of potentially dangerous pollutants even where scientific evidence is not conclusive, if the balance of likely costs and benefits justifies it."

The meaning of the principle was considered in *R. v. Secretary of State for Trade and Industry, ex p. Duddridge*.[39] As has been said, this was an action for judicial review by the parents of three children concerned that their exposure to power cables would increase the risk of leukaemia. The applicants submitted that the government had misunderstood the precautionary principle by setting the threshold of preventive action

---

[36] See Justice Stephen Breyer, Supreme Court of the U.S., *Institutions for Regulating Risk*, 1995.
[37] *This Common Inheritance*, Cm. 1200 (1990).
[38] *ibid*.
[39] (1995) J.E.L. Vol. 7(2) 224, Q.B.D.

where a *significant* risk of damage arises. They argued that the principle required action to be taken as soon any *possible* risk was demonstrated. In rejecting this argument, the court observed that:

> "There is at present no comprehensive and authoritative definition of the precautionary principle. It is an expression which has in recent years been used in a number of international declarations and treaties to some of which the U.K. is a party . . . in none of these documents is the principle comprehensively defined."

Smith J. was of the view that the principle: " . . . is primarily intended to avoid long term harm to the environment itself rather than damage to human health from transitory environmental conditions."

Perhaps all that can be said with certainty about the precautionary principle is that:

> "[It] is a culturally framed concept that takes its cue from changing social conceptions about the appropriate rôle of science, economics, ethics, politics and the law in pro-active environmental protection and management. [It] is a rather shambolic concept muddled in policy advice and subject to the whims of international diplomacy and the unpredictable public mood over the true costs of sustainable living."[40]

## (3) The philosophies behind environmental regulation

The principles of environmental law are formulated on the basis of certain philosophical ideas about the purpose of protecting the environment. To a large extent, then, the difficulties inherent in interpreting the principles are due to a lack of coherence in these underlying philosophies, and to a lack of consensus about which of a number of different philosophical approaches is appropriate. Arguably, judgments in environmental cases reveal the existence of a number of contrasting philosophies. Broadly speaking, there may be said to be three different philosophical viewpoints underlying the principles of environmental law. These are, respectively, the "anthropocentric", the "biocentric", and the "ecocentric" viewpoints.

*"Anthropocentric" values*

The basic tenet of anthropocentric thought is that mankind is inherently separate from the rest of nature, and that natural resources are to be exploited for the benefit of mankind. The welfare of mankind is therefore to be accorded primary importance in any regime for environmental protection. Conservation of natural resources and environmental amenities is justified on the basis of "stewardship", that is to say, present generations should hold environmental assets in trust for future generations of mankind. The conservation of flora and fauna is justified only on the basis of the scientific and aesthetic benefits which it brings to mankind. Lord Goff's words, which began this chapter, reveal an anthropocentric approach to environmental protection.

---

[40] *Interpreting the Precautionary Principle* (eds Tim O'Riordan and James Cameron), p. 23.

### "Biocentric" values

Those who adhere to a biocentric viewpoint argue that, in any scheme for environmental protection, animals should have rights which are equal to those of humans. On this view, animals are not at the service of mankind. Rather they co-exist with him in nature and are deserving of protection for their own sake.

### "Ecocentric" values

Ecocentric thought is more radical. It adopts a holistic approach to the environment and holds that humans, animals and plants have value only as part of an ecological system. Natural ecosystems are therefore seen as having an intrinsic value, irrespective of the existence of animals and mankind. Plants are thought to have an intrinsic right to protection which is independent from the uses to which they are put by animals and human beings. This kind of "deep ecology" does not necessarily rule out human intervention in nature, but it does require that such intervention should be strongly justified if it presents any risk of upsetting the existing balance of the ecosystem. Traditional materialist values are seen as of little importance, and all human members of the ecosystem are thought to have a responsibility to participate in preserving its well-being. Ecocentric thought might, perhaps, be identified in the judgments of Lord Denning, whose reasoning often displays a romantic view of nature and of the interdependence between nature and mankind.[41]

Early environmental protection measures, designed to alleviate insanitary living conditions, were motivated solely by an anthropocentric approach. The terminology of recent statutes, however, *may* reflect a shift away from this position. We have noted that the Environmental Protection Act 1990 defines "harm" as including " . . . harm to the health of *living organisms* or other interference with the *ecological systems* of which they form part". We have also noted that Smith J., in *ex p. Dudderidge*,[42] recently analysed the precautionary principle in terms of avoiding harm to the "*environment itself*". What is unclear, however, is whether this apparent shift in statutory language and in judicial reasoning is to be explained simply in terms of preserving the environment for future generations of mankind (an "anthropocentric" viewpoint), or whether it reflects a move towards biocentric, or even ecocentric thought.

## TECHNIQUES FOR ENVIRONMENTAL REGULATION

This book examines *one* response of society to the need for environmental protection — the response embodied in environmental law. This response is to be distinguished from other societal responses — civil disobedience, political campaigning, or the voluntary adoption of environmentally friendly lifestyles, for example. A number of responses to environmental problems are possible. Although most of these responses will require legal intervention if they are to be put into effect, this is not true in every case. The various ways in which *governments,* as opposed to individual members of the public, can respond to environmental problems may be identified as follows:

---

[41] See, for example, *New Windsor Corporation v. Mellor* [1975] Ch. 380.
[42] (1995) J.E.L. Vol. 7(2) 224, Q.B.D.

- By simply educating the public about environmental issues and leaving it to them to decide on an appropriate lifestyle;

- By relying on market forces to dictate environmentally friendly lifestyles;

- By using economic instruments (taxes on certain forms of behaviour) to encourage environmentally friendly lifestyles;

- By passing legislation which prohibits or restricts certain forms of environmentally harmful behaviour (the so-called "command and control" technique).

All of these techniques find expression to some extent within U.K. environmental policy, although the last of these — that of command and control — is by far the most pervasive. This technique also requires the greatest amount of legal intervention in order for it to be implemented. It is an examination of the laws which implement the command and control technique, then, to which most of this book is devoted. Environmental education, however, may be facilitated by legal intervention, and legal intervention is necessary, of course, to give effect to economic and fiscal policy.

## Education and Information

Public access to environmental information is a key aspect of environmental protection. If people are in possession of the relevant facts, they are well placed to make their own decisions about the importance of environmental amenities and to exert pressure for change as consumers, investors, lobbyists and electors. The solutions to environmental problems are not usually straightforward. They require decisions to be made about lifestyle. A new industrial process, for example, may create jobs and national wealth but diminish the quality of the landscape or the air we breathe. Economic growth and environmental protection are both desirable, but often cannot be achieved simultaneously. In a democratic society, balancing these conflicting desires can best be resolved through public participation in the decision-making process, so that a fair balance may be struck between the interests of different parties.

All of the media-specific pollution control regimes in the U.K., as well as the integrated pollution control regime, require the enforcing authorities to maintain public registers containing detailed information about the various parties who have applied for licences to carry out polluting activities and the activities to which those licences relate. In theory, public scrutiny of these registers can provide ammunition for lay critics of the regimes. In practice, however, the registers are seldom consulted by ordinary members of the public. Another feature of the regimes is that applications for licences to pollute must be advertised in newspapers, and that representations from interested members of the public must be entertained before licences can be granted.

Whilst it is obvious that the attitudes of the public can initiate laws for environmental protection, what is less obvious, perhaps, is that *the passing of environmental laws can shape the attitudes of the public*. Environmental protection measures which necessitate very small (and therefore politically acceptable) changes in lifestyle (the use of lead-free petrol, for example) serve to heighten the public's awareness of environmental problems generally with the result that, over time, society becomes conditioned into accepting ever more stringent controls on the understanding that they are of benefit. At this stage in its development, then, environmental law might be said to be as much about environmental *education* as it is about environmental *protection*. That this is so is clearly recognised in E.C. and U.K. policy, which attaches great importance to the public availability of environmental information.

## Reliance on Market Forces

It is widely recognised that a non-interventionist approach to environmental regulation, which relies on market forces alone to dictate environmentally-friendly lifestyles, is insufficient to produce the level of environmental protection which the electorate expects. The reason why this is so is that there is no "market", in a traditional sense, for environmental amenities like clean air, clean water and unspoilt countryside. Traditionally, environmental resources have been treated as "free goods" of which there is a virtually unlimited supply. The problem with this attitude, however, is that treating goods as if they are in infinite supply will create an infinite demand for them. We know that the actual supply of environmental amenities is being diminished daily by polluting activities, and that it will, at some point in the future, be incapable of satisfying this demand. In time, of course, a non-interventionist approach to the environment, coupled with a diminishing supply of environmental amenities, would allow for the development of a traditional market in those amenities. Arguably, such a market is already developing in relation to drinking water, which in many parts of the world must be bought in bottles. But to allow such a situation to develop, for example, in relation to air for breathing, would be highly undesirable.

## Economic Instruments

Economic instruments can be used to control the operation of the free market where this would produce adverse environmental consequences. The most obvious example of the use of an economic instrument in the U.K., perhaps, is the tax incentive given to users of unleaded petrol. A tax on waste disposal by landfill, the proceeds of which are to be used to reduce national insurance contributions, has also recently come into effect. The government's view, expressed in its 1990 White Paper,[43] is that economic instruments are a viable and effective alternative to command and control regulation. They have the advantage of allowing producers and consumers, rather than government regulators, to decide, through the mechanism of market choice, the extent to which environmental protection is to be secured.

Several European countries, including Denmark, Norway and the Netherlands, have introduced wide-ranging pollution taxes. Sweden's use of fiscal incentives to encourage cleaner diesel has drastically reduced emissions of sulphur dioxide, a cause of acid rain. The international community debated the concept of economic instruments when formulating the 1992 UN Framework Convention on Climate Change, where the concept of "emission credits" was discussed. It was suggested that, within individual States, companies might meet their obligations to limit emissions of greenhouse gases

---

[43] *This Common Inheritance*, Cm. 1200 (1990).

in two ways: they could either reduce their emissions to the required standard, or they could "buy in" emission credits from other companies who had reduced their emissions to below the required standard, and so had some "spare" permission to pollute.

Economic instruments seek to put a "price" on environmental amenities (like the clean air which is polluted by leaded petrol). Ideally, this "price" will reflect the true "environmental costs" of the activities to which it is applied. However, because these costs can seldom, if ever, be accurately defined (for reasons which are illustrated below), economic instruments are used simply as a device for discouraging environmentally harmful behaviour and for encouraging other forms of behaviour.

## Valuing the Environment

One of the principal difficulties for environmental policy-makers who wish to make use of economic instruments has been to find a way of valuing the environment. It is clear that most people do attach some "value" to the availability of a clean environment. The precise extent to which this is so, however, is very difficult to measure; this is because people have grown accustomed to using *money* as a measure of their well-being. The environment does not lend itself to being valued in money terms because, as has been said, environmental amenities like clean air and clean water, have traditionally been regarded as "free goods" for which no-one has to pay.

Economists, however, have taken the view that it is desirable, if possible, to attach a monetary value to environmental amenities. Only when this is done, it is argued, will society, which is wedded to the idea of measuring its well-being in terms of material wealth, be able to make informed choices about sacrificing traditional indicators of prosperity for environmental benefits. It is important to value the environment in money terms so that environmental benefits (like clean air or clean water) can be compared not only with each other, but with other benefits (like fast cars) which have an ascertainable money value. The idea is that if particular environmental amenities were to have an ascertained "price", it would then be possible for that "price" to be added to the market price of goods, in the form of a tax, so that the amount which the consumer paid for the goods would reflect the true "environmental costs" of their production and use.

Whilst the idea of valuing environmental amenities so as to give them a market price is immensely attractive, it has, in practical terms, been virtually impossible to implement. This is because of the sheer number of different factors which need to be taken into account in calculating "environmental costs". There is also a lack of consensus amongst policy-makers about which factors should be taken into account and about how much weight should be attached to each factor. In a sense, then, the economists who seek to engineer an "artificial market" for environmental amenities are faced with a circular argument: on the one hand, they argue that only when environmental amenities are measured in money terms will any clear picture emerge of how much the public are willing to pay for them, but on the other hand, they cannot create the market needed to find out environmental "prices" without somehow fixing those prices initially, which they cannot do because, in the absence of a market, they have no accurate data about where the prices should be fixed. A simple example will serve to illustrate the difficulties of determining the "environmental costs" associated with different forms of behaviour.

It is commonly assumed that re-usable consumer products are more "environmentally friendly" than disposable ones. To take a particular example, it may be thought that old-fashioned washable nappies should be used in preference to disposable ones. The environmental problems associated with disposable nappies are well-known. Once the nappy has been used, the cotton and paper used in its manufacture cannot be recycled and must be disposed of either by landfill (burying in the ground) or by incineration. Both of these methods of disposal cause environmental damage. Environmental damage caused at the manufacturing stage must also be considered — the use of energy, water and bleaching agents, for example — as must the damage caused by distributing the product to the consumer (for example by road, causing air and noise pollution).

The environmental problems associated with washable nappies, however, are less obvious. They must, of course, be manufactured and eventually disposed of, but this will cause fewer problems than in the case of disposable nappies, because fewer nappies will be used. The environmental consequences of washing the nappies must then be considered. Washing uses fresh clean water — a valuable environmental amenity. This must be distributed to the home. Electricity may be needed to supply the fresh water and to carry away the waste water to the sewage works. Generating this electricity has adverse environmental consequences. The waste water will have to be purified so that it may be used again, which will involve removing and disposing of the detergent present in the water. The environmental consequences of manufacturing the detergent, and of distributing it to the home, must also be considered. There are adverse environmental consequences associated with the manufacture and distribution of a washing machine and with its consumption of electricity. The washing of the nappies will produce wear and tear on the machine, hastening the time when it must be disposed of, perhaps by landfill, so some way must be found of calculating the environmental consequences of this. The picture is more complicated still if a tumble dryer is used.

The methodology used to calculate the "environmental costs" of washable nappies, then, so that they might be compared with those of disposable nappies, will have to be extremely complex. Moreover, *implementing* this methodology will produce adverse environmental consequences, such as the environmental costs of running a research establishment. Indeed, these consequences might, at the end of the day, *outweigh* any "environmental saving" which can be achieved by knowing the answer to the problem and encouraging people to use one type of nappy or the other. Therefore, in the absence of accurate information about all aspects of the problem, we simply trust our instincts in adopting the course of action which appears to us to be the most environmentally friendly, but we have no real way of knowing whether our instincts are misplaced.

# THE FUTURE OF ENVIRONMENTAL REGULATION

## Sustainable Development

The concept of "sustainable development", which, as we have noted, is one of the principles of environmental law, is beginning to have a profound influence on the development of environmental regulation in the U.K.

The concept is a vague one. It has been estimated that there are over 200 definitions of it. Nevertheless, it has been described as having achieved, in recent years, a popularity approaching that of "democracy".[44] Sustainable development is more fully discussed elsewhere in this book. In summary, however, the concept originated in a realisation that the world's environment, its economies and the ways in which it treats its human and animal inhabitants are all interlinked. The Brundtland Report, which first gave prominence to the concept, illustrated this fact by reference to the famine in Africa during the 1980s. Although its immediate cause was drought, its underlying causes were more complex. They included rapidly rising populations and debts owed by African countries. Inability to pay these debts forced African nations, relying on sales of agricultural commodities, to over-use their fragile soils, turning good land into desert.

Although the concept of sustainable development originated in international law, it has quickly gained currency in environmental debates at all levels, and is now accorded great importance in U.K. environmental law and policy. As has been noted, achieving sustainable development is the principal aim of the Environment Agency.[45] Guidance on the meaning of sustainable development, and on the nature of the contribution which the Agency should make towards attaining it, is to be issued to the Agency by Ministers.

During the second reading of the Environment Bill in the House of Commons, the Secretary of State for the Environment commented on the meaning of sustainable development in the following terms:

> "Balance is at the heart of sustainable development. The two words, sustainability and development, need to be held together if we are to get a sensible answer. We need to grow, if we are to provide the resources our people need, but at the same time we need to grow in a sustainable way . . . When people talk about sustainability but fail to talk about growth, they are talking about the destruction of society, for a society without the resources for improvement, change and betterment is not one in which we would wish to live. Those who talk about growth without giving any indication of how to make it sustainable are betraying the next generation. The two words must be kept permanently together. This means reconciling the needs of the environment and of economic development, rather than pursuing one at the cost of the other. It means placing the concept of the environment at the centre of decision-making, rather than as an add-on extra."[46]

## Implementing Sustainable Development

### An Integrated Approach

The idea of "policy integration", to which the Secretary of State lastly refers, is a principle which is likely to assume increasing importance in environmental law. It

[44] See William M. Lafferty, "The Politics of Sustainable Development: Global Norms for National Implementation", (1996) *Environmental Politics*, Vol. 5, p. 185.
[45] EA 1995, s.4.
[46] *Hansard*, H.C., April 18, 1995, cols 37–38.

requires that a consideration of environmental policy should form an integral part of all other policy decisions, particularly those relating to transport and energy. The E.C. has recognised the importance of this approach. Article 130R of the E.C. Treaty provides that environmental protection should be a component of other E.C. policies.

Implementing sustainable development may also require a shift in policy away from "environmental protection" towards "environmental management". There is a tendency for existing legislation to concentrate on regulating the release of polluting substances created by industrial processes, rather than on the uses which those processes make of energy and natural raw materials. The U.K.'s integrated pollution control regime, discussed in Chapter 6, has adopted a restricted interpretation of "Best Practicable Environmental Option" which does not allow for a consideration of these factors. The European Environment Agency, however, has noted that reductions in substance emissions are often insufficient, by themselves, to achieve an improvement in environmental quality.[47]

## Adapting the Law

The need to achieve sustainable development, which demands that environmental problems must be approached from a wide economic and social perspective, has led to an awareness that there are particular difficulties inherent in tackling the problem of environmental protection through traditional legal mechanisms. It has been recognised that solving environmental problems requires that the law must adopt a novel and innovative approach.

Environmental concerns may come before the courts in a number of different ways. The variety of available legal mechanisms means that sometimes there will be a multiplicity of hearings which all deal with the same substantive issues. Consider an example.[47a]

Imagine that there is an explosion on board an oil tanker which is discharging its cargo at a port. Under conventional procedures, the Secretary of State might hold a public inquiry to investigate what has happened and to make certain recommendations. Pending the outcome of this inquiry, other legal proceedings might be deferred, so that the trauma of those who have been affected by the incident will be prolonged. If the explosion has caused death, there will be an inquisition before a coroner. There may also be criminal proceedings in which the company responsible for the tanker may be charged with manslaughter. In addition, claims in negligence may be brought by those who have suffered as a result of the explosion. The merits of the decision of the enforcing authority which permitted the discharge of oil at the port may be called into question, and this may necessitate a review of licensing policy.

In each of these sets of proceedings, then, the relevant tribunal will to some extent be hampered by a concern not to frustrate the other tribunals' ability to do justice. Moreover, the costs of pursuing all of these different proceedings, both to the public and to the individual litigants, may be enormous.

---

[47] *Europe's Environment: The Dobris Assessment* (eds David Stanners and Philippe Bourdeau) (1996, The European Environment Agency).
[47a] *op cit.,* n.48, below.

There is another sense in which the mechanism of law has presented problems. In traditional legal disputes, there are two or more distinct and ascertainable parties. The court's task is to find a solution to a factual problem which strikes the most appropriate balance between the interests of these parties. In environmental law, however, the position is different. Environmental damage is often invisible and its effects on ascertained individuals are not readily apparent. The effects of environmental damage on ascertained individuals may become apparent only after a number of years (as has been the case with the use of asbestos, for example), or they may become apparent only to future generations of mankind. In environmental cases, therefore, the "victim" of environmental damage — the other party to the dispute with whom the law is so familiar — is often "the environment itself", or "mankind in general". Unlike the victims of traditional civil and criminal wrongs, "the environment", or "mankind in general" have no legal personality and consequently no rights which are recognised in law.

Both of these problems have led to calls for the creation of a new, specialist tribunal, which could deal exclusively with environmental issues. Such a tribunal might adopt an inquisitorial, rather than an adversarial approach, and might be given a certain amount of discretion to determine its working methods. It might, for example, appoint a High Court judge to make initial findings of fact on which it could base its decisions, as many public inquiries now do. An environmental court might have the power to impose financial penalties and to refer appropriate matters to other courts. In addition, counsel might be engaged by the tribunal and instructed to present arguments on behalf of members of the general public, and ultimately, perhaps, on behalf of "the environment itself".[48]

On a more philosophical level, it might be thought that the very nature of law is inappropriate for solving environmental problems. The law is fond of placing things in compartments. This is often the reason for its success in finding workable solutions to problems which would prove insoluble to the philosopher or logician. Therefore, when a new and complex problem becomes apparent, as, over the last century, has the need to protect the environment, the law is inclined to distinguish each *aspect* of the problem, as and when it arises, from all other aspects of the same problem. As Clarence Morris put it, in *How Lawyers Think*:

> "Problems occur in gross. The unit which appears to be a single problem at first glance is usually a complex of related difficulties, a confluence of more specific problems. Often, the initial urge is to dismiss the whole difficulty with some easy, impulsive solution . . . "[49]

The adverse effects of this compartmentalist approach have been illustrated only too clearly by the *ad hoc* and unstructured development of environmental law. It has been recognised that implementing sustainable development will require, from those involved in the legal system, a shift in focus away from "everyday rules", towards underlying principles and philosophies. As one commentator has noted:

> "While the legal practitioners argue after the meaning of 'significant harm' . . . or whether cement fuel is or is not a waste . . . they will be excluded from the larger

---

[48] See Sir Harry Woolf, " Are the Judiciary Environmentally Myopic?", (1992) J.E.L. Vol. 4(1) p. 1.
[49] Clarence Morris, *How Lawyers Think*, 1937.

policy debates currently being conducted by economists, philosophers, and scientists . . . For the lawyers, the challenge is to lift their eyes to the hills . . . above all they must learn to be artists not tradesmen."[50]

[50] Macrory, "Challenges beyond the Foothills", Garner Environmental Law Lecture, 1996, *UKELA Environmental Law*, Vol. 10(3) p. 12.

# Chapter 2

# INTERNATIONAL ENVIRONMENTAL LAW

*"In the middle of the 20th century, we saw our planet from space for the first time. Historians may eventually find that this vision had a greater impact on thought than did the Copernican revolution of the 16th century. From space we see a small and fragile ball dominated not by human activity and edifice but by a pattern of clouds, oceans, greenery and soils."[1]*

## Introduction

In 1986, an explosion at the Chernobyl nuclear power plant blasted 50 tonnes of nuclear fuel into the atmosphere. A northwesterly wind carried the radioactive particles across the Baltic Republics and to much of western Europe, leading to the pollution of land, air and water, and to an increased risk of cancer in humans. In 1986, following a fire in a warehouse in Switzerland, agricultural chemicals, solvents and mercury flowed into the River Rhine killing millions of fish and threatening the safety of drinking water in the Federal Republic of Germany and in the Netherlands.

It is not only environmental catastrophes such as these, however, that illustrate the impossibility of confining pollution within a country's borders. Land degradation causes millions of environmental refugees to cross national borders. In Africa, along the Sahel's 3,000 mile front, 10 million refugees have been displaced by barren soil.[2] Forest cutting in Nepal has increased the severity of floods in neighbouring India and Bangladesh. Acid rain, which can destroy crops, is carried by the water cycle and may fall in countries sometimes thousands of miles away from the source of the air pollution which causes it. The effects of global warming, caused by the emission of greenhouse gases, will be experienced worldwide, as will the consequences of the destruction of the ozone layer.

Clearly, these environmental problems can be effectively tackled only when many, if not all, countries of the world act together. An international law of the environment is fast developing to respond to this need. This chapter considers whether there can be said to be an international law of the environment, and if so what its main principles are.

---

[1] Report of the World Commission on the Environment and Development: "Our Common Future" (1987) (The Brundtland Report).
[2] Stone, Christopher D., *The Gnat is Older than Man* (1993).

## State Territory and "Global Commons"

It is important to appreciate that environmental damage on an international scale can occur in, and can be caused by activities which take place in, three distinct types of geographical region:

- Within the sovereign territory of a State, over which that State has exclusive jurisdiction;

- Within "Global Commons", over which all States share jurisdiction. (The only true "Global Commons" are, in fact, the deep sea bed and the moon);

- Within areas over which, although not "Global Commons", jurisdiction is exercised by a large number of different States together in accordance with the provisions of treaties (Antarctica, for example, or the High Seas).

## Basic Principles of International Law

To understand international environmental law, it is necessary to appreciate that international law is fundamentally different from the domestic legal system of a nation state. In international law there is no supreme source of authority. The law is therefore effectively formed by a consensus of behaviour and of ideas between nation states, which creates a system of rules of general application. Moreover, compliance with these rules by States is largely voluntary, because the availability of sanctions in international law is limited. Although States may impose economic sanctions or, as a last resort, wage war to ensure compliance with rules of international law, enforcement of international law depends for the most part on the persuasive powers of diplomats and on the idea that States will comply with international provisions in order to preserve their standing within the international community.

Because of this absence of any supreme authority, international law develops very gradually. It is only recently that commentators have begun to consider whether there may be said to be an international *law* on the environment, as opposed to a mere international *policy* on environmental matters, evidenced by a number of treaties which deal with problems with an environmental flavour. Some of those commentators have been cautious in holding that international environmental policy has yet developed into a regime of international law.[3]

## Sources of International Law

Article 38 of the Statute of the International Court of Justice is generally regarded as a complete statement of the sources of international law. It refers to:

- International conventions (treaties);

---

[3] See, for example, Birnie and Boyle, *International Law and the Environment* (1992).

- International custom;
- General principles of law;
- Judicial decisions and academic writings.

## Treaties

Treaties (also called conventions) create obligations and norms of behaviour for the States which are parties to them. In principle, treaties are binding only on the signatory States, but where a large number of influential States sign a treaty, their explicit acceptance of certain rules of behaviour has a strong law-making effect. Consistent compliance with the provisions of a treaty by many States and for a number of years may provide evidence of customary international law with which all States must comply. Treaties usually become binding on States only after they have been ratified (formally adopted) by a certain specified number of States. In environmental law, treaties have tended to require only a low number of ratifications before their provisions come into force. Even where a treaty is not yet technically in force, however, it can have persuasive force and may therefore have some law-making effect by generating rules of customary international law. Treaties on the environment fre-quently follow the approach of adopting, initially, a framework treaty which sets out the general obligations of the parties. Protocols are subsequently adopted which set out the details of those obligations.

Treaties, like customary law (below), establish legally binding obligations and may therefore be regarded as a source of "hard law". The provisions of international declarations, on the other hand, may be regarded as rules of "soft law". The Stockholm Declaration[4] and the Rio Declaration[5] (discussed below), which are of great significance in international environmental law, are not binding on States but have significant persuasive force. They have played an important rôle in the development of international environmental law by pointing to the form which formally binding treaty obligations are likely to take in the future and by informally establishing acceptable norms of behaviour. Certain provisions of these declarations are sometimes thought of as reflecting or codifying existing rules of customary law.

## Customary Law

Rules of customary international law arise where there is a general recognition among States that certain practices and norms of behaviour are obligatory. In international environmental law, customary rules generally play a subordinate rôle to the law contained in treaties, because their existence is difficult to establish. To show that a rule of customary law is in existence, not only must the uniformity, consistency and generality of the practice of States be examined, but so too must the length of time during which that practice has been adhered to. Therefore, because environmental concerns are of comparatively recent origin, few rules of customary international law have yet developed in relation to them.

[4] The Declaration of Principles for the Preservation and Enhancement of the Human Environment, June 16, 1972. UN Doc. A/CONF. 48/14; 11 I.L.M. 1416 (1972).
[5] Rio de Janeiro Declaration on Environment and Development, June 16, 1992. UN Doc. A/CONF. 151/5.

## General Principles of Law

Certain fundamental principles are generally observed by all nations. The most important of these is the principle that a State is sovereign within its own borders. As has been noted[6]:

"The sovereignty and equality of States represents the basic constitutional doctrine of the law of nations . . . The principal corollaries of [this] are:

(1) A jurisdiction *prima facie* exclusive over a territory;
(2) A duty of non-intervention in the area of exclusive jurisdiction of other States."

The doctrine of sovereignty, as we shall see, has the potential to come into conflict with international laws for the protection of the environment.

## Judicial Decisions and Academic Writings

Judicial decisions of international courts and tribunals provide evidence of the consensus between States in relation to particular rules or practices. The writings of academics perform a similar, albeit less significant, function. Academic commentary plays a much greater rôle in international law than it does in many domestic legal systems, including that of the U.K. Like international declarations, judicial decisions and academic writings are not so much sources of international law *per se*, but are means by which the existence and scope of international law may be determined.

# THE DEVELOPMENT OF INTERNATIONAL ENVIRONMENTAL LAW

International law on environmental concerns dates from the early nineteenth century. At that time, attention centred on the exploitation of natural resources as a result of growing industrialisation. A number of bilateral treaties were signed with the aim of conserving fishing stocks, but pollution and other ecological issues were not addressed. The international response to resource management was characterised by *ad hoc* reactions to immediate problems, but was significant nonetheless because it recognised that co-operation between States was necessary.

In 1893, a dispute between the U.S. and Great Britain over the exploitation of seals for fur was submitted to international arbitration.[7] The finding of the tribunal established an important principle which is still significant today, namely that States did not have the right to assert jurisdiction over natural resources which were outside their territory in order to ensure their conservation.

In 1941, a dispute between Canada and the United States over the emission of sulphur fumes from a Canadian smelting works, which caused damage to crops, trees and pasture in the U.S., led to what has been described as "a crystallizing moment for

---

[6] Brownlie, *Principles of Public International Law* (4th ed., 1990).
[7] *The Pacific Fur Seals Arbitration* (1893) 1 *Moore's International Arbitration Awards* 755.

international environmental law".[8] The two States agreed to submit the matter to arbitration, and the tribunal held that under international law:

" . . . no State has the right to use or permit the use of its territory in such a manner as to cause injury by fumes in or to the territory of another or the properties or persons therein, when the case is of serious consequence and the injury is established by clear and convincing evidence."[9]

In 1945, the creation of a global organisation — the United Nations — after the destruction caused by the Second World War, provided an institutional framework within which to develop an international law on the environment. Although the UN Charter did not refer explicitly to environmental protection, its mandate has proved wide enough to include environmental matters. The UN is the main forum for the creation of international legal rules and has played an important rôle in developing international environmental law.

## The Stockholm Conference

By 1972, a significant body of environmental obligations had been established at both a regional and global level. International concern was no longer focused only on the conservation of flora and fauna but was addressing issues such as oil pollution and the effects on the atmosphere of nuclear tests. In 1972, the first international conference on the environment — the United Nations Conference on the Human Environment — held in Stockholm, marked a turning point in the development of international environmental law. Attended by 114 States, the conference provided an opportunity to formulate a coherent analysis of environmental problems. It placed environmental issues firmly on the international legislative agenda, and a declaration issued by the participating States proclaimed that: " a point has been reached in history when we must shape our actions through the world with a more prudent care for their environmental consequences."[10]

The Stockholm conference produced a declaration of principles (the Stockholm Declaration[11]) which may be regarded as the foundation of modern international environmental law. Its provisions have formed the basis of numerous subsequent conventions. The most significant provisions include the requirement for international co-operation to:

" . . . effectively control, prevent, reduce and eliminate adverse environmental effects resulting from activities conducted in all spheres, in such a way that due account is taken of the sovereignty and interests of all States."[12]

The declaration requires States to co-operate in developing international environmental law,[13] and provides that States are responsible for ensuring that activities within

[8] Sands, *Principles of International Environmental Law* (1995).
[9] *Trail Smelter Case* (1941) 3 R.I.A.A. 1905.
[10] UN Doc. A/CONF. 48/14/rev.1 (UN Pub. E73, IIA (1973), adopted June 16, 1972.
[11] The Declaration of Principles for the Preservation and Enhancement of the Human Environment, June 16, 1972. UN Doc. A/CONF. 48/14; (1972) 11 I.L.M. 1416.
[12] Principle 24.
[13] Principle 22.

their jurisdiction or control do not cause damage in other States or in geographical areas beyond national jurisdiction.[14]

The 1972 conference also created the United Nations Environment Programme (U.N.E.P), as a body to guide the future development of international environmental law, and established the UN Environment Fund, to which signatory States make voluntary contributions. By acting as a co-ordinating body between States, U.N.E.P. has greatly stimulated the development of international environmental law. Since 1972, protection of the environment has become one of the central objectives of the international legal system as a whole,[15] and, in less than 25 years, international environmental law has become one of the most dynamic areas of the international legal regime.[16] Between 1972 and 1992, several hundred bilateral and multilateral environmental agreements were concluded between nations. This constitutes a huge output in terms of the usual pace at which international agreements proceed.

## The Brundtland Report

In the 1970s and 1980s, the nature and extent of the world's environmental problems were changing rapidly, not only because the rate at which human activity was affecting the environment increased dramatically, but also because of increased scientific knowledge in relation to the global warming effects of fossil fuel emissions and of mass deforestation. In 1987, a report by the World Commission on Environment and Development, known as the Brundtland Report,[17] noted that during the 1980s there had been a marked increase in the incidence of environmental crises of a "global nature", such as the drought in Africa, which triggered an environmental and development crisis putting some 35 million people at risk and killing perhaps a million. The report concluded that if natural resources continued to be used at the current rate, if the plight of the poor was ignored, and if pollution and wasting of resources continued, a decline was to be expected in the quality of life of the world's population. It called upon wealthy nations to make changes in their lifestyle by recycling waste, conserving energy and land, and by rehabilitating damaged landscapes. The publication of the Brundtland Report led to growing pressure for further international action on the environment and eventually to the holding of the 1992 United Nations Conference on the Environment and Development in Rio de Janeiro, Brazil.

## The Rio Conference

The UN conference in Rio de Janeiro was attended by approximately 10,000 delegates from 176 States. Its effect has been described as starting an "environmental revolution" which, if it succeeds, will rank with the agricultural and industrial revolutions as

---

[14] Principle 21.
[15] Michael Bowman, "Environmental Litigation and the International Legal System" (1995) *Environmental Liability.*
[16] Dunoff, "From Green to Global: Towards the Transformation of International Environmental Law", (1995) *Harvard Environmental Law Review* Vol. 19, no. 2, p.441.
[17] Report of the World Commission on the Environment and Development: "Our Common Future" (1987) ("The Brundtland Report").

one of the great economic and social transformations in human history.[18] The conference produced the following results:

- A Declaration on Environment and Development (the Rio Declaration[19]), which defines the rights and responsibilities of States.

It has been suggested that the Rio Declaration must be taken to reflect — to the extent that any international instrument can do so — the current consensus of values and priorities in the environment and development.[20] The Declaration, therefore, goes some way towards remedying the problem noted by the Brundtland Report, namely that:

" . . . at present international environmental law is scattered throughout numerous conventions and other instruments, all of which are limited in scope and only deal with ecological issues in a sectoral, piecemeal fashion."

- A global action plan for all States on development and the environment (Agenda 21).

This is also significant because it reflects the consensus of States. It was negotiated over a period of two years and accepted by all of the participating States.

- Two legally binding multilateral treaties, which were opened for signature: the Convention on Biological Diversity[21] and the UN Framework Convention on Climate Change.[22] These were signed by representatives of more than 150 countries.

Multilateral treaties have, since 1972, been the main source of obligations in relation to marine pollution, protection of the atmosphere, wildlife conservation and conservation of international watercourses. The increased use of multilateral (as opposed to bilateral) treaties is significant because it has moved international environmental law beyond the protection of what might be termed "private rights" between States into the arena of obligations owed to the international community — and by implication to mankind — as a whole.

Whilst traditional treaties and rules of customary law had concentrated on the territorial jurisdiction of States and on States' liability for transboundary pollution, the underlying concern in more recent treaties has been protection of the wider environment. Modern treaties have increasingly focused on global, rather than transboundary pollution, on the conservation of entire ecosystems rather than the preservation of particular species, and on the conservation of common global resources, rather than those of individual States. For example, in 1970 it was recognised that the sea-bed and

---

[18] Brown, Lester R., *An Environmental Revolution*.
[19] Rio de Janeiro Declaration on Environment and Development, June 16, 1992, UN Doc. A/CONF. 151/5.
[20] Porreas, Ileana M., "The Rio Declaration: A New Basis for International Co-operation" in *Greening International Law* (ed. Phillippe Sands) (1993).
[21] Convention on Biological Diversity, June 5, 1992, Rio de Janeiro, 31 I.L.M. 822 (1992).
[22] UN Framework Convention on Climate Change, May 9, 1992, New York, 31 I.L.M. 849 (1992).

the ocean floor were the "common heritage of mankind" and therefore were beyond the jurisdiction of any one State.[23] Other areas which *might* be so described include the ozone layer, the global climate, the tropical rain forests and sites of importance to world heritage, such as the Taj Mahal.

It should not be thought, however, that the best response to environmental problems is always a global one. Global regulation may sometimes be less flexible; it must be painted with a broad brush because of the impossibility of taking into account domestic circumstances in each and every contracting State. Moreover, global institutions are inevitably slower than national governments to respond to environmental problems. It is to be noted that the U.S. and Canada have successfully countered a number of environmental problems bilaterally.[24]

One of the problems with the creeping "globalisation" of environmental law, as evidenced by the Rio Conference and by the use of multilateral treaties, is that developing nations and developed nations often have very different priorities. This is largely because the environmental problems of developing nations are often directly related to poverty, whilst environmental problems in developed nations are related to excessive industrialisation and high-consumption lifestyles. This divergence of priorities was particularly apparent at the Rio Conference. The developed nations were concerned to protect the environment, but many of the developing nations only agreed to participate in the conference largely because the issue of development was on the agenda. Many felt threatened by the idea of environmental protection, which they saw as likely to impede rapid economic growth.

A common criticism of international environmental law is that the concerns of developed nations dominate its agenda at the expense of the more immediate concerns of developing States. Thus, for example, there is much international activity and debate in relation to climate change and ozone depletion, even though the harm which they cause is to some extent still unproven and their effects have yet significantly to be felt. Developing nations are faced with more pressing environmental problems. Approximately one billion third world citizens drink dirty water which fails to meet any basic safety standards. In addition, acute respiratory infection, caused by unsafe air, kills an estimated 4.3 million people in developing nations every year. As one writer has put it:

> "Although global warming has yet to kill a single human being, and may not do so for centuries, it has received enormous attention and resources. At the same time silent emergencies that are killing people every day . . . do not attract the same kind of screaming headlines and well funded action plans."[25]

It has been suggested that the Rio Declaration, on balance may be judged as a victory for developing countries, in so far as it evidences a shift away from the traditional dominance of developed countries in dictating international norms and priorities.[26]

---

[23] *Declaration of Principles Governing the Sea-Bed and the Ocean Floor, and the Subsoil Thereof, Beyond the Limits of National Jurisdiction*, G.A. Res. 2749 (XXV), December 17, 1970, 10 I.L.M. 230 (1970).
[24] Stone, *The Gnat is Older than Man* (1993).
[25] Dunoff, "From Green to Global: Towards the Transformation of International Environmental Law", (1995) *Harvard Environmental Law Review* Vol. 19, no. 2.
[26] Porreas n.20 above.

Nevertheless, at present, the international regime for environmental protection caters considerably less for the specific and immediate needs of developing countries than it does for the more general concerns of developed nations.

Since the Rio Conference in 1992 there have been few dramatic developments in international environmental law. Rather, the picture has been one of steady development and consolidation. The Council of Europe, however, has adopted a Convention on Civil Liability for Environmental Damage, which provides for access to information and for national pollution remedies in civil law, both of which were called for at Rio. In addition, the Programme for the Development and Periodic Review of Environmental Law (The Montevideo Programme), which originated in 1981 under the guidance of U.N.E.P., was revised in 1992. The programme aims to identify the principles of international environmental law so that they may be developed. Most ironically, however, no specific principles are mentioned in the programme because of disagreement amongst States, although the programme does identify the need for action on, *inter alia*, the ozone layer, hazardous waste, and transboundary air pollution.

The period since Rio has also been characterised by increasing debate on the question of how to integrate environmental considerations into other areas of policy-making, in particular economic policy, at an international level. Moves in this area have been facilitated by the establishment of an Environment Department within the World Bank, and by the integration of formal environmental obligations in the articles of association establishing the European Bank for Reconstruction and Development.

## THE PRINCIPLES OF INTERNATIONAL ENVIRONMENTAL LAW

Because, as has been said, international law is formed by a consensus of ideas and behaviour between States, it is extremely difficult to determine at what stage a mere idea, or isolated examples of behaviour, can be said with certainty to have formed a binding principle of international law. It is clear that a number of principles are emerging in the field of international environmental law, but it is too early to say whether all or any of these principles are sufficiently established to be relied upon in an international court. The principles may be stated as follows:[27]

(1) The principle of State sovereignty over, and environmental responsibility for, the use of natural resources;

(2) The principle of good neighbourliness and co-operation;

(3) The principle of preventive action;

(4) The precautionary principle;

(5) The polluter pays principle;

(6) The principle of common but differentiated responsibility;

(7) The principle of sustainable development.

---

[27] Sands, *Principles of International Environmental Law*, (1995) Vol. 1, chap. 6.

Each of these principles is examined in turn below.

## (1) Sovereignty and environmental responsibility in the use of natural resources

In spite of the rhetoric favoured by the developed countries at the Rio conference, which included globalising certain selected environmental resources (such as the rain forests), the principle that a State retains sovereignty over the resources within its territory remains a cardinal principle of international law. This is so despite the increasing focus of international law on agreements which restrain environmentally harmful activities within national borders and which thereby aim to qualify the traditional doctrine of State sovereignty.

The principle of state sovereignty is recognised in the Stockholm Declaration, Principle 21 of which states that: "States have . . . the sovereign right to exploit their own resources pursuant to their own environmental policies . . . "

A State's freedom to exploit its resources, however, carries with it a responsibility. Thus, Principle 21 goes on to impose on States: " . . . the responsibility to ensure that activities within their jurisdiction or control do not cause damage to the environment of other States or of areas beyond the limits of national jurisdiction."

Both of these ideas are combined in a single Principle of the Rio Declaration, Principle 2, which states:

> "States have, in accordance with the Charter of the UN and the principles of international law, the sovereign right to exploit their own resources pursuant to their own environmental and developmental policies, and the responsibility to ensure that activities within their jurisdiction or control do not cause damage to the environment of other States or to areas beyond their jurisdiction."

It should be noted that the wording of The 1972 Stockholm Declaration: " . . . pursuant to their own environmental policies . . . ", may have implied merely that States should be free to select the methods which best suited them when implementing environmental protection measures, whilst the wording of Principle 2 of the Rio Declaration may imply that "development" can be a *justification* for the depletion of resources. It has been suggested that the inclusion of "developmental" policies as reasons which can justify a State's exploitation of resources may have upset the "delicate balance between the sovereign use of natural resources and the duty of care for the environment" which was reflected in the Stockholm Declaration.[28]

The concept of State responsibility for environmental harm, or of an "environmental duty of care" owed by States, inevitably begins to transform the accepted relationship between a State and its natural resources from one of ownership — in which the State is free to exploit its resources in accordance with its national policies and priorities — into one of trusteeship, or "stewardship", in which the State is required to consider the interests of (and perhaps to consult with) the international community before taking

---

[28] Marc Pallemaerts, "International Environmental Law From Stockholm to Rio: Back to the Future?" in *Greening International Law* (ed. Sands) (1993).

any action which may deplete the world's resources. Thus it has been noted that it may be possible to envisage a redefinition of the principle of sovereignty so that it entails "a commitment to co-operation for the good of the international community at large".[29]

## (2) The principle of good neighbourliness and international co-operation

The principle that States should co-operate in the field of environmental protection is affirmed in virtually all international environmental agreements. The preamble to the Convention on Biodiversity, for example, stresses the necessity and importance of promoting international, regional and global co-operation among States. The necessity for co-operation is mentioned six times in the Rio Declaration.

## (3) The principle of preventive action

The principle of preventive action requires that States take action to protect the environment at an early stage, and ideally before any damage has occurred. Whilst the concept of State responsibility not to cause environmental damage (above) requires that States must not exploit their resources so as to cause environmental harm *to other States*, the principle of preventive action has been interpreted in terms of placing States under an obligation to prevent damage to the environment within their *own* territories.[30] That both the Stockholm Declaration and the Rio Declaration make reference to this principle, as do a number of treaties, is good evidence of its status as a binding principle of international environmental law. The principle is endorsed by the Rio Convention on Biodiversity, which refers in its preamble to the vital necessity of anticipating, preventing and attacking at source the causes of loss of biodiversity. The European Community Treaty also makes reference to the principle.

## (4) The precautionary principle

The precautionary principle is to be found in a number of different forms, so that its substantive content cannot be stated with certainty. Broadly, however, the principle embodies the idea that States should err on the side of caution when taking steps to prevent environmental damage. Because the elements of the principle are still evolving, it cannot yet be said to be an established tenet of international law. The Treaty on European Union refers to the principle, but gives no definition of it. A commonly cited definition, however, is that contained in 1990 Bergen Ministerial Declaration on Sustainable Development:

> "Environmental measures must anticipate, prevent and attack the causes of environmental degradation. Where there are threats of serious or irreversible

[29] Birnie and Boyle, *International Law and the Environment* (1992), p. 14.
[30] Sands, *Principles of International Environmental Law* (1995), p. 195.

damage, lack of full scientific certainty should not be used as a reason for postponing measures to prevent environmental degradation."

Principle 15 of the Rio Declaration is couched in the same terms: "Where there are threats of serious or irreversible damage, lack of full scientific certainty shall not be used as a reason for postponing cost-effective measures to prevent environmental degradation."

The difference between the preventive principle and the precautionary principle, then, is that the former requires States to take action where there is a foreseeable risk of damage to the environment, whilst the latter requires action where the risks associated with an activity are suspected but are not fully known.

In its strongest form, the precautionary principle may be said to entail a reversal of the onus of proof *vis-a-vis* the potential polluter and the State whose territory may be polluted. In other words, the polluter must demonstrate that the activities he proposes will not cause harm to the environment, instead of the State's demonstrating that they *will* cause such harm. The key question, however, to which there is yet no answer, is: what level of risk is necessary before action must be taken? The Ozone Convention,[31] in common with other international instruments, requires States to act when they have reasonable grounds for believing that activities may cause harm to the environment. The difficulties which have emerged in persuading States to take action with respect to global climate change, however, indicate that as yet there is no international consensus on the application of the precautionary principle.

## (5) The "polluter pays" principle

This principle may be said to embody the idea that the polluter should bear the expenses of carrying out measures decided upon by public authorities as necessary to ensure that the environment is in an acceptable state. One way of giving effect to this principle is to ensure that the costs of environmental protection measures are reflected in the prices of goods and services which cause pollution, either by their production or in their consumption, through the use of economic instruments. The difficulties involved in doing this are considered in Chapter 1.

Although the principle is mentioned in a number of treaties, such as the European Community Treaty,[32] which requires that action by the Community shall be based on the principle, the precise means by which the principle is to be given effect are not clarified by international instruments. The principle is referred to in the Rio Declaration, which states:

"National authorities should endeavour to promote the internalization of environmental costs and the use of economic instruments, taking into account the approach that the polluter should, in principle, bear the cost of pollution, with due regard to the public interest and without distorting international trade and investment."

[31] Convention·on the Protection of the Ozone Layer, March 22, 1985, Vienna, 26 I.L.M. 1529 (1987).
[32] Treaty Establishing the European Economic Community, Rome, March 25, 1957, 298 UNTS 267.

## (6) The principle of common but differentiated responsibility

In essence, this principle embodies the idea that some States have different environmental concerns and responsibilities from others. Thus, Principle 7 of the Rio Declaration states:

> "In view of the different contributions to global environmental degradation, States have common but differentiated responsibilities. The developed countries acknowledge the responsibility that they have in the international pursuit of sustainable development in view of the pressures their societies place on the global environment and of the technologies and financial resources they command."

Underlying the principle is the concept of "intragenerational equity", or equality of treatment, as between present generations of mankind, in terms of shouldering the burden of action to secure environmental benefits. The principle is based on the recognition that developing countries have special needs to which priority must be accorded. At Rio, developing nations made it clear that they would only participate in international environmental protection measures if they were given an incentive to do so. They took the view that it was unfair for the economically developed world, which had been able to industrialise at the expense of the environment, to deny the developing world a similar opportunity in the name of environmental protection.

As a result of the views expressed at Rio, much of the developed world has now accepted that it must pay the developing world to refrain from polluting activities. The preamble to the Convention on Climate Change notes that *per capita* emissions of greenhouse gases in developing countries are still relatively low, and recognises the special difficulties of developing countries, whose economies are particularly dependent on fossil fuel production and use. Whereas developed countries are required under the Convention to limit their greenhouse gas emissions to 1990 levels by the year 2000,[33] developing countries are required only to limit their emissions in accordance with the extent to which the developed nations have fulfilled their commitments to transfer finance and technologies to the developing countries for that purpose.[34]

## (7) Sustainable development

The principle of sustainable development is perhaps the most important principle to have emerged from international activity on the environment. The most widely accepted definition of sustainable development is that given in the Brundtland Report[35]: "Development that meets the needs of the present without compromising the ability of future generations to meet their own needs."

The principle is incorporated into U.K. law by the Environment Act 1995,[36] which places the Environment Agency under a duty to exercise its functions so as to achieve

[33] Art. 4(2)(a)(b).
[34] Art. 4(7).
[35] Report of the World Commission on Environment and Development: Our Common Future (1987) ("The Brundtland Report").
[36] EA 1995, s.4.

sustainable development. A concrete definition of the phrase, however, indicating in practical terms what the Agency must do to fulfil its duty, is notably absent from the statute. During the passage of the Environment Bill, Lord Moran commented on the inclusion of the phrase in the following way:

> "The term gives rise to endless ambiguity and confusion . . . I do not like to see such a misleading term included in legislation; but, if it is, it should be rigorously defined and clarified on the face of the Bill."[37]

## Sustainable Development: The Brundtland Report

The Brundtland Report, in which the concept of sustainable development originated, provides a useful starting point in determining its meaning. The report noted that nations had traditionally compartmentalised human activity and its environmental effects within sectors such as energy, agriculture and trade, and also within broad areas of concern such as "environmental", "economic", or "social". These compartments, however, had now begun to dissolve. The "crises" of the 1980s, such as the chemical leak from the Bhopal factory, which killed 2,000 and injured 200,000, and the Rhine River incident (above) were not separate crises, but constituted crises of environment, development and energy combined.

The report isolated poverty as the cornerstone of environmental problems. Not only were the developing nations promoting industrial growth on the scale of their more developed neighbours, which brought with it associated environmental problems, but measures to tackle poverty on the most basic level were causing environmental damage. For example, the destruction of vegetation to obtain food, or timber for fuel or building, left land unprotected from above, so that its soil was washed away by rain. Without adequate soil, the land no longer retained water and became incapable of producing further food or timber, forcing the population to turn to new land and repeat the process of destruction.

The report concluded that in order for development to be sustainable, the basic needs of the world's population must be met and the opportunity extended to all to fulfil their aspirations for a better life. It was proposed that this could be achieved by a number of mechanisms:

- Effective economic growth for poor nations;
- The participation of citizens in decision-making;
- The adoption, by the more affluent nations, of lifestyles within the planet's ecological means, particularly by reducing their use of energy;
- The control of population growth.

## Sustainable Development: The Rio Declaration

The Rio Declaration consolidated these concepts and placed them firmly on the international agenda. However, whilst the Declaration clearly attaches great importance to sustainable development, and makes numerous references to it, it does not

[37] *Hansard,* H.L., December 15, 1994, col. 1409.

define it. Its meaning therefore has to be deciphered from the principles outlined in the Declaration.

The first principle of the Declaration states that "human beings are at the centre of concern for sustainable development." It goes on to say that they are entitled to a healthy and productive life in harmony with nature. This reflects an anthropocentric approach to the environment in which man's interests in the environment take precedence over its intrinsic value. The Declaration goes on to say that:

- The right to development must be fulfilled so as to meet equitably developmental and environmental needs of present and future generations (Principle 3), and that

- In order to achieve sustainable development environmental protection shall constitute an integral part of the development process and cannot be considered in isolation from it (Principle 4).

These two principles have proved controversial. The reference to a right to development, in Principle 3, was seen as a victory for developing States, because this was the first time it had ever been referred to in an international instrument. Principle 3, however, with its reference to meeting environmental as well as development needs, may be taken to imply that development must sometimes be compromised to achieve environmental goals.

Principle 4 reflects a commitment to bring environmental considerations and objectives from the periphery of international relations into the core of international law as it relates to economic development. Indeed, according to one commentator,[38] sustainable development may be seen as firmly integrated into the international law of human rights. On such a view, the achievement of sustainable development is supported by three pillars: international environmental law, international human rights law, and international economic law. In this way, the principle overarches a broad range of disciplines. The link between the environment and human rights is evidenced by growing international interest in the concept of a human right to a healthy environment.[39] A further illustration of this multi-disciplinary approach is the policy of the European Bank for Reconstruction and Development, which aims to integrate environmentally sound and sustainable development with the rule of law, market economies and multi-party democracy.[40]

The integration of environmental, economic and human rights issues is also apparent in Principle 5 of the Declaration, which, as a prerequisite of attaining sustainable development, exhorts all States and all peoples to co-operate in eradicating poverty, in order to decrease international disparities in standards of living, and better to meet the needs of the majority of the world's population. It has been questioned, however, whether a multi-disciplinary approach is entirely helpful. One commentator

[38] McGoldrick, "Sustainable Development and Human Rights: An Integrated Conception" [1996] 45 I.C.L.Q. 796.
[39] See, for example: Ksentini, "Human Rights and the Environment", UN Doc. E. CN. 4/sub.2/1994/9, July 6, 1994 (special report of the UN Sub-Commission on Prevention of Discrimination and Protection of Minorities).
[40] McGoldrick, "Sustainable Development and Human Rights: An Integrated Conception" n. 38 above.

has suggested that the Rio Declaration smothers international environmental law and policy by merging it, as it were, with international economic and developmental law.[41]

Principle 8 of the Declaration states that:

"To achieve sustainable development and a higher quality of life for all people, States should reduce and eliminate unsustainable patterns of production and consumption and promote appropriate demographic policies."

This, of course, is in accordance with the views expressed by the Brundtland Commission, which saw unsustainable farming methods as one of the fundamental problems behind the world's environmental crisis. Principle 8, then, exhorts States to promote sustainable development at its most basic level, for example by encouraging crop rotation and birth control.

Both the Brundtland Report and the Rio Declaration provide a useful analysis of sustainable development, but it must be remembered that they are in essence non-legal documents. Few attempts have been made to give sustainable development a hard and fast legal meaning and, in the U.K., legislation and explanatory guidance generally ascribe to the phrase the same vague meaning as was attached to it by the Brundtland Report. For example, under the Environment Act 1995, Ministers are required to give guidance to the Environment Agency as to the contribution which it should make to achieving sustainable development.[42] Although no guidance has yet been prepared for the Environment Agency in England, draft guidance to the Scottish Environmental Protection Agency simply employs the Brundtland Report's definition of the phrase.

## General Principles of Sustainable Development

In essence sustainable development may be said to incorporate a number of core principles:

- "Intergenerational equity" (meeting the needs of future generations);
- The sustainable use of natural resources;
- The equitable use of natural resources (or "intragenerational equity");
- The integration of environmental protection and economic development.

These principles, each of which is examined below, are supplemented by the operation of the other general principles of international environmental law, such as the preventive and precautionary principles and the polluter pays principle, which have been examined above.

### Intergenerational Equity

Whilst the concept of "*intra*generational" equity is concerned with the distribution of environmental resources between present generations of mankind, or, in other words,

---

[41] Marc Pallemaerts, "International Environmental Law From Stockholm to Rio: Back to the Future?" in *Greening International Law*, (ed. Sands) (1993).
[42] EA 1995, s.4(2).

with fulfilling the first requirement of the Brundtland Commission's vision of development — meeting the "needs of the present" — the concept of "*inter*generational" equity is concerned with considering the needs of future generations of mankind when making decisions about the present. In particular, it is concerned with the need to preserve environmental resources for the benefit of future generations. The theory of intergenerational equity assumes that each generation receives a natural and cultural legacy in trust from previous generations and holds it in trust for future generations. The U.K. government has interpreted this in terms of the concept of "stewardship" of the world.[43]

Opinion differs as to whether or not intergenerational equity is an accepted principle of international environmental law. The idea of holding the world in trust for future generations, however, is relatively well-known to international law. Principle 1 of the Stockholm Declaration, for example, states that man bears: " . . . a solemn responsibility to protect and improve the environment for present and future generations."

Article 3 of the Convention on Climate Change refers to the principle, stating that the parties should protect the global climate for *present and future* generations. It has been noted, however, that this reference is specific to the particular theme of the Convention and that it is therefore unlikely to constitute sufficient evidence that the principle is of binding general application.

Principle 3 of Rio also refers to intergenerational equity: "The right to development must be fulfilled so as to equitably meet developmental and environmental needs of present and future generations."

The confusion surrounding the principle of intergenerational equity is to some extent compounded by the fact that there are two different versions of it. On one view, the principle holds that the next generation of mankind must inherit a stock of environmental assets, no less than the stock inherited by the present generation. On another, wider view, however, the principle of intergenerational equity may be satisfied by leaving to the next generation a stock of assets which comprises environmental assets, technological assets and "know-how".[44] This view recognises that in some respects environmental resources can be "traded-off" against technology. A future generation which has a safe and abundant source of alternative energy, for example, will not need to inherit large stocks of fossil fuels. Thus, technology can be *substituted* for environmental assets, whilst still securing an appropriate standard of living for the next generation. Whilst this wider idea of intergenerational equity is no doubt useful, a large amount of disagreement exists about the precise extent to which technological assets can properly be substituted for environmental ones.

## *The Sustainable Use of Natural Resources*

States have a general obligation to ensure the sustainable use of both living and non-living natural resources. This obligation is evidenced by the adoption of standards in treaties governing the rate at which resources may be exploited, for example, commitments to limit catches of tuna. The Convention on Climate Change accords the

---

[43] *This Common Inheritance*, Cm. 1200 (1990).
[44] Pearce, Markandya and Barbier, *Blueprint for a Green Economy* (1989).

parties a right to sustainable development,[45] but does not elaborate on this. Similarly, the Convention on Biodiversity refers, in Article 1, to the "sustainable use" of resources, but gives no clear definition of the concept. It has been noted that international instruments which refer to the principle of sustainability seldom specify exactly *how* resources are to be used in a sustainable way. Nor do they specify particular resources such as fossil fuels. At present, therefore, there is no general obligation of States not to exhaust non-renewable energy resources.[46]

## The Equitable Use of Natural Resources

This principle (known as "intragenerational equity") implies that use of resources by one State must take account of the needs of other States. The concept of equity, or fairness, is increasingly becoming the focus of conflict in negotiating and implementing international environmental instruments. The traditional notion of equity has been the sovereign right of a State to exploit its own resources, but this notion has been deteriorating and a new one emerging in its place. The new concept of sovereignty may be seen in the principle of common but differentiated responsibility (above) as expressed in terms of the priority needs of developing States, and in the agreement of the developed nations that finance for environmental protection must be provided by them to developing nations. The practical effects of the principle, however, have yet fully to emerge.

## Integration of Economic Development and Environmental Protection

As has been said, Principle 4 of the Rio Declaration states that, in order to achieve sustainable development, environmental protection shall constitute an integral part of the development process and cannot be considered in isolation from it. This means that environmental considerations must be taken into account in economic decisions and development decisions and that, in turn, environmental decisions must take account of economic and social development. The fundamental difficulty underlying the application of this principle is that of finding acceptable methods of "valuing" the environment (see Chapter 1). Nevertheless, mechanisms have been put in place to implement the concept of integrated decision-making, for example the establishment of an environment department within the World Bank, which is likely to make a contribution in future environmental conferences and treaty negotiations.

## Sustainable Development: Conclusions

It will now be apparent that the interpretation of sustainable development is in its infancy. Whilst the concept has been criticised because of its vagueness, it is arguable that, at least during the early stages of its emergence, this vagueness has assisted the formation of the concept and has contributed to its strength and pervasive force by allowing for various interpretations and applications of it to be made in different

---

[45] Art. 3(4).
[46] Sands, *Principles of International Environmental Law* (1995).

contexts. Organisations making use of the concept have been able to interpret it in terms of their own activities and needs. However, as was pointed out by Lord Moran during the passage of the Environment Bill, the flexibility of the concept is in one sense undesirable because it has meant that developers are able to use the concept to *justify* development. His Lordship rightly pointed out that the phrase "sustainable development":

> " . . . actually means the opposite of what it is generally supposed to mean. 'Sustainable' is an adjective which qualifies the noun 'development'. So a developer or polluter can reasonably claim that the phrase means the continuance of his developing or polluting operations, while the World Wildlife Fund argues that the phrase must mean environmental sustainability, not economic sustainability."

The extent to which sustainable development is a principle of international *law*, rather than merely one of *policy,* is unclear. Although there has been intense media interest in the principle, on an international scale, this, of course, cannot make it part of international law.

It has been noted that in arguing that the principle is an accepted part of international law, commentators have often shown a tendency to point to the widespread international endorsement of sustainable development as a central concept of international environmental *policy* as support for the status of the principle as a principle of international environmental *law*.[47] Endorsement of a principle, however, in the absence of clear evidence of *action* on the part of States, is unlikely to be sufficient to establish a rule of customary international law. Nevertheless, the endorsement of the principle at Rio was significant because, albeit to a limited degree, it consolidated and crystallised the concept of sustainable development. Although some have questioned whether the media "hype" surrounding the Rio Conference was justified by the results achieved, it must be remembered that international law, which depends for its formation on the establishment of an international consensus, cannot emerge overnight.

# THE FUTURE OF INTERNATIONAL ENVIRONMENTAL LAW

## A Human Right to a Healthy Environment

The first Principle of the 1972 Stockholm Declaration proclaims that: "Man has the fundamental right to freedom, equality and adequate conditions of life in an environment of a quality that permits a life of dignity and well-being."

References to the right to a healthy or decent environment have appeared in several global and regional human rights treaties, for example the African Charter on Human Rights. In 1994, the UN Sub-Commission on Prevention of Discrimination and Protection of Minorities published a report on the relationship between human rights

---

[47] Birnie and Boyle, *International Law and the Environment* (1992).

and the environment which recommended the adoption of a set of principles.[48] The Sub-Commission found that the constitutions of over sixty States contained specific provisions relating to the protection of the environment, and that an increasing number of constitutions explicitly recognised, and placed the State under a duty to protect, the human right to a satisfactory environment.[49] The final report stated that research had revealed an acceptance of environmental rights at national, regional and international levels, concluding that there had been "a shift from environmental law to the right to a healthy and decent environment", and that since this right was part of existing international law, it was therefore capable of immediate implementation by human rights organisations. The substantive elements of the right, it seems, include the right to development, life and health. The right also implies a right to the due process of law, to public participation in environmental decision-making, and to access to effective national remedies.[50] These rights are included in the draft principles, which are annexed to the Sub-Commission's report.

In spite of the Sub-Commission's conclusion that a human right to the environment is *de facto* accepted as part of existing international law, by virtue of its presence in national constitutions, at an international level, environmental human rights are seldom explicitly referred to in international instruments. Rather, they are evidenced by such things as the right to development contained in the Rio Declaration, and by the elements of that Declaration which deal with the procedural aspects of environmental policy within States. Principle 10 of the Declaration, for example, affirms that environmental issues are best handled with the participation of all concerned citizens at the relevant level, and that, at a national level, each individual shall have appropriate access to information concerning the environment held by public authorities, together with the opportunity to participate in decision-making processes. Principle 10 also requires States to provide effective access to judicial and administrative proceedings in environmental matters.

The debate continues as to what form environmental human rights should take. Whilst some commentators favour environmental rights which are principally procedural in character, so that environmental protection may be achieved through democracy and informed debate,[51] others argue that procedural rights alone do not provide effective protection, and favour the adoption of a substantive right to a clean environment. The continuing uncertainty and debate about the link between human rights and the environment may explain why emphasis on this link, which was present in the 1972 Stockholm Declaration, was not apparent in the Rio Declaration some twenty years later. The Rio Declaration avoids explicit reference to human rights, stating merely that human beings are at the centre of concerns for sustainable development.

---

[48] Ksentini, " Human Rights and the Environment" (above).
[49] UN Sub-Commission, First Progress Report, UN Doc. E/CN.4/Sub.2/1992/7,428.
[50] Boyle, "The Role of International Human Rights Law in the Protection of the Environment," in *Human Rights Approaches to Environmental Protection* (eds Boyle and Anderson) (1996).
[51] Cameron and MacKenzie, "Access to Environmental Justice and Procedural Rights in International Institutions" in *Human Rights Approaches to Environmental Protection*, (eds Boyle and Anderson) (1996).

# Chapter 3

# European Community Environmental Law

*"Within the Community, the long-term success of the more important initiatives such as the Internal Market and economic and monetary union will be dependent upon the sustainability of other policies . . . but each of these policies . . . is dependent on the carrying capacity of the environment . . . "* [1]

## Introduction

Europe's environment is damaged. In many places her landscapes are disappearing. Her plants and animal species are declining. 65 per cent of her population is exposed to noise levels exceeding those which cause annoyance. The quality of air in her cities is a continuing problem.[2] This is all despite numerous measures over the past two decades to combat air pollution, deterioration of the urban environment, climate change and acidification.[3]

European Community environmental law constitutes a highly developed and sophisticated body of international law. It has exerted, and continues to exert, a profound influence on the content and development of U.K. environmental law. It is for this reason that E.C. law and policy in relation to different aspects of environmental protection are considered in each individual chapter below, alongside the domestic law relevant to each particular subject. The aim of this chapter, however, is to consider the general principles of European Community environmental law and policy, and to examine how these affect the law in the U.K. The basic general principles of European Community law are not covered in any great detail. These may be found in a number of excellent textbooks on the subject, which the reader is encouraged to consult.[4] The following paragraphs, however, provide a brief overview for readers unfamiliar with the workings of the European Community.

[1] Fifth Action Programme on the Environment, [1993] O.J. C138/11.
[2] See *Europe's Environment: The Dobris Assessment* (eds David Stanners and Philippe Bourdeau) (The European Environment Agency, 1996).
[3] See "Report on the State of the Environment" COM (92) 23 Final — vol. III, published in conjunction with the Fifth Action Programme on the Environment [1993] O.J. C138/1.
[4] See, for example, Josephine Steiner, *Textbook on E.C. Law* (4th ed.).

## INSTITUTIONS OF THE EUROPEAN COMMUNITY

### The Commission

This is essentially the "think-tank" of the European Community. The Commission proposes and formulates new E.C. policy, based on information gathered from Member States. The Commission also has a vital ancillary rôle as the first port of call where a Member State has failed to comply with E.C. law. If a complaint is made to the Commission that a Member State has failed properly to implement an E.C. Directive or Regulation, the Commission may issue a "reasoned opinion" expressing its disapproval and warning that it may take action against the Member State in the European Court of Justice.

### The European Parliament

This is not a Parliament in the traditional sense, because it has no power to make laws by itself, or to raise taxes. Rather, the European Parliament acts as an advisory body. If the Commission proposes policies with which Parliament is unhappy, the most that Parliament can normally do is to delay matters by passing a "motion of censure" and referring those policies back to the Commission for reappraisal. In this sense, then, the European Parliament operates in much the same way as does the House of Lords at Westminster, fulfilling an important consultative function, but with little real power. However, under the "co-decision" procedure, which applies to certain types of law made by the Community (see below), the European Parliament has the power to veto legislation indefinitely in order to secure amendments to it.

### The Council of Ministers

The Council of Ministers may be thought of as the "executive branch" of the E.C. law-making system. It is comprised of government ministers, one from each Member State, who review, and formally enact as law, the proposals of the Commission. The Council may also initiate policy of its own motion by passing "resolutions", but before these can become law, the Commission and the European Parliament must be consulted.

### The European Court of Justice

The European Court of Justice (ECJ) deals with non-compliance with E.C. law by Member States. As has been said, the Commission will sometimes bring a Member State before the ECJ for non-compliance. Moreover, courts in Member States are obliged to interpret provisions of their own domestic law so as to be consistent with E.C. law. Where, within a Member State, a dispute arises between the parties as to the appropriate interpretation of E.C. law, the domestic court will refer the case to the European Court of Justice, whose judgment is binding on the courts of Member States. In the U.K., therefore, the European Court of Justice may be seen as the final court of appeal, superior to the Judicial Committee of the House of Lords, but only in cases where the application of E.C. law is called into question.

## The European Environment Agency

The European Environment Agency (E.E.A.) aims to provide the European Community and Member States with objective, reliable and comparable information at a European level. It was created because of a lack of reliable, standardised environmental data supplied to the Community by Member States. The importance of obtaining accurate scientific information on the environment was recognised as early as 1972, when a report from the Commission noted that:

" . . . the environment suffers the effects of natural phenomena and human activities alike as a result of vastly complex interactions marked by countless transfers of material and energy between the individual component parts of the environment. A full understanding of the problems is rarely possible. It is only by increasing knowledge of how pollutants move through and affect the environment that the environment can be better regulated. As regards Europe, the Commission has found it a constant problem that the availability of data from Member States is not plentiful and is not based on standard measurements or sampling materials."

The information collated by the E.E.A. provides a basis for future environmental protection measures, assists in assessing the results of current measures, and ensures that the public is properly informed about the state of the environment.[5] A report by the House of Lords has welcomed the creation of the Agency,[6] and in particular has noted that the Scientific Committee, which forms part of the Agency, will make a valuable contribution to the work of the Commission. Their Lordships were of the view that the Commission had thus far failed to take sufficient account of up to date scientific knowledge and methodology in formulating its proposals, and felt that the Agency could contribute to greater transparency in the implementation and enforcement of environmental legislation.

## SOURCES OF E.C. LAW

The European Treaties may be thought of as the "primary legislation" (or the "statutes") of the European Community. They set out the powers of the Community to make law through its institutions. The substance of that law is contained in Regulations and Directives, which may be thought of as the "secondary legislation" (or "statutory instruments") of the Community. The law contained in Regulations is binding in Member States as soon as the Regulation is issued, whilst the law contained in Directives usually requires implementation by a Member State in the form of domestic legislation before it will become binding within that State. Most E.C. environmental law is passed in the form of Directives.

---

[5] The E.E.A. was established by Regulation 1210/90; [1990] O.J. L120/1.
[6] Select Committee on the European Communities, the House of Lords (Session 1994–1995) Fifth Report, H.L. Paper 29.

## THE ADVENT OF E.C. ENVIRONMENTAL POLICY

European law on the environment is today firmly established as part of the European Community's regime of regulation. This is despite the fact that, until 1987, there was no proper legal basis for legislation on the environment in the European Community Treaty. The fact that by the time such a basis became available there was already in place a coherent philosophy on environmental protection, together with a considerable body of legislation, bears testimony to the innovative stance towards environmental protection adopted by the institutions of the Community. The development of E.C. environmental law may be conveniently divided into two stages: before 1987, and after 1987.

### Before 1987

The European Community originated in 1957, when six Western European countries — Belgium, France, Germany, Italy, Luxembourg and the Netherlands — decided to create a common market. The aims of this were to promote harmonious development of economic activities, continuous and balanced economic expansion, increased stability, an increased standard of living, and closer relationships between Member States. These aims were given effect to by the Treaty of Rome[7] but this contained no provisions in relation to the environment. It is a basic principle of E.C. law that the measures which the E.C. adopts must have some foundation in Treaty provisions, so that in the absence of relevant Treaty provisions, environmental legislation could not be adopted.

Nevertheless, a number of the economic measures which were adopted had an impact on environmental matters; for example, the 1967 Directive on the classification, labelling and packaging of dangerous substances. The Community's concern in enacting these early measures, however, was to avoid disparities in national environmental policies which might affect the free circulation of goods within the common market, or which might distort market competition between Member States. There was no concern to protect the environment itself.

In 1972, acting on the impetus generated by the UN Conference on the Human Environment, held in Stockholm, the Member States of the European Community adopted a Declaration, which stated that: "As befits the genius of Europe, particular attention will be given to intangible values and to protecting the environment so that progress may really be put at the service of mankind."

A year later, in 1973, the Council of Ministers adopted its First Action Programme on the Environment.[8] There have to date been five Action Programmes on the Environment, the last of which was published in 1993.[9] These provide a statement of the aims and policies of the E.C. on environmental matters.

As time went on, the growing emphasis on protecting the environment *per se* began to show itself in the wording of Directives. Whilst, for example, the 1970 Directive on

[7] Treaty Establishing the European Economic Community, Rome, March 25, 1957; 298 U.N.T.S. 267.
[8] First Programme of Action on the Environment, [1973] O.J. C112/1.
[9] Second Action Programme on the Environment (1977–1981), [1977] O.J. C139; Third Action Programme on the Environment (1982–1986) [1983] O.J. C46; Fourth Action Programme (1987–1992), [1987] O.J. C328; Fifth Action Programme (1993) [1993] O.J. C138/1.

air pollution from cars had justified itself in terms of establishing a common market, the 1984 Directive on pollution from industrial plants[10] refers first to the Action Programmes on the Environment and to the importance of preventing and reducing air pollution, and only later to the necessity of avoiding the distortion of competition. In 1985, the ECJ ruled that even in the absence of an express reference to the environment in the Treaty of Rome, protection of the environment was one of the Community's "essential objectives", which could justify placing certain limitations on the principle of the free movement of goods enshrined in the Treaty.[11]

## 1987: The Single European Act

The Single European Act 1987[12] gave formal recognition to the informal development of environmental policy which had taken place in preceding years. It amended the Treaty of Rome, inserting into it a chapter on the environment which outlines the objectives and principles of European Community action on the environment. The amended Treaty of Rome stated that the environment is to be preserved, protected and improved, that natural resources are to be used with care, and that human health is to be protected.[13] Armed with new powers to legislate specifically for environmental protection, the Community was able to take action of a more sophisticated nature, including, for example, legislation prohibiting television advertisements which encourage behaviour prejudicial to the protection of the environment.[14]

## The Treaty on European Union

In February 1992, the Treaty on European Union was signed at Maastricht.[15] It came into force in November 1993. The treaty comprises two separate parts. The second part is concerned with political moves to establish a closer European Union, and provides for closer co-operation with a view to Community action in such areas as foreign and security policy. The first part of the treaty renames the "E.E.C. Treaty", the "E.C. Treaty" to reflect the fact that its provisions are now wider than economic. It also establishes a mechanism for the E.C. to move towards economic and monetary union and the adoption of a single currency by January 1, 1999.

The E.C. Treaty (as already amended by the Single European Act 1987) is further substantially amended, in particular to give effect to the principle of "sustainable development", which aims to place environmental protection within the wider context of economic and social policies. Included among the basic tasks of the Community are now the promotion of sustainable and non-inflationary economic growth and the formulation of a policy in relation to the environment. The treaty therefore

---

[10] Council Dir. 84/360/EEC of June 28, 1984 on Combating Air Pollution from Industrial Plants [1984] O.J. L188/20).
[11] Case 240/83 *Procureur de la Republique v. Association de Defense des Bruleurs d'Huiles Usages* [1985] E.C.R. 531.
[12] February 17, 1986, Luxembourg, and February 28, 1986, The Hague.
[13] Art. 130r.
[14] Dir. 89/552/EEC [1989] O.J. L298.
[15] Treaty on European Union, February 7, 1992, Maastricht [1992] O.J. C224/1.

strengthens the E.C.'s commitment to environmental protection. The provisions of the (amended) E.C. Treaty which relate specifically to environmental legislation are considered more fully below.

## THE LEGAL BASIS OF E.C. ENVIRONMENTAL LEGISLATION

As has been said, it is a basic principle of E.C. law that the measures which the E.C. adopts must have some foundation in treaty provisions. During the years before the Single European Act 1987, when there was no explicit legal basis for legislation on the environment, Articles 100 and 235 of the treaty were used as the basis for environmental legislation. Article 100 permitted Directives designed to harmonise laws within Member States which directly affected the establishment or functioning of the common market, whilst Article 235, which is a "catch-all" provision, gave the Council power to legislate on matters necessary to achieve the operation of the common market even where the treaty did not explicitly provide for the legislation in question. Thus, for example, the Birds Directive, which is based on Article 235 of the treaty, was justified on the basis that:

> " . . . the conservation . . . of . . . wild birds . . . is necessary to attain, within the operation of the common market . . . the Community's objectives regarding the improvement of living conditions, a harmonious development of economic activities throughout the Community and a continuous and balanced expansion, but the necessary specific powers to act have not been provided for in the Treaty."[16]

The Single European Act 1987 introduced two Articles on which environmental measures could be based: Article 130s and Article 100A. Article 130s was to be used for action taken by the Community with respect to the environment. Article 100A was to be used for measures aimed at progressively establishing the internal market (an area without internal frontiers in which the free movement of goods, persons, services and capital is ensured). Each of these Articles required the use of a different voting procedure for the passing of legislation. The Treaty on European Union further complicated matters by providing, within the two amended Articles, a total of four voting procedures.

It is important to distinguish in broad terms between the different procedures, because some may arguably provide for a higher level of environmental protection than others. The following analysis of the procedures is simplified. Readers are referred to the diagram of the "co-decision" voting procedure, which illustrates the complexity of that particular procedure.[16a]

---

[16] Sixth recital to Dir. 79/409/EEC [1979] O.J. L103/1.
[16a] The diagram was produced for the European Parliament's Environment Committee by David Earnshaw.

# Diagram 2: The Co-decision Procedure (Article 198b)

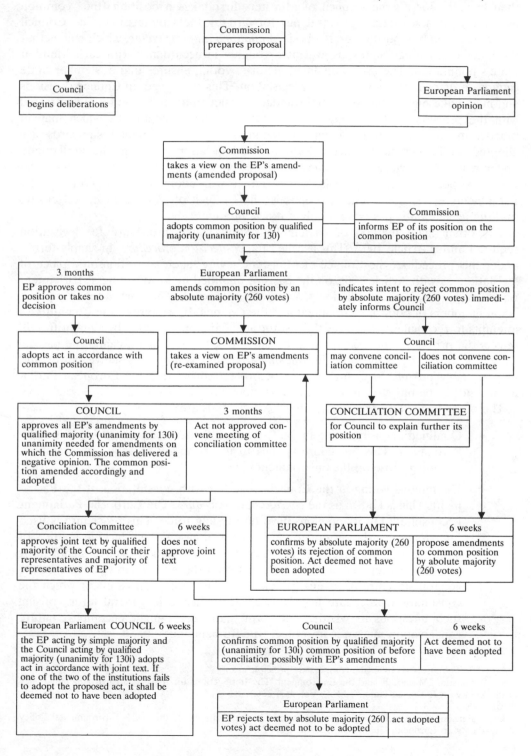

The usual basis for environmental legislation will be Article 130s. The procedure will then be as follows[17]: the Council of Ministers first takes a position (the "common position") on a legislative proposal put forward by the Commission. The Council adopts the common position on the basis of *qualified majority voting*, which means that the votes of Member States are weighted roughly in accordance with each Member State's population. The use of qualified majority voting ensures that a Member State cannot on its own veto a proposal for legislation. This can speed up Council decisions and may make higher environmental standards easier to agree.[18] It is to be contrasted with the procedure which requires the Council to be in unanimity, which may in practice mean that "lowest common denominator" environmental standards are adopted. Following the Council's decision, the legislation passes to the Parliament, under what is known as the *co-operation procedure*. Parliament may agree with the Council's position, in which case the Council will adopt the legislation. If the Parliament rejects the Council's proposals, the Council of Ministers can still ensure that the legislation is passed, but only if it acts unanimously.

The other main method of passing legislation is the procedure for legislation required under Article 100A. This is called the *co-decision procedure*. In simple terms, under this procedure, the Council of Ministers having taken a position on a piece of legislation, as with Article 130s, on the basis of qualified majority voting, if Parliament rejects a proposal, a Conciliation Committee is formed. The committee comprises equal members of both the Parliament and the Council. If, in spite of the Committee's attempts to reconcile the views of the institutions, Parliament, acting by a majority, still rejects the proposal, and asks for it to be amended, the legislation cannot be passed. This procedure, then, gives the European Parliament genuine legislative power and may arguably provide for a higher level of protection because the European Parliament tends to be more environmentally conscious than the Council.

The other two voting procedures under Article 130s are:

- Qualified majority voting in the Council, together with "co-decision" for the Parliament. This procedure applies to the adoption of action programmes, including those on the environment.

- Unanimous voting in the Council, together with consultation of the Parliament. This is known as the *consultation procedure*. The European Parliament is consulted, but its opinions have no binding force. This procedure is used for passing legislation in certain exceptional cases which include matters of land use, the management of water resources, and measures significantly affecting a Member State's choice between different energy sources or the general structure of its energy supply.[19] The circumstances under which the consultation procedure may be used are couched in general terms, raising such questions as whether the term "land use" might encompass nature conservation measures to protect wildlife habitats.[20]

---

[17] Art. 130s. See also Art. 189c (the co-operative principle).
[18] See Wilkinson, "Maastricht and the Environment: The Implications for the E.C.'s Environmental Policy of the Treaty on European Union", J.E.L. Vol. 4(2) 221.
[19] Art. 130s.
[20] See Wilkinson, "Maastricht and the Environment: The Implications for the E.C.'s Environmental Policy of the Treaty on European Union", J.E.L. Vol. 4(2) 221.

A number of cases brought before the European Court of Justice have sought to establish which of the two Articles (130s or 100A) is the correct legal basis for Directives on the environment. In Case 300/89, *Commission v. Council*,[21] the ECJ held that Article 100A could be used for environmental matters which also contributed to the establishment of the internal market. The decision concerned the Titanium Dioxide Directive,[22] which aimed to harmonise programmes for the reduction of waste from the titanium dioxide industry, and had been based on Article 130s. In the circumstances, the Court annulled the Directive because it had been based on the wrong Article, and held that it should have been based on Article 100A. This was seen as a landmark decision and has been interpreted as widening the circumstances under which Article 100A may be used.[23] Commentators have noted, however, that the decision in Case 300/89 was not without constitutional difficulties, because of the strained interpretation which the Court gave to the concept of "contributing to the establishment of the internal market" under Article 100A.

In a subsequent case, the ECJ has held that the legal basis for a Directive should depend on what the court has called its "centre of gravity". In Case C155/91, *Commission v. Council*,[24] which concerned the correct basis for a Directive amending the Framework Directive on Waste, the court held that, on balance, the principal concern of the Directive (its "centre of gravity") was environmental protection, and not the establishment of the internal market. The proper basis for the Directive, therefore, was Article 130s. The Commission had argued that because the Directive harmonised national laws, *inter alia*, by introducing a single definition of "waste", it could be justified under Article 100A as contributing to the establishment of the internal market. The ECJ, however, took the view that the Directive's effect on the internal market was incidental to its primary function, which was environmental protection, so that use of Article 100A could not be justified. The conclusion to be drawn from this decision, then, is that environmental protection measures must now generally be taken under Article 130s, but that Article 100A may, in exceptional circumstances, be used for environmental protection legislation, provided that this has a significant and direct effect on the internal market.

# THE PRINCIPLES OF E.C. ENVIRONMENTAL LAW

The Treaty lists certain objectives, principles and factors to be taken into account with respect to E.C. action on the environment[25]:

---

[21] [1991] I–E.C.R. 2687.
[22] Dir. 89/428/EEC [1989] O.J. L201/56.
[23] *ibid.*
[24] [1993] I E.C.R. 939.
[25] Arts. 130r, 130s and 130t.

## Objectives: (Article 130r(1))

- To preserve, protect and improve the quality of the environment;
- To contribute towards the protection of human health;
- To ensure a prudent and rational utilisation of natural resources;
- To promote measures at an international level to deal with regional or worldwide environmental problems.

## Principles: (Article 130r(2))

- Community policy on the environment shall aim at *a high level of protection*, taking into account the diversity of situations in the various regions of the Community;
- Policy is to be based on the precautionary principle;
- Policy is to be based on the principles that preventive action should be taken, and that environmental damage should, as a priority, be rectified at source;
- The polluter should pay for the costs of environmental damage;
- Environmental protection requirements must be integrated into the definition and implementation of other Community policies.

## Factors to be Taken into Account: (Article 130r(3))

In preparing its policy on the environment, the Community shall take account of:

- Available scientific and technical data;
- Environmental conditions in the various regions of the Community;
- The potential benefits and costs of action or lack of action;
- The economic and social development of the Community as a whole and the balanced development of its regions.

Member States are free to maintain or introduce more stringent protective measures than those adopted by the E.C., provided that they are compatible with the E.C. Treaty.[26]

# THE DEVELOPMENT OF E.C. ENVIRONMENTAL POLICY

In the early years, the Community had adopted a reactive approach to environmental policy, placing emphasis on reducing pollution once it had occurred. The emphasis

[26] Art. 130t.

was, in the words of Article 130r(1), on "preserving and protecting" the quality of the environment, rather than on *improving* its quality. Quickly, however, this emphasis changed, so that now a proactive policy is apparent which aims to prevent pollution in advance even before the activities giving rise to it have commenced.

The Second Action Programme on the Environment (1977 - 1981) put forward the idea of "Environmental Impact Assessment". This required studies to be undertaken of the environmental impacts of certain development projects before decisions were taken whether or not to proceed with them. Environmental Impact Assessment has now become an important feature of Community policy. In 1985, a Directive made an assessment mandatory for a number of different categories of project, and there are currently proposals to amend the 1985 Directive so that its scope is extended.

Aligned with this increasingly sophisticated approach came a recognition that protection efforts should not be limited to a single environmental medium. Early Directives had focused specifically on the protection of individual environmental media, such as water or air. Pollutants, however, do not necessarily confine themselves to one medium. The recognition that this is so led to the formulation of the Directive concerning Integrated Pollution Prevention and Control,[27] which is discussed in Chapter 6.

Ensuring a "prudent and rational utilisation of natural resources" (the third objective of Article 130r(1)) is a much wider objective than preserving and protecting the environment. It requires the E.C. to make fundamental decisions about the nature of individuals' lifestyles within the Community and, perhaps, to place limits on economic growth. The E.C.'s Third Action Programme explicitly recognised the link between the environment and the economy and noted that environmental resources set limits to, and therefore must form the basis of, economic and social policy. Thus it was important that environmental considerations should form an integral part of economic and social policies. This is reflected in Article 130r(2) of the Treaty (above). Recognition of the link between the environment and the economy reached its height in the Fifth Action Programme, which addressed the concept of "sustainable development", the achievement of which it refers to as one of the principal challenges facing the E.C in the 1990s.

## Sustainable Development

Sustainable development is now at the centre of Europe's strategy on the environment. The concept, which originated in international law (see Chapter 2), is given effect in E.C. law by the Treaty on European Union. The treaty requires that economic growth be sustainable, non-inflationary, and that it should respect the environment.[28] Although, as has been said, this strengthens the E.C.'s commitment to environmental protection, the term "sustainable growth" (rather than "sustainable development") has been criticised as being too close to the idea of "sustained growth" and too similar to the original phrasing of the Treaty, in 1957, which referred to "continued and balanced expansion" as one of the tasks of the Community.

[27] Dir. 96/61 E.C. [1996] O.J. L257/26.
[28] Art. 2.

The Fifth Action Programme gives some indication of the means by which sustainable development is to be achieved. The programme lists a number of environmental problems: climate change; acidification of waterways; air pollution; depletion of natural resources and of biodiversity; deterioration of the urban environment; deterioration of coastal zones, and waste management. These, the programme states, are merely symptoms of the real cause of environmental damage, which is current patterns of human consumption and behaviour within the Community. Effecting changes to these consumption patterns requires "shared responsibility", or in other words the involvement of all sectors of society, including public administration, public and private enterprise and the general public.

The enthusiasm with which the E.C. has embraced what was originally an international law concept reflects its increased awareness of the global dimension of environmental law. Indeed, the Treaty on European Union has added to the Community's other environmental objectives that of promoting measures at an international level to deal with regional or worldwide environmental problems.[29] This objective, which was not provided for in the Single European Act 1987, reflects the sentiments expressed in the Fifth Action Programme, namely that global concerns about climate change, deforestation and energy consumption, together with the political and economic changes in central and eastern Europe, have all added to the responsibilities of the E.C. in the international arena.[30]

## SPECIFIC ENVIRONMENTAL PRINCIPLES OF THE E.C. TREATY

Two principles, in particular, are specifically referred to in the treaty as forming the basis for environmental policy and legislation:

### The "Precautionary" Principle

The precautionary principle was made part of Community policy for the first time by the Treaty on European Union. Given the current state of scientific knowledge, it is rarely possible for us fully to understand the mechanisms by which the environment is damaged. The danger, therefore, is that given the uncertainty surrounding the causes of environmental deterioration, legislation to protect the environment may be passed too late to be of any use, or may not be passed at all. The precautionary principle, however, requires measures to be taken despite scientific uncertainty about the likelihood of harm, and even in cases where there is no scientific proof of a causal link between the emissions in question and their effects. The problem is that there is no definition of the principle in the treaty and no agreement as to what, in practical terms, the principle means. At most, therefore, it provides a rather vague guide for policy-makers.

---

[29] Art. 130r.
[30] Fifth Action Programme Executive Summary.

## The "Polluter Pays" Principle

The "polluter pays" principle has been a declared policy of the European Community since its First Action Programme in 1972. In essence, the principle requires that the polluter, rather than society at large, must pay for his polluting activities. The Fourth Action Programme stated that the application of the "polluter pays" principle was of decisive importance in the E.C.'s strategy for making the best possible use of resources. Apportioning to polluters the costs of protecting the environment in accordance with the principle gave polluters an incentive to reduce the pollution caused by their activities and to develop less polluting technologies and products.

The problem for policy-makers, however, has been how to translate the broad concept of the principle into practical methods of collecting fair and adequate payments from polluters. It is clear that the polluter should pay for the damage he causes to the environment, but the precise amounts he should pay have proved difficult to calculate. This is because, as is discussed elsewhere in this book, no appropriate formula has been developed for valuing environmental amenities.

## The Legal Status of the Treaty Principles

The principles are to be found in Article 130r, which states that they are to form the basis of Community policy on the environment. It appears from case law in the ECJ that the principles outlined in Article 130r are not justiciable and cannot therefore be used to challenge legislative measures by Member States.

In the case of *Peralta Re*,[31] the ECJ stated that Article 130r was confined to defining the general objectives of the Community in relation to the environment and that its principles were designed to provide guidance to the Council in formulating policy. They could not be used as the basis for a declaration that an Italian domestic law was invalid. Courts in the U.K. have adopted a similar approach. In *R. v. Secretary of State for Trade and Industry, ex p. Dudderidge and Others*,[32] it was held that the Secretary of State is not required to apply the "precautionary principle" in taking action where possible risk of environmental harm or harm to human health arises. According to the court, Article 130r, when examined in its context, laid down principles on which Community policy on the environment was to be based. It did not impose any immediate obligation on Member States to act in a particular way.

# REGULATORY TECHNIQUES IN E.C. ENVIRONMENTAL LAW[33]

Over the years, the regulatory techniques employed by the E.C. for environmental protection have grown increasingly sophisticated.

---

[31] Case 379/92 (1995, ECJ, unreported). See *Environmental Law and Management* (1996), Vol. 8(1), p.6.
[32] *The Independent,* October 4, 1994, Q.B.D.
[33] See Macrory, "Enforcement of Community Environmental Laws: Some Issues" 29 C.M.L.R. 347.

## "Command and Control" Legislation

The earliest Directives were examples of "command and control" legislation. They prescribed explicit and precise goals which had to be achieved within a given sector.[34] The Fifth Action Programme, however, noted that responsibility for the environment can be more effectively shared within the Community by broadening the range of instruments used to protect the environment beyond traditional "command and control" legislation. This broadening of approach was already apparent in some Directives which laid down certain goals but gave Member States discretion in how those goals were to be achieved.[35]

## "Horizontal" Directives

So-called "horizontal" Directives are a more recent Community innovation in regulatory technique. Instead of applying to a specific area of environmental regulation (such as water or air) and requiring substantive results, the Directives may be described as "procedural" in their nature. They focus on the *methods* by which environmental protection is to be achieved. Examples of such Directives are the Directive on Environmental Impact Assessment and the Directive on Access to Environmental Information.

(i) *Environmental Impact Assessment*

Impact Assessment requires that certain development proposals must be assessed to determine their environmental effects before permission for development is granted. The Directive on the Assessment of the Effects of Certain Public and Private Projects on the Environment[36] applies, *inter alia*, to crude oil refineries, thermal power stations, installations for the storage of radioactive waste, installations for the extraction of asbestos, and to the construction of motorways and trading ports. Impact assessment is mandatory for these projects.

In addition, Member States are required to adopt all measures necessary to ensure that, before consent is given, certain other projects likely to have significant effects on the environment, by reason of their nature, size or location are subject to an environmental assessment. The assessment aims to identify, describe and assess the direct and indirect effects of the project on humans, fauna, flora, soil, water, air, climate, landscape, material assets and cultural heritage. In order to give effect to the Directive, the U.K. has had to pass 20 or so individual laws in different legal areas.

(ii) *Information on the environment*

The Fifth Action Programme recognises that many of the Community's environmental problems are caused by society's vast consumption of resources in the absence of any awareness of the environmental degradation which this causes. The programme puts

---

[34] See, for example, Dir. 80/779/EEC on air quality limit values and guide values for sulphur dioxide and suspended particulates, [1980] O.J. L229/30.

[35] For example, Dir. 78/659 on the quality of freshwaters needing protection or improvement in order to support fish life, [1978] O.J. L229/11.

[36] Dir. 85/337/EEC; [1985] O.J. L175/40.

forward the idea that once the public is in possession of relevant information about environmental damage, it will put pressure on industry to reduce pollution and will provide a mandate for further pollution control legislation. Access to information is now seen as an important aspect of E.C. environmental policy and is achieved by various methods:

(a) The Directive on Freedom of Access to Information on the Environment was adopted in 1990.[37] This is intended to ensure, throughout the Community, free access to, and wide dissemination of environmental information held by public authorities. Member States are under a duty to ensure that public authorities make information on the environment available to any natural or legal person in the E.C. who requests it. A request may only be refused on certain specified grounds, for example that the information would prejudice national security or is *sub judice*.

(b) Eco-labelling.[38] The Community's eco-labelling scheme aims to promote the design, production, marketing and use of products with a reduced environmental impact without compromising the product, or worker safety, or significantly affecting a product's essential useful properties. The aim is also to provide consumers with the information they need in order to enable them, when purchasing products, to choose those which have the least environmental impact. Eco-labels are awarded on the basis of fulfilment of specified Community criteria. As yet, the scheme has not been a success. At the time of writing there are only a handful of "eco-labelled" products in the shops and the scheme has been described as "flagging".[39]

(c) Eco-auditing.[40] The objective of the eco-auditing scheme is to promote continuous improvement in the environmental performance of participating companies through the establishment of environmental policies, programmes and management systems and their regular review or audit. The scheme is a voluntary one for industry, under which companies publish a report on the success with which they have implemented environmentally-friendly practices, thus providing the public with more information on their environmental performance. The report is compiled from the results of an "environmental audit" which measures the company's performance against the objectives and policies which it has set out and provides a basis for ascertaining how that performance might be improved.

## Market-Based Instruments

The use of market-based instruments is a regulatory technique that is of increasing interest to the E.C. The Fifth Action Programme emphasised the importance of

---

[37] Dir. 90/313/EEC [1990] O.J. L158.
[38] See Regulation 880/92; [1992] O.J. L99/1, the Community's ecolabel award scheme).
[39] ENDS 257, p. 25, June 1996.
[40] Council Regulation (EEC) No. 1836/93; [1993] O.J. L168/1; Regulation allowing voluntary participation by companies in the industrial sector in a Community eco-management and audit scheme.

market instruments in regulating the environment. Whilst the use of "command and control" instruments had been useful in setting fundamental levels of protection, market-based instruments, such as taxes and permits, which aimed to ensure that products reflected the environmental costs of their manufacture, had a vital rôle to play in persuading producers and consumers to be responsible in their use of natural resources.

## The Impact of Subsidiarity on the E.C.'s Regulatory Techniques

Subsidiarity is essentially a political doctrine governing the appropriateness of Community action. Its effect is that legislation by the Community, rather than by Member States themselves, should be passed as an exception rather than as a rule, and only when Community action is essential. As Article 3B of the Treaty puts it:

> "In areas which do not fall within its exclusive competence, the Community shall take action, in accordance with the principle of subsidiarity, only if and in so far as the objectives of the proposed action cannot be sufficiently achieved by the Member States, and can, therefore, by reason of the scale or effects of the proposed action, be better achieved by the Community. Any action by the Community shall not go beyond what is necessary to achieve the objectives of this Treaty."

The European Community, therefore, must demonstrate a clear need for each new piece of Community legislation, and show that legislation affecting the Community as a whole secures advantages which cannot be attained by domestic legislation in individual Member States.

The doctrine of subsidiarity is underpinned by the doctrine of proportionality. This requires that E.C. legislation must not go further than is reasonably necessary to tackle a particular problem, or, in other words, that the legislative solution to a problem should be *proportional* to its extent.[41] The House of Lords Select Committee on the European Community has noted that the use of Directives as the main legislative instruments in E.C. law may be said to safeguard to some extent the principle of subsidiarity, because Directives usually give Member States some discretion as to how to achieve the objectives they prescribe.[42] Further, the ability of Member States, under the Treaty, to enact environmental measures that are more stringent than E.C. measures[43] allows them a certain "local" control of environmental regulation.

In order to give effect to the principle of subsidiarity, the E.C. is beginning to consolidate and to simplify certain environmental Directives. In 1992, the European Council declared that, in accordance with the principle of subsidiarity, the Commission intended to simplify the various Directives on water quality. The Community intended to set essential quality and health parameters, whilst leaving Member States free to add further standards which they considered necessary.

---

[41] See Commission Report to the European Council on the adaption of Community legislation to the subsidiarity principle, COM (93) 545.
[42] House of Lords Select Committee on the European Communities (Session 1991 — 1992) 9th Report, H.L. Paper 53-I.
[43] Art. 130t.

The principle of subsidiarity is essentially political, rather than legal, in effect. It is stated in the Treaty in very general terms. It would be difficult, therefore, for a Member State to challenge, in the ECJ, E.C. activity in a particular sphere as being inconsistent with the principle.

## THE EFFECT OF E.C. ENVIRONMENTAL LAW ON U.K. LAW

E.C. law is a particular species of international law. The Treaty of Rome — the basic constitutional code of the Community — was originally conceived as an international agreement between States binding in international law.[44] The approach of the U.K. is that international law is not regarded as part of our own legal system unless it is incorporated into U.K. law by an Act of Parliament. This was done by section 2(1) of the European Communities Act 1972 which provides that E.C. law is to form part of the law in the U.K: "All such rights . . . arising under the Treaties . . . are without further enactment to be given legal effect".

In spite of this general provision, the *extent* to which individual E.C. laws are part of the U.K. legal system will depend upon the particular "effect" of each individual E.C. legislative instrument. Any given legislative instrument may have an effect on U.K. law in one or more of three ways. First, it may have "direct effect" in U.K. law. Secondly, it may be given effect by national courts indirectly. Thirdly, it may be effective by means of the *Francovitch* principle.

### Direct Effect

If a provision of E.C. law is "directly effective", or "capable of direct effects", domestic courts must apply it as it stands. As E.C. law takes priority over domestic law,[45] domestic courts must apply it in preference to national provisions.

Most E.C. environmental law is contained in Directives. The conditions necessary for a Directive to have direct effect are that it must be sufficiently clear and precise, and it must be unconditional, leaving no room for the Member State to which it is addressed to exercise discretion in the method by which it is implemented.[46]

Opinion differs as to the extent to which Directives on the environment have direct effect. Many Directives are simply concerned to instruct Member States to draw up rehabilitation programmes, or to undertake monitoring activities, leaving national governments with a degree of discretion as to how these things are to be done. Directives of this kind, then, clearly cannot have direct effect. There are, however, a number of Directives in which the position is unclear. The ECJ's approach to the matter is illustrated by the decision in *Comitato di Coordinamento per la Difesa della Cava v. Regione Lombardia*.[47] The issue in that case was whether Article 4 of a Waste Directive[48] had direct effect. The Directive was framed in the following terms:

---

[44] See Jason Coppel, "Rights, Duties and the End of *Marshall* ", 57 M.L.R. 859.
[45] *Costa v. ENEL* (Case 6/64) [1964] E.C.R. 585; *Internationale Handelsgesellschaft GmbH* (Case 11/70) [1970] E.C.R. 1125.
[46] *Yvonne v. Duyn v. Home Office* (Case 41/74) [1974] I E.C.R. 1337.
[47] [1994] I E.C.R. 0483.
[48] Dir. 75/442/EEC.

"Member States shall take the necessary measures to ensure that waste is disposed of without endangering human health and without harming the environment, and in particular without risk to water, air . . . [etc]."

The Court held that the Directive could not have direct effect, because it was not unconditional and not sufficiently precise. It merely indicated a programme for Member States to follow and defined a framework for action.

E.C. Directives on the environment may be divided into a number of categories[49]:

- Directives which lay down maximum permissible levels of discharges or emissions. These values are precise and must be adhered to unconditionally by Member States. Such Directives, therefore, are likely to have direct effect.

- Directives which prohibit entirely the use of certain substances or their discharge into the environment. Again, such prohibitions are generally couched in absolute terms and will therefore have direct effect.

- Directives which require Member States to perform certain acts, for example to draw up and carry out environmental rehabilitation programmes, or programmes to reduce waste. This is the most commonly used form of Directive. Such Directives do not have direct effect because the nature of the programmes will depend upon the particular extent of the environmental problems within each Member State and upon the Member State's response to those problems.

## *"Horizontal" Direct Effect*

Discussion has centred so far on whether a Member State is obliged to give effect to a Directive in its dealings with individuals. But can an individual rely on a Directive as against a water company or a waste haulage firm?

It has been established by the ECJ[50] that an individual cannot rely on a Directive in a national court as against an individual. This is on the basis that Directives are addressed to Member States. A directly effective provision can only be invoked against a government body. This ruling has the potential to produce harsh consequences, because whether or not an individual has the protection of E.C. law will depend on whether he is taking action against a public or a private body. Therefore, the ECJ has mitigated the effects of the rule by defining the notion of "State" widely. An examination of the Court's jurisprudence demonstrates that this concept encompasses municipalities, local authorities and professional societies entrusted with public functions.[51] In *Foster v. British Gas plc*,[52] the ECJ held that direct effect could be relied on against:

"a body, whatever its legal form, which has been made responsible, pursuant to a measure adopted by the State for providing a public service under the control of

---

[49] See Ludwig Kramer, "The Implementation of Community Environmental Directives within Member States: Some Implications of the Direct Effect Doctrine", (1991) J.E.L. 39.
[50] *Marshall v. Southampton and South West Hampshire Area Health Authority (Teaching)* Case 152/84 [1986] I E.C.R. 723.
[51] Bebr, Joined Cases C6/90 and C9/90 *Francovich v. Italy* C.M.L.R. 29, pp. 557–558, 570.
[52] Case C188/89 [1990] I E.C.R. 3313.

the State and has for that purpose special powers beyond those which result from the normal rules applicable in relation between individuals."

*Commission v. Ireland*[53] suggests that this would include private bodies whose activities are subject to direct or indirect control. This would mean, for example, that the privatised water companies or private waste disposal companies might be held liable for breaches of E.C. Directives.

## Indirect Effect

The doctrine of "indirect effect" requires national courts to interpret domestic legislation so as to be consistent with, and so as to give effect to, European Community law.[54] This will be so even where the national provisions in question were adopted after the Directive.[55] It follows that where domestic legislation purports to give effect to the provisions of a Directive, that legislation will not be effective in so far as it may actually be inconsistent with the Directive. The U.K. courts, however, have been wary of using the doctrine of indirect effect in this way to strike out legislation as *ultra vires* where it fails properly to implement a Directive. Thus, in *R. v. Swale Borough Council and Medway Ports Authority, ex p. RSPB*,[56] the court, in reviewing a planning authority's decision to grant planning permission in the absence of an environmental impact assessment, focused exclusively on interpreting the relevant regulations, and failed to consider the wording of the Directive which they purported to implement.

## The "*Francovich* Principle"

The "*Francovich* principle" enables individuals to obtain compensation from a Member State for its breach of an E.C. environmental obligation.

The case of *Francovich and Others v. Italian Republic*,[57] concerned a number of Italian employees who were to lose large sums of money in unpaid salaries following the bankruptcy of two Italian firms. Italy had failed to implement a Directive that would have ensured payment of these salaries. The European Court of Justice held that it was a general principle, inherent in the scheme of the Treaty, that a Member State is liable to make good damage to individuals caused by a breach of Community law for which it is responsible. There were, however, a number of conditions to be met before a Member State would be found liable. First, only breach of a "fundamental Community obligation" had the potential to give rise to liability. There were three further conditions:

> (1) The result required by the Directive must include the conferring of rights for the benefit of individuals;

---

[53] Case 249/81 [1982] E.C.R. 4005.
[54] *Von Colson v. Land Nordrhein-Westfalen,* Case 14/83 [1984] E.C.R. 1891.
[55] *Marleasing S.A. v. La Commercial Internaciona de Alimentacion S.A.* [1992] 1 C.M.L.R. 305.
[56] [1991] J.P.L. 39.
[57] Cases C6/90 and C9/90 [1991] I E.C.R. 5357.

(2)  The content of these rights must be identifiable by reference to the Directive;

(3)  There must exist a causal link between the breach of the State's obligations and the damage suffered by the persons affected.

The effect of this principle, which has been clarified in subsequent cases,[58] is that the success of those seeking to sue a Member State for breach of an environmental Directive will depend upon whether the Directive in question creates rights for the benefit of individuals. Directives on the environment often merely require Member States to draw up programmes of action. These Directives cannot reasonably be construed as creating rights for the benefit of individuals. However, the European Court of Justice has accepted that the Directive on Dangerous Substances in Groundwater[59] and the Directive on Sulphur Dioxide and Suspended Particles in Air[60] both create rights for individuals.[61] Other Directives which might be held to create rights for the benefit of individuals include those of a procedural nature, for example the Directives on Environmental Impact Assessment[62] and on Freedom of Information,[63] as well as Directives made for the purpose of protecting human health.[64]

# ENFORCEMENT OF E.C. ENVIRONMENTAL LAW

Enforcement of E.C. obligations is particularly important with respect to the environment, because the environment often cannot be restored to its former condition once it is damaged. The environment has no legal voice of its own and cannot, therefore, counter the voice of industry, which has an interest in depleting environmental resources.

Failure by Member States properly to implement their obligations under environmental Directives is a serious problem throughout the Community. The House of Lords, reporting on the enforcement of environmental legislation, noted that there was a "substantial body of evidence" that Community legislation was being "widely disregarded", and that there was an "absence of an appropriate political response to this evidence." A communication published by the European Commission in October 1996 states that E.C. environmental policy is now at a crucial point in its development. The communication continues:

> "Following two decades of formulating a legal framework, we are now moving into a second stage of strengthening and consolidating the established body of law by attempting to ensure that it is properly enforced in all Member States."[65]

---

[58] *Brasserie du Pecheur S.A. v. Republic of Germany and R. v. Secretary of State for Transport, ex p. Factortame,* Joined cases C46/93 and C48/93 [1996] I E.C.R. 1029.
[59] Dir. 80/68/EEC; [1980] O.J. L20/43.
[60] Dir. 80/779/EEC; [1980] O.J. L229.
[61] See Case C131/88 *Commission v. Germany* [1991] I E.C.R. 825 and Case C361/88 *Commission v. Germany* [1991] I E.C.R. 2567.
[62] Dir. 85/337/EEC; [1985] O.J. L175.
[63] Dir. 90/313/EEC; [1990] O.J. L158.
[64] Dir. 80/779 on air quality limit values and guide values for sulphur dioxide and suspended particulates.
[65] ENDS 261, p. 41, October 1996.

It is not to be thought that simply because a Member State has passed legislation which purports to give effect to the provisions of a Directive, that legislation will amount to compliance with the requirements of the Directive. Often, the discretion which a Member State has in choosing the method by which the requirements of a Directive are met is exercised in such a way as to fall short of fulfilling the purpose of the Directive, sometimes leaving the question of proper implementation to be decided by the European Court of Justice at the behest of the Commission. There are numerous examples in U.K. environmental law of *purported* compliance with Directives which may not amount to *de facto* compliance because the legislation in question fails to make sufficient changes to the pollution control or conservation regime which is in place. One such example is the Drinking Water Directive,[66] which is discussed in Chapter 9. Another is the Natural Habitats Directive,[67] discussed in Chapter 12.

The problem of non-implementation has become particularly acute in recent years. A number of environmental E.C. Directives were issued during the 1970s and early 1980s which gave Member States a considerable length of time for implementation. At the time, this meant that no onerous action was necessary, but such action is necessary now that the time limits for compliance have run out. Moreover, the current jurisprudence of the ECJ towards Member States' implementation of Directives entails harsh consequences for a Member State which defaults in implementing a Directive, including compensating any individual who has thereby suffered loss. Such consequences were not evident in the 1970s and 1980s and have now effectively transformed the legal status of Directives from mere declarations of policy and intention into instruments creating genuine legal obligations.[68]

As has been said, the European Commission is responsible for bringing enforcement proceedings against Member States in the European Court of Justice. It does this under Article 169 of the Treaty of Rome. Following the Treaty on European Union, the ECJ has the power to impose a penalty against a Member State which has failed to comply with a judgment against it.[69] In practical terms, however, the Commission is faced with a number of problems in relation to enforcement.

The procedure under Article 169 is reactive, and so cannot be used to prevent harm from occurring. The Commission has a limited staff for investigating and dealing with infringement complaints. In the process of establishing the European Environment Agency, the European Parliament pressed hard for the Agency to have a rôle in enforcing Community law. Their efforts, however, were unsuccessful, so that the Agency's rôle is confined to the collection and analysis of environmental data, largely in co-operation with national authorities.

The Commission suffers from a lack of information about infringements of Community law. It cannot, of course, deal with infringements unless it is aware of them. Individuals and environmental organisations have proved helpful to the Commission by acting as environmental watchdogs, but they themselves have very limited access to domestic courts and to the ECJ. It is the Commission which decides whether

---

[66] Dir. 80/778/EEC [1989] O.J. L229/11.
[67] Dir. 92/42/EEC [1992] O.J. L167/17.
[68] See Macrory, "Enforcement of Community Environmental Law" 29 C.M.L.R. 347.
[69] Art. 171.

or not to bring proceedings against a Member State, and it does so only in a small number of cases. Individuals and pressure groups cannot compel the Commission to take proceedings, and they often lack the funds and institutional structures necessary to pursue protracted litigation themselves. Moreover, the number and nature of complaints often depends upon the particular interests of environmental organisations. For example, the large number of reported infringements of water pollution law in the U.K. has been attributed to the strength of campaigns on this issue by U.K. pressure groups, whilst in France the focus of similar groups has been on hunting and the protection of wild animals.

The idea of allowing individuals or organisations access to domestic courts to speak on behalf of the environment is strongly advocated by some commentators and is increasingly gaining acceptance.[70] Indeed, the E.C.'s Environment Commissioner has recently pledged to "leave no stone unturned" in her efforts to improve access to the courts for environmental groups and individuals who wish to address infringements of E.C. legislation.[71] The Commission is currently considering a range of proposals to improve enforcement of environmental Directives, including measures to improve public interest groups' access to national courts and asking the ECJ, as a matter of course, to impose sanctions on Member States which fail to comply with its rulings.[72]

[70] See Kramer, "Public Interest Litigation in Environmental Matters before European Courts" (1996) J.E.L. vol. 8(1).
[71] See "Implementing Community Environmental Law," COM(96) 0500 Final.
[72] ibid.

# Chapter 4

# THE COMMON LAW AND THE ENVIRONMENT

*". . . public bodies, both national and international, are taking significant steps towards the establishment of legislation which will promote the protection of the environment . . . given that so much well informed and carefully structured legislation is now being put in place for this purpose, there is less need for the courts to develop a common law principle to achieve the same end and indeed it may well be undesirable that they should do so."*[1]

## Introduction

Although the modern trend in environmental law is for regulatory agencies to control the environment under authority derived from statute, the common law may also be used to control environmental damage. The primary function of the common law, however, is to protect private rights, and there are a number of ways in which this overriding concern of the common law can operate to the detriment of environmental amenities.

The common law tends to reward the exploitation of natural resources by man. Wild animals, for example, may be killed or taken into ownership under the common law, subject only to the prior claims of the owner of the land on which they are found. Similarly, a public right to fish in tidal waters is enshrined in the common law, as are the private fishing rights of the owner of land adjacent to non-tidal waters. The common law regards fish simply as profits of the land, and cares nothing for their protection. A further example is the distinction drawn in the common law, absurd in ecological terms, between water which percolates beneath the ground and water which flows in defined channels. Percolating groundwater cannot be owned until it is abstracted.[2] It follows that a landowner has an absolute right to abstract percolating water from beneath his land, irrespective of the consequences to his neighbours or to the surrounding community, who have no recognised interest in the water.[3]

Many environmental amenities are "public property", in the sense that they are not owned by ascertained individuals. Therefore, the extent to which common law rules can provide protection for them is limited. Moreover, the manner in which the

---

[1] *per* Lord Goff in *Cambridge Water Company v. Eastern Counties Leather Co. plc* [1994] 1 All E.R. 53 at 76.
[2] See Clayberg, "The Law of Percolating Waters" (1915) 14 Mich. L.R. 119.
[3] *Bradford Corporation v. Pickles* [1895] A.C. 587.

common law develops — by decisions in individual cases — is ill-suited to the process of developing rules for environmental protection, which requires the balancing of a wide range of competing interests. The only interests that can be considered in an adversarial courtroom battle are those of the individual litigants. Because the common law can operate only where harm has been caused to an ascertained individual, rather than to the environment *per se*, its effectiveness is limited to the resolution of what may be termed "neighbourhood" environmental problems. To this extent, then, the common law retains an important, albeit ancillary, function in environmental law.

The predominant method of environmental control at common law is through the nuisance action. Closely related to this is the action for the escape of noxious things from land, brought under what is known as "the rule in *Rylands v. Fletcher*".[4] Following the decision of the House of Lords in *Cambridge Water Company v. Eastern Counties Leather*,[5] this is perhaps more properly regarded as an offshoot of the tort of nuisance rather than as a distinct cause of action. Consideration of the law of nuisance, then, forms the bulk of this chapter. Also related to common law nuisance is the operation of Part III of the Environmental Protection Act 1990, which prescribes certain "statutory nuisances". These, although they are not, of course, actions at common law, are also dealt with here for the sake of convenience. In addition, the torts of trespass and negligence, which have some limited utility in protecting the environment, are briefly considered.

## NUISANCE

In summary, there are three types of nuisance:

- Private nuisance;
- Public nuisance;
- Statutory nuisance.

## PRIVATE NUISANCE

Private nuisance may be defined as: ". . . unlawful interference with a person's use or enjoyment of land or some right over, or in connection with it."[6]

It is an important mechanism for the protection of the individual's private right to freedom from pollution. Typical situations which may give rise to liability in nuisance include incursions on to the plaintiff's property, or interference with his enjoyment of that property, by water, smoke, smell, fumes, gas, noise, heat, vibrations, electricity, animals and vegetation.[7] Disease or germs brought onto property by the act of another can also found an action in nuisance.[8]

---

[4] (1868) L.R. 3, H.L. 330.
[5] [1994] 1 All E.R. 53.
[6] Rogers, *Winfield and Jolowicz on Tort* (14th ed., 1994), p. 408.
[7] Salmond and Heuston, *Law of Torts*, p. 57.
[8] *per* Viscount Maugham in *Sedleigh-Denfield v. O'Callaghan* [1940] A.C. 880 at 888, H.L.

The range of interests protected by the law of nuisance, however, is limited. In contrast with other legal systems, English law has persistently refused to condemn aesthetic nuisances. Thus, ruining a view can create no cause of action, for it is a matter only of "delight" not of "necessity".[9] Similarly, the right to clear television reception is not protected. In *Hunter and Others v. Canary Wharf Ltd*,[10] Pill L.J. said:

> "I accept the importance of television in the lives of very many people. However, in my judgment the erection or presence of a building in the line of sight between a T.V. transmitter and other properties is not actionable as an interference with the use and enjoyment of land."

The law of private nuisance, then, protects a person's interest in the use and enjoyment of his land. Long before planning and environmental legislation placed limits on a person's freedom to use his land exactly as he pleased, it was recognised that the very exercise of a freedom to enjoy land creates, as its corollary, an obligation of non-interference with the freedoms enjoyed by owners of neighbouring land. In other words, the freedom to use land can never be absolute, but must be exercised so that it does not unreasonably prevent a neighbouring landowner from enjoying *his* freedom. Therefore, in an action for private nuisance, the court strives to strike an appropriate balance between the rights of one owner of land to use that land as he wishes and the rights of his neighbour to do the same. To assist them in performing this "balancing act", the courts have developed and applied a number of general principles which are examined below.

## The Plaintiff

In contrast with the position in relation to public nuisance and statutory nuisance, it has traditionally been necessary for a plaintiff who wishes to bring an action in private nuisance to show that he has a legal interest in the land affected by the nuisance. This is because, historically, the tort of private nuisance arose as an offshoot of land law, so that a plaintiff's lack of a legal right to occupy or enjoy his land was fatal to a nuisance claim. In 1993, however, the decision of the Court of Appeal in *Khorasandjian v. Bush*[11] appeared to sweep this requirement aside. The decision in *Khorasandjian*, in which a daughter living in the parental home was granted standing to sue in respect of harassing telephone calls, shed little light on the precise nature of the connection (if any) which the plaintiff must establish between himself and the land on which the nuisance was experienced. It therefore threatened to blur the distinction between public and private nuisance and to transform the tort of private nuisance from a tort against land into a tort of personal harassment. In *Hunter and Others v. Canary Wharf Ltd*,[12] the plaintiffs included wives, husbands, partners, children and other relatives

---

[9] *per* Wray C.J. in *Aldred's case* (1610) 9 Co.Rep. 57.
[10] [1996] 2 W.L.R. 348. Affirmed H.L., *The Times,* April 25, 1997.
[11] (1993) 137 Sol. Jo. LB 88.
[12] [1996] 2 W.L.R. 348, C.A., reversed on *locus standi* point by H.L., *The Times,* April 25, 1997. (Preserving the rule, however, that a reversioner may sue if he can establish that the nuisance is sufficient to damage his reversionary interest.)

who shared a home with householders affected by a nuisance. Relying on *Khorasand-jian*, they sought damages for interference with their television reception and for the effects of dust caused by the construction of a link road. The Court of Appeal, allowing them standing to sue, held that although the existence of a "substantial link" between the plaintiff and the land affected by the nuisance was essential, occupation of the property as a home would suffice to enable an occupier to sue in private nuisance. The House of Lords, however, reversing the decision of the Court of Appeal and overruling the decision in *Khorasandjian*, reasserted the traditional view that only those who have exclusive possession of the land affected by the nuisance are entitled to sue in private nuisance.

## The Defendant

A person will be liable in nuisance if he bears "some degree of personal responsibility" for the nuisance.[13] Thus, the potential defendants in a nuisance action include the creator of the nuisance and the person who, being an occupier of land on which a nuisance has arisen, fails to take reasonable steps to remedy the state of affairs giving rise to the nuisance. As was noted by Veale J. in *Halsey v. Esso Petroleum Company*,[14] there appears to be no requirement that the acts complained of must emanate from land belonging to the defendant.

## Physical Damage to Land

The courts have distinguished two types of act which may constitute a private nuisance:

- An act which causes unreasonable interference with a person's *enjoyment* of his land, for example by the ingress on to the land of fumes or noise;

- An act which causes *physical damage* to a person's land.

The distinction between these two types of private nuisance is important for this reason: in cases of interference with enjoyment, such as by noise or smell, the plaintiff must show that the defendant's activities constituted an unreasonable use of his land *given the characteristics of the locality in which the land is situated*, whilst in cases of physical damage to property, so long as the damage is more than trivial, liability follows automatically on proof of the damage, the character of the neighbourhood being irrelevant.[15] This distinction, which originated during the Industrial Revolution, when noises or smells were trivial problems compared with the thick black soot from factories which destroyed crops, is, perhaps, less easy to justify today.

## Interference with the Enjoyment of Land

Where the act complained of causes an interference with the plaintiff's enjoyment of his land, but does not damage the land, it becomes relevant for the court to consider

---

[13] *per* Lord Atkin in *Sedleigh-Denfield v. O'Callaghan* [1940] A.C. 880 at 897.
[14] [1961] 1 W.L.R. 683.
[15] *St Helen's Smelting Co. v. Tipping* (1865) 11 H.L. Cas. 642.

whether or not the defendant is making reasonable use of his own land *vis-à-vis* the plaintiff. In answering this question, the courts have recognised that a certain level of inconvenience is to be tolerated as part and parcel of modern life, and have held that the interference complained of must be substantial if it is to amount to an actionable nuisance. Thus, according to Knight-Bruce V.C. in *Walter v. Selfe*,[16] the question for the court is:

"... ought this inconvenience to be considered in fact as more than fanciful, more than one of mere delicacy and fastidiousness, as an inconvenience materially interfering with the ordinary comfort physically of human existence, not merely according to elegant and dainty modes or habits of living, but according to the plain and sober and simple notions among the English people? "

A trivial interference with enjoyment, then, cannot be a nuisance. However, the loss of just one night's sleep because of excessive noise has been held to constitute a nuisance,[17] as has the use of adjoining premises as a sex shop.[18]

There is no precise test for deciding whether the plaintiff's use of his land is unreasonable, the matter being dependent on the facts of each particular case. However, the extent and nature of the harm alleged, the duration of the nuisance, the utility of the defendant's activities, the abnormal sensitivity of the plaintiff, malice on the part of the defendant, and the character of the neighbourhood in which the activity is carried on, have all been identified as relevant considerations.

## The Character of the Neighbourhood

Where the nuisance complained of constitutes mere interference with the plaintiff's enjoyment of his land, the character of the neighbourhood in which the defendant's activities are undertaken is a relevant consideration. It follows that certain forms of activity are permissible in industrial areas which would constitute a nuisance if carried on in a residential area. As Thesiger L.J. put it in *Sturges v. Bridgman*[19]: "What would be a nuisance in Belgrave Square would not necessarily be so in Bermondsey."

Recent case law has suggested that a grant of planning permission may change the character of the neighbourhood, and thereby permit certain activities which, prior to that change, would have been actionable nuisances. In *Gillingham B.C. v. Medway (Chatham) Dock Co. Ltd*,[20] the defendants were granted planning permission to change a little-used naval dock into a commercial port, with the result that levels of noise and disturbance to local residents increased dramatically. The council, on behalf of the local residents, brought an action in nuisance and sought an injunction to restrict the movement of vehicles at night. Buckley J. held that the grant of planning permission had changed the character of the neighbourhood so that 24 hour access to the dock was permissible. It followed that, since the question of the reasonableness of

---

[16] (1851) 4 De G. & Sm. 315.
[17] *Andreae v. Selfridge & Co. Ltd* [1938] Ch. 1.
[18] *Laws v. Florinplace Ltd* [1981] 1 All E.R. 659.
[19] (1879) 11 Ch.D. 852.
[20] [1993] Q.B. 343.

the defendants' activities fell to be decided by reference to the character of the neighbourhood, there could be no actionable nuisance. Buckley J. was influenced by the fact that, before granting planning permission, a local planning authority would balance the interests of the community against those of individuals and took the view that, this having been done, the environmental controls imposed through planning law must prevail over those available in private law. The learned judge put the matter in the following terms:

"... planning permission is not a licence to commit a nuisance and a planning authority has no jurisdiction to authorise nuisance. However, a planning authority can through its development plans and decisions, alter the character of a neighbourhood. This may have the effect of rendering innocent activities which, prior to the change, would have been an actionable nuisance."

It is respectfully submitted that this *dictum* is, in a sense, a contradiction in terms, for if a local planning authority in fact sanctions development which has the effect of obliterating claims for private nuisance, what is the authority doing *but* "licensing" the commission of nuisances? In *Gillingham*, Buckley J. clearly saw the grant of planning permission as determinative of the character of the neighbourhood. His reasoning seems to have been based on an analogy between planning permission and statutory authority, which may operate as a defence to a nuisance action (see below).

The validity of this analogy, however, has subsequently been firmly rejected by the Court of Appeal in *Wheeler v. J.J. Saunders Ltd.*[21] The plaintiffs brought an action in nuisance when the smell from the defendants' neighbouring pig farm interfered with their enjoyment of their property. The units housing the pigs had been erected in accordance with planning permission. The court held that the existence of the planning permission could not operate as a defence to the nuisance claim because, in contrast with the position in *Gillingham*, the planning permission had not sufficiently altered the character of the neighbourhood. It was held that the analogy between the grant of planning permission and the defence of statutory authority could not be justified because, whilst Parliament may be entitled to authorise the commission of nuisances under statute, a local planning authority has no such power. Although this suggests that the *dictum* of Buckley J. in *Gillingham* should be treated with caution, it should be remembered that the key finding in *Wheeler* was that the planning permission for the housing of pigs was *insufficient* to alter the character of the neighbourhood. Therefore, the possibility remains that where, as in *Gillingham*, the planning permission in question is of a strategic character and is designed to promote the regeneration of a large area, it may in practical terms extinguish residents' claims in private nuisance.

## The Utility of the Defendant's Activities

Clearly, because in a nuisance action the courts are concerned with what is reasonable as between the plaintiff and the defendant, the purpose to be served by the defendant's activities is a relevant consideration. This is, of course, apparent in the decision in

[21] [1995] 2 All E.R. 697.

*Gillingham* (above), where the activities in question were of general benefit to the community in terms of urban regeneration and job creation.

Similarly, in *Harrison v. Southwark and Vauxhall Water Co.*[22] it was said that for a man to pull down a house for the purposes of rebuilding on his land would be a reasonable use of the land, and therefore not an actionable nuisance, provided that he took all reasonable care to avoid causing inconvenience to his neighbours. This would be so even where considerable inconvenience was caused and the operation lasted for several months, for progress would be unduly hampered if the law of nuisance were to prevent the development of land. However, where serious damage is being done to the plaintiff's property or livelihood, the court will not accept the argument that the plaintiff alone should bear the burden of the activity from which the community as a whole will benefit.[23] Nor will a court grant damages in lieu of an injunction, since this would amount to expropriation of rights without the sanction of Parliament. Thus, in *Bellew v. Cement Co.*[24] an Irish court granted the plaintiff an injunction which had the effect of closing for three months the only cement factory in Ireland at a time when building was an urgent public necessity.[25]

## Malice

It follows that if the utility of the defendant's activities is relevant, then where the act in question is maliciously perpetrated and therefore has no social utility, the court will more readily presume that it constitutes an actionable nuisance. Thus in *Christie v. Davey*,[26] North J. was prepared to grant an injunction restraining the defendant from annoying the plaintiff by banging on a party-wall, beating tea-trays, whistling and shrieking. The defendant had taken these actions in protest at noise from music lessons given by the plaintiff next door. North J. stated that, "if what has taken place had occurred between two sets of persons both perfectly innocent, I should have taken an entirely different view of the case."

Similarly, in *Hollywood Silver Fox Farm Ltd v. Emmett*,[27] where the defendant, motivated by spite, caused guns to be fired on the boundary of his land in order to frighten the plaintiff's foxes and prevent them from breeding, Macnaghten J. considered that the intention of the defendant was relevant in determining liability for nuisance and awarded damages together with an injunction.

In both of these cases, the courts were concerned to protect a recognised legal right to the enjoyment of property. Where no such right exists, however, the position is different.[28] Thus, in *Bradford (Mayor of) v. Pickles*,[29] where the defendant deliberately abstracted groundwater from his land, which diminished the plaintiff's water supply, in order to induce the plaintiff to purchase his land, the House of Lords stated that a malicious motive could not make unlawful an act which was otherwise lawful. Because

---

[22] [1891] 2 Ch. 409.
[23] Bohlen, *Studies in the Law of Torts*, p. 429.
[24] [1984] Ir.R. 61.
[25] Rogers, *Winfield & Jolowicz on Tort* (14th ed., 1994), p. 408.
[26] [1893] 1 Ch. 316.
[27] [1936] 2 K.B. 468.
[28] Rogers, *Winfield & Jolowicz on Tort* (14th ed., 1994), p. 414.
[29] [1895] A.C. 587.

it had previously been established by case law that no legal interest can exist in percolating groundwaters before those waters have been abstracted, no recognised interest of the plaintiff had been infringed and the motive of the defendant was therefore irrelevant.

## "One-Off" Events

There is some authority for the proposition that an isolated incident cannot found an action in nuisance. In *Bolton v. Stone*[30] the plaintiff, who was standing on the highway, was injured by a cricket ball which had been hit from the defendant's land. Oliver J., at first instance, stated that a nuisance must be: ". . . a state of affairs, however temporary, and not merely an isolated happening."[31]

In the Court of Appeal, however, the nuisance was regarded not as the isolated hitting of the ball on to the highway, but as the carrying on of a cricket game adjacent to the highway. This illustrates the tendency of the courts, where the event complained of is a "one-off", to hold that the essence of the nuisance is the state of affairs which gives rise to the event rather than the event itself. Thus, in *Spicer v. Smee*,[32] where defective electrical wiring installed in the defendant's bungalow caused a fire which damaged the plaintiff's adjacent bungalow, Atkinson J. held that the defendant was liable in nuisance because he had permitted a dangerous state of affairs to exist on his land. Where, however, the isolated event falls within the rule in *Rylands v. Fletcher* (below), there is no need to show that the event is referable to a "state of affairs". Further, there seems to be a developing rule that statutory nuisances may be caused by one-off incidents.

## Abnormal Sensitivity of the Plaintiff

If the plaintiff, or his use of his land, is abnormally sensitive to the interference of which he complains, he will not be granted relief. The principle is illustrated by the decision in *Robinson v. Kilvert*.[33] The defendant carried on a business in the lower part of a building which required certain hot and dry air conditions and he heated the basement accordingly. This had the effect of heating the plaintiff's premises above, where the plaintiff stored a quantity of brown paper. As a result of the heat, the brown paper dried and diminished in value. There was no evidence that the levels of heat inconvenienced the plaintiff's workmen, or that it would cause damage to paper generally. Refusing to grant an injunction, the court held that: "a man who carries on an exceptionally delicate trade cannot complain because it is injured by his neighbour doing something which would not injure anything but an exceptionally delicate trade."[34]

However, where it can be shown that the activity of the defendant is such as would inconvenience a plaintiff who is *not* abnormally sensitive, then the fact that the

---

[30] [1951] A.C. 850.
[31] See Rogers, *Winfield & Jolowicz on Tort* (14th ed., 1994), p. 412.
[32] [1946] 1 All E.R. 498.
[33] (1884) 41 Ch.D. 88.
[34] *per* Lopes L.J. at 97.

plaintiff's activity is particularly sensitive will not prevent him from recovering losses which result from its interruption. Thus, in *McKinnon Industries Ltd v. Walker*,[35] the plaintiff recovered in respect of his inability to grow orchids in circumstances where the defendant's interference with his enjoyment of his land was substantial.

# PUBLIC NUISANCE

Unlike private nuisance, which is only a tort, the commission of a public nuisance is also a criminal offence. A nuisance is said to be a public nuisance when it "materially affects the reasonable comfort and convenience of the life of a class of Her Majesty's subjects"[36] The number of people required to establish that a "class" of people has been affected is a question of fact in each case. In *Attorney-General v. P.Y.A. Quarries Ltd*, Denning L.J. held that the correct approach was not specifically to count the numbers of people affected, but to assess whether the nuisance was so widespread and indiscriminate in its effect that it would not be reasonable to expect one person, rather than the community at large, to take action to put a stop to it. Denning L.J. gave as an example the non-repair or blocking of a public footpath used by few people. The obstruction nevertheless affects indiscriminately everyone who may wish to walk along it. Public nuisances include carrying on an offensive trade, keeping a disorderly house, selling food unfit for human consumption, throwing fireworks in the street and holding a badly organised pop festival.[37]

## Special Damage

A public nuisance only becomes actionable at the suit of an individual where he can show that he has suffered some special damage over and above that which has been suffered by the other members of the public whom the nuisance affects. Thus, if a public highway is obstructed the plaintiff will not succeed in public nuisance if he can prove no damage beyond being occasionally delayed or having to make a detour, because every other user of the highway has incurred a similar inconvenience.[38] If, however, the plaintiff falls over the obstruction and sustains injury, then he has suffered some particular or special damage not suffered by all users of the highway and will therefore be entitled to bring an action.

## Differences between Public and Private Nuisance

Traditionally, the key difference between an action in private nuisance and an action by a person suffering special damage because of a public nuisance has been that the plaintiff in a private nuisance action had to show that his interest in land was affected, whilst the plaintiff in public nuisance had standing to sue irrespective of whether or not

---

[35] [1951] 3 D.L.R. 577.
[36] *per* Romer L.J. in *Attorney-General v. P.Y.A. Quarries Ltd* [1957] 2 Q.B. 169 at 184.
[37] Rogers, *Winfield & Jolowicz on Tort* (14th ed., 1994), p. 402.
[38] *Winterbottom v. Lord Derby* (1867) L.R. 2 Ex. 316, *op. cit.* at n.34, above.

this was the case. For a time, the decision of the Court of Appeal in *Khorasandjian v. Bush*[39] threatened to blur the distinction between public and private nuisance by permitting a claim in private nuisance where the plaintiff had no legal interest in land. However, it is clear from the recent decision in *Hunter and Others v. Canary Wharf Ltd*[40] that it is still necessary for the plaintiff in private nuisance to show exclusive possession of the affected land. This is not required of a plaintiff who sues in public nuisance.

Although in many cases what is a public nuisance will also amount to a private nuisance, this is not always the case. The distinction between the two forms of nuisance is illustrated by the decision in *Tate & Lyle Industries Ltd v. G.L.C.*[41] Ferry terminals constructed by the defendants in the Thames caused silting of the river bed which prevented large vessels from accessing the plaintiffs' jetty. The plaintiffs' claim in private nuisance was dismissed because the jetty itself had not been affected and they had no proprietary interest in the bed of the river. The silting, however, had caused an interference with a *public* right of navigation. It was held that because the plaintiffs had incurred considerable expense in dredging the river in order to carry on with their business, they had suffered special damage and were therefore entitled to recover in public nuisance.

## The Relevance of Public Nuisance Today

Public nuisance at common law once had a useful rôle in safeguarding the local environment. However, over the last hundred years or more, virtually the entire area which was traditionally the province of public nuisance has been covered by statute. Although the common law of public nuisance still fulfils a residual rôle, particularly in relation to matters concerning pollution of the highways, it will often be cheaper and more convenient for an individual affected by a public nuisance to complain to the local environmental health officer, who may bring an action to abate the nuisance under the provisions relating to "statutory nuisances" (below). However, because the remedy for a statutory nuisance is abatement of the nuisance, the law of statutory nuisance can do little to *compensate* a person who has been the victim of a continuing nuisance. The common law action for public nuisance therefore remains an effective tool for those determined to seek compensation in addition to a cessation of the defendant's activities.

# DEFENCES TO A COMMON LAW NUISANCE ACTION

## Prescription

Under the doctrine of prescription, if an activity which constitutes a private nuisance continues for a period of twenty years it will become immune from suit. Commission

---

[39] (1993) 137 Sol.Jo. LB 88.
[40] *The Times*, April 25, 1997.
[41] [1983] 2 A.C. 509.

of a public nuisance, however, cannot be made legal in this way. In practice, it is extremely difficult to prove a prescriptive right to commit a nuisance. This is because the 20 year time period does not commence until there is an actionable nuisance in existence. The point is illustrated by the facts of *Sturges v. Bridgman*.[42] For more than 20 years a confectioner had used a large mortar and pestle on his property which adjoined the garden of the plaintiff doctor. This was not a nuisance to the doctor until he built a consulting room at the end of his garden when he found, for the first time, that the noise and vibration interfered with the running of his practice. In granting an injunction to restrain the defendant from using the mortar and pestle, the court held that the defendant had not acquired a prescriptive right to commit the nuisance because there had not been in existence an actionable nuisance for a continuous period of 20 years.

## Statutory Authority

In practice, statutory authority is the most important defence to an action in nuisance. Many activities which might constitute a nuisance are carried out by private and public bodies authorised by Parliament to undertake those activities. Broadly speaking, where the statute places the body under a duty to do the act which is complained of and it is unavoidable that the act must be done in the particular place where it causes a nuisance, the body will be immune from suit in a nuisance action. Thus in *Smeaton v. Ilford Corporation*,[43] where frequent eruptions of sewage from a manhole overflowed into the plaintiff's premises causing considerable discomfort, a claim in nuisance failed because the overflow was caused by excess sewage that the defendants were bound by statute to accept into their drains. Although the whole sewage system was inadequate, it was held that the proper remedy was to complain to the relevant Minister.

Where, however, on a proper construction of the statute, the body is given a discretion as to *where* to do the act in question, the body may be liable in nuisance if it could reasonably have undertaken the activity in another location where no nuisance would be caused. Similarly, where the statute confers a *power* to act, rather than a *duty*, then the power must be exercised in such a way as not to interfere with private rights.[44]

Where a nuisance is the "inevitable" result of an activity authorised by statute, the body responsible for the activity will be immune from suit. It is a matter of statutory interpretation in each particular case whether or not the nuisance is "inevitable". In *Allen v. Gulf Oil Refining Ltd*,[45] for example, the defendant company was authorised by statute compulsorily to acquire land for the purpose of constructing an oil refinery. The defendants built the refinery and then operated it in such a way as to cause a nuisance to the plaintiffs. The court held that the statutory authority to *construct* a refinery impliedly carried with it the authority to *operate* the refinery when it was constructed. It followed that the company enjoyed immunity with respect to nuisances that were the inevitable result of an oil refinery being built. Lord Wilberforce stated that the establishment of an oil refinery was bound to involve some alteration of the

---

[42] (1879) 11 Ch.D. 852.
[43] [1954] 1 Ch. 450.
[44] *Metropolitan Asylum District Managers v. Hill* (1881) 6 App.Cas. 193, H.L.
[45] [1981] A.C. 1001.

environment, and so of the standard of amenity and comfort which neighbouring occupiers might expect. Therefore, to the extent that the environment had been changed from peaceful unpolluted countryside to an industrial complex, to which different standards apply, Parliament must be taken to have authorised the nuisances.

## Other Defences

The plaintiff's consent to the existence of a nuisance is a defence. Act of God, or act of an unidentified third party, may also provide a defence, except in cases where the defendant can be said to have "adopted" the nuisance, in the sense that he knows of its existence but fails to abate it where it is within his power to do so. Moreover, where negligence is the essence of liability, the defendant may have a defence of inevitable accident. The Law Reform (Contributory Negligence) Act 1945 is applicable to nuisance and can therefore operate to reduce an award of damages where the plaintiff, through carelessness, has contributed to his own loss. In certain cases, ignorance of the circumstances in which the nuisance arises can also provide a defence. Thus, in *Noble v. Harrison*,[46] a branch of a tree which overhung the highway fell on to the plaintiff's car. The branch fell because of a "secret and unobservable operation of nature" for which the defendant could not be held responsible.

The following are NOT defences to an action in nuisance.

## That the Plaintiff "Comes to the Nuisance"

It is not a defence to a claim in nuisance for the defendant to argue that "he got there first", or in other words the plaintiff "came to the nuisance". Thus, in *Bliss v. Hall*,[47] where the defendant set up a tallow-chandlery which emitted noise and offensive smells to the annoyance of the plaintiff, it was held to be no defence for the defendant to argue that the factory had been in existence for three years before the plaintiff's arrival. When the plaintiff moved into his house, he "came to the house . . . with all the rights which the common law affords, and one of them is a right to wholesome air."[48]

## That the Nuisance is Due to Many

It is no defence that the nuisance complained of is due to the actions of other people acting together with the defendant and that the defendant's act, considered in isolation, would not have amounted to a nuisance. In assessing what is reasonable conduct on the part of the defendant, the court will take account of all the surrounding circumstances, including the conduct of others.

## That the Defendant's Activity is Socially Useful

Whilst the utility of the defendant's conduct is relevant in determining whether his activities are reasonable, it is not, of itself, a defence for a defendant to show that his

---

[46] [1926] 2 K.B. 332.
[47] (1838) 4 Bing. N.C. 183.
[48] *per* Tindal C.J., *ibid.* at 186.

activities are socially worthwhile. Thus in *Adams v. Ursell*,[49] the defendant opened a fish and chip shop in what had hitherto been a "well to do" residential area. In resisting the grant of an injunction to stop a nuisance caused by smells from the shop, the defendant argued that, in effect, he was providing a social service and that closing the shop would cause hardship to the "less well off" in the area, who were his customers. This argument was rejected, the court holding that the defendant should have located his shop in the area where his customers lived, presumably because, being of a lower class, they would not be offended by the smell of fish and chips!

# REMEDIES

The principal remedies available to the plaintiff in an action for nuisance are an award of damages and/or an injunction. In addition, the plaintiff has the "self-help" remedy of abatement.

## Damages

An award of damages aims to evaluate the loss to the plaintiff which results from the defendant's activities and to put the plaintiff in the position he would have been in had the nuisance not occurred. The traditional method of quantifying damages is to assess the diminution in the market value of the plaintiff's property. Whilst this method has the advantage of relative simplicity, it may be criticised as often underestimating the subjective value of the property to the resident owner. The diminution in value test assumes that the property is worth no more to the plaintiff than its market value and fails to take account of the emotional and psychological damage which can flow from a disturbance in the home.

## Injunction

An injunction has the effect of preventing the defendant from carrying out the activity that is being complained of, or of restricting the scope of that activity. Exceptionally, an injunction may be mandatory in its terms, requiring the defendant to perform some positive act rather than to forbear from doing the act complained of. Unlike an award of damages, an injunction is an equitable remedy, so that the plaintiff is not entitled to it as of right, but must have the discretion of the court exercised in his favour. In exercising this discretion, the courts take the view that injunctive relief is generally preferable to an award of damages but that in certain circumstances damages in lieu of an injunction are appropriate. Thus, where the plaintiff has acted maliciously in retaliation against the nuisance, as in *Christie v. Davey* (above), he may be deprived of injunctive relief.

In deciding whether or not to grant damages instead of an injunction, the courts will not consider the social and economic effects on third parties of granting an injunction.

---

[49] [1913] 1 Ch. 269.

The law is concerned to protect individual property rights which, in the absence of legislation to the contrary, prevail over the public interest. Thus, in *Shelfer v. City of London Electric Co.*[50] the court refused to award damages in lieu of an injunction despite the defendants' argument that the public at large derived a benefit from their supplying electricity. Similarly, in *Kennaway v. Thompson*[51] the court rejected the proposition that the public interest could justify the continuance of a nuisance and refused to grant damages in lieu of an injunction where this would amount to permitting the defendant to "buy" the right to continue the nuisance.

## Abatement

Traditionally, where a plaintiff is affected by a nuisance he is entitled in law to take steps himself to abate the nuisance without recourse to legal proceedings. Thus in *Lemon v. Webb*[52] the plaintiff was held to have acted legally when he trimmed the branch of a tree which overhung his land. The remedy of abatement, however, must be exercised within narrow confines. In particular, notice must be given to the defendant by the plaintiff prior to his taking action unless he can abate the nuisance without going on to the defendant's land, the abator must not do unnecessary damage to the defendant's land in abating the nuisance, and, where there is more than one method of abating the nuisance, the abator must select the course of action which causes least harm to the defendant financially, except where this would have a detrimental effect on innocent third parties or on the public.

## STATUTORY NUISANCES

As has been noted above, most of the activities which once constituted public nuisances at common law are now statutory nuisances. The law in relation to statutory nuisances has its origin in legislation dating from 1848 and was consolidated by the Public Health Act 1936. The law was further consolidated in Part III of the Environmental Protection Act 1990. The statutory nuisance regime provides a fast and cheap remedy by comparison with common law public nuisance, and although a prosecution for statutory nuisance will normally be brought by a local authority, aggrieved individuals have a statutory right to apply to a magistrates' court for the abatement of a nuisance.[53]

Under the Environmental Protection Act 1990, district councils and London borough councils are under a duty to inspect their areas for statutory nuisances.[54] Although the duty is to carry out inspections periodically, it has been suggested that if a member of the public complains of a statutory nuisance and the authority fails or refuses to inspect, an action for judicial review will lie to compel the authority to do

---

[50] [1895] 1 Ch. 287.
[51] [1981] Q.B. 88.
[52] [1895] A.C. 1.
[53] EPA 1990, s.82.
[54] EPA 1990, s.79.

so.[55] The Act lists a number of activities which are statutory nuisances. In addition, it provides that certain other activities specified in other legislation as constituting a statutory nuisance are to be governed by the provisions of the Act. These activities include, for example, those prescribed under the Noise and Statutory Nuisance Act 1993. Under the Environmental Protection Act 1990, the principal criterion for establishing that an activity is a statutory nuisance is whether or not it is "prejudicial to health or a nuisance".

## The Meaning of "Prejudicial to Health or a Nuisance"

For the purposes of the statutory regime, the word "nuisance" has the same meaning as attached to it by the common law.[56] "Prejudicial to health" is defined by the Environmental Protection Act 1990 as "injurious, or likely to cause injury, to health".[57] In *Coventry City Council v. Cartwright*,[58] a resident complained of a statutory nuisance (under the Public Health Act 1936) emanating from a nearby refuse tip owned by the council. The Divisional Court held that because the rubbish accumulated on the site was inert rather than putrescible, so that there was no likelihood that vermin or disease would emanate from the site, the site could not be said to be "prejudicial to health". The chance that people might be caused injury by walking on the site was not sufficient to make the site prejudicial to their health.

## Categories of Statutory Nuisance

The following categories of statutory nuisance are set out in the Environmental Protection Act 1990. Many of these relate to problems of atmospheric pollution, and are considered more fully in Chapters 10 and 11 below.

- Any premises in such a state as to be prejudicial to health or a nuisance;

- Smoke emitted from premises so as to be prejudicial to health or a nuisance;

- Fumes or gases emitted from premises so as to be prejudicial to health or a nuisance;

- Dust, steam, smell or other effluvia arising on industrial, trade or business premises and being prejudicial to health or a nuisance;

- Any accumulation or deposit which is prejudicial to health or a nuisance;

- Any animal kept in such a place or manner as to be prejudicial to health or a nuisance;

- Noise emitted from premises so as to be prejudicial to health or a nuisance;

- Any other matter declared by any enactment to be a statutory nuisance.

---

[55] Ball and Bell, *Environmental Law* (3rd ed., 1995), p. 193.
[56] *National Coal Board v. Thorne* [1976] 1 W.L.R. 543.
[57] EPA 1990, s.79(7).
[58] [1975] 1 W.L.R. 845.

## Abatement Notices

If the authority is satisfied that a statutory nuisance exists, it is under a duty to serve an abatement notice on the person responsible for the nuisance or, in cases where he cannot be found, the owner or occupier of the premises on which the nuisance arises.[59] The local authority has no discretion whether to take action. It is under a duty to do so. In *R. v. Carrick District Council, ex p. Shelley and Another*[60] the Divisional Court held, on an application for judicial review, that a local authority had not discharged its duty under section 80 of the Environmental Protection Act 1990, when, having discovered the existence of a statutory nuisance, it resolved that it was not appropriate to serve a notice but that it would continue to monitor the situation.

The notice will require the recipient to stop the nuisance altogether, or to restrict its occurrence. In addition, it may require him to take certain specified steps (including the carrying out of positive works) in order to comply with the notice. Failure to comply with the requirements of an abatement notice without reasonable excuse is an offence. The recipient of an abatement notice may appeal against it to a magistrates' court on the grounds that the notice is not justified, that there has been an error in the service of the notice, that the authority has unreasonably refused to accept alternative methods of complying with the notice, that its requirements are unreasonable or unnecessary, that the period for compliance is unreasonably short, or that the best practicable means were used to abate the nuisance.[61]

## Defences

A number of defences are available to a person prosecuted for statutory nuisance. In particular, the defences of reasonable excuse and best practicable means. In determining whether or not a person has a reasonable excuse to commit the nuisance, an objective test is appropriate, the question for the court being "would a reasonable person think that the excuse given was consistent with a reasonable standard of conduct?"[62] Thus, in *Wellingborough B.C. v. Gordon*,[63] the defendant was held not to have a reasonable excuse when he argued that there had been a three year delay between the service of the abatement notice and its breach and that no-one had complained about the breach because the inconvenience caused was minimal.

Where the nuisance emanates from trade or industrial premises, it will be a defence for the accused to show that he used the best practicable means to prevent the occurrence of a nuisance.[64] In deciding whether or not this is the case, the court must take into account local conditions, the current state of technical knowledge and the design and operation of the defendant's plant and machinery, as well as the financial implications for the defendant of compliance with the abatement notice.[65] In addition, certain special defences are available where the nuisance consists of noise.[66]

[59] EPA 1990, s.80.
[60] *The Times*, April 15, 1996.
[61] Statutory Nuisance (Appeals) Regulations 1990 (S.I. 1990 No. 2276) and Statutory Nuisance (Appeals) (Amendment) Regulations 1990 (S.I. 1990 No. 2483).
[62] Ball and Bell, *Environmental Law* (3rd ed., 1995), p. 198.
[63] [1993] Env. L.R. 218.
[64] EPA 1990, s.70.
[65] *ibid.*, s.79(9).
[66] *ibid.*, s.80(9).

# THE RULE IN *RYLANDS V. FLETCHER*

## The Rule

The so-called "rule in *Rylands v. Fletcher*" has its origins in a case of that name.[67] The defendants were owners of a mill who wanted to improve their water supply. To this end, they engaged a firm of independent contractors to construct a reservoir on their land. During the course of the works, the contractors discovered a number of disused mines and passages under the land on which the reservoir was to be built. They failed to seal off these passages, with the result that, when the reservoir was filled with water, the water ran through the passages and flooded the plaintiff's mine.

The defendants could not be liable in nuisance because the damage was a "one-off" event (if the case were decided today, however, nuisance liability may be likely — see, for example, *Spicer v. Smee* above). Nor was it clear that the contractors should have foreseen that their activities would cause harm to the plaintiff, so it was unlikely that the plaintiff would have succeeded in negligence. An action in trespass may have failed because the damage caused to the plaintiff was not a direct and immediate consequence of the defendants' activities.[68] Therefore, according to the traditional view of the case, Blackburn J. in the Court of Exchequer created a new principle on which liability could be founded. As was pointed out by Lord Goff, however, in the subsequent case of *Cambridge Water Co. v. Eastern Counties Leather plc*[69] Blackburn J., in *Rylands v. Fletcher*, was not enunciating any new principle of law. Rather, he was extending liability in nuisance to cover cases of an isolated escape. Indeed, the terms in which his famous *dictum* is phrased indicate that he thought he was stating an established principle of law, rather than creating a new one, when he said:

> "We think that the true rule of law is, that the person who for his own purposes brings on to his lands and collects and keeps there anything likely to do mischief if it escapes, must keep it in at his peril, and, if he does not do so, he is *prima facie* answerable for all the damage which is the natural consequence of its escape."

This statement of principle by Blackburn J. was explicitly approved of by Lord Cairns L.C. on appeal to the House of Lords. His Lordship, however, added the requirement that the defendant must be making a "non-natural use" of his land in order for liability to follow under the principle. The rule, therefore, has a number of elements, each of which is examined below.

## Accumulation of Things on Land

Blackburn J. referred to the defendant "bringing" things on to his land. Thus, where the escape causing the damage is of something which arises naturally on the land or

---

[67] (1868) L.R. 3 H.L. 330.
[68] Dias and Markesinis, *Tort Law* (2 ed.), p. 344.
[69] [1994] 1 All E.R. 53.

has accumulated there by natural forces, no liability will follow under the rule (although it may, of course, follow in nuisance where the defendant fails to deal with the accumulation). In *Giles v. Walker*,[70] for example, an escape of thistle seeds was not covered by the rule, nor, in *Smith v. Kenrick*[71] was a natural accumulation of rain water.

## "For his own Purposes"

As formulated by Blackburn J., the rule appears to apply only to things which the defendant has accumulated on land for his own purposes, so that if the things are brought on to the land by the defendant for the purposes of another he cannot be liable. The position in this regard is unclear. However, in *Rainham Chemical Works v. Belvedere Fish Guano Co.*,[72] where two parties engaged in the manufacture of explosives had, in breach of the terms of their lease, assigned their tenancy of a factory to a company which they had formed, the House of Lords held that the parties were liable when an explosion occurred because they could not have under their lease, and therefore had not, effectively divested to the company their occupation of the premises. Lord Parmoor, however, was of the opinion that if the company had become the tenant and had entered into exclusive occupation of the premises, then the materials brought on to the premises could not be said to have been for the purposes of the two individuals, but for the purposes of the company, so that it would be the company, and not they, who were liable.

## "Likely to do Mischief"

The question has arisen whether it is a requirement of the rule that the thing which escapes from the defendant's land must be inherently dangerous.[73] Although, not surprisingly, much of the relevant case law makes reference to the "dangerousness" of the various things which have given rise to liability, in *Read v. Lyons Ltd* (below), Lord Macmillan stated that it would be impractical for the law to draw a distinction between "dangerous" and "non-dangerous" things. The Law Commission has come to a similar conclusion.[74] In practical terms, therefore, it is likely that Blackburn J.'s requirement that the thing concerned be "likely to do mischief" is not a separate requirement, but is part of the general requirement of non-natural use, so that the more dangerous the thing which the defendant brings on to his land, the less likely it is that the defendant's use of land will be "natural".[75]

---

[70] (1890) 24 Q.B.D. 656.
[71] (1849) 7 C.B. 515.
[72] [1921] 2 A.C. 465.
[73] Stallybrass, "Dangerous Things and the Non-Natural User of Land" (1929) 3 C.L.J. 376.
[74] Civil Liability for Dangerous Things and Activities (1970) (Law Com. 32).
[75] Pitchfork, *Tort Textbook* (1996).

## "Escape"

For liability to arise, the thing which the defendant has on his land must "escape". Thus, in *Read v. Lyons Ltd*,[76] where the plaintiff was injured by the explosion of a shell inside the defendants' war-time munitions factory, the defendants were not liable under the rule because the explosion was confined to within their premises.

## Non-Natural Use of the Land

The requirement that the defendant's use of his land be "non-natural" has led to particular difficulties. In adopting an expansive interpretation of this requirement it appears that the courts, over the years, had unwittingly narrowed the scope of *Rylands v. Fletcher* liability.[77] An examination of the use of the words "natural" and "naturally", as they appear in the judgments in *Rylands v. Fletcher*, reveals that for both Blackburn J and Lord Cairns L.C., the word "natural" meant "in accordance with nature". However, in a line of cases culminating with the famous decision in *Rickards v. Lothian*,[78] the sense in which Blackburn J. and Lord Cairns had used that word was misconstrued by the courts so that a "natural" use of land came to mean a use of land which was "ordinary" or "usual".

In *Rickards v. Lothian*, the plaintiff's offices were flooded when water flowed into them from the defendants' premises two floors above. The flooding was caused by the blocking of a lavatory basin which had overflowed because a "malicious person" had left a tap running into it. The Privy Council held that the defendants were not liable under the principle in *Rylands v. Fletcher*, Lord Moulton stated:

> "It is not every use to which land is put that brings into play that principle. It must be some special use bringing with it increased danger to others, and must not merely be the ordinary use of the land or such a use as is proper for the general benefit of the community."

In *Cambridge Water Co. v. Eastern Counties Leather plc*, however, where the defendants, in the course of their business, had stored chemicals on their land, Lord Goff expressly rejected the trial judge's finding that the activities of the defendants constituted a "natural" use of the land in the sense that they were proper for the general benefit of the community because they created employment. Lord Goff stated that: ". . . the storage of substantial quantities of chemicals on industrial premises should be regarded as an almost classic case of non-natural use."

His Lordship suggested that in future the courts should interpret the requirement of "non-natural use" so as to give it the function which it originally had, namely that of drawing a distinction between a naturally occurring event (such as a natural flood) and an event which occurs because of something artificial (such as the flooding of a reservoir).

In the light of *Cambridge Water*, then, it might be thought that liability under *Rylands v. Fletcher*, which for many years had been difficult to establish because of the

---

[76] [1947] A.C. 156.
[77] Newark, "Non-Natural User and *Rylands v. Fletcher*" (1961) 24 M.L.R. 557.
[78] [1913] A.C. 263.

restrictive interpretation which had been given to the concept of "non-natural use", would be very much back on the agenda as an environmental cause of action. This is only partially true, however, because, having widened the potential for liability under the rule in one way, the House of Lords in *Cambridge Water* have considerably narrowed it in another by holding that reasonable foresight by the plaintiff of the kind of damage caused to the defendant is a prerequisite of liability (see below).

## Strict Liability

Liability under the rule in *Rylands v. Fletcher* is often described as "strict liability". "Strict liability" can mean a number of things in different contexts. In the context of *Rylands v. Fletcher* liability, however, it simply means that absence of negligence is no defence. In other words, where there is an "escape" from the defendant's land, he will be liable for the consequences even where he shows that he took all reasonable care to prevent that escape. This follows from Blackburn J.'s insistence that the defendant must "keep [the thing] in at his peril". (There are, however, a number of defences to an action under the rule in *Rylands v. Fletcher* which serve to undermine this principle — see below.)

A further meaning of the phrase "strict liability" implies that the defendant will be liable even where he cannot foresee that the escape of the thing in question will cause damage to the defendant. This type of "strict liability" is the sort of liability which arises under certain environmental statutory provisions which give effect to the "polluter pays" principle, for example those related to liability for contaminated land.[79] For some time it was thought that the rule in *Rylands v. Fletcher* could also give rise to this form of "strict liability", and this was what the plaintiffs contended for, unsuccessfully, in *Cambridge Water Company v. Eastern Counties Leather plc*.[80]

## The Decision in *Cambridge Water*

The defendants, Eastern Counties Leather, had operated a tannery in Sawston near Cambridge for over 100 years. Until 1976, solvents for use in their business had been delivered to them in 40 gallon drums and transported for storage using fork-lift trucks. Over the years there had been a considerable number of spillages on the site. The spilled solvents had leached into the soil beneath the defendants' premises and had permeated the watercourse below. They had then travelled through the underground watercourse and percolated towards a borehole some 1.3 miles away, which the plaintiffs were using to abstract domestic drinking water for their customers. Cambridge Water Company began to use the borehole in 1979 and, before doing so, had established that the water was "wholesome" in accordance with the standards of water quality which were then current. In 1980, however, a new E.C. Directive relating to the particular solvents in question meant that the water could not be lawfully supplied as drinking water. The plaintiffs, who sought to recover their expenses in locating a new source of groundwater, brought an action in negligence, nuisance and under the rule in *Rylands v. Fletcher*.

[79] See Chapter 7, below.
[80] [1994] 1 All E.R. 53.

At first instance, the trial judge, finding that it could not be foreseen in 1976 that the spillages which had occurred would give rise to contamination of the watercourse in this way, dismissed the plaintiffs' claims. The Court of Appeal, overturning the decision of the trial judge, followed *Ballard v. Tomlinson*,[81] and held that since what was complained of was interference with a right akin to a property right (the right to abstract water), then liability would follow without foreseeability, the only issue being whether the defendants had caused the interference. On appeal to the House of Lords, their Lordships allowed the appeal by Eastern Counties Leather on the basis that foreseeability of the relevant damage was necessary to found liability in nuisance, negligence *and* under the rule in *Rylands v. Fletcher*.

As a matter of policy, the House of Lords was reluctant to impose liability for pollution without foreseeability of the relevant harm because to do so would, in effect, impose retrospective liability on a defendant. The idea of retrospective liability is generally alien to the U.K. legal system, although it appears to be provided for now in relation to contaminated land.[82] Their Lordships took the view, therefore, that liability for "historic pollution" (*i.e.* pollution which occurs at a time when it is not known that the substance being released into the environment is a pollutant) is a matter for Parliament rather than for the courts. As Lord Goff put it:

> "I incline to the opinion that, as a general rule, it is more appropriate for strict liability in respect of operations of high risk to be imposed by Parliament than by the courts . . . .It is of particular relevance that the present case is concerned with environmental pollution. The protection and preservation of the environment is now perceived as being of crucial importance to the future of mankind, and public bodies, both national and international, are taking significant steps towards the establishment of legislation which will promote the protection of the environment and make the polluter pay for damage to the environment for which he is responsible . . . But it does not follow from these developments that a common law principle such as the rule in *Rylands v. Fletcher* should be developed or rendered more strict to provide for liability in respect of such pollution. On the contrary, given that so much well-informed and carefully structured legislation is now being put in place for this purpose, there is less need for the courts to develop a common law principle to achieve the same end and indeed it may well be undesirable that they should do so."

On one view, Lord Goff's *dicta* can be seen as *inviting* Parliament to come up with a coherent and integrated answer to the problem of contaminated land, which must inevitably involve the imposition of retrospective liability. Since *Cambridge Water* was decided, this has indeed been done. Part IIA of the Environmental Protection Act 1990, which was inserted by the Environment Act 1995, contains detailed provisions in relation to contaminated land, which are considered in Chapter 7 below.

---

[81] (1885) 29 Ch.D. 115 (see Chapter 9, below).
[82] See Chapter 7, below.

## Defences to an Action under *Rylands v. Fletcher*

As has been said, liability under *Rylands v. Fletcher* is "strict" in the sense that it is no defence for the defendant to show that he took all reasonable care to prevent the escape. It therefore differs from common law liability in negligence. However, although absence of negligence is not *generally* a defence, there are certain circumstances in which it will be:

*Statutory authority*

If the dangerous thing is operated under statutory authority, the defendant will not be liable unless he is shown to have been negligent. Thus, in *Green v. Chelsea Waterworks*,[83] where a watermain burst without any negligence on the part of the defendants, it was held that since statute had authorised the defendants to lay the watermain and to maintain a continuous supply of water, the statute had also impliedly exempted them from liability in the absence of negligence.

*Act of stranger*

This defence provides that where the damage is caused by the actions of a third party which were not foreseeable by the defendant, he will not be liable. Thus, in *Perry v. Kendrick Transport Ltd*,[84] where two boys ignited the fuel tank of a bus injuring the plaintiff, the Court of Appeal held that the plaintiff had failed to show that the removal of the petrol cap by a third party was the type of act which the defendants ought reasonably to have foreseen and taken precautions against. Obviously, the operation of this defence somewhat dilutes the idea that the defendant must keep in the dangerous thing at his peril and, where the actions of third parties are involved, approximates liability under *Rylands v. Fletcher* to liability in negligence.

*Act of God*

As in a nuisance action, the defendant will escape liability if he can show that the damage has been caused by an Act of God. According to Lord Westbury in *Tennant v. Earl of Glasgow*,[85] the defence will operate in circumstances which are:

> ". . . circumstances which no human foresight can provide against, and of which human prudence is not bound to recognise the possibility, and which when they do occur, therefore, are calamities that do not involve the obligation of paying for the consequences that may result from them."

## TRESPASS

In essence, the tort of trespass requires that the defendant's conduct be intentional rather than careless (as in the tort of negligence[86]), or "unreasonable" (as in nuisance).

---

[83] (1894) 70 L.T. 547.
[84] [1956] 1 W.L.R. 85.
[85] (1864) 2 M. (H.L.) 22.
[86] *Letang v. Cooper* [1965] 1 Q.B. 232.

Moreover, for trespass to be established, the damage which results to the plaintiff must be a direct, rather than indirect, consequence of the defendant's activities. The point was illustrated by Fortescue J. in *Reynolds v. Clarke*[87]:

". . . if a man throws a log into the highway and it hits me I may maintain trespass because it is an immediate wrong; but if, as it lies there, I tumble over it and receive an injury, I must bring an action upon the case [*i.e.* an action in negligence] because it is only prejudicial in consequence."

For these reasons, the tort of trespass is of limited utility in environmental protection. The requirement of "directness" is particularly difficult to overcome because, where substances are released into the environment and may affect any number of persons in a number of different ways, the damage is inevitably "consequential" in nature.

Despite these difficulties, an action in trespass may have a number of advantages. In particular, in *Jones v. Llanrwst Urban District Council*,[88] where faecal matter deposited by the council came to rest on the plaintiff's river bed, the court refused to allow a defence of statutory authority to succeed, holding that a private individual was entitled to an injunction to restrain the council from allowing sewage to escape from a sewer, notwithstanding that the council was under a statutory duty to accept and dispose of the sewage. A further advantage of trespass is that, unlike nuisance, it is actionable without the plaintiff's needing to show that he has suffered, or is likely to suffer, any damage. This makes it easy for the plaintiff to obtain an injunction in cases where the gathering of evidence to prove that damage has occurred would be time-consuming or costly.

# NEGLIGENCE

An action in negligence, which requires the plaintiff to show that the defendant owes him a duty of care, that he has breached that duty (in that his conduct has fallen below the standard required of the "reasonable man"), and that the damage caused by the breach is of a kind which is reasonably foreseeable, is also of limited use in environmental matters. There have, however, been cases in which it has succeeded. In *Tutton v. A.D. Walter Ltd*,[89] for example, a farmer who, contrary to the advice of the manufacturers and of government, sprayed his land with insecticide when oil seed rape was in flower, was held to have been negligent when he caused the death of a number of the plaintiff's bees. More controversially, perhaps, in *Scott-Whitehead v. National Coal Board*,[90] a regional water authority was held liable in negligence for failing to advise a farmer that the water which he was abstracting for irrigation purposes was contaminated.

---

[87] (1725) 1 Stra. 643.
[88] [1911] 1 Ch. 393.
[89] [1985] 3 W.L.R. 797.
[90] (1987) 53 P. & C.R. 263.

## RIPARIAN RIGHTS

The owner of land adjacent to water has certain common law rights of a quasi-proprietary nature in the soil beneath the water. These are important in the context of water pollution and are therefore considered in Chapter 9, below.

# Chapter 5

# PLANNING LAW AND THE ENVIRONMENT

*"The purpose of the planning system is to regulate the development and use of land in the public interest . . . The material question is not whether the occupiers of neighbouring properties would suffer financial or other loss from a particular development but whether the proposal would affect the locality generally and unacceptably affect amenities that ought in the public interest to be protected."*[1]

## Introduction

The availability of land, of course, is essential to mankind. It is needed for homes, transport, industrial activity and the production of food. The aesthetic qualities of landscapes are also of benefit to mankind. The amount of land used in the U.K. has increased dramatically over the last century or so, in line with the expansion of the population, and the ways in which land has been used have profoundly affected the environment. In many cases they have changed the nature of land irrevocably, so that future generations are deprived of the choices enjoyed by present generations about the uses to which land can be put. In deciding whether and how to develop land, then, the advantages of development must be balanced against the advantages of conserving land in its undeveloped state for the benefit of both present and future generations. The principal legal mechanism for striking this balance is the planning system. In England, around 480,000 applications to develop land are made each year. Of these, between 85 per cent and 90 per cent are granted planning permission.

The planning system operates in conjunction with other statutory regimes for environmental protection. The importance of the planning system in protecting the environment, however, should not be underestimated. For example, in spite of the far-reaching statutory provisions in relation to contaminated land which have been introduced by the Environment Act 1995 (discussed in Chapter 7), the problems of contaminated land are to be tackled primarily through the planning system. The Department of the Environment has stated that: "The government believes that the normal process of development and redevelopment provides the best means of tackling much past contamination."[2]

---

[1] Planning Policy Guidance Note 1.
[2] *Framework for Contaminated Land* (DoE, 1994).

93

The law of planning is a vast subject. To cover it in its entirety is beyond the scope of this work. This chapter, however, aims first to explain the basic principles of planning law and secondly to consider the ways in which the operation of the planning system is related to the operation of the various pollution control regimes examined elsewhere in the book.

## The History of Planning Law

In the aftermath of the Second World War, the U.K. was left with ruined towns and cities which needed to be redeveloped. Industry, which needed to adapt to serve the peacetime market, also required land for development. There was perceived an opportunity, and indeed a need, to create a new and comprehensive planning regime which could impose some coherence on development. To this end, the Town and Country Planning Act 1947 was passed. This repealed all previous planning legislation and provided the basis for the modern planning system.

A series of subsequent Acts completed the modern system. In 1962 and 1971 there were certain repeals of previous legislation. A further repeal and consolidation took place in 1990 with the passing of the Town and Country Planning Act 1990, the Planning (Listed Buildings and Conservation Areas) Act 1990 and the Planning (Hazardous Substances) Act 1990. The provisions of these Acts, however, were swiftly amended by the Planning and Compensation Act 1991 which made a number of amendments and additions to the new system. The Town and Country Planning Act 1990 (as amended) is the most important statute.

## Features of the Modern Planning System

The following may be identified as the most significant features of the modern planning regime:

(1) Ownership of land entails merely the right to go on using it for its existing purposes or for very similar purposes. An owner has no *right* to "develop" his land. That is to say he has no *right* to build on the land or substantially to change the use to which it is put.

(2) Control of development is achieved by means of flexible "development plans", drawn up by the planning authority, which afford the planning authority some discretion in whether or not to grant planning permission. Such a system is to be contrasted with a rigid "zoning" system, under which, once the development plan has marked out an area of land for a particular purpose, development within that area which does not fulfil that purpose will be prohibited absolutely.

(3) Almost all development requires planning permission before it can proceed.

(4) Planning permission, once granted, cannot normally be revoked without payment of compensation.

(5) Whilst there is a right of appeal against a *refusal* to grant planning permission, there is no right of appeal where planning permission has been granted.

(6) The planning regime is administered at a local level by planning authorities, but strong control over the regime is retained by central government.

The Town and Country Planning Act 1990 confers wide discretionary powers on the Secretary of State for the Environment. As a result, the nature of planning control is dictated by central government policy as expressed by the Secretary of State. This policy is set out in White Papers, Policy Planning Guidance Notes (PPGs), Regional Policy Guidance Notes (RPGs), Department of the Environment Circulars and Ministerial Statements. PPGs and RPGs are now the principal source of guidance on general planning *policy*, whilst Circulars are the main source of guidance on the interpretation of legislation and on procedural matters.

# THE REGULATORY AUTHORITIES

## Local Planning Authorities

The decision whether planning permission should be granted is made by a local planning authority. Local planning authorities are differently constituted in different parts of the country. At the time of writing, in England,[3] in the six metropolitan counties (Greater Manchester, Merseyside, South Yorkshire, Tyne and Wear, West Midlands and West Yorkshire), the local planning authority is the district council. In Greater London the local planning authority is the borough council for each of the 32 boroughs. In the rest of the country, that is to say in the 47 non-metropolitan counties (or "shire" counties), the county council is the planning authority for the whole county, whilst the district council is the planning authority for each district. Thus, the district council will consider all applications for planning permission, save for "county matters", such as mineral working or development within a National Park, which will be adjudicated on by the county council. There may well be changes to this system following a report by the Local Government Commission which recommended that the two tier system of government in 21 of 39 county areas should be replaced by an all-purpose (or unitary) form of local government.[4]

## The Secretary of State

The Secretary of State for the Environment can "call in" any planning application for determination by him rather than by the local planning authority.[5] This tends to occur with applications that the local planning authority does not propose to refuse, but which the Secretary of State believes should be more closely scrutinised before permission is granted. The applications called in will involve planning issues of more than local importance, that is to say those which have effects beyond the immediate

---

[3] For the position in Wales, see the Local Government (Wales) Act 1994.
[4] Local Government Commission for England, *Renewing Local Government in the English Shires — A report on the 1992–1995 Structural Review.*
[5] TCPA 1990, s. 77.

locality, those which give rise to substantial regional or national controversy, and those which conflict with national policy on important matters.

## THE MEANING OF "DEVELOPMENT"

The planning system regulates the "development" of land. The statutory definition of "development" has been described as "the very essence of the Town and Country Planning Act 1990 — the pivot on which the whole system of day-to-day control of land development under the 1990 Act turns and depends."[6] An understanding of this definition, then, is vital in order to appreciate the extensive scope of planning law. Development is defined in the Act[7] as:

(1) The carrying out of building operations, engineering operations, mining operations or other operations in, on, over, or under land; or

(2) The making of any material change in the use of any buildings or other land.

The Act provides that "development" can occur even where the land in question is not physically altered. In addition, the following four matters are specifically mentioned as constituting development:

(1) The use of a single dwelling-house for the purpose of two or more separate dwellings[8];

(2) The deposit of refuse or waste materials on an existing dump if either:

    (a) The superficial area of the dump is extended, or

    (b) The height of the dump is extended and exceeds the level of the land adjoining the dump;

(3) The placing or assembly of a tank in any inland waters for the purpose of fish farming;

(4) The display of an advertisement on the external part of a building not normally used for such display.[9]

### "Building Operations"

Building operations include the demolition of buildings, rebuilding, structural alterations or additions to buildings, and any other operations normally undertaken by a person carrying on business as a builder.[10] Internal works in a house, however, do not constitute building work.[11] The courts have taken the view that a "building" is an

---

[6] Heap, *An Outline of Planning Law* (11th ed., 1996), p. 115.
[7] TCPA 1990, s.55 and s.336(1).
[8] *ibid.*, s.55(3)(a).
[9] *ibid.*, s.55(5) and s.222.
[10] *ibid.*, s.55(2).
[11] *ibid.*, s.55(2)(a).

object attached to land, even if it is very small (*eg.* a model village). Where something is attached to the land as a permanent structure, it will usually be a "building", whilst something that has been wheeled on to the land may not necessarily be a "building".[12]

## "Engineering Operations"

The 1990 Act gives little guidance on the meaning of "engineering operations". They have been broadly defined by the courts as "operations of the kind usually undertaken by engineers".[13]

## "Mining Operations"

The Act defines "mining operations" so as to include the removal of material of any description from a mineral working deposit or from a deposit of pulverised fuel ash or other furnace ash, the removal of clinker from a deposit of iron, steel or other metallic slags, and the extraction of minerals from a disused railway embankment.[14]

## "Material Change of Use"

A change of use occurs when there is a change in the use to which the land, building or structure is currently put. The courts have taken the view that the question whether or not a change of use is "material" is a matter of fact and degree for the local planning authority to decide. They will only interfere with a decision if it is one to which no reasonable authority could have come.[15] Changes of use will include, for example, changes from commercial to residential use and *vice versa*, as where a residential house is used for offices. Certain changes of use, however, do not constitute development and are therefore exempt from the requirement of planning permission (see below).

## Exemptions from the Need to Apply for Planning Permission

Some forms of activity do not require an application for planning permission. This may be for one of two reasons. Some activities are exempt from this requirement because they *do not constitute development*. Other activities are exempt because, although they constitute development, permission is *granted* for those operations by legislation.

*Matters which do not constitute development:*

The following seven matters do not constitute development[16]:

    (1)  Internal or external improvements, alterations or maintenance works none of which materially affects the external appearance of the building so treated;

---

[12] See *Encyclopedia of Planning Law and Practice,* vol. 2, para. 55.10.
[13] *Fayrewood Fish Farms Ltd v. Secretary of State for the Environment* [1984] J.P.L. 267.
[14] TCPA, s.55(4).
[15] *Bendles Motors Ltd v. Bristol Corporation* [1963] 1 W.L.R. 247.
[16] TCPA 1990, s.55.

(2) Maintenance or improvement works carried out by a local highway authority to and within the boundaries of, a road;

(3) The breaking open of streets etc. for the inspection, repair or renewal of sewers, mains, pipes, cables etc. by a local authority or by a statutory undertaker;

(4) The use of any buildings or other land within the curtilage of a dwelling house for any purpose incidental to the enjoyment of the dwelling house;

(5) The use of land for agriculture or forestry and the use for those purposes of any building occupied in connection with land so used;

(6) The demolition of any description of building specified in a direction given by the Secretary of State to local planning authorities generally or to a particular local planning authority;

(7) In the case of buildings or other land used for a purpose of any class specified in an Order made by the Secretary of State, the use thereof for any purpose within the same class.

## The Use Classes Order

The Use Classes Order,[17] made by the Secretary of State, provides that certain changes in the use of land do not constitute development. The aim of the Order is to reduce the need for planning permission where it is unnecessary because the change of use will not damage the amenity of the area. In this way, property owners are given greater freedom and the burden of planning control is lifted in relation to a variety of commercial activities.

Thus, for example, where a post office is changed to become a travel agency, this would not constitute development, so that no planning permission would be required. If, however, the post office were to change into a take-away selling hot food, a change of use not permitted by the Use Classes Order would have taken place, so that planning permission would be necessary. The reason why this should be so is clear. In contrast with a post office, a take-away might be open late at night. People will congregate outside. Litter might be deposited. These matters have the potential to affect the amenity of the surrounding area by creating a nuisance. The Use Classes Order, then, divides uses of land into different "classes", according to their potential to affect the amenity of the area. Changes of use within the same class are permitted, as is a change from within a "bad for local amenity" use class to a "better for local amenity" use class.

### Matters for which planning permission is granted by legislation

Some operations are exempt from control by planning authorities because planning permission is *granted* for them by regulations or by primary legislation. This is sometimes referred to as "deemed" planning permission. These include:

---

[17] Town and Country Planning (Use Classes) Order 1987 (S.I. 1987 No. 764) (as amended by S.I. 1995 No. 297).

(i) *Development permitted under a Development Order*

Under the Act, the Secretary of State may make "Development Orders" which grant planning permission for certain types of development.[18] Eighty four classes of development are permitted. These include:

(a) Marginal development, such as enlarging a dwelling house or erecting a gate;

(b) Development by certain types of developers, such as local authorities, highways authorities and water authorities;

(c) Development connected with development allowed under other statutory provisions.

(ii) *Development in an Enterprise Zone*

Enterprise zones are areas designated by the government in order to encourage industrial and commercial activity.[19] In such zones, developers do not have to go to the trouble and expense of applying for planning permission for every kind of development.

(iii) *Development in a Simplified Planning Zone*

Any development in a Simplified Planning Zone that conforms with the terms of the scheme laid down for that area does not require planning permission. The planning regime in such a zone is similar to that in an Enterprise Zone, but whilst Enterprise Zones have other advantages, Simplified Planning Zones relate solely to planning freedom. Such zones are part of the government's policy of deregulation in order to reduce the burden on businesses.

## DEVELOPMENT PLANS

Development plans set out the planning policies of each local planning authority. There are three types of plan. In the "shire" counties, two different plans are prepared — a "structure" plan and a "local" plan — whilst in other areas of the country there is only one "unitary" plan.

The Secretary of State for the Environment has the power to supervise the making of all development plans. He is a statutory consultee at the preparation stage, where he can object to the plan and make a direction that it should be modified. Exceptionally, he can call in all or part of the plan for approval or rejection.[20] Although these powers are rarely used, their purpose is to ensure that development plans do not become greatly out of step with government policy.

### Structure Plans

Structure plans are prepared in relation to a substantial region, such as a whole county. The policies in structure plans deal only with the major uses of land in the county, and

---

[18] TCPA 1990, s.59 The orders currently in force include the Town and Country Planning (General Permitted Development) Order 1995 (S.I. 1995 No. 418) and the Town and Country Planning (General Development Procedure) Order 1995 (S.I. 1995 No. 419).

[19] Local Government Planning and Land Act 1980, Sched. 32 para. 17(1).

[20] TCPA 1990, s.35A (structure plans) and s.44 (local plans).

set out broad policies in relation to future development. The Act requires structure plans to include policies with respect to the conservation of the natural beauty and amenity of the land, the improvement of the physical environment, and the management of traffic.[21] In addition, structure plans will include policies on housing, green belts, the conservation of the natural and built environment, the urban and rural economies, transport, waste management, tourism, leisure and energy generation (including the use of renewable energy).[22]

## Local Plans

Local plans translate the broad strategic issues dealt with in the structure plan into specific policies and proposals. Each local plan will comprise a map, designating particular areas of land for the implementation of particular policies, together with a written statement detailing those policies. The local plan forms the basis for determining planning applications. If a developer wishes to see what he can do with his land, he can easily consult the local plan to find out what policy restrictions attach to his land and the purpose for which it has been designated. These matters will usually determine whether or not his application for planning permission will succeed, although they are not conclusive. The difference between structure plans and local plans can be illustrated by looking at the way in which they deal with housing policy. The structure plan will allocate a specific number of houses to each district, whilst the local plan will allocate these to specific sites.

## Unitary Development Plans

For metropolitan areas there is only one plan which covers both broad policy and specific details. This is known as a "unitary development plan". It consists of a Part 1 and a Part 2, which have the same functions as a structure plan and a local plan respectively. The structural review of local government, which took place between 1994-1996, abolished five of the 39 shire counties, so that these areas will also have unitary plans.

# THE GRANT OF PLANNING PERMISSION

## Determination of Planning Applications

Once an application for planning permission has been made, the local planning authority has eight weeks in which to notify the applicant of its decision. The application can be decided by a committee or by an officer of the local planning authority.[23] The local planning authority can grant planning permission unconditionally, grant it with conditions, or refuse it.

---

[21] TCPA 1990, ss.12(3A) and 31(3).
[22] See PPG 12, para. 5.9 (DoE).
[23] Local Government Act 1972, s.101.

When deciding an application for planning permission, the local planning authority must have regard to the development plan so far as is material to the application and to "any other material considerations".[24] Section 54A of the Act (discussed below) requires that determination of the planning application shall be in accordance with the plan unless material considerations indicate otherwise. Material considerations will include local and national planning policies, as expressed in RPGs, PPGs and other guidance. The authority must also consider any representations or objections which have been made to the development proposal. In certain cases, it has a duty to consult with another body, such as the Environment Agency or one of the nature conservancy councils. Such bodies are known as "statutory consultees". The very general nature of all these duties, however, enables the local planning authority to exercise a considerable amount of discretion in determining planning applications.

## The Presumption in Favour of Development

During the 1980s, it was government policy that planning permission should always be granted unless there were good reasons for not doing so. This was known as the "presumption in favour of development". Thus, in 1988, government guidance stated:

> "The planning system fails in its function whenever it prevents, inhibits or delays development which can reasonably be permitted . . . [T]he developer is not required to prove the case for the development he proposes to carry out . . . the onus is on [the local planning authority] to demonstrate clearly why the development cannot be permitted."[25]

## The Presumption in Favour of the Development Plan

The position has now changed, however, because of the enactment of section 54A of the Town and Country Planning Act 1990, which was inserted into that Act by the Planning and Compensation Act 1991. Section 54A states:

> "Where, in making any determination under the planning Acts, regard is to be had to the development plan, the determination shall be made in accordance with the development plan unless material considerations indicate otherwise."

In the light of this section, which replaces the old duty to "have regard to" the development plan with a new duty to act "in accordance with" the plan, the situation has changed from one of "developer-led" planning policy to one of "plan-led" policy. In other words, now, in contrast with the position in the 1980s, where the development plan states that development in a particular area should not be permitted, there will be a presumption in favour of following the plan and not allowing the development to proceed. The presumption in favour of following the plan can be rebutted, however, if the applicant produces convincing reasons why the development should go ahead.

---

[24] TCPA 1990, s.70(2).
[25] PPG 1, 1988, para. 15 (DoE). (This guidance has now been amended.)

Material considerations indicating that the development should go ahead must be weighed against the development plan in making the decision. One such consideration is how up to date are the policies contained in the development plan.

## Material Considerations

As has been said, the planning authority is required to have regard to the development plan and to "any other material considerations". The Act offers no guidance as to what considerations might be regarded as material. It has therefore fallen to the courts to determine this matter. Cooke J., in *Stringer v. Minister of Housing and Local Government*,[26] stated:

> "In principle . . . any consideration which relates to the use and development of land is capable of being a planning consideration. Whether a particular consideration falling within that broad class is material in any given case will depend on the circumstances."

Material considerations must be genuine planning considerations, that is to say they must be related to the purpose of planning legislation, which is to regulate the development of land in the public interest. For a consideration to be material, it must also "fairly and reasonably relate to the proposed development".[27] Material considerations, then, will include the number of buildings to be constructed, their size, their layout, where they are situated, how they are designed, and the means by which they are to be accessed. Consideration of their impact on the neighbourhood and their effects on supporting infrastructure (*e.g.* the sewage system and the transport system) will also be material. The question of whether a development is economically worthwhile, however, is not a material consideration.[28]

## Planning Conditions

Almost all planning permission granted is subject to conditions. The issue is often not whether the development should be permitted but on what terms it may be permitted. Conditions may be used by a planning authority to keep the nature of the development under tight control. The government's policy in relation to planning conditions is that, if used properly, conditions can enhance the quality of development and enable many development proposals to proceed where it would otherwise have been necessary to refuse planning permission.[29]

The planning authority has the power to attach to planning permission whatever conditions it thinks fit.[30] It is also given a specific power to attach conditions to land under the control of the applicant which is not part of the land which he proposes to develop.[31] A condition may also be imposed to the effect that planning permission will

---

[26] [1971] 1 All ER 65 at 77.
[27] *R. v. Westminster County Council, ex p. Monahan* [1989] 3 W.L.R. 408.
[28] *Walters v. Secretary of State for Wales* [1979] J.P.L. 171.
[29] Circular 11/95, July 20, 1995, *The Use of Conditions in Planning Permission* (DoE).
[30] TCPA 1990, s.70.
[31] *ibid.*, s.72(1)(a).

last only for a limited period, so that the development must commence, or must be completed, within a specified time.[32] In exceptional cases, a condition may be imposed which limits the duration of the time for which the development can remain in existence. The advantage of this approach is that where objections are made to a particular development, a "trial run" of the development may be permitted to see whether the objections are well founded. Thus, where a developer wished to attach a large fibreglass fish to the exterior of his house, and concerns were expressed that this might prejudice road safety by surprising passing drivers, the planning Inspector granted planning permission for the fish to remain for three years.

Although the local planning authority has wide discretion in deciding what conditions to impose, its discretion is not totally unfettered. The following limits to the discretion were identified in *Newbury District Council v. Secretary of State for the Environment*[33]:

(1) The condition may only be imposed for a "planning" purpose and not for any ulterior purpose;

(2) The condition must fairly and reasonably relate to the development permitted by the planning permission;

(3) The condition must not be so unreasonable that no reasonable planning authority could have imposed it.

In *R v. Hillingdon London Borough Council, ex p. Royco Homes Ltd*,[34] for example, a condition of planning permission which required a proposed residential development to be occupied by people on a local authority's housing waiting list was held to be *ultra vires* because it had been imposed for an improper purpose. It represented an attempt by the local authority to use its planning powers to shift the burden of the duty to house people in need on to the developer. This was not permissible, because the duty was imposed by the law on a housing authority. Similarly, in *Newbury District Council v. Secretary of State for the Environment*,[35] a condition attached to a planning permission to use aircraft hangars to store rubble for 10 years, which required that the hangars be demolished after that time, was held to be invalid because it did not relate to the development permitted, which was the use of the hangars. In *Hall & Co Ltd v. Shoreham-by-Sea Urban District Council*,[36] a condition which had the effect of requiring the developer to construct a public road at his own expense was held to be unreasonable.

## Appeals

If the local planning authority refuses to grant planning permission, or grants it subject to conditions, the applicant can appeal to the Secretary of State within 28 days of the

[32] *ibid.*, s.72(1)(b).
[33] [1981] A.C. 578.
[34] [1974] Q.B. 720.
[35] [1981] A.C. 578.
[36] [1964] 1 W.L.R. 240.

decision.[37] The Secretary of State (on the recommendations of a planning inspector whom he appoints to hear the appeal) may allow or dismiss the appeal or may vary the decision by imposing different conditions. An appeal takes the form of a rehearing[38] which can be conducted either by way of an oral hearing before a planning inspector, known as a local inquiry, or by way of written representations by the parties, which produces a faster result.

If an applicant is dissatisfied with the Secretary of State's decision, he may appeal to the courts, as may any other person aggrieved by an order or action of the Secretary of State, challenging the validity of the decision. The general principles of review are that the Secretary of State acted perversely, failed to take account of relevant material, took into account irrelevant material, failed to abide by statutory procedures, and that, where, on the basis of new evidence, the Secretary of State has departed from the inspector's recommendations, he has failed to allow the parties the opportunity to make further representations.[39]

## Planning by Agreement

By section 106 of the Town and Country Planning Act 1990, an applicant for planning permission may enter into an agreement with the local planning authority, or give a unilateral undertaking, to carry out certain activities on his land or to refrain from using the land. Thus, for example, the developer may agree to provide a community centre, a creche, or sewage facilities, or to make a contribution to the cost of widening a road where his development will increase the amount of traffic on the road. Where the developer offers to do such things, he is said to be offering the planning authority a "planning gain" in return for permitting his development to proceed.

In contrast to the position in relation to the imposition of planning conditions, the planning authority has a virtually unregulated discretion to enter into planning agreements. This means that such agreements may be made for purposes which would be unlawful if pursued by way of planning conditions, as for example where the developer agrees to provide housing for people on the local authority's waiting-list. Where planning gain is offered, the authority is able to grant the permission on the basis that the benefits associated with the proposed development are material considerations which outweigh its adverse effects. This means, of course, that the nature of the planning gain must be capable of being a material consideration. It cannot simply be a "bribe" to the planning authority.

The practice of accepting planning gain, which is followed by different local planning authorities in different parts of the country operating under widely different rules, has the potential to become, in effect, a system of local taxation on development. Although planning gain cannot be *demanded* by the planning authority, in real terms, where a developer offers it, he will often know that it is a precondition to his proposals being accepted. A government circular has attempted to address this problem by providing that planning obligations should be sought only where they are *necessary* for the development to proceed and *relevant* to the proposed development. The circular states

---

[37] TCPA 1990, s.78.
[38] *ibid.,* s.79.
[39] *Seddon Properties v. Secretary of State for the Environment* [1978] J.P.L. 835; 248 EG 950.

that unacceptable development should never be permitted because of unrelated benefits offered by the applicant.[40]

The House of Lords, in *Tesco Stores Ltd v. Secretary of State for the Environment*,[41] has effectively drawn a distinction between planning obligations which are *required* by the local planning authority and planning obligations *offered* by developers. As regards the former, the clear limits outlined in the circular apply. As regards the latter, the circular is less relevant. In reality, however, where a formal application for planning permission in relation to a large development is preceded by lengthy preliminary negotiations with the planning authority, and by the submission of outline proposals, it will often be very difficult to draw the distinction which their Lordships have suggested between situations where planning gain is "offered" and situations where it is "required" by the authority. Planning gain remains a very controversial topic, because, although it has the potential significantly to affect the environment, it remains virtually unregulated by statute.

## ENFORCEMENT OF PLANNING CONTROLS

Enforcement of planning controls is primarily designed to prevent breaches of planning control rather than to punish the wrongdoer. Carrying out development without planning permission, or failing to comply with a condition imposed on planning permission, is a breach of planning control. It is not, however, a criminal offence. The occurrence of a breach enables the planning authority to serve a variety of notices designed to remedy the breach. It is failure to comply with the requirements of such notices which constitutes a criminal offence.

### Planning Contravention Notices

Where it appears to the local planning authority that there *may* have been a breach of planning control, it may serve a planning contravention notice requiring information about the operations which are being carried out on the land. The aim of such notices is to enable planning authorities to obtain information so as to resolve the matter by co-operation without further recourse to enforcement procedures. Failure to provide the information can result in a fine of £1,000.

### Breach of Condition Notices

If planning permission is granted subject to conditions and any of those conditions are not complied with, the planning authority may serve a breach of condition notice requiring compliance with the conditions. This notice will specify a time within which certain steps necessary to comply with the condition must be carried out, after which time the person responsible for the breach will be guilty of an offence.

[40] Circular 16/91 (DoE).
[41] [1995] 1 W.L.R. 759.

## Enforcement Notices

If the local planning authority decides not to use either of the above procedures, or uses them but without success in remedying the breach, it may serve an enforcement notice (not to be confused with a notice of the same name served by the Environment Agency to enforce the IPC regime, discussed in Chapter 6, below). The notice will outline the matters constituting the breach of planning control and the steps to be taken to remedy the breach. The notice will specify a time limit within which the requisite steps must be taken. After this time, the planning authority may enter the land and carry out the specified steps itself. It may then recover the expense of so doing from the owner.[42] It is a criminal offence to fail to comply with an enforcement notice.[43] The maximum fine in the magistrates court is £20,000, whilst the fine in the Crown Court is unlimited. In determining the amount of the fine, the court can take into account any financial benefit which has accrued or appears likely to accrue to the developer in consequence of the offence.[44] The service of an enforcement notice may be appealed against by any person having an interest in the land to which it relates or by the occupier of the land. The appeal is to the Secretary of State.[45] Once an appeal is brought, the enforcement notice is of no effect until the appeal has been decided or until the appeal is withdrawn.[46]

## Stop Notices

If a serious breach of planning control is being committed and the planning authority considers that it should be stopped immediately, it can issue a Stop Notice at the same time as the enforcement notice or at any time afterwards.[47]

## Injunctions

The local planning authority has an express power to obtain an injunction to restrain an actual or threatened breach of planning control.[48] This power was given to planning authorities for the first time by the Planning and Compensation Act 1991. Prior to this Act, injunctions could only be sought in exceptional cases, and as a last resort, under section 222 of the Local Government Act 1972, to restrain breaches of the criminal law. The courts have held that the new powers are much wider than those under section 222 and that their exercise is not subject to the same restrictions.

## Limitations on Enforcement

It is a significant restriction on the ability to enforce planning controls that there are time limits on the taking of enforcement action:

[42] TCPA 1990, s.178.
[43] *ibid.*, s.179(2).
[44] *ibid.*, s.179(9).
[45] *ibid.*, s.174(1).
[46] *ibid.*, s.175(4).
[47] *ibid.*, s. 183.
[48] *ibid.*, s.187B (inserted by the Planning and Compensation Act 1991).

(a) If operations have been carried out on land without planning permission, no enforcement action can be taken four years after the operations were substantially completed.[49]

(b) If a change of use is made to a building to convert it to a single dwelling house, in breach of planning controls, no enforcement action can be taken after the end of four years from the date on which the breach occurred.[50]

(c) No enforcement action can be taken for any other breach of planning controls after the end of 10 years following the date of the breach.[51]

## ENVIRONMENTAL CONSIDERATIONS IN THE PLANNING SYSTEM

Having considered the mechanics of the planning regime, it is now appropriate to examine the ways in which it is used to protect the wider environment and to consider the nature of its relationship with other forms of environmental control.

The planning system is primarily designed to control the local built environment. In formulating policy and in making planning decisions, the regulatory authorities' terms of reference are to consider the effect of development on the "amenity of the locality". *Prima facie*, then, this, by definition will not include consideration of the impacts of development on the wider environment. There are, however, a number of ways in which such considerations do form part of planning policy and procedure. These are examined in the remainder of this chapter.

It should be noted that because of its heavy reliance on the discretion of planning authorities, planning *policy* is rarely capable of affording land absolute immunity from development for the protection of the wider environment. This is usually only possible by designation of a site as a National Nature Reserve and by appropriation of the site by a Nature Conservancy Council. These matters are discussed in Chapter 12. As U.K. environmental law moves increasingly towards a more integrated and coherent approach to environmental problems, however, with national environmental strategies for waste management and for air quality, it may be that the discretionary nature of the planning system will change slightly and that planning law will assume a greater rôle in implementing absolute standards relating to certain forms of development or development in certain areas.

In *individual planning decisions,* an awareness of the wider environment has become increasingly apparent in recent years. It is clear, however, that protection of the wider environment is only one factor amongst many which must be balanced in making a decision whether to grant planning permission. PPG 9 states that local planning authorities should not refuse planning permission if other material factors are sufficient to override nature conservation considerations. Sometimes, however, the planning system simply has no opportunity to consider the wider environment. The use of any land for the purposes of agriculture or forestry is exempt from the need for

---

[49] *ibid.,* s.171B.
[50] *ibid.,* s.171B(2).
[51] *ibid.,* s.171B(3).

planning permission because it does not constitute development.[52] Although intensive farming is one of the main causes of habitat destruction, then, it cannot be regulated from within the planning system.

## Sustainable Development

Sustainable development has become a central theme of planning guidance. Indeed, the Secretary of State for the Environment has described the concept of sustainable development as the "touchstone" of government planning policy. Government guidance explicitly recognises the driving force of sustainable development in a planning context. PPG 1 states:

> "The government has made clear its intention to work towards ensuring that development and growth are sustainable. It will continue to develop policies consistent with the concept of sustainable development. The planning system, and the preparation of development plans in particular, can contribute to the objectives of ensuring that development and growth are sustainable. The sum total of decisions in the planning field, as elsewhere, should not deny future generations the best of today's environment."[53]

### Transport Policy

Transport policy is at the centre of the government objective of making development more sustainable.[54] Its principal aims are to reduce the number and length of motorised journeys and to encourage alternative means of travel which are more environmentally-friendly, so as to reduce people's reliance on private cars. This will reduce the need for fuel, which will in turn reduce emissions of greenhouse gases and other pollutants.

Transport policy is to be implemented by ensuring, where possible, that housing, employment, retail, leisure and education should be located close to public transport, and as close as possible to one another, so as to avoid the need for travel. Parking is to be controlled, cyclists and pedestrians provided for, and local authorities are to assist in public transport provision. Journeys are also to be reduced by encouraging development in town centres, as well as development which mixes residential and business uses. Thus, a revival of the former trend for people to live above shops is to be encouraged. This idea marks a change in policy. Formerly it had been thought that out of centre locations had a distinctive rôle to play in providing for new retail development in a way which could relieve congestion in high streets.

### Use of Renewable Energy[55]

Renewable energy sources are sources of energy which occur naturally and repeatedly in the environment. They include energy from the sun, the wind, the sea and the fall of

---

[52] *ibid.,* s.55.
[53] PPG 1, para. 3 (DoE, 1992).
[54] See PPG 13.
[55] PPG 22, "Renewable Energy" (DoE, February 1993).

water. Renewable energy sources offer the possibility of increased diversity and security of energy supply, as well as of reducing the greenhouse gas emissions which occur with traditional methods of energy generation in large and centralised power stations burning fossil-fuel. They also avoid the risks associated with nuclear power. Some renewable energy sources, such as hydro-power, have already been widely commercially exploited, whilst others, such as wind, are on the verge of wide-spread commercial exploitation. The government's policy is to encourage the exploitation and development of renewable energy sources through the planning system wherever they have prospects of being economically attractive and environmentally acceptable.

## Development Plans

The presumption in favour of following the development plan in making planning decisions, which has now displaced the presumption in favour of development, is welcomed by environmentalists, because plans are required to reflect environmental considerations. Government guidance on the drawing up of development plans is contained in PPG 12, which advises on the importance of environmental considerations in plan preparation:

> "Local planning authorities should take account of the environment in the widest sense in plan preparation. They are familiar with the 'traditional' issues of Green Belt, concern for landscape quality and nature conservation, the built heritage and conservation areas. They are familiar too with pollution control planning for healthier cities. The challenge is to ensure that newer environmental concerns such as global warming and the consumption of non-renewable resources are also reflected in the analysis of policies that forms part of plan preparation".[56]

The guidance states that planning authorities must have regard to environmental considerations in preparing their general policies and proposals in structure plans and unitary development plans. Most policies and proposals, in all types of plan, will have environmental implications which should be appraised as part of the plan preparation process.[57] The guidance does not require planning authorities to conduct a full environmental impact assessment in relation to its policies[58] (see below), although such a requirement may yet be imposed under proposals currently under consideration by the E.C. The existing obligation is merely to appraise the environmental implications of development policy. Such an appraisal entails identifying, quantifying, weighing up and reporting on the environmental and other costs and benefits of the measures which are proposed. All the implications of the different policy options should be analysed, including their financial, social and environmental effects. The guidance states that such a systematic appraisal ensures that the objectives of planning policy are clearly laid-out and that any "trade-offs" are clearly identified and assessed.[59]

---

[56] PPG 12.
[57] *ibid.*, para. 5.52; Town and Country Planning Development Plan Regulations 1991 (S.I. 1991 No. 2794), reg.9.
[58] PPG 12, para. 5.2.
[59] *ibid.*, para. 5.52.

Planning authorities are also required to have regard to other government guidance in preparing their development plans.[60] Such guidance requires, for example, that a planning authority should take account of any designations affecting land (see below) and weigh up the need to encourage rural enterprise with the need to protect the landscape, wildlife habitats and historic features. Plans must include policies encouraging the management of features of the landscape which are of major importance for wild fauna and flora (defined as being those features that are essential for the migration, dispersal and genetic exchange of wild species).[61] The structure plan should indicate how the balance between development and conservation has been struck.[62]

Development plans should also include policies for the clean up and re-use of contaminated land, for the protection of groundwater resources, for the environmental effects of new water services, and for the siting of hazardous installations and mineral extraction operations. They should also contain policies which have the potential to reduce the deposit of refuse and waste material.[63]

## Consultation at the Planning Stage

In drawing up the plans, a statutory process of public consultation and debate takes place.[64] This is the primary means of reconciling conflicts between the need for development and the need to protect the environment. The reality is that this is the most important point for integrating environmental considerations into the planning process, because, once the plan is in place, decisions whether or not to grant planning permission, and decisions about planning conditions, will depend upon the content of the plan.

Planning authorities are required to consult, *inter alia*, the Environment Agency and English Nature when drawing up development plans. Once a plan has been prepared it will be "deposited" for a time. During this time, interested parties are able to object to policies in the plan. For local plans, objectors have the right to have their objections considered at a local plan inquiry held by an inspector appointed by the Secretary of State. The inspector can recommend modifications to any of the plan's policies and his recommendations will be considered by the planning authority. If modifications to the plan are made, there is a further period of consultation. If new issues are raised during this period, a further inquiry can be held. For structure plans, the process is similar, except that objections to the plan are considered at an examination in public (EIP) presided over by a panel. No person has the right to be heard at an EIP, so that representations can only be made by those who have been invited to speak.

## Consultation at the Decision Stage

There are statutory requirements on a local planning authority to consult with a number of expert bodies in the making of a planning decision[65]:

---

[60] TCPA 1990, ss.12 and 31.
[61] Conservation (Natural Habitats, etc.) Regulations 1994 (S.I. 1994 No. 2716), reg. 37.
[62] PPG 12.
[63] PCA 1991, Sched. 4.
[64] TCPA 1990, ss.13 and 33.
[65] General Development Procedure Order 1995.

- If development is likely to affect land in a National Park, the National Park Authority must be consulted;

- If the development is likely to affect the site of a scheduled ancient monument, the Historic Buildings and Monuments Commission must be consulted;

- If the development is in or likely to affect a Site of Special Scientific Interest (SSSI) of which notification has been given to the local planning authority, or is in a notified area within two kilometres of an SSSI, the relevant Nature Conservancy Council must be consulted;

- The Environment Agency is a statutory consultee for certain classes of development with a high water pollution potential.

## Environmental Considerations as Material Considerations

The impact of noise from a development on a local community is a material consideration, as is the need to preserve an ancient monument.[66] The fact that a site is designated as a World Heritage Site (as are Blenheim Palace and Stonehenge, for example) is a key material consideration in any decision whether or not to grant planning permission.[67] Planning Policy Guidance Notes which refer to the wider environment are, of course, an important material consideration. The problem, however, is to determine how much weight is to be attached to these broad statements of policy in the light of the evidential problems in relation to environmental degradation. In *Bolton M.D.C. v. Secretary of State for the Environment*,[68] for example, the court recognised the enormous evidential problems of determining the amount of carbon dioxide which would be generated by traffic because of a proposed new shopping centre, so that it might be compared with the amount generated by shoppers using existing shops.

## Environmental Impact Assessment

Assessment of the environmental effects of proposed development before planning permission is granted is, of course, a normal part of the decision-making process for planning authorities. The E.C. Directive on Environmental Impact Assessment,[69] however, establishes the need for planning authorities to prepare a formal statement indicating the environmental effects of certain proposed projects before planning permission is granted. The Directive is implemented by a number of statutory instruments, the main regulations being set out in the Town and Country Planning (Assessment of Environmental Effects) Regulations 1988.[70]

---

[66] *Hoveringham Gravels Ltd v. Secretary of State for the Environment* [1975] Q.B. 754.
[67] PPG 15.
[68] [1994] J.P.L. B37.
[69] Directive on the Assessment of the Effects of Certain Public and Private Projects on the Environment (Dir. 85/337/EEC [1985] O.J. L175/40).
[70] S.I. 1988 No. 1199.

The Regulations, which in essence repeat the contents of the Directive, establish two classes of project for which a formal environmental impact assessment is appropriate. For projects listed in Schedule 1 of the regulations, a formal assessment is mandatory, whilst for those listed in Schedule 2, a formal assessment may be undertaken at the discretion of the planning authority. Projects listed in Schedule 1 include crude oil refineries, thermal power stations, and the construction of motorways. Those listed in Schedule 2 include such activities as pig farming, glass making and paper manufacturing.

At the time of writing, a proposal to amend the Directive, which was put forward by the European Council, has been approved by the European Parliament.[71] The proposed amendments extend the remit of the assessment procedure beyond individual development decisions to cover Community or national *programmes* likely to have environmental effects. The amendments were felt necessary in view of the fact that often the biggest decisions affecting the environment are taken when plans are prepared, before individual applications for projects are made. The amendments are also concerned with establishing a more uniform and rigorous methodology for impact assessment within Member States. In the U.K., as we have noted, there is a general requirement to conduct an environmental appraisal of policies in development plans. As yet, however, this does not appear to meet the requirements envisaged by the E.C.

## Preservation of the Countryside

Preservation of the countryside is discussed more fully in Chapter 12. For present purposes, however, it should be noted that the guiding principle of government policy is that development in the countryside should benefit the rural economy as well as maintaining or enhancing the environment. Any development in open countryside away from existing developed areas should be strictly controlled. In areas which have been designated as worthy of special protection, however, different rules apply. Sites of Special Scientific Interest (SSSIs), National Nature Reserves (NNRs), Marine Nature Reserves, and sites designated under Limestone Pavement Orders, are discussed more fully in Chapter 12. Some other forms of site designation which have an impact on planning law are also briefly considered below.

### National Parks

National Parks are designated under the National Parks and Access to Countryside Act 1949. Their statutory purpose[72] is the conservation and enhancement of natural beauty, wildlife and cultural heritage and the promotion of opportunities for public understanding and enjoyment of their special qualities. National Park land covers 8 per cent of the land area of England. Responsibility for the detailed running of the parks rests with a National Park Authority, which must prepare local plans covering the whole of its area. The government's policy is that conservation of the natural beauty of the countryside should be given great weight in planning policies relating to, and

---

[71] [1995] O.J. C287/83.
[72] As amended by the Environment Act 1995.

development decisions affecting, National Parks. Major development should not take place in the National Parks save in very exceptional circumstances. Because of the serious impact that major developments may have, applications for such developments must be subject to rigorous examination.

## Areas of Outstanding Natural Beauty

Areas of Outstanding Natural Beauty (AONBs) are designated to conserve the natural beauty of the landscape. These form 16 per cent of the total land area in England. They are different from National Parks in that promotion of recreation is not an objective of designation. In general, policy and development control decisions affecting AONBs should favour conservation of the natural beauty of the landscape. Thus it would normally be inconsistent with the aims of designation to permit the siting of major industrial or commercial development within such an area.

## Green Belts

The purpose of a Green Belt is to act as a "buffer zone" between the countryside and large built-up areas so as to stop the outward expansion of those built-up areas from encroaching on the countryside. They also assist in preserving the special character of historic towns. Within green belts, there is a general presumption that inappropriate development will not be permitted.[73]

## Special Areas of Conservation

The Conservation (Natural Habitats etc.) Regulations 1994,[74] which implement the E.C.'s Natural Habitats Directive (discussed in Chapter 12), make significant alterations to the planning system with respect to the Special Areas of Conservation (SACs) designated under the regulations. The Regulations require that where an SAC has been designated, planning permission which has been granted for projects within the area must be reconsidered, and, where development has not yet taken place, may be revoked unless there are reasons of overriding public interest for not doing so, or unless conditions can be imposed to prevent ecological damage. The regulations also effectively extinguish rights of permitted development within such areas, so that an application for planning permission becomes necessary for development to proceed.

# Planning and the Pollution Control Regimes

Government guidance states that the rôle of the planning system is to focus on whether the development is an acceptable use of the land, rather than to make development decisions in every case by reference to the development's likely impact on the wider environment.[75] In making decisions, then, the planning authority must

---

[73] See PPG 2 (DoE, January 1995).
[74] S.I. 1994 No. 2716.
[75] PPG 23 "Planning and Pollution Control" (DoE, 1994).

assume that the risk and impact of pollution from the proposed development will be dealt with fully by the relevant pollution control authority. Under the U.K. pollution control regime, most operations with the potential to cause pollution, such as the use of land as a landfill site, or for an industrial activity prescribed under Part I of the Environmental Protection Act 1990, will require a licence, either from the Environment Agency or from the local authority. Such operations will, of course, also require planning permission where they involve development of the land on which they take place.

The granting of a licence will not exempt the operator of an industrial or waste management process from the need to obtain planning permission for his activities where they constitute development, and the fact that a licence has been granted does not mean that planning permission will automatically follow, because the local planning authority will have a different range of interests to balance in deciding whether or not to permit the development in its area than will the pollution control authority in deciding whether to grant a licence.

The interrelationship between planning and other environmental controls was considered in *Gateshead Metropolitan Borough Council v. Secretary of State for the Environment*,[76] The case concerned an application for planning permission to build a clinical waste incinerator. The Secretary of State had granted outline planning permission for the project on the basis that the controls available under the Environmental Protection Act 1990 were such that it would have no unacceptable impact on the environment. Although the extent of likely atmospheric pollution was a material consideration, so was the existence of a stringent pollution control regime. The council appealed. In upholding the grant of planning permission, Glidewell L.J. referred to the government's guidance on the interrelationship between pollution control and planning control, and stated that: "It is not the job of the planning system to duplicate controls which are the statutory responsibility of other bodies."

It followed that issues concerning air quality policy which were raised during the appeal were properly to be considered by HMIP, rather than by the Secretary of State in the exercise of planning control. It also followed that the grant of planning permission did not necessarily mean HMIP had to grant an authorisation for the operation of the incinerator.

[76] (1993) 67 P. & C.R. 179.

# Chapter 6

## INTEGRATED POLLUTION CONTROL

*". . . different approaches to controlling emissions into air, water or soil separately may encourage the shifting of pollution between the various environmental media rather than protecting the environment as a whole."*[1]

### Introduction

The Integrated Pollution Control regime in the U.K. is a relatively recent and innovative method of pollution control, designed for certain types of industrial processes that discharge significant quantities of harmful substances, or very small amounts of highly toxic material. It is based on a holistic approach to the management of pollution and is implemented by Part I of the Environmental Protection Act 1990.

### The Nature of Integrated Pollution Control

Integrated Pollution Control (IPC) is based upon a recognition that a pollutant, when discharged, may enter more than one environmental medium and indeed may travel through several environmental media. The concept of Integrated Pollution Control recognises that solving one pollution problem may create another. For example, dust that would otherwise be emitted to the air may be removed by the use of water sprays. This leaves polluted water that must then be disposed of. The water may be piped into a lagoon to settle and dry out, creating solid waste. Disposing of the solid waste may create a worse problem than if the dust that had caused the original problem had been widely dispersed through a tall chimney.[2] As an alternative the dust might be filtered from the air by the use of large extractor fans, but solving the air pollution problem in this way may create a noise pollution problem. Moreover, extractor fans use a lot of power. This must be generated at a power station which, in turn, may cause atmospheric pollution. When these factors are taken into account, it can be seen that the proposed solutions to the problem may cause greater pollution than if the air from the factory had been discharged without having the dust filtered from it.

---

[1] Preamble to Council Dir. 96/61 E.C., September 24, 1996, concerning integrated pollution prevention and control, [1996] O.J. L257/26.
[2] *op. cit.,* n.3, below.

The Royal Commission on Environmental Pollution, in its fifth report,[3] recognised that previous pollution control regimes in the U.K. had not addressed these difficulties. The pollution of air, land and water had been treated as three separate issues and controlled by different authorities acting under various legislation. Regulation in this manner had been inefficient. Pollutants would be disposed of in a haphazard manner without considering the best solution for the environment as a whole. Resources for pollution control would not necessarily be targeted where the pollution problems were most severe. A fragmented approach to pollution control enabled polluters to seek out the easiest and cheapest media to pollute.

The theory of Integrated Pollution Control allows for a consideration of the holistic nature of environmental problems. The traditional focus in pollution control had been on the media that were polluted: air, water and land. An integrated approach to pollution control, on the other hand, focuses on the *pollutant* and on reducing the effect it can have on *any* and *all* environmental media. It is therefore appropriate to apply an IPC regime to industrial processes which are likely to discharge substances into more than one environmental medium. It will be seen, however, that in many respects the practical implementation of the IPC regime in the U.K. has fallen short of the theoretical concept upon which it is based.

## The Environmental Protection Act 1990

The law in relation to Integrated Pollution Control is expressed by way of an enabling statute, supplemented by a multiplicity of subordinate legislation, some of which deals with quite complex and technical matters. As was noted in Chapter 1, the advantage of this approach to environmental legislation is that regulations can be made quickly to address changes in technology and scientific thought. The disadvantage is that knowledge of what the law requires in a particular case becomes relatively inaccessible, even to the trained lawyer.

Part I of the Environmental Protection Act 1990 implements the Integrated Pollution Control regime. The main objectives of the regime are to:

(a) Prevent or minimise the release of certain prescribed harmful substances into the environment and to render harmless any other substances which are released.[4]

(b) Develop an approach to pollution control that takes into account the effect of discharges from industrial processes on the environment as a whole.[5]

The term "Integrated Pollution Control", as it is used in the U.K.'s statutory regime, does not *necessarily* refer to the control of industrial processes which release substances into more than one environmental medium. Some of the industrial processes which have been prescribed for Integrated Pollution Control by the Secretary of State under

---

[3] Royal Commission on Environmental Pollution Fifth Report: *Integrated Pollution Control,* Cmnd. 6371 (1976).
[4] EPA 1990, s.7(2).
[5] See *IPC — A Practical Guide* (DoE/Welsh Office).

the Environmental Protection Act 1990 may discharge substances into only one environmental medium. The prescribed processes are, however, generally the most hazardous and complex industrial processes. Part I of the Act also implements a regime for controlling emissions to air alone from generally less hazardous and complex industrial processes. This regime is enforced by local authorities, which have the same powers of control over these processes (but only in relation to air pollution) as does the Environment Agency in relation to the more hazardous and complex processes prescribed for IPC.[6]

It is the responsibility of the operator of any process which has been prescribed for Integrated Pollution Control to prevent or, where this is not practicable, to minimise the release into the environment of prescribed substances. Prescribed substances are those deemed by the Secretary of State to be potentially polluting so as to warrant control.[7] In preventing or minimising the release of these substances, process operators are required to use the *Best Available Techniques Not Entailing Excessive Cost* (BATNEEC). In applying BATNEEC to processes which are likely to discharge substances into more than one environmental medium, operators are further required to achieve the *Best Practicable Environmental Option* (BPEO) for the discharge of those substances. This necessitates a consideration of which environmental media will suffer the least damage in receiving the substances.

Regulation of the operators is by a system of prior approval by the Environment Agency, which, in April 1996, took over the functions of Her Majesty's Inspectorate of Pollution (HMIP). An operator cannot carry on a prescribed process without consent, in the form of an authorisation, from the Agency.[8]

## Prescribed and Non-Prescribed Substances

The control of substances is at the heart of the IPC regime. The Act distinguishes between prescribed substances and other substances. It requires that the release of prescribed substances into the particular environmental medium for which they have been prescribed is to be prevented using BATNEEC or, where this is not practicable, minimised using BATNEEC.

All other (non-prescribed) substances come within a second, wider tier of control: the Act requires that *any* substance, whether prescribed or not, which might cause harm if released into the environment must be rendered harmless using BATNEEC before it is released. Harm is defined widely in Part I of the Act to include harm to the health of living organisms or other interferences with the ecological systems of which they form part and includes, in the case of man, offence to any of his senses or to his property. "Harmless" has a corresponding meaning.[9]

At first sight, this definition of "harm" seems fairly clear cut. On closer analysis, however, it proves to be too wide for practical application. For example, the odour emanating from a particular activity, or its visual impact on the landscape, may be

---

[6] See Chapter 10.
[7] See the Environmental Protection (Prescribed Processes and Substances) Regulations 1991 (S.I. 1991 No. 472) (as amended by S.I. 1992 No. 614).
[8] EPA 1990, s.6(3).
[9] EPA 1990, s.1(4).

offensive to some but inoffensive to others. Further, it must be accepted that a certain minimal background level of pollution is "harmless" in the sense that, provided it has no serious long term consequences, it is to be tolerated as an ordinary incident of modern living. For these reasons, HMIP, the predecessor to the Environment Agency, developed a practical approach to the assessment of harm which takes into account not only the magnitude of substance releases but also the composition, response and function of the receiving environment. The Environment Agency, in continuing with this approach, proposes to use statutory Environmental Quality Standards (EQSs). These are published mathematical figures which define the maximum level of concentration of a particular substance in the environment which can be considered tolerable.[10]

## Prescribed Processes

In practice the method by which the control of prescribed substances is achieved is by control of the processes which use those substances. To this end, the Secretary of State has prescribed certain industrial *processes* as involving potentially polluting *substances* so as to warrant control.

The definition of "process" was given a wide scope in a prosecution brought by HMIP against *Safety-Kleen U.K.*[11] for the leakage of 13,000 litres of Cemfuel (a controversial cement kiln fuel produced from solvent wastes) from a loaded tanker while it was parked overnight. The company had argued that the tanker was outside the conceptual boundary of the process regulated, in particular because the parking of product-tankers had not been mentioned specifically in the company's application or in the authorisation issued by HMIP. HMIP in turn argued it was not necessary to have a specific reference in the application or authorisation for the activity to be subject to control. It relied on Schedule 2 of the 1991 Regulations[12] to determine the scope of IPC. The regulations provide that any description of a process prescribed for control under IPC includes any other process carried on at the same location by the same person as part of that process. HMIP also cited the definition of "process" in section 1 (5) and (6) of the Act: a process means any activity including the keeping of a substance capable of causing pollution. The court accepted HMIP's argument and held that the keeping of a tanker load of the product on the same site as the process was within the definition of "process".

## The Methods by which Releases of Substances are Controlled

Once a process has been prescribed for Integrated Pollution Control, process operators, as has been said, are required to use the *Best Available Techniques Not Entailing Excessive Cost* (BATNEEC) to prevent or minimise the release of substances into the environment. In addition, if the process is likely to involve the release of substances into more than one environmental medium, an operator must achieve the

---

[10] See Draft Technical Guidance Note E 1, vol. 1, p. 8 (DoE).
[11] ENDS 236, p.41 September 1994.
[12] S.I. 1991 No. 472, n.7, above.

*Best Practicable Environmental Option* (BPEO). BATNEEC and BPEO have proved difficult to define and HMIP experienced a number of problems in the practical application of these concepts.

## Definition of BATNEEC

Despite its importance as a guiding principle, BATNEEC is not defined in the Environmental Protection Act 1990. It therefore falls to be defined by reference to the policies behind the Act and by guidance issued by the Department of the Environment and by HMIP.

*A basic definition*

BATNEEC is essentially the means by which economic, environmental and (in theory perhaps) social costs and benefits are to be compared and weighed up in establishing the best method for controlling the particular pollutant in question.[13]

*The components of BATNEEC[14]*

**"Best":** The best techniques are simply those which are the most effective in preventing, minimising or rendering harmless polluting emissions. There may be more than one set of techniques that achieve comparable effectiveness and thus there may be more than one set of "best" techniques.

**"Available":** A technique must be available in the sense that it must be within the capabilities of the operator to procure and use it. The guidance, however, adopts a tough approach to the concept of "availability". Techniques which have been developed only on a pilot scheme level are "available" if they can be implemented in the relevant industrial context with business confidence. If there is only a monopoly supplier, the technique counts as being available provided that an operator can procure it. Technology or "know-how" which can only be procured from outside the U.K. is nevertheless "available" and the existence of an open and competitive market for the supply of the technique is not required.

**"Techniques":** The Act provides for the consideration of a wide range of factors in deciding upon the "techniques" to be used to combat pollution. The technology used in the process should be taken into account as well as the numbers, qualifications, training and supervision of the people employed in the process and the design, construction, lay-out and maintenance of the building in which it is carried on.[15] By not requiring the use of specific technology, the formula allows for the continuing development of cleaner technology and gives operators a choice of means to achieve the given standards.

**"Not entailing excessive costs":** The presumption is that the best available techniques for combatting pollution will be used, but this presumption may be displaced by economic considerations. This can occur where the costs of applying the best available techniques would be excessive in relation to the level of environmental protection

---

[13] Andrew Jordan "IPC and the Evolving Style and Structure of Environmental Regulation in the U.K.", (1993) *Environmental Politics,* vol. 2(3), p. 405.
[14] See *IPC — A Practical Guide,* above.
[15] EPA 1990, s.7(10).

which could be achieved. The NEEC part of the formula must be considered in two contexts depending on whether it is applied to "new" processes (*i.e.* processes which have not yet commenced operation) or to "existing" processes (*i.e.* processes which were in operation at the time the Act came into force). As a guide to its application to "new" processes, pollution should, in principle, be abated to the point where the extra benefit to society from further abatement equals the extra cost to society of this abatement.[16]

A strict application of this principle would entail valuing environmental benefits in money terms in order to compare them with abatement costs. However, in the absence of any widely accepted techniques for doing this, the decision whether or not a particular cost is "excessive" is, in practice, a matter for the expert judgment of the Environment Agency. Thus, if there is a choice between one technology which reduces the emission of a polluting substance by 90 per cent and another which reduces the emission by 95 per cent but at four times the cost, the proper view may be that, because of the small benefit and the great costs, the second technology would entail excessive costs. On the other hand, if the emissions are particularly dangerous, the additional costs may not be excessive.

In relation to "existing" processes which need to be upgraded to meet the requirements of IPC, the configuration of the existing plant is a relevant consideration. This may make it excessively costly (in relation to the harm which would be avoided) to fit particular types of pollution abatement technology. The disruption which may be caused to existing operations (and resulting loss of profit to the operator) as a consequence of the immediate deployment of new techniques is also relevant. Thus the immediate introduction of the best available techniques may entail excessive costs where the phased introduction of those techniques would not.

The particular financial circumstances of an individual operator, however, are not relevant in determining the question of excessive costs. Where an operator lacks the balance sheet strength to raise finance for investment which is needed to achieve an acceptable level of environmental protection, the fact that the operator cannot afford to reduce emissions to the required level is disregarded by the Environment Agency in setting the conditions of the authorisation.[17]

An important question in relation to the meaning of "excessive costs" was succinctly framed by Lord McNair in a House of Lords debate on the Environmental Protection Bill[18]: ". . . who is to decide what is an 'excessive cost': industry or the individuals at risk of being harmed?"

The obvious answer, of course, is that the Environment Agency makes the decision, acting with the mandate of those individuals. But this is only a partial answer because it leaves unresolved the question of whose costs are relevant to the decision.

At present, it would seem that the "costs" of a technique refer only to the financial costs to industry. So-called "social costs", either to a local community (redundancy, for example) or to the wider community (for instance, the social cost of reduced access to a public utility like electricity should it become more expensive), do not fall to be considered in the application of BATNEEC. It is submitted, however, that there is no good reason why they should not be so considered.

[16] See RCEP Fifth Report, above.
[17] Draft Technical Guidance Note E1, above.
[18] *Hansard* H.L. 1989–90, vol. 519, col. 480.

An interpretation of "Best Practicable Means", the precursor of BATNEEC, which was given by the Chief Inspector of the Alkali Inspectorate nearly 30 years ago, supports this contention. He took the view that the economic effects of a chosen process should be considered not only in relation to the operator concerned but also in relation to the surrounding community. He justified this on the grounds that ultimately it was the public who paid for clean air and that it was the duty of the inspectorate to see that money was wisely spent on the public's behalf.[19]

This view, however, does not accord with that of the Royal Commission, which, in its twelfth report, indicated that it would not endorse political reasons for failing to implement environmental controls. The commission cited as an example a decision not to close an outdated plant for employment reasons and stated that this would involve a compromise which was in its view unacceptable.[20] Unemployment, however, is of direct financial cost to members of a local community. Once it is accepted that financial costs are a legitimate reason to compromise environmental protection, it is submitted that there can be no logical reason for confining a consideration of such costs to those of industry.

## Definition of BPEO

It will be recalled that where a process is likely to involve the release of substances into more than one environmental medium, the process operator is required to use BATNEEC to achieve the Best Practicable Environmental Option (BPEO) for the environment as a whole. BPEO is not defined in the Environmental Protection Act 1990. The accepted definition, and that which was adopted by HMIP for use in the IPC regime, was given by the Royal Commission in its twelfth report:

> "A BPEO is the outcome of a systematic, consultative and decision-making procedure which emphasises the protection and conservation of the environment across land, air and water. The BPEO procedure establishes for a given set of objectives *the option that provides the most benefit or least damage to the environment as a whole at acceptable cost in the long term as well as in the short term.*"[21]

There are very significant differences, however, between the theoretical concept of BPEO, as put forward by the Royal Commission, and the way in which BPEO is implemented under the Act. The Royal Commission favoured an "imaginative response" to pollution control which involved considering an industrial process in its widest possible environmental context. Thus the BPEO for a given process was to be decided by reference not only to the substances released from the process, but also by reference to the environmental consequences of its use of raw materials and energy and the methods by which any waste it produced could be disposed of. On such a wide interpretation of BPEO, it was conceivable that the BPEO for a specific process might

---

[19] (1967) 103rd Annual Report of the Chief Inspector, p. 3 (HMSO).
[20] Royal Commission on Environmental Pollution. Twelfth Report: *Best Practicable Environmental Option*, Cmnd, 310 (1988).
[21] Authors' emphasis.

involve a higher than normal level of substance releases for the sake of using less energy or raw materials.

Under the current IPC regime, however, this is not possible because the Best Practicable Environmental Option for a process must be one that allows certain Environmental Quality Standards to be met in relation to every substance released.[22] This, in practice, means that fixed emission limits, set by the Environment Agency, must be applied in relation to each substance released. It is therefore not possible to "trade off" an increase in substance emissions above the prescribed limit against a decrease in the use by a particular process of energy and raw materials, even though this might secure the greatest long term environmental benefit.

HMIP was at pains to point out that, in interpreting BPEO, it was constrained by the powers given to it by legislation,[23] Section 7 (7) of the Act requires that where a process is likely to involve the release of substances into more than one environmental medium:

> ". . . the best available techniques not entailing excessive cost will be used for minimising the pollution which may be caused to the environment taken as a whole by the releases having regard to the best practicable environmental option available *as respects the substances which may be released*."[24]

The Environment Agency is therefore restricted (as was HMIP) to a consideration of the BPEO in respect of substance releases only. It does not have the power to consider wider issues such as the environmental effects of the production and delivery of raw materials and the production of energy off-site. The issue of whether BPEO should be given a wider interpretation, more in keeping with that envisaged by the Royal Commission, was considered by Parliament in the context of the Environment Bill and the creation of the Environment Agency. The Agency has greater scope than did HMIP for implementing BPEO in its wider sense. For example, unlike HMIP, it regulates not only the amount of solid and liquid waste produced from an IPC process, but also the manner in which that waste is disposed of. However, a radical change in the meaning of BPEO did not find its way into the Environment Act 1995. The Agency is therefore hampered by the existing statutory definition in the same way as was HMIP, and although it has a duty to promote sustainable development, it can do so only in accordance with existing statutory provisions.[25]

## BPEO in Practice

The concept of BPEO, as it is employed by the Environment Agency, requires the comparison of many different options for the release of substances from an industrial process in order to determine which of those options produces the least harmful effect on the environment as a whole. This necessitates a comparison of the effects of each substance on each environmental medium.

[22] Draft Technical Guidance Note E 1, above.
[23] *ibid.*, vol. 1, p. 13.
[24] Authors' emphasis.
[25] EA 1995, s.4(1).

The accurate assessment of the effects of a substance on an environmental medium is extremely difficult, if not impossible, given the limits of current scientific knowledge. The effect of a substance will depend on many factors, including the rate at which the substance is released, the velocity and temperature at which the substance is released, the propensity of the receiving medium to disperse the substance or to transfer it to other media, the concentration in the medium of other substances with which the released substance may react and the nature of those reactions. If there were complete knowledge about all these factors, it would, in principle, be possible to measure and predict the effects of substances using monitoring and modelling techniques.

In practice, however, knowledge about these factors is limited. Although progress is being made in developing predictive mathematical models and data bases for use as assessment tools, assessment by these methods is time-consuming and costly. The Environment Agency takes the view that a balance has to be struck between ensuring that resources targeted at environmental protection are not mis-allocated and, on the other hand, expending greater resources on the assessment process itself than could be justified by the resulting choice of a particular environmental option.[26] To this end, it has developed a simplified methodology for determining the BPEO for a given process.

The Agency's "simplified methodology" for comparing the effects of substances on different environmental media, and for comparing the costs of implementing various process options to determine whether an option is "practicable" within the meaning of BPEO, is nevertheless fairly complex. Its application entails the comparison of statistics.

In very broad terms, the Agency has prescribed, as a mathematical figure, an "Environmental Assessment Level" (EAL) for each substance in each medium.[27] The EAL represents the concentration of each substance in each medium which is considered tolerable by the Environment Agency. Often this will be the concentration of a substance at which no appreciable effect on the environment can be discerned. The EAL will then be compared with an estimated "Process Contribution" (PC) from the proposed plant, for each substance in each medium. This is calculated as the predicted annual average concentration of a substance at the relevant location in the receiving medium. The "relevant location" for air (and for depositions on land from air) is at ground level and for water is after an appropriate "mixing zone".

An "Environment Quotient" (EQ) for each substance in each medium is then calculated as the ratio of the "Process Contribution" to the "Environmental Assessment Level". Mathematically:

$$EQ \text{ (substance, medium)} = \frac{PC}{EAL}$$

The Environment Quotients for all substances released to a particular environmental medium are then added together to achieve an Environment Quotient for that medium:

---

[26] Draft Technical Guidance Note E1, vol. 1., p. 15.
[27] *ibid*. The EALs are to be published in vol. 3 (Technical Data).

$$EQ \text{ (Medium)} = EQ \text{ (a)} + EQ \text{ (b)} + EQ \text{ (c) etc.}$$

where a . . . c are the substances released into a particular medium.

The Environment Quotients for each medium are then added together to give a value for the overall effect of all substances in all media. This is termed the "Integrated Environmental Index"(IEI):

$$IEI = EQ \text{ (Air)} + EQ \text{ (Water)} + EQ \text{ (Land)}$$

The Integrated Environmental Index thus provides a mechanism for ranking and comparing various process options according to their environmental effects. It is not the only factor considered in the assessment procedure. Further mathematical indicators are used to represent each option's potential for global warming, ozone creation and the production of solid and liquid waste.[28] Odours, visible smoke plumes and the exceeding of critical loads, particularly by foreseeable but unplanned for releases, are amongst the other factors considered. Taken together, these factors are used to determine the "Best Environmental Option" (BEO).

If this is not the option preferred by the operator, it is made the subject of a further assessment procedure by which the implementation and operating costs of various options are compared with their environmental benefits. In theory, the BPEO is achieved where the cost of making any further increase in environmental protection is just equal to the value of the resulting benefit to the environment.[29] However, in the absence of any robust and commonly accepted means of valuing environmental benefits, this criterion is largely academic. In practice, whether the Best Environmental Option is "practicable", in the sense of being economically worthwhile, is (as is the decision whether costs are "excessive" under BATNEEC) a matter for the judgment of the Environment Agency.

The Agency have stressed that the BPEO assessment procedure should not be applied in a mechanistic way[30] and that the final justification of a BPEO should be based on a weighing up of all relevant factors and upon the expert judgment of operators and site inspectors. The benefit of a uniform and structured assessment methodology, however, is that it will allow for closer scrutiny of the way in which BEO is applied: operators will be required to produce an "audit trail" which shows the calculations which they have made and the decisions which they have taken at each stage of the procedure.

## Application for an Authorisation[31]

Before a prescribed process can be carried on by any person, he or she must apply to the Environment Agency for an authorisation.[32] The application must be in writing and provide details of the applicant, a description of the proposed process, a list of the prescribed substances that will result from the process, a description of the techniques

[28] *ibid.*, pp. 45–48.
[29] *ibid.*, p. 71.
[30] *ibid.*, p. 19.
[31] See the Environmental Protection (Applications, Appeals and Registers) Regulations 1991 (S.I. 1991 No. 507).
[32] EPA 1990, s.6.

to be used for preventing or minimising the release of those substances, an assessment of the environmental consequences of their release, proposals for monitoring, and, where substances will be released into more than one environmental medium, a BPEO assessment. In addition, the Environment Agency may, by notice in writing, require "any person" to furnish any other information that it reasonably needs to decide the application. [33] The prospective operator is required to publish details of the application in a newspaper circulated daily in the locality of the proposed process and in *The London Gazette*.[34]

Before determining the application, the Agency is required to notify, and to receive representations from, certain other bodies (the "statutory consultees").[35] Those required to be consulted include the Health and Safety Executive,[36] the Ministry of Agriculture Fisheries and Food, sewerage undertakers (where releases to sewers are involved) and English Nature (where Sites of Special Scientific Interest may be affected).

If the Agency considers that the applicant will be able to comply with the necessary conditions, it must grant the authorisation, otherwise the authorisation must be refused.[37] The Secretary of State may give the Agency directions as to whether or not to grant a particular authorisation.[38] He also has power to "call in" an application and appoint a person to decide it on his behalf or cause a local inquiry to be held.[39] (This power is exercisable in relation to any individual application, or any class of applications.) The Act makes provision for an authorisation, once granted, to be transferred from one operator to another.[40] Every authorisation which is in force must be reviewed by the Agency at least once every four years.[41]


## Authorisation Conditions

The Environment Agency must include in every authorisation conditions which ensure that the objectives of IPC are met.[42] Conditions might, for example, stipulate for the use of specific abatement technology such as desulphurisation chambers to remove sulphur dioxide from emissions to the air. Specific conditions will also be necessary to give effect to any directions given by the Secretary of State implementing either E.C. or international obligations and to ensure that any Environmental Quality Standards (*i.e.* prescribed maximum emission levels for the concentration of any substance in a particular medium) which have been set are complied with.

---

[33] *ibid.*, s.19(2). Note that the power to require information is not confined to applicants; it is exercisable in relation to "any person".
[34] S.I. 1991 No. 507, as amended by S.I. 1996 No. 979.
[35] EPA 1990, Sched. 1 para. 2.
[36] reg. 4(1).
[37] EPA 1990, s.6(4).
[38] *ibid.*, s.6(5).
[39] *ibid.*, Sched. 1, para. 3.
[40] *ibid.*, s.9.
[41] *ibid.*, s.6(6).
[42] *ibid.*, s.7.

## The "Residual" Condition

Because specific conditions can never cover every eventuality, there is implied into every authorisation a condition that the process will use BÁTNEEC to prevent or, where this is not practicable, minimise the release of prescribed substances and render harmless the release of all other substances.[43] This implied condition (the residual condition) applies to all aspects of a process which are not regulated by a specific condition.[44]

The advantage of regulation by specific conditions is that it leaves an operator in no doubt as to what he must do to comply with a condition. The enforcement of specific conditions is easier than the enforcement of the residual duty to use BATNEEC because it is more readily apparent when specific conditions have been breached. On the other hand, the residual obligation to use BATNEEC has the advantage of being ongoing throughout the operational life of a plant. It therefore forces operators to respond to developments in pollution control techniques and ensures that, if techniques become available that can be applied to an aspect of the process which has not been regulated by a specific condition, investment will be made in those techniques.

The courts have stressed that the obligation on operators is to prevent or minimise the release of substances by using BATNEEC; it is not merely to use BATNEEC. Jeremy Sullivan Q.C., in his judgment in *Gateshead Metropolitan Borough Council v. Secretary of State for the Environment and Northumbria Water Group plc.*,[45] rejected any assumption that, where an emission would be harmful, HMIP should nevertheless grant an authorisation merely because BATNEEC had been employed. The Court of Appeal accepted this.[46] Glidewell L.J. said that if, in the end, the inspectorate conclude that the best available techniques, etc., would not achieve the results required by sections 7(2) and 7(4), it may be proper for it to refuse an authorisation.

According to section 7(2) of the Act, the issue of whether the release of a substance should be prevented entirely or simply minimised by the use of BATNEEC depends on whether or not complete prevention is "practicable by such means". The wording of the Act therefore leaves unanswered the question whether, once a technique which would entirely prevent the release of substances has been identified as one not entailing excessive costs, it is still possible to argue that it is not "practicable" to prevent a release entirely by that technique.

"Practicable" is not defined in the Environmental Protection Act 1990 and, if a traditional statutory meaning of "practicable" is adopted, it is unclear what purpose is served by the word's inclusion in this section. The statutory definition of "practicable" in the Clean Air Act 1956[47] allows for consideration of the financial implications of implementing a technique.

The meaning of "practicable" under the Coal Mines Act 1911 was considered in *Edwards v. National Coal Board*,[48] The court took the view that in every case the risk of

---

[43] *ibid.*, s.6(4).
[44] *ibid.*, s.7(6). A successful prosecution was brought against ICI for failing in its residual duty to use BATNEEC following the escape of chemicals at its Wilton works. ENDS No. 241 February, 1995, p. 37.
[45] [1994] Env. L.R. 11.
[46] [1995] Env. L.R. 37.
[47] s.34(1).
[48] [1949] 1 K.B. 704.

an accident had to be weighed against the measures necessary to eliminate that risk. The greater the risk, the less should be the weight given to the factor of cost. In *Adsett v. K&L Steelfounders and Engineers*,[49] Singleton L.J., in determining the meaning of "practicable" under the Factories Act 1937, referred to the definition of "practicable" contained in *Webster's Dictionary*, holding that "practicable" meant "possible to be accomplished with known means or known resources". Clearly, this allows for a consideration of financial resources. In the context of BATNEEC, however, it is submitted that a consideration of what is "practicable" in this sense can add little to a decision whether to prevent or minimise the release of a substance, because financial considerations will already have been addressed in the "Not Entailing Excessive Costs" part of the formula. In real terms, therefore, any argument that it is not "practicable" to prevent a release using BATNEEC must amount to a simple assertion that preventing the release by such means is not "possible".

## Enforcement of the IPC Regime

It is a criminal offence to operate a prescribed process without an authorisation or in breach of the conditions to which an authorisation is subject.[50] The maximum penalty is a fine of £20,000 if the offence is tried by magistrates or an unlimited fine and two years' imprisonment where the offence is tried in the Crown Court. The first prosecution by HMIP was brought in March 1993 against the Devon Timber Company,[51] who were fined £1,650 for operating a process prescribed for control under the IPC regime without the necessary authorisation.

There is no defence of reasonable excuse for the breach of an authorisation condition.[52] It is not necessary to prove an intention to pollute or that any pollution has in fact been caused by the breach, and ignorance of the condition being contravened is no defence. These matters are apparent from the decision in *HMIP v. Drum Laundry Services*,[53] The defendant was prosecuted for breach of its authorisation conditions when waste from the firm's storage area discoloured a brook which flowed into the River Blackwater. The leak had been caused by a contractor who, unbeknown to the firm, had put a pipe in a wall surrounding the storage area. The firm entered a guilty plea, was fined £5,000 and ordered to pay £5,000 costs. HMIP did not have to prove that environmental damage was caused. (It is interesting to note that the contractor who installed the pipe could also have been charged with the offence: section 158 of the Act states that where the commission by a person of an offence under Part I of the Act is due to the act or default of some other person, that other person may be charged with and convicted of the offence whether or not proceedings are taken against the first-mentioned person. No prosecution has yet been brought under this provision.)

---

[49] [1953] 1 W.L.R. 773.
[50] EPA 1990, s.23(1).
[51] *HMIP v. Devon Timber Company* (1993) ENDS 218 44.
[52] The defence is, however, available in relation to offences concerning failure to co-operate with visiting inspectors or to furnish information: EPA 1990, s.23(1)(d) and (g).
[53] (1993) ENDS 218 44.

## Enforcement Notices

If The Environment Agency believes that an operator is contravening any of the conditions of an authorisation, it may serve an "enforcement notice".[54] This will outline the matters constituting the contravention and require specific steps to be taken, within a set period, to prevent the breach from continuing. Failure to comply with the requirements of an enforcement notice is an offence.[55]

The Agency may also serve a notice where no breach of a condition has occurred if it is of the opinion that a breach is likely to occur. Such a notice was served on the Isle of Wight County Council in October 1994.[56] HMIP had issued an authorisation for the council to operate a plant which manufactured fuel from waste. It was a condition of the authorisation that the height of one of the plant's chimneys be increased. The council accepted this, obtained planning permission for the venture, and allocated finance to the project. Despite these steps, HMIP chose to serve an enforcement notice to emphasise its continuing interest in the project and to ensure that the condition would be complied with. It is submitted that in this case HMIP may have been acting outside its statutory remit, since, given the steps taken by the council to comply with the condition, there was no indication it was likely to be breached.

## Prohibition Notices

Where the Environment Agency considers there is an *imminent risk of serious pollution to the environment* it is under a duty to serve a "prohibition notice".[57] This effectively suspends the operation of a process, or part of a process, and may be served even though there has been no breach of the authorisation.[58] Failure to comply with the requirements of a prohibition notice is an offence.[59]

The provision was not intended to be used as a punitive measure. Rather, it was to be applied in the unusual event that substances present in the environment as the result, for example, of an accident at another plant could react with those normally released from the process in question, thereby creating a toxic effect.[60] Although the process in question may be being operated in accordance with its authorisation, it may need to be suspended to prevent a serious pollution incident. The reported case law, however, suggests that prohibition notices have been used as a punitive measure. For example, in October 1994 HMIP served a prohibition notice on Medical Energy[61] in respect of a clinical waste incinerator because of concerns it had about some technical aspects of the process. This caused the incinerator to be shut down until the company had demonstrated that the areas of concern had been addressed. There was no suggestion that a serious pollution incident was imminent or that the receiving environment contained potential reagents which were not normally present.

---

[54] EPA 1990, s.13.
[55] *ibid.,* s.23(1)(c).
[56] February 1995, p. 14.
[57] EPA 1990, s.14(1).
[58] *ibid.,* s.14(2).
[59] *ibid.,* s.23(1).
[60] *per* Lord Reay, *Hansard,* H.L., 1989–90, Vol. 520, col. 877.
[61] *Environmental Law and Management,* February 1995, p. 14.

The prohibition notice must specify the nature of the imminent risk, the steps which must be taken to remove the risk and the time within which they must be taken. In addition, the Environment Agency may impose further, temporary conditions relating to any part of the process the operation of which is not suspended.[62]

What constitutes "serious pollution to the environment" in this context has yet to be clearly established. The Act defines "pollution of the environment" as: "pollution due to the release of substances which are capable of causing harm to man or to any other living organisms supported by the environment."[63]

The definition of "harm" includes offence to the senses of man.[64] "Serious pollution", however, is left undefined. It is submitted that it is unlikely that mere offence to the senses of man (for example by foul odour) would constitute serious pollution.

The maximum penalty for failure to comply with any requirement imposed by an enforcement or prohibition notice is a £20,000 fine in the magistrates' court or an unlimited fine and two years' imprisonment in the Crown Court.[65] Compliance with a notice may be difficult if the notice is not accurate or precise enough. Although the point has not been considered by the courts in relation to notices issued under the Act, it is submitted that a notice which is vague is liable to be quashed on an application for judicial review. An analogy may be made with planning enforcement notices, where the test for the validity of a notice is whether it tells the wrongdoer "fairly what he has done wrong and what he must do to remedy it".[66] The attitude of the courts to abatement notices issued under the statutory nuisance provisions of Part III of the Environmental Protection Act 1990 is also instructive. In *Network Housing Association Ltd v. Westminster City Council*,[67] a noise abatement notice was quashed as being invalid on the grounds that it specified a decibel limit that had to be adhered to, but did not specify how this was to be achieved. The court was influenced first by the fact that the issue was a technical one, and secondly by the fact that any recipient of a notice would face penal sanctions in the event of non-compliance with the notice. Both of these factors are applicable to enforcement notices under the IPC regime.

## Variation of Authorisations

The Act provides for the conditions of an authorisation to be varied. This can be done either at the behest of the Environment Agency or at the behest of a process operator. The Agency has a duty to vary an authorisation if it appears that new or different conditions are necessary to meet the objectives of the IPC regime.[68]

If the Agency decides to vary the conditions of an authorisation, it must serve a "variation notice" on the operator of the process. The notice will specify the variations which the Agency has decided to make and the date(s) on which the variations are to take effect.[69] It will require an operator to notify the Agency what action (if any) he

---

[62] EPA 1990, s.14(3).
[63] *ibid.*, s.1(3).
[64] *ibid.*, s.1(4).
[65] *ibid.*, s.23(2).
[66] *per* Upjohn L.J. in *Miller Mead v. Minister of Housing and Local Government* [1963] 2 Q.B. 196.
[67] [1995] 93 L.G.R. 280, Q.B.D.
[68] EPA 1990, s.10(1).
[69] *ibid.*, s.10(2).

proposes to take to ensure that the process is carried on in accordance with conditions as varied by the notice.[70] Failure to comply with a variation notice is not, in itself, an offence, so that an operator who neglects to notify the Agency commits no crime. However, if any action which is required in order to comply with the varied conditions is not taken by the operator, he is liable to be charged with operating the process in breach of his authorisation.

If the Agency is of the opinion that variation of an authorisation will involve a "substantial change in the manner in which the process is being carried on", the proposed variation must be advertised, notice of it must be given to the statutory consultees, and any representations made by them and by the public must be considered by the Agency before deciding upon a variation.[71] "Substantial change" is defined by the Act as: "a substantial change in relation to the substances released from the process or in the amount or any other characteristic of any substance so released".[72]

Whilst this definition clarifies what sorts of changes will constitute a "substantial change", it gives no guidance on the meaning of "substantial". This is clearly a matter of fact and degree for the Environment Agency, although an E.C. Directive, which deals with limit values for certain dangerous substances, provides some guidance.[73] The Directive refers to a "substantial increase" in the context of an increase in a plant's capacity for handling substances. The Department of the Environment has interpreted "substantial" under the Directive as an increase of 20 per cent.[74] However, the Directive on Integrated Pollution Prevention and Control refers to an increase of 5 per cent or more as substantial.[75] It remains to be seen whether the Environment Agency will adopt this more stringent interpretation.

The holder of an authorisation who wishes to make a change to the process must notify the Environment Agency. The Agency will then determine whether the proposed change involves a breach of any conditions of the authorisation. It this is so, it will notify the operator, who may then apply for the conditions to be varied.[76] However, if the operator is certain that the change will constitute a breach of conditions, he may bypass this stage and make an immediate application for a variation.[77] If the Agency decides to grant the application, it will then serve an appropriate variation notice. An operator may apply for a variation even where he is not proposing to make any changes to the process. (This may be appropriate where he wishes to transfer the authorisation to another operator).[78] Where the change in the process proposed by the operator would amount to a "substantial" change, the application for a variation must be advertised and the statutory consultees consulted.

The power to vary authorisations is an important one because it allows environmental standards to be tightened as pollution control techniques improve.[79] It is underpinned by the Environment Agency's duty to keep abreast of developments in

[70] *ibid.,* s.10(4).
[71] *ibid.,* Sched. 1, Part II. para. 6.
[72] *ibid.,* s.10(7).
[73] Dir. 86/280 [1986] O.J. L181/16 EEC on limit values and quality objectives for discharges of certain dangerous substances included in List I of the Annex to Dir. 76/464/EEC ([1986] O.J. L181/16 ).
[74] Circular 7/89, para. 22 (DoE).
[75] Directive on Integrated Pollution Prevention and Control 1993 ([1993] O.J. L257/26).
[76] EPA 1990, s.11.
[77] *ibid.,* s.11(6).
[78] *ibid.,* s.11(5).
[79] See *IPC — A Practical Guide* (DoE/Welsh Office).

pollution abatement techniques[80] and by its duty to review the conditions of an authorisation every four years,[81] which allows for new techniques to be incorporated into the authorisation.

## Revocation of Authorisations

The Environment Agency has a general power to revoke an authorisation by written notice at any time.[82] Clearly, revocation might be appropriate where an operator has persistently flouted the conditions of an authorisation.[83] In certain circumstances, as an alternative to variation, it may also be appropriate to revoke an existing authorisation as a condition precedent to the grant of a new one. The Act provides that, in particular, the Agency may revoke an authorisation where it has reason to believe that the process for which the authorisation is in force has not been carried on for a period of 12 months.[84]

The Secretary of State has the power to direct the Environment Agency whether or not and how to exercise its powers in relation to enforcement and prohibition notices, variation and revocation. In relation to prohibition notices and powers of variation, he may give directions either in respect of a particular case or in respect of particular circumstances, whilst in relation to enforcement notices and powers of revocation, he may only give directions in respect of particular operators and particular authorisations.[85] The operator has a right of appeal to the Secretary of State against decisions taken by the Agency in the exercise of all of these powers.[86]

## Appeals

The Secretary of State may determine an appeal himself or refer it to any other person whom he has appointed for the purpose of determining appeals.[87] An appeal against revocation of an authorisation has the effect of suspending that revocation until the withdrawal or final determination of the appeal,[88] but appeals against enforcement, prohibition and variation notices do not have the effect of suspending these notices.[89] Where the operator appeals in respect of a notice, the Secretary of State can either quash the notice, modify it, or allow it to stand.[90] An operator may also appeal against a refusal to grant an authorisation or against any of the conditions which have been attached to an authorisation.

The Act does not specify whether conditions of an authorisation which has already been granted are to remain in force pending the outcome of an appeal to which they

---

[80] EPA 1990, s.4(9).
[81] *ibid.,* s.6(6).
[82] *ibid.,* s.12(1).
[83] HMIP revoked an authorisation on these grounds for the first time in 1995. The firm involved, A. W. Stokes & Sons, had failed to carry out an improvement programme stipulated for in its authorisation conditions despite several extensions to the timetable. Reported at ENDS No. 240 (Jan 1995) p. 8.
[84] EPA 1990, s.12(2).
[85] *ibid.,* s.13(3) (enforcement notices); s.14(4) (prohibition notices); s.10(6) (variation); s.12(5) (revocation).
[86] EPA 1990, s.15.
[87] EA 1995, s.114.
[88] EPA 1990, s.15(8).
[89] *ibid.,* s.15(9).
[90] *ibid.,* s.15(7).

are subject. This point has, however, been raised in the Divisional Court. The action arose when a company, which had appealed to the Secretary of State against the conditions of its authorisation, also sought leave for judicial review of those conditions, together with an injunction restraining HMIP from enforcing the conditions pending the outcome of the appeal. The court refused leave, holding that the company must first exhaust its statutory remedies. Refusing to grant an injunction, it expressed the view that whether or not the conditions were to remain in force pending the appeal was a matter for the Secretary of State.[91]

## Powers of Inspectors

Under the Environment Act 1995, general powers are given to the Environment Agency for the purposes of:

- Determining whether any provision of the pollution control enactments is being, or has been, complied with;

- Exercising or performing one or more of their pollution control functions;

- Determining whether, and if so how, such functions should be exercised or performed.

The powers given to an inspector of the Agency are as follows:

- To enter at any reasonable time (or, in an emergency, at any time and if need be, by force) any premises which he has reason to believe it is necessary for him to enter;

- On entering any premises, to take with him any other person authorised by the Agency, or a constable if necessary, and any necessary equipment or materials;

- To make such examination and investigation as may in the circumstances be necessary;

- To direct that any premises be left undisturbed as long as is necessary for the purposes of the investigation;

- To take any necessary measurements, photographs and samples;

- To require an article to be dismantled, or subjected to tests, if it appears to have caused, or to be likely to cause pollution, and then to take possession of it and detain it;

---

[91] The case is unreported. (Source: DoE).

- To require any person to answer questions if it appears that they are able to give any information relevant to any investigation.

If an authorised person has reasonable cause to believe that an article or substance is presenting an imminent danger of serious pollution of the environment or serious harm to human health, he may seize it and cause it to be rendered harmless.[92]

It is a criminal offence for a person to intentionally obstruct an authorised person in the exercise or performance of his powers or duties.

The powers outlined above give inspectors sweeping powers of entry, investigation and interview. According to one source, the Agency's inspectors will be "trained to expect violent situations". They will wear clip-on ties (to prevent their clothing being used to strangle them), carry "ultrasonic stun guns" and undergo courses in unarmed combat.[93]

## Enforcement in Practice

The Environment Agency has a wide discretion to decide whether and how to take enforcement action. In certain cases it may take the view that it is more important to ensure that an operator complies with the requirements of an enforcement or prohibition notice than to punish him. Where this can best be achieved by maintaining a co-operative relationship with the operator, prosecution will be seen as a last resort.

In other cases the Agency may be of the opinion that prosecution will afford an inadequate remedy. There is an obvious danger that operators who breach the conditions of their authorisations will treat financial penalties as part of the operating costs of a process and will absorb fines by passing them on to customers in the form of increased charges for their product or services. It may be that, whilst the sanction of imprisonment is thought too draconian, the likely level of fine in respect of a breach is not sufficient to punish or deter by adversely affecting an operator's profit or goodwill when passed on in this way. This will be especially true in the case of large organisations, or where the market for a particular service or product is not highly competitive.

Therefore, as an alternative or in addition to prosecution, the Agency may take proceedings against an operator in the High Court for an injunction ordering compliance with the requirements of an enforcement notice.[94] Such proceedings may also be taken to ensure compliance with a prohibition notice. In the event that an immediate shut-down of a process is required to prevent a serious pollution incident, an injunction may prove to be an important means of securing compliance by a reluctant operator. HMIP did not, however, find it necessary to seek the assistance of the High Court in enforcing the IPC regime; it was of the view that the wide powers available to it to issue enforcement and prohibition notices were sufficient to contain any problems,[95] and it remains to be seen whether the Agency will do so.

---

[92] EA 1995, s.109.
[93] *Time Out*, March 20–27, 1996. See also: William Upton and Richard Harwood, "The Stunning Powers of Environmental Inspectors" [1996] J.P.L. 623.
[94] EPA 1990, s.24.
[95] Source: HMIP.

Where an operator has been convicted of an offence involving breach of an authorisation or failure to comply with an enforcement or prohibition notice, the convicting court may, instead of or as well as imposing a penalty, order that the person convicted of the offence take specified steps within his power to remedy the matters which gave rise to the commission of the offence.[96] This power was used for the first time in a prosecution against a chemical company, Einchem,[97] for a chemical spill. The court required the company to fit alarms which would detect any overflow from the tanks storing the chemical in question.

In addition, the Environment Agency, with the written approval of the Secretary of State, is empowered to arrange for reasonable steps to be taken (*i.e.* by a private contractor) to remedy any harm caused as a result of such an offence. The Act also provides that he may recover the full costs of this clean up operation from the guilty operator.[98] These costs will, of course, be in addition to any fine imposed by way of a criminal sanction. This provision effectively allows the Environment Agency to impose a financial penalty which is far in excess of any fine likely to be imposed by the courts. Its inclusion in the Act marked an acceptance in the U.K. of the principle so often propounded by the E.C. that the polluter should pay the full costs of any environmental damage caused by his activities.

The Act provides that where an offence committed by a body corporate is proved to have been committed with the consent or connivance of, or because of the neglect of, any director, manager, secretary or similar officer of that body, that officer is liable to be punished for the offence as well as the body corporate itself.[99] Such punishment may include a prison sentence imposed by the Crown Court. Imprisonment of a guilty operator is, of course, a sanction of last resort.

## Private Prosecutions

The Act makes no specific provision for prosecutions to be brought by members of the public. As a general principle of constitutional law, however, private prosecutions may be brought for statutory offences where this is not expressly precluded by the statute in question, and might therefore be brought under the Act. Public participation in the enforcement of pollution control, however, depends to a large extent on public knowledge both of the law and of the occurrence of illegal activities.

## Public Registers

The Act provides for registers to be kept which contain details of the IPC regime. These are designed to ensure that the public, and in particular environmental pressure groups, have the information they need in order to scrutinise the effectiveness of the regime.

The Environment Agency is required to maintain registers which contain "all particulars" of the following matters[1]: applications for authorisations; authorisations

---

[96] EPA 1990, s.26.
[97] ENDS 238 p. 40 (Nov 1994).
[98] EPA 1990, s.27.
[99] *ibid.,* s.157.
[1] Environmental Protection (Applications, Appeals and Registers) Regulations 1991 (above).

granted; information furnished by an applicant in response to a written notice from the Agency; variation, enforcement and prohibition notices; any representations made by the statutory consultees or by the public; any notice given by an operator of proposed changes to a process; any determination by the Agency of whether this will require variation of the conditions; applications for variation; the withdrawal of any prohibition notice which has been issued; any appeals to the Secretary of State; any directions given to the Agency by the Secretary of State; any convictions for offences under the Act; any monitoring data collected by the Agency or furnished by an operator or, where this is omitted, a statement by the Agency indicating whether the conditions have been complied with; any report published by the Agency relating to an assessment of the local environmental consequences of carrying out a prescribed process.[2]

An operator may apply for information to be excluded from the register on grounds of commercial confidentiality. Commercially confidential information is defined as information the inclusion of which on the register "would prejudice to an unreasonable degree the commercial interests" of the individual involved.[3] It is for the Environment Agency or, on appeal, the Secretary of State to decide whether information should be excluded from the register on these grounds.[4] If information is so excluded, a statement must be included in the register indicating the existence of commercially confidential information.[5] Any determination as to whether information is commercially confidential must be made within 14 days of the date of the application, and if no determination is made within that time, the information is deemed to be commercially confidential.[6] If information is not determined to be commercially confidential, it is not entered in the register for a period of 21 days, during which an appeal may be made to the Secretary of State.[7]

However, even where information has been determined to be commercially confidential, the Secretary of State may direct that it, or parts of it, should be included in the register because the public interest so requires.[8] This might be necessary, for example, following a major pollution incident like Chernobyl, when confidential information might need to be disclosed to allay public anxiety.[9] The Secretary of State may also give directions to the Environment Agency requiring that certain information should be excluded from the register on the grounds that its inclusion would be contrary to the interests of national security.[10] The register does not have to indicate that information has been excluded for this reason.

The Department of the Environment has indicated that it will look sceptically on applications for the exclusion of information and that it will require specific and cogent evidence that disclosure of the information in question would prejudice to an unreasonable degree the business interests of the person concerned. Such prejudice

---

[2] EPA 1990, s.20(1).
[3] *ibid.*, s.22(11).
[4] *ibid.*, s.22(1).
[5] *ibid.*, s.20(5).
[6] *ibid.*, s.22(3).
[7] *ibid.*, s.22(5).
[8] *ibid.*, s.22(7).
[9] *per* Lord Hesketh June 19, 1990 *Hansard,* H.L., 1990 Vol. 509, col. 907.
[10] EPA 1990, s.21.

might include revealing the secrets of a new technological process, the use of a particular raw material, or some other specific feature of a process which, if known to competitors, might diminish a legitimate commercial advantage. General claims, for example that disclosure might damage the reputation of the operator concerned, will not be entertained.[11]

The case law on the subject indicates that consideration will be given to how relevant the information is to the grant of an authorisation. In 1991, PowerGen plc appealed against a decision to include in the register forecast schedules of emissions for 1991.[12] Following a 12 day private hearing, their appeal was dismissed. It was held that the information was so significant that it ought to be made available to the public as part of the process of determining PowerGen's applications for authorisations. However, when National Power plc appealed against the inclusion of data concerning the type and quality of fuel which it planned to burn in 1991,[13] the appeal was successful. The Secretary of State was satisfied that this information was not directly relevant to the determination of the applications.

## THE INFLUENCE OF THE E.C. ON THE IPC REGIME

### Introduction

The inclusion of public registers in the IPC regime, the provision for fixed emission limits to be set by the Secretary of State, the high penalties which may be imposed for breach of pollution control and the statutory provision which allows the Environment Agency to recover the full costs of clean-up operations from a convicted operator are all reflections of European policy. This includes greater communication with the public about the environment, the adoption of clear environmental quality standards in preference to loose objectives and informal negotiations with industry, the principle that environmental measures should be preventive and precautionary rather than remedial, and the principle that the polluter should pay for the environmental consequences of his activities.

The IPC regime has been aptly described as "a true hybrid; a peculiar concretation of British and continental philosophy and practice which is only loosely modelled on the [Royal Commission for Environmental Pollution's] initial recommendations".[14]

The Environmental Protection Act was implemented, *inter alia*, to give effect to the U.K.'s obligations under the Air Pollution Directive[15] and the Directive limiting emissions from large combustion plants.[16] The Secretary of State has a general power to amend Part I of the Act to give effect to E.C. obligations or international obligations arising from an agreement to which the U.K. is party.[17]

---

[11] DoE News Release No. 51, January 30, 1990.
[12] *Encyclopedia of Environmental Law,* vol. 2 D433 (note to EPA, s.22) (Sweet & Maxwell).
[13] *ibid.*
[14] Andrew Jordan, (1993) *Environmental Politics,* vol. 2, no. 3, p. 405.
[15] Dir. 84/360/EEC ([1984] O.J. L188/20).
[16] Dir. 88/609/EEC ([1988] O.J. L336/11).
[17] EPA 1990, s.156.

## The E.C. and BATNEEC

Prior to the Act, industry had been required to use the "Best Practicable Means" (BPM) available to combat pollution. The concept of BPM originated in the middle of the nineteenth century. It was applied to control smoke emissions and, later, noxious emissions from alkali works. The Air Pollution Directive introduced the concept of "Best Available Techniques Not Entailing Excessive Cost". This coincided with a change in environmental thinking in the U.K. which was to lead to the U.K.'s abandoning the concept of "Best Practicable Means".

There had been growing concern in the 1980s, expressed both by environmental pressure groups and by politicians, that the application of the BPM test was characterised by such flexibility and informality that "cosy relationships" between industry and its regulators were a possibility, if not a reality. Moreover, the U.K.'s fragmented approach to environmental regulation was clearly becoming incompatible with European policy, which was moving towards an integrated approach to regulation, administered by a single enforcement agency. A fresh approach was required.

As the mechanics of implementing the IPC regime were being worked out, the concept of BATNEEC was conveniently borrowed from the Air Pollution Directive and used to replace BPM as the principle to be applied to each environmental medium considered in isolation. The inclusion of BPEO as a further principle to be considered when a process may cause pollution in more than one medium reflected a wish on the part of the Royal Commission to retain some of the more positive aspects which it had identified in the way the BPM test had been applied.[18] In particular, it was recognised that, in applying the BPM test, the Alkali Inspectorate had acted as consultants and advisors to industry rather than as mere law enforcers. It was hoped that in applying BPEO some of this atmosphere of co-operation might be retained.

## The Use of Registers

Another principle upheld and emphasised by the E.C. has been the importance of public access to information on the environment. E.C. Action Programmes on the environment have repeatedly stated that public awareness is vital to ensure public acceptance of environmental protection measures. Moreover, unless the public has access to information, it is unable to judge the effectiveness of any pollution control regime. The judgment of the public has an important rôle to play in ensuring that industry complies with its environmental obligations. It is not good business to be seen as a polluter by potential customers and investors. Indeed, HMIP expressed the view that one of the reasons why they faced relatively few legal challenges to the implementation of the IPC regime is the concern companies have had for their public image.

The Directive on freedom of access to information on the environment,[19] which has been incorporated into U.K. law by way of regulations,[20] supplements the system of public registers established under the Act. The Directive aims to promote the

---

[18] See RCEP (1976) Fifth Report: *Integrated Pollution Control* (above).
[19] Dir. 90/313/EEC [1990] O.J. L158/56.
[20] The Environmental Information Regulations 1992 (S.I. 1992 No. 3240).

dissemination of environmental information held by public authorities, and sets out the basis on which such information should be made available to the public. Member States are required to ensure that public authorities make available information relating to the environment to any person on request and without his having to prove an interest. Information can, however, be refused where it would, *inter alia*, affect national security.

## Quality Standards *versus* Quality Objectives

The Air Pollution Directive,[21] the Water Pollution Directive[22] and the Directive limiting emissions from large combustion plants[23] allowed for fixed limits to be set on the emission of certain substances. This is a concept which the U.K. has only recently adopted in response to the lead from Europe. Environmental Quality Standards (EQSs) have been set in relation to many substances,[24] and in relation to substances for which no EQS has yet been set, the Environment Agency has set, for each substance, an Environmental Assessment Level (EAL) which indicates the level of emissions which it will consider acceptable.

Section 3 of the Act provides the means by which the requirements of E.C. Directives, as they are issued, may be incorporated within the IPC regime. Under this section, the Secretary of State may make regulations establishing standards, objectives or requirements in relation to particular prescribed processes or substances. He may, for example, set standard limits for the concentration of any substance to be released from a process[25] or standard requirements for the measurement of substances so released.[26] He may also establish quality objectives or quality standards in relation to any non-prescribed substances which may be released, and draw up plans for the progressive reduction of emissions,[27] for example by the phased introduction of increasingly more stringent emission standards.

There has been a long running ideological dispute between the United Kingdom and the rest of the European Community over the merits and demerits of fixed emission standards. Continental Europe has tended to favour setting limits on discharges of particular contaminants from particular sources. These limits must then be met by all operators irrespective of whether and how these contaminants may react with the receiving environment, and without considering the raw materials and energy needed to comply with them. The traditional approach in the U.K., on the other hand, has been to identify environmental *objectives*; for example to make River X clean enough to support certain fish in certain numbers. Emission standards are then set in order to achieve those objectives.

Environmental Quality *Standards* provide a quicker and administratively simpler solution to pollution problems. However, a cogent argument can be made in favour of placing environmental *objectives* at the heart of pollution control. Such an argument is

---

[21] See n.15, above.
[22] Dir. 76/464/EEC ([1976] O.J. L129/23).
[23] See n.16, above.
[24] These are contained in Draft Technical Guidance Note E 1, vol. 3 (Technical Data), above.
[25] EPA 1990, s.3(2)(a)(i).
[26] *ibid.,* s.3(2)(b).
[27] *ibid.,* s.3(4). A national plan for the reduction of sulphur dioxide and nitrogen oxide was adopted in 1990.

predicated on the assumptions that resources are limited and that a certain degree of pollution is tolerable in a modern society. It focuses on the need to accommodate pollution within a given land mass whilst preserving the benefits of an unspoilt environment in certain areas. It follows that where the nature of a site's receiving environment is recreational, more stringent pollution control is required than where the receiving environment is industrialised or, as is often the case, already so polluted by past industrial activities that its reclamation to an unspoilt state is not economically feasible. The proponents of such an argument point out that it makes economic sense to allocate financial resources to environmentally sensitive areas, where fixed emission standards may not provide adequate protection, and to secure those resources by making savings in areas where pollution control in excess of a certain level will be wasted on the receiving environment.

For these reasons, industry in the U.K. has traditionally favoured an approach to pollution control which is geared towards meeting Environmental Quality *Objectives* rather than Environmental Quality *Standards*. The Chemical Industries Association has distinguished between "pollution"; which poses or causes harm to the environment, and "contamination"; which is the mere presence in the environment of a foreign substance that may well be harmless. It does not believe that this distinction is either made or understood in Europe.[28]

A further objection to Environmental Quality Standards is sometimes raised on the grounds that guidelines of dubious scientific validity are used to establish emission limits. There is a lack of knowledge about what actually happens to pollutants once they enter the environment, and in particular how they combine with other substances. It is contended that for as long as it remains scientifically impossible to determine, effectively and accurately, the capacity of the environment to absorb pollution, any fixed emission standards which are set are virtually meaningless.

When considered in the light of current practice, however, the Environmental Quality Objectives/Environmental Quality Standards controversy reveals itself to be somewhat academic. Both the U.K. and continental countries have traditionally adopted a combination of methods.[29] For example, U.K. standards for discharges into rivers have historically shown a high degree of uniformity.[30] With the widespread adoption of Environmental Quality Standards in the U.K., it seems likely that the debate will become marginalised and, in the short term at least, relegated to the world of academia. It is submitted, however, that any society in which financial resources are limited overlooks at its peril the arguments made by economists in favour of an approach to pollution control driven by environmental quality objectives rather than by the blanket application of emission standards.

---

[28] See Royal Commission on Environmental Pollution (1984). Tenth Report: *Tackling Pollution — Experience and Prospects,* Chapter III: *Domestic Traditions and International Influences,* Cmnd. 9149 (1984).
[29] *ibid.*
[30] For a further discussion, see Michael Carpenter, former head of European Commission Directorate General for the Environment, Consumer Protection and Nuclear Safety (DG XI), in *New Scientist,* 1991, pp. 416–417: "[The EQO/EQS controversy is] an artificial argument. It is more a battle of principles than of realities."

## PRACTICAL IMPLEMENTATION OF THE IPC REGIME

The introduction of Integrated Pollution Control represented a dramatic overhauling of the pollution control regime in the United Kingdom. Although IPC makes use of a number of elegant academic concepts, there have been problems putting these into practice. The Act is principally an enabling statute. It gives powers to the Secretary of State and to the Environment Agency and leaves it to them to shape the theories of BATNEEC and BPEO into workable tools. It is perhaps not surprising, therefore, that some practical difficulties have emerged.

HMIP did not succeed in developing a coherent approach to interpreting the notion of "excessive cost", nor has the Environment Agency clarified how it intends to resolve the fundamental conflict between growth of the economy and environmental protection. Prior to its adoption of a statistically based BPEO assessment procedure, HMIP was criticised for having only a crude methodology for determining permissible levels of pollution. In April 1994, it responded to these criticisms by issuing details of the new procedure, which makes use of the Integrated Environmental Index. However, the procedure has met with criticism from the Chemical Industries Association, who have described the Index as having no scientific or logical basis and have expressed the view that HMIP selected Environmental Assessment Levels arbitrarily, for example by adopting World Health Organisation guidelines without questioning them.

HMIP's difficulties were compounded by the fact that pollution can cause a number of different types of harm yet there are no commonly accepted criteria for determining which type of harm is the more worthy of prevention. For example, emissions of sulphur into the atmosphere from all U.K. sources, including transport and industry, were cut from 6.423m. tonnes a year to 3.482m. tonnes a year between the years 1970 and 1992. This has helped asthma sufferers. However, to produce an optimum yield, crops need a correct balance of nutrients, of which sulphur is one. Yields are now lower as crops increasingly suffer from deficiencies in sulphur.[31]

The inadequate use of public registers and the failure of the register system to provide a failsafe mechanism for accountability may also be identified as significant failings of the IPC regime. The registers are technical and unwieldy. Moreover, the fear persists that important decisions may be taken in "off the record" discussions between the Environment Agency and process operators.

In the early years of Integrated Pollution Control, HMIP adopted an "arm's length" policy towards industry in order to reassure the public that it was an objective and independent body which would set stringent standards and ensure that they were met. This policy was in keeping with the views of the Royal Commission, who had reported that it was not acceptable that decisions on emissions which affected the everyday lives of so many people should be taken by a small, specialist body consulting only with industry. They were of the opinion that greater public participation and accountability were needed. The "arm's length" approach to regulation, however, was soon abandoned, primarily because the first applications for authorisations were of such poor quality that HMIP found itself having to work in close co-operation with industry to elaborate the standards to which it was expecting industry to conform and the methods

---

[31] *Financial Times*, February 28, 1995.

by which they could be met. A relationship between HMIP and industry characterised by *some* degree of co-operation was, of course, in keeping with the Royal Commission's view that the determination of BPEO should involve a consultative and advisory rôle on the part of HMIP. It was felt that, in applying BPEO, HMIP could retain a co-operative stance whilst the system of registers would provide the safeguard of accountability.

In practice, however, it proved difficult for HMIP to maintain its dual rôle as advisor and enforcer without sacrificing accountability. The advice given by HMIP to industry has undoubtedly improved the quality of applications, but the unfortunate consequence has been a decline in the transparency of the system. A register which reveals the details of an application which is the product of consultation, together with the particulars of an authorisation granted in response to that application, may tell the public little about how successful the Environment Agency has been in curbing an operator's initial desire to pollute. This might, of course, be apparent from pre-application correspondence between the Agency and the operator, but, although the regulations require the disclosure of "all particulars of any application",[32] a strict construction of those words does not require the inclusion of pre-application correspondence or, indeed, minutes of informal negotiations. Whether the "audit trails" which are required of applicants under the BPEO assessment procedure will be diligently entered on the register remains to be seen.

As part of its duty to review authorisations[33] the Environment Agency is required to undertake "audit monitoring". This means that it is required to supervise the effectiveness of an operator's environmental monitoring techniques by carrying out further monitoring for comparative purposes. Audit monitoring is designed to ensure that operators carry out effective monitoring and that they report their findings accurately. The inclusion of audit monitoring results in the register is important to maintain public confidence in the pollution control regime. However, a survey conducted in 1994 by the Environmental Data Service (ENDS)[34] revealed no report of audit monitoring on the public registers at the time of its visits. ENDS described this as a clear breach of statutory responsibility and a serious blow to the transparency and credibility of the system. Further, ENDS found that files were missing from registers and that registers were generally poorly maintained, indicating HMIP did not take its obligations seriously enough.

HMIP also met with the criticism that the standards which it set for new processes were not stringent enough and did not always correspond to what could be achieved by the use of the best available techniques. For example, guideline standards for incinerators and combustion plants have been found by the Environmental Data Service to be significantly less stringent than those in force in some other European countries.[35] Where HMIP has allowed the use of cheaper but less effective pollution control technology, there is the possibility of the validity of authorisations being challenged by environmental pressure groups. HMIP indicated that it expected an increase in applications for judicial review of authorisations in the light of the decision

[32] Environmental Protection (Applications, Appeals and Registers) Regulations 1991 (above), reg. 15(a).
[33] EPA 1990, s.6(6).
[34] *IPC. The first three years* ENDS, January 1994.
[35] *ibid.*

in *R. v. HMIP, ex p. Greenpeace*,[36] following which the previously prohibitive rules on the standing of pressure groups are no longer applicable.

## THE FUTURE OF THE INTEGRATED POLLUTION CONTROL REGIME

### The E.C. Directive on Integrated Pollution Prevention and Control

In September 1996, the European Community adopted a Directive concerning Integrated Pollution Prevention and Control.[37] The Directive defines its purpose as being to achieve integrated prevention and control of pollution. It lays down measures designed to prevent, or where that is not practicable, to reduce, emissions to the air, water and land. It also includes measures concerning waste, in order to achieve a high level of protection for the environment taken as a whole. To a large extent, the policy which it expresses conforms to that of the U.K. Indeed, the U.K.'s IPC regime has been a significant influence in shaping the Directive.

There are, however, a number of significant differences between the U.K.'s IPC regime and that proposed by the E.C., so that the U.K. may be required to effect certain changes to the IPC regime in order to meet its obligations under the Directive. The Directive uses the formula "Best Available Technique" (BAT) rather than BATNEEC. The absence of any direct reference to the costs of pollution prevention techniques may suggest a more radical approach to environmental protection. However, in defining BAT, Article 1 refers to techniques developed on a scale which allows implementation in the relevant industrial sector under economically and technically viable conditions, taking into consideration the costs and advantages.

Within the Directive can be seen the beginnings of a policy shift away from environmental *protection* towards a more holistic approach to environmental problems which might be termed "environmental *management*". The preamble of the Directive refers to ensuring "the prudent management of natural resources".

If the U.K. is to give effect to this policy shift, it may have to modify the IPC regime so that a consideration of the raw materials used by a process is brought within the purview of BATNEEC and BPEO. This would accord with the views of the Royal Commission, which has stated that BPEO has been implemented in a much narrower context than it had envisaged.[38]

At present, the selection of raw materials for a process is largely a matter for the operator. The rôle of the Environment Agency is confined to ensuring that pollution does not result from the way in which those raw materials are processed. However, if a wider interpretation of BATNEEC and BPEO were adopted, it would be open to the Agency to refuse an authorisation on the grounds that the use of a particular raw material, where a more environmentally acceptable substitute is available, is not the Best Available Technique or the Best Practicable Environmental Option. For example, the use of tungsten by industry is seen as environmentally acceptable, because very

---

[36] [1994] 2 C.M.L.R. 548.
[37] Council Dir. 96/61/EC of September 24, 1996 concerning Integrated Pollution Prevention and Control ([1996] O.J. L257/26).
[38] See ENDS 234, pp. 34–35 July 1994.

little pollution results. It is not at present open to the Agency to prevent its use on the grounds that this entails the depletion of a scarce natural resource.

It must be accepted, however, that if such wide powers were granted to the Environment Agency, a fundamental reconsideration and redefinition of its functions and purposes would be required. Individual site inspectors would inevitably become involved in far-reaching political decisions about the operations of industry which, arguably, are more appropriately addressed by central government through the mechanism of primary legislation. Clear acceptance of these new functions and purposes by industry, the public and the judiciary would be necessary to ensure the effective implementation of any wider powers granted to the Agency.

Given that the Part I of the Environmental Protection Act 1990 is couched in terms of substance control, and given the vigilant eyes of administrative lawyers, it seems unlikely that the Royal Commission's original concept of BPEO can be comfortably accommodated within existing legislation. The Environment Act 1995 goes some way towards promoting a holistic approach to environmental problems by placing the Agency under a duty to have regard to such matters as building conservation, the protection of flora and fauna, and the effect of environmental controls on rural communities.[39] However, the ethos of existing environmental legislation is over-whelmingly one of pollution control. It may be that the only effective way to displace this in favour of a truly conservationist and managerial approach is by fresh primary legislation.

---

[39] EA 1995, s.7.

# Chapter 7

# POLLUTION ON LAND

*"Dumping refuse in worked-out quarries and holes in the ground has been the established — and the cheapest — form of waste disposal in this country for centuries. The legacy is thousands of closed landfill tips concealing a cocktail of contamination which may or may not be disastrous for the surrounding land and rivers."*[1]

## Introduction

Land pollution can occur in a number of different ways. It can be caused when, in the course of industrial activity, pollutants are deliberately released, either in the form of dust, which settles on land, or in the form of liquids, which permeate land. In addition, substances may be released unintentionally when they leak or are spilled on to the land on which they are stored. Common examples of contaminated sites in the U.K. include old gas works, which leave a legacy of coke, coal, tar and other chemical by-products, and old sewage works where the concentration of metals in the soil may be high. A significant cause of land pollution has been the deliberate practice of burying waste in landfill sites. Most of the solid waste which the U.K. produces has traditionally been disposed of in this way, and this has resulted in a considerable number of contaminated sites. Contaminated landfill sites present environmental problems not only because they are incapable of being developed for beneficial use, but also because of the danger of explosions caused by the build-up of gas from decaying matter within the site and because of the likelihood of water pollution occurring when rainwater drains through the contaminated soil, carrying contaminants with it to the watercourse below.

A number of incidents in recent years have served vividly to illustrate the consequences of using land as a general repository for waste materials. In 1986, for example, an explosion destroyed a bungalow in Loscoe, Derbyshire. The three occupants survived, although they were trapped in rubble for a considerable time. An investigation found the cause of the explosion to be gas from decomposing waste in a nearby landfill site. The incident at Loscoe had been preceded by events at Lekkerkerk, in the Netherlands. Between 1972 and 1975, 268 houses were built on the site of a forgotten chemical waste dump. Toxic chemicals leaked into the domestic water

---

[1] Amanda Seidl, "Take Your Fill", (1996) EG vol. 9615, p. 42.

supply and caused illness amongst the residents. In 1980 it was discovered that some 1,600 drums, containing waste chemicals from the dyestuffs industry, had been deposited illegally on the site in the past. The site was finally evacuated in 1981, when the waste was removed at a cost (in 1981) of £156,000.[2]

The most striking example of the effects on land of historic pollution comes from the United States. Between 1947 and 1953, nearly 22,000 tonnes of chemical waste was dumped on a site at Love Canal, in New York state. The site was then sold, on condition that it should never be disturbed. However, in the 1950s, shortly after the sale, a 16 acre development, comprising a school and houses, was built on the site. Residents reported illness in 1976. The basements of their houses smelt of chemicals and children returned from the school with holes in their shoes caused by chemical burns. In 1978, children and expectant mothers were evacuated from the site and a state-sponsored clean-up programme was initiated which involved the evacuation of some 900 families and the demolition of hundreds of homes. The site was finally declared habitable in 1988 at a cost of in excess of $250 million.[3]

Pollution of land poses a special danger to the environment because it is generally of a more permanent character than pollution of the other environmental media. Small doses of air or water pollution can sometimes be blown or washed away. Natural forces work to dilute and disperse pollution in these media so that its effect is diminished. This is seldom the case with pollution on land. Although accidental events like fires, floods and explosions can cause the migration of pollutants from land, they rarely leave behind them land in an unpolluted state.[4]

The problem of land pollution divides into two main issues:

- The cleaning up of land that has been polluted in the past ("contaminated land"), and

- The management of land currently in use, and in particular, the management of waste disposal operations.

This chapter focuses on the problem of contaminated land and examines the statutory regime introduced by the Environment Act 1995. The control of waste disposal operations is considered in Chapter 8.

## Contaminated Land

In essence, "contaminated land" is land containing substances which may represent a hazard to humans or to the environment. It is not known precisely how much land in the U.K. is contaminated. Estimates suggest, however, that about 500,000 acres may have been polluted at some time by industrial use, landfill or mining. The Confederation of British Industry has estimated that the cost of investigating all potentially contaminated sites and of cleaning them up, is likely to be around £20 billion.[5]

---

[2] Tromans and Turrall-Clarke, *Contaminated Land* (1994).
[3] *ibid.* See also *The Independent,* March 31, 1989.
[4] Tromans and Turrall-Clarke, *Contaminated Land* (1994).
[5] See (1996) *Environmental Liability* 4 (4) pp. 67–74.

Land which has been contaminated presents the government with a number of difficult problems. In many cases, the activity which has caused the contamination occurred at a time when its danger was not appreciated. The decision whether and how to clean up the land is hampered by the limits of scientific knowledge about how pollutants affect land, particularly in combination with one another. Land is usually contaminated by a cocktail of chemicals in varying concentrations, and little is known about the long term effects of low level exposure to many of these chemicals.

A number of issues, therefore, need to be decided:

- How much or how little land contamination is acceptable?

- Who determines what level of contamination is acceptable?

- Is the land to be restored to its pristine state, or to a state where future damage is avoided and the site is suitable for a limited range of uses?

- Who is responsible: the polluter or the present owner of the land?

- How is liability to be apportioned where there are several persons or legal entities responsible?

- How is causation to be established?

- Who pays if the polluter cannot be traced or lacks funds; the taxpayer?

- Should the polluter have to pay even if he has not been negligent and could not reasonably have foreseen the damaging outcome of his activities?

- Should the user of land who is a potential polluter be compelled to insure against all environmental liabilities?

## Legal Control of Contaminated Land

Contaminated land is regulated by both the common law and by statute. The common law has always existed to enable a person who finds his land has been contaminated to seek compensation through an action in negligence, nuisance, or under the rule in *Rylands v. Fletcher.*[6] The common law, however, is of limited applicability to contaminated land. The breadth and flexibility of the tort of nuisance has given rise to a number of uncertainties. Negligence is of limited use because the plaintiff must show that the defendant owed him a duty of care and because, in many cases, the loss suffered will be economic. Where the vendor of land is sued by the new owner in contract, the issue will inevitably be one of *caveat emptor*. The requirement of foreseeability of harm has proved to be a significant stumbling block for liability under

---

[6] (1868) L.R. 3, H.L. 330. For a more detailed discussion, see Chapter 4, above.

the rule in *Rylands v. Fletcher*. This is discussed in Chapter 4. In *Cambridge Water Company v. Eastern Counties Leather*,[7] Lord Goff stated:

> "I incline to the opinion that, as a general rule, it is more appropriate for strict liability in respect of operations of high risk to be imposed by Parliament than by the courts. If such liability is imposed by statute, the relevant activities can be identified and those concerned know where they stand. Furthermore, statute can, where appropriate, lay down precise criteria establishing the incidence and scope of such liability."

Prior to the Environment Act 1995, which introduced what the government has called "the modern contaminated land power", there were no satisfactory statutory provisions dealing with the issue. In 1989, a report by the House of Commons Select Committee on the Environment referred to a lack of clarity in relation to legal liability for contaminated land, noting that this was not in the interests of landowners or the public, and recommending that urgent attention should be given to creating statutory liability for damage caused by contaminated land. The report noted that "various pieces of legislation touch on the problem . . . but the overall effect is patchy and little or no thought has been given to the big central questions such as who should pay for contaminated land." The Select Committee expressed its concern about the passive approach which had been adopted in relation to contaminated land, which meant that no official action need be taken in relation to a site unless and until it was developed, and concluded that there was a lack of coherent policy with respect to the issues raised by historic contamination of land.

Part III of the Environmental Protection Act 1990 provided some scope for the regulation of contaminated land under the provisions relating to statutory nuisances. Thus, a statutory nuisance may be caused by: "any premises in such a state as to be prejudicial to health or a nuisance", or "any accumulation or deposit which is prejudicial to health or a nuisance".

Under these provisions, local authorities were empowered to require owners or occupiers to clean up contaminated land, but the provisions have rarely been used for this purpose. The 1990 Act also saw the government's first attempt specifically to address the problem of identifying the extent of contaminated land in the U.K. Section 143 of that Act required the registration of all land which was subject to contaminative uses. In 1989, the House of Commons Select Committee on the Environment had identified a startling lack of information about the extent of contaminated sites in the U.K., and had recommended that a duty should be placed on local authorities to identify, and to compile registers of, all land which was contaminated.[8] The government did not fully implement this recommendation. Instead, it decided that registers should be compiled (under section 143) of land which was being used in a way which had the potential to cause contamination, rather than of land which was already contaminated. The committee's report had identified 19 potentially contaminating uses

---

[7] [1994] 1 All E.R. 53.
[8] House of Commons Environment Committee, Session 1989–1990, First Report, vol. I, p. xi.

of land including petrol stations, textile manufacturing, timber treatment, paper-making and printing.[9]

The decision to adopt a "use-based" approach to registers was prompted by fears on the part of industrialists and property developers that land which was labelled "contaminated" by inclusion on a register would be subject to "property blight" and would effectively be unsaleable, regardless of the extent and nature of the contamination. The government therefore adopted a "developer-friendly" policy on registers, which found expression in section 143 of the Environmental Protection Act 1990. Under this section, the Secretary of State was empowered to specify certain uses of land as "contaminative" and to require local authorities to maintain registers of land subject to those uses.

The gentleness of the government's approach, however, was not enough to allay developers' fears of blight being caused to their land simply by its having been identified as subject to a contaminative use, and, for this reason, section 143 was never implemented.[10] The fears of the property world were to some extent justified: under section 143, all land that was subject to contaminative uses was to be registered, regardless of whether or not actual contamination had occurred. Moreover, the scheme was incomplete, because it made no provision for remedial action to be taken in respect of land which was in fact contaminated.

In March 1993, the government, prompted by the uncertainties which were affecting the land market, initiated a review of the issue of contaminated land.[11] Following a protracted consultation period, the government expressed its views as follows:

" . . . the statutory nuisance powers have provided an essentially sound basis for dealing with contaminated land. However, in order to improve clarity and consistency, the government now considers that it is necessary to replace these powers — in respect of contaminated land only — with a modern, specific contaminated land power."[12]

The government's recognition of the persistent need to identify contaminated land, then, prompted a change of heart towards the fears of property developers and necessitated the adoption of a tougher approach than that which had led to the abandonment of section 143 registers. This approach finds expression in the Environment Act 1995, which puts in place a comprehensive regime for dealing with contaminated land. The Environment Act 1995 inserted into the Environmental Protection Act 1990 a new Part IIA. At the time of writing, Part IIA is not yet fully in force. Like many recent statutory environmental measures, the provisions of the Act are to be supplemented by detailed guidance, which is to be published after consultation with those whom it will affect.

[9] *ibid.*, para. 12.
[10] DoE Press Notice 209, March 24, 1993.
[11] See *Paying for our Past: the Arrangements for Controlling Contaminated Land and Meeting the Cost of Remedying Damage to the Environment*, (DoE, March 1994).
[12] See *Framework for Contaminated Land*, (DoE, November 1994).

## Diagram 3: The "Modern Contaminated Land Power"

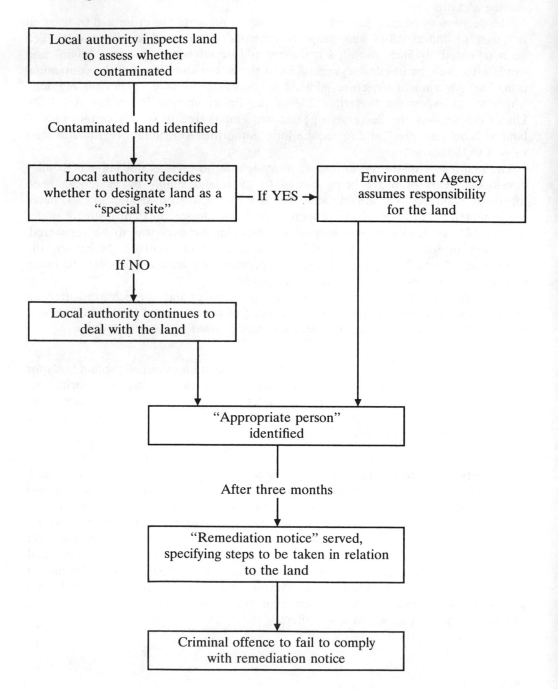

Local authority inspects land to assess whether contaminated

Contaminated land identified

Local authority decides whether to designate land as a "special site"

If YES →

Environment Agency assumes responsibility for the land

If NO

Local authority continues to deal with the land

"Appropriate person" identified

After three months

"Remediation notice" served, specifying steps to be taken in relation to the land

Criminal offence to fail to comply with remediation notice

## The Environment Act 1995

In the same way that Part I of the Environmental Protection Act 1990 divides responsibility for the control of air pollution between local authorities and the Environment Agency, so Part IIA divides responsibility for contaminated land. In broad terms, contaminated land which is likely to cause *serious* harm to the environment or to controlled waters is to be designated by the local authority as a "special site", over which the Environment Agency exercises responsibility, whilst control over contaminated land which poses a risk of *significant* (but not *serious*) harm to the environment is exercised by the local authority.

In any event, and whether or not the contamination in question warrants the designation of a particular site as a "special site", the first stage in the operation of the regime is for the local authority to identify all contaminated sites within its area, in accordance with guidance issued by the Secretary of State. All guidance which the Secretary of State proposes to issue in connection with Part IIA of the Environmental Protection Act 1990 must be laid before, and approved by, both Houses of Parliament.[13]

## Definition of "Contaminated Land"

For the purposes of Part IIA, contaminated land is defined as land which appears to the local authority in whose area it is situated to be in such a condition, by reason of substances in, on or under it, that either:

(a)  It is causing significant harm, or there is a significant possibility of its causing such harm, or

(b)  It is causing or is likely to cause pollution to controlled waters.[14]

In Part IIA, "harm" is given a narrower definition than that which appears in Part I of the Act (which is concerned with Integrated Pollution Control and Local Authority Air Pollution Control). As in Part I, the definition of "harm" includes harm to the health of living organisms and interference with the ecological systems of which they form part. In relation to man, however, the definition in Part IIA extends only to harm to his property. Offence to senses of man is not part of the definition.[15] This omission was motivated by the government's desire to prevent land from being regarded as contaminated merely because it is the source of a foul odour or is unpleasant to look at. Since man is a "living organism", his health is protected by the definition of "harm". However, offence to his senses cannot in itself be sufficient to constitute harm to his health. This point is reinforced by the draft guidance on identifying contaminated land, issued for consideration by Parliament during the passage of the Environment Bill,[16] which states that a local authority should disregard harm to the health of man other than death, serious injury and clinical toxicity.

---

[13] EPA 1990, s.78YA.
[14] *ibid.*, s.78A(2).
[15] *ibid.*, s.78A(4).
[16] DoE, May 5, 1995.

Part IIA makes no distinction between the concept of "contamination" and the concept of "pollution", although logically it is possible to do so. Most land which is contaminated has the *potential* to cause pollution if and when substances escape from it on to other land, into the air, or into the watercourse. However, even where substances are not escaping from land, logically it might be said to be in a state of *contamination*, although it is not a source of *pollution*. Such land nevertheless poses an environmental problem because often it cannot be disturbed without becoming a source of pollution. It is therefore often unsuitable for the kind of development which is most needed in the area where it lies.

The House of Commons Select Committee on the Environment, whose proposals helped to shape the policy behind Part IIA, noted that the Department of the Environment had not generally drawn a distinction between "contaminated" and "polluting" sites. In evidence to the Committee, the Department stated that it regarded contaminated land as land which represented: " . . . an actual or potential hazard to public health or to the environment as a result of current or previous use."

It is this view which has found expression in the definition of contaminated land in the Environment Act 1995. Therefore, land which is "contaminated" *but presents no threat of pollution* is (confusingly) *not* "contaminated land" in the context of Part IIA of the Environmental Protection Act 1990. Consequently, the problems associated with such land, although addressed to some extent by the operation of planning control, are not directly addressed by U.K. legislation.

## The "Suitable for Use" Approach

The Act provides that the questions of what harm is to be regarded as "significant", and of whether there is a "significant possibility" of harm being caused, are to be decided by the local authority in accordance with guidance to be issued by the Secretary of State.[17] Although no such guidance has formally been issued, the draft guidance indicates that local authorities will be required to adopt a pragmatic approach. The question of whether or not a particular site should be regarded as contaminated will depend on the use to which the land in question is to be put.[18] For example, consider a scrapyard contaminated by traces of metal. This form of contamination would present a hazard if the land were subsequently developed for agricultural use, but would be of no account in the construction of an office block.[19]

The site-specific appraisal of environmental problems in relation to land represents a departure from the approach adopted towards pollution in other environmental media. The approach makes use of environmental quality *objectives* rather than a uniform application of environmental quality *standards* (*i.e.* precise standards that must be met in relation to *all* land). In this regard it differs from the approach taken in determining BATNEEC and BPEO, which are defined by reference to fixed Environment Assessment Levels (EALs).[20]

---

[17] EPA 1990, s.78A(5).
[18] This is also the policy expressed in *Framework for Contaminated Land* (DoE, 1994), to which the draft guidance refers.
[19] This example was used in evidence given to the House of Commons Select Committee by the Department of the Environment.
[20] See Chapter 6, above.

The nature of land pollution is such that it necessitates a more flexible approach than pollution control regimes in other environmental media. The most obvious difference is that, in the case of contaminated land, the problem is one of pollution which has already occurred. Indeed, the extent of the problem is such that no amount of financial resources could solve it entirely. During the second reading of the Environment Bill, it was acknowledged in the Lords that it would be technically and scientifically impossible to regenerate all contaminated land to a virgin state. It is this impossibility which justifies the use of environmental quality objectives. Absolute quality standards are inappropriate in relation to contaminated land not merely because their use would entail an inefficient allocation of resources, but because, as a method of pollution control, they are simply *incapable* of fully addressing the problem.

## The Duties of Local Authorities

Under Part IIA of the Environmental Protection Act 1990, local authorities (county councils, district councils and London borough councils) are required, in accordance with guidance issued by the Secretary of State, to inspect all land in their area for the purposes of identifying contaminated sites and deciding whether or not any of those sites should be designated as "special sites".[21] Once a local authority has identified a contaminated site, it must notify the Environment Agency, the owner of the site and any person in occupation of the site.

It must also notify the person whom it considers to be the "appropriate person" in relation to that site[22] (which person may, in certain circumstances, also be the owner or occupier) who may then be required to clean up the land himself, or bear the cost of clean-up operations undertaken by the local authority or by a third party. In addition, he may be required to bear the cost of any inspection and scientific analysis of the land necessary to assess, more fully, its condition. All of the foregoing actions are encompassed by the word "remediation" as it is defined for the purposes of the Act.[23] Each aspect of the regime's operation is considered more fully below.

## Identifying Contaminated Land

The approach which local authorities are to adopt in identifying contaminated land is described in the draft guidance. This sets out a methodology based on risk assessment.[24] Each local authority is required to identify *source-pathway-target* relationships in respect of all land which it suspects may be contaminated. The government's view is that this methodology will contribute to market confidence by setting out a regulatory framework which does not place unnecessary burdens on industry.[25]

The first step in the process is the identification of potential *targets* for the effects of contamination. These will include humans, certain ecosystems and habitats (*e.g.* SSSIs

---

[21] EPA 1990, s.78B(1).
[22] *ibid.,* s.78B(3).
[23] *ibid.,* s.78A(7).
[24] This is compatible with the approach described in the *Guide to Risk Assessment and Risk Management for Environmental Protection,* (DoE, 1995).
[25] *Draft Guidance on Identifying Contaminated Land,* (DoE, May 5, 1995), para. 9.

and those protected under the Natural Habitats Directive and the Birds Directive), and property (including livestock) present on the land in question. The authority will draw on its current holdings of information to identify human targets, and will consult with English Nature about the presence of protected ecosystems and habitats.[26]

Once the potential targets are identified, the local authority will proceed to an identification of likely *sources* of contamination in the land on which the targets are present. In doing this, the local authority will consider the previous history of the site.[27] However, historical information, or information based solely on a visual inspection of the site, will not afford sufficient grounds for the authority to conclude that the site is contaminated. It can do so only on the basis of an exploratory survey which reveals the actual presence of substances in the land.[28] Clearly, this provision of the guidance is necessary to ensure that local authorities do not require the landowner, by way of remediation, to conduct a survey at his own expense merely for the purpose of furnishing the authority with information from which it can conclude that a site is contaminated. The power to require remediation is exercisable only once a local authority has, at its own expense, identified contaminating substances in the land.

The next stage in the identification process requires a local authority to identify the presence of *pathways* by which the sources of contamination may affect the targets. It is at this stage in the methodology that account is taken of the use to which the land is put.

For example, if the local authority identifies children as the potential targets of contamination, and cadmium in the soil as the source of contamination, it will then consider the pathways by which that source is accessible to the children. The possible pathways might include ingestion or inhalation of the contaminated soil, skin contact with the soil, and the consumption of contaminated vegetables. If a child has access to the soil in one of these ways then a *source-pathway-target* relationship can be established. If, however, the soil is beneath a concrete hardstanding, then such a relationship is unlikely to have been established.[29]

Where *source-pathway-target* relationships are established, the local authority will proceed to the final stage of the identification process. This involves determining whether, by virtue of those relationships, significant harm is being caused, or whether there is a significant possibility of such harm (*i.e.* whether the land is "contaminated" within the meaning of the Act).[30] The authority may use as a starting point a "worst case scenario". However, this will not normally be sufficient to indicate that the risk of harm is such that the land should be classified as contaminated. In this context, "risk" is defined as the combination of the probability (or frequency) of the occurrence of a particular hazard and the magnitude of the consequences.

Each authority will set its own criteria for determining the point at which the risk of harm warrants classification of the land. Disparity of practice may therefore emerge between authorities in different areas. Indeed, this is envisaged by the draft guidance,[31] which concedes that different local authorities face different patterns of development

---

[26] *ibid.,* para. 39.
[27] *ibid.,* para. 41.
[28] *ibid.,* paras. 48–52.
[29] This example is taken from the draft guidance at para. 44.
[30] *ibid.,* para. 54 *et seq.*
[31] *ibid.,* para. 28.

and land use within their areas, as well as different geological conditions which can affect the magnitude of the risk posed by substances in land. In the absence of more detailed information about the risks posed by specific substances, local authorities may make use of guideline values for concentrations of contaminants in soil which have been provided in other contexts (for example, those provided by the World Health Organisation) to determine the magnitude of the risk of harm. However, the authority must demonstrate that its use of such guidelines is appropriate in view of the use and characteristics of the particular land in question.[32]

## Special Sites

Once a local authority has identified a contaminated site, it must go on to consider whether or not that site should be designated as a "special site".[33] Special sites are sites in relation to which the Environment Agency, rather than the local authority, is the enforcing authority. The powers and duties exercisable by the Environment Agency in relation to special sites are identical to those exercisable by local authorities in relation to ordinary contaminated sites. These powers and duties are examined below, where, as in Part IIA of the Environmental Protection Act 1990, the words "enforcing authority" are used to connote either the local authority or the Environment Agency, depending on whether the land in question has been designated as a special site.

The Secretary of State is empowered to make regulations prescribing the circumstances in which land is to be designated as a special site.[34] The Act provides that in doing so he may have regard, amongst other things, to whether certain types of contaminated land are likely to cause *serious* harm or *serious* pollution to controlled waters, and to the fact that the Environment Agency may have particular expertise not possessed by local authorities in relation to certain types of contamination.[35]

The Act sets out a fairly complex (and inevitably slightly bureaucratic) system for the designation of special sites, which aims to ensure co-operation between the local authority and the Environment Agency and which makes provision for resolving disputes which may arise between them. Before deciding to designate any site as a special site, the local authority is required to seek the advice of the Agency and to have regard to that advice.[36] If it then decides to designate the land, it must notify the Environment Agency, as well as the owner of the site, any persons in occupation of the site, and any persons who appear to be "appropriate persons" to take responsibility for the state of the land (the "relevant persons").[37]

The local authority's decision to designate takes effect as a designation of the site in question after the expiry of a period of 21 days from the date on which the Agency was notified, except in cases where, prior to the expiry of that period, the Agency gives notification to the local authority that it agrees with its decision to designate, in which case the decision takes effect as a designation as soon as this notification is given.[38] If,

[32] *ibid.*, para. 55.
[33] EPA 1990, s.78B(1)(b).
[34] *ibid.*, s.78C(8). Note that, unlike guidance, regulations issued under Part IIA do not require the approval of Parliament.
[35] EPA 1990, s.78C(10).
[36] *ibid.*, s.78C(3).
[37] *ibid.*, s.78C(1).
[38] *ibid.*, s.78C(6).

however, within 21 days, the Agency notifies the local authority that it disagrees with its decision to designate, the decision does not take effect as a designation and the matter must be referred to the Secretary of State for determination.[39]

The Environment Agency may at any time notify the local authority in respect of any particular land which it considers should be designated as a special site.[40] Where it does this, the local authority is required to consider the matter for itself and to decide whether or not to designate the site. If it decides not to designate, however, the Agency may, within 21 days, give notice to the local authority that it disagrees with this decision and that it is still of the opinion that the land should be designated, in which case, similarly, the matter is referred to the Secretary of State.

In either case where a dispute between the Agency and the local authority has been referred to him, the Secretary of State may reverse or confirm the local authority's decision with respect to the whole or any part of the land to which it relates.[41] Where a local authority's decision to designate is confirmed, or its decision not to designate is reversed by the Secretary of State, his decision does not take effect as a designation until he has given notice of his confirmation or reversal to the relevant persons.[42]

The duty to consider whether land should be designated as a special site is a continuing one. It arises both at the time land is first identified as contaminated land and throughout the period during which the land remains classified as contaminated.[43] This means that if contamination on a particular site, which is causing significant harm at the time of its identification, begins to cause serious harm, or begins to cause problems with which the Environment Agency are especially equipped to deal, the site can be designated as a special site and control over it can be transferred from the local authority to the Environment Agency. The Environment Agency can at any time terminate the designation of a special site and convert it into an ordinary site by giving notice to the Secretary of State and to the local authority.[44] Where this is done, however, it does not prevent the site from being re-designated on a subsequent occasion.

## The Appropriate Person

The Act adopts a hierarchical approach towards apportioning liability for contaminated land. Because contaminated land is often the result of the activities of polluters who can no longer be found, there is an obvious difficulty in giving full effect to the "polluter pays" principle. However, the Act makes an attempt to reconcile the implementation of this principle with the practical need to identify a person on whom to place responsibility for pollution on land.

In the first instance, the "appropriate person" to bear responsibility for the contaminating substances in, on or under land is the person who "caused or knowingly permitted" those substances to be there.[45] The meaning of this phrase, which is

[39] *ibid.,* s.78D(1).
[40] *ibid.,* s.78C(4).
[41] *ibid.,* s.78D(4).
[42] *ibid.,* s.78D(5) and (6).
[43] *ibid.,* s.78C(1).
[44] *ibid.,* s.78Q.
[45] *ibid.,* s.78F(2).

discussed below, is central to determining liability. If, however, after reasonable enquiry, such a person cannot be found, the owner or occupier of the contaminated land is made the "appropriate person".[46] The idea of placing liability on an owner or occupier who is not at fault in having caused or permitted the contamination was sharply criticised, during the passage of the Environment Bill, by the Earl of Lytton, who said:

> " . . . making an economic scapegoat out of an individual for matters which in times gone by were at least partly a collective responsibility is wrong as a general principle. I have to say that I do not think it would work in practice."

Where two or more persons are "appropriate persons", either because they were jointly responsible for causing or knowingly permitting the pollution, or because they are co-owners or co-occupiers of land in relation to which no original polluter has been found, then they are made to bear the cost of cleaning-up the land in appropriate proportions, to be determined by the enforcing authority in accordance with guidance issued by the Secretary of State.[47] The Act specifically provides that the enforcing authority may, in accordance with this guidance, determine that one or more persons should be absolved of responsibility and should not be treated as an appropriate person.[48] It remains to be seen whether, in the case of co-owners or co-occupiers who have not caused or knowingly permitted the contamination, the guidance will enable the authority simply to fix responsibility on the person with the deepest pocket, or whether questions of the intensity or profitability of their respective uses of the land will fall to be considered. What is clear, however, is that where there are one or more persons who have caused or knowingly permitted the contamination, the liability of one polluter can extend only to the particular substances (and to the amount of those substances) which he, rather than his co-polluter, caused or knowingly permitted to be in the land.[49]

## The Meaning of "Causing or Knowingly Permitting"

Because substances, once in land, can degrade or combine with other substances to produce new substances entirely distinct from the substances originally deposited, the Act provides that a person who caused or knowingly permitted the presence in, on or under land of any substance (substance A) shall be treated as having also caused or knowingly permitted the presence of any other substance (substance B) which is there as a result of any chemical reaction or biological process affecting substance A.[50]

The case law on the meaning of "causing or knowingly permitting", which evolved in clarifying that phrase as it was used in water pollution legislation, establishes that the words create offences of strict liability.[51] It is not necessary to show that the pollution

---

[46] *ibid.*, s.78F(4).
[47] *ibid.*, s.78F(7).
[48] *ibid.*, s.78F(6).
[49] *ibid.*, s.78F(3).
[50] *ibid.*, s.78F(9).
[51] The meaning of "causing or knowingly permitting" is discussed further in Chapter 9, below.

was caused intentionally or through negligence. It will therefore be no defence to a prosecution to show that, in the light of scientific knowledge at the time of its original deposit, it was not possible to foresee that a substance would be a source of contamination.

It is to be noted that the criteria for determining environmental strict liability under Part IIA of the Environmental Protection Act 1990 differ considerably from those applied in determining (so-called) strict civil liability for pollution at common law, under the rule in *Rylands v. Fletcher,*[52] as that rule has emerged from the opinion of the House of Lords in *Cambridge Water Company v. Eastern Counties Leather plc.*[53] In cases where the defendant has only recently been informed of some newly-discovered harmful effect of substances on his land, under Part IIA (unlike the position at common law) liability for the state of the land will follow if it can be shown that he caused or knowingly permitted those substances to be there, it being irrelevant that foreseeability of contamination was not present at the time those substances were originally deposited.

## Retrospective Liability

There is, of course, a sense in which the kind of strict liability imposed by the offences of causing and knowingly permitting allows for the imposition of retrospective liability. As has been said, a person who caused or knowingly permitted substances to be deposited on land at a time when it was not known that those substances were pollutants, may nevertheless be held responsible for their subsequent environmental effects when those effects are later identified in the light of increased scientific knowledge. It is to be noted that this element of retrospective liability makes statutory offences of environmental strict liability quite distinct from other forms of statutory strict liability. Traditionally, where statutes have created strict liability, the risks inherent in the activity from which the liability arises are well known, so that the person who engages in the activity can make an informed decision about the likely costs of assuming the risk and insure himself accordingly. Traditional strict liability arises where the legislature has thought it appropriate to allocate the risk associated with a particular activity to one party (often the party who can abate or absorb the risk at least cost) rather than to another. This often occurs in the field of employers' liability. For example, in *John Summers & Sons v. Frost*[54] it was held that the statutory duty created by section 14 (1) of the Factories Act 1961 required an employer to guard a grinding wheel even though to do so would render the machine unusable.

Where, however, as a matter of policy, legislation operates to shift losses in this way, the philosophical justification for shifting the liability lies in the fact that the magnitude of the risk is foreseeable (and can be given a finite monetary value in terms of an insurance premium), and the employer is free to make a business decision about whether or not to accept the risk as part of the price he pays for the profits he derives from his activities. Clearly this is not possible in relation to many environmental activities, the risks of which can often be appreciated only with the benefit of hindsight

[52] (1868) L.R. 3 H.L. 330.
[53] [1993] 2 W.L.R. 53.
[54] [1955] A.C. 740.

and have, in practical terms, proved to be uninsurable. This raises the controversial question of whether environmental offences of strict liability which have the potential to impose retrospective liability are contrary to fundamental principles of fairness and natural justice. There can be no easy answer to this question, save for the bald statement that where environmental problems exist, they must be solved in the interests of society as a whole and, in a democratic state, it is not politically viable for government to finance environmental solutions entirely through general taxation. The inevitable consequence of this may be that through retrospective liability an unlucky few are made to bear the cost of resolving environmental problems which are not solely their fault.

## Remediation Notices

Once a local authority has identified any contaminated land within its area, it (or the Agency in relation to a special site) may serve on each "appropriate person" a "remediation notice" specifying what that person is required to do by way of remediation and the time periods within which each of the things specified are to be done.[55] Where the contamination is the result of the presence of several different substances for which more than one "appropriate person" is responsible, then several remediation notices may be served, one on each appropriate person, and those notices may require different things to be done by each person.[56] Where a remediation notice requires the doing of one activity by two or more "appropriate persons", it must state the proportion of the cost of that activity which each of them is liable to bear.[57]

Where there is an imminent danger of serious harm, or of serious pollution being caused to controlled waters, the enforcing authority may serve a remediation notice as soon as it has identified the contaminated land and has given the required notification.[58] However, under ordinary circumstances there is a statutory "cooling-off" period of three months, beginning with the date on which notice identifying the contaminated land is given to the appropriate person, during which no remediation notice may be served on him. In addition, a number of conditions have to be satisfied before a remediation notice can be served. The enforcing authority is required reasonably to endeavour to consult the appropriate person as well as the owner and the occupier of the contaminated land (where he is not also the appropriate person).[59] It must also reasonably endeavour to consult any third parties likely to be affected by things done by way of remediation.

The "cooling-off" period gives the enforcing authority and the appropriate person time to negotiate a solution to the problem and if, at the end of the three month period, the authority is satisfied that things are being done, or will be done, by way of remediation without the need for a remediation notice, then it need not serve one.[60] Where this is the case, however, the person who is doing or will do those things must

---

[55] EPA 1990, s.78E(1).
[56] ibid., s.78E(2).
[57] ibid., s.78E(3).
[58] ibid., ss.78G(4) and 78H(4).
[59] ibid., s.78H(1).
[60] ibid., s.78H(5)(b).

prepare and publish a "remediation statement" setting out the action he is taking or proposes to take.[61] If he fails to do so within a reasonable time, then the enforcing authority itself may prepare and publish such a statement and recover the costs of doing so from the defaulter.[62]

Alternatively, the authority may decide that, having regard to the likely cost of remediation in relation to the harm which could be prevented, there is nothing which can reasonably be done by way of remediation, in which case it will not serve a remediation notice.[63] In neither of these cases, however, is the authority precluded from "changing its mind". The authority can serve a remediation notice if a person defaults in carrying out remediation which it seemed likely would be undertaken voluntarily at the time when a decision not to serve a notice was made. Similarly, a notice may be served if the authority later decides, perhaps in accordance with revised guidance, that remediation which at the time of its decision it was precluded from requiring would not now be unreasonably costly.[64]

## Appeal against a Remediation Notice

A person on whom a remediation notice has been served has 21 days in which to appeal to a magistrates' court (if the notice was served by a local authority) or to the Secretary of State (if the notice was served by the Environment Agency).[65] The appellate authority may quash, confirm or modify the notice. In particular, it may extend the period specified in the notice for doing what is required. The Act provides for regulations to be made in relation to the grounds on which appeals may be brought, the parties who are entitled to appeal, and whether or not and in what circumstances a notice is to be suspended pending the outcome of an appeal.

## Breach of a Remediation Notice

It is an offence to fail, without reasonable excuse, to comply with the requirements of a remediation notice.[66] However, the Act provides that where the remediation notice in question is one which required the person charged with the offence to bear only a proportion of the cost of remediation, together with others, it is a defence for that person to prove that the only reason why he has failed to comply with the notice is that one or more of the other persons who were required to share with him the cost of remediation refused or was unable to pay his share of the cost.[67]

The offence is triable only in the magistrates' court, where the penalty for the offence differs according to whether or not the land in question consists of "industrial, trade or business premises". These are defined to include premises on which matter is burnt in connection with any industrial, trade or business purpose, whether or not those premises are also used for that purpose.[68]

---

[61] *ibid.,* s.78H(7).
[62] *ibid.,* s.78H(9).
[63] *ibid.,* s.78H(5)(a).
[64] *ibid.,* s.78H(10).
[65] *ibid.,* s.78L.
[66] *ibid.,* s.78M(1).
[67] *ibid.,* s.78M(2).
[68] *ibid.,* s.78M(6).

In a normal (non-industrial) case, the maximum penalty is an initial fine of an amount equal to level 5 on the standard scale, together with further fines of one tenth of that sum in respect of each day after conviction on which the breach of the requirement in the remediation notice continues. For industrial offenders, however, the maximum penalty is a fine of £20,000, plus an additional fine of one tenth of that sum in respect of each day on which the breach of the notice continues after conviction.[69] The amount of the maximum fine for industrial offenders may be increased by order of the Secretary of State, provided that the order has been approved by both Houses of Parliament.[70] If the enforcing authority is of the opinion that prosecution would provide an ineffectual remedy, it may seek an injunction in the High Court to secure compliance with a remediation notice.[71]

## The Nature of Remediation

As has been said, the term "remediation" embraces a number of activities which the enforcing authority may require the appropriate person to perform. In particular, he may be required to conduct or finance an assessment of the condition of the contaminated site so that the local authority may determine what action, if any, needs to be taken in respect of it. He may also be required to take steps to prevent or minimise the effects of the contaminated site, or to restore the site to its former condition, and to carry out subsequent inspections for the purpose of reviewing the condition of the land.[72]

The draft guidance makes it clear that the appropriate person cannot be required, by way of remediation, to finance initial investigations to assist the local authority in fulfilling its duty to determine whether or not the land is contaminated.[73] In the absence of further guidance, however, it is unclear whether, once land has been identified by the local authority as contaminated, the appropriate person can be required, by way of remediation, to assess the condition of his land to assist the authority in determining whether or not it should be designated as a special site. Arguably, this is a primary duty of the local authority[74] which must be discharged before any remediation can be required.

The nature of the action which the enforcing authority may require by way of remediation is, however, limited in a number of important respects. First, where the contaminated land is causing or is likely to cause pollution to controlled waters, but no significant harm is being caused or is likely to be caused (which might, for example, be the case where substances are entering a river or watercourse which has the capability to dilute and disperse them so that no harm is likely), the authority has no power to require remediation of any land or waters, although it can carry out remediation itself without recovering the cost.[75]

Secondly, the Act provides that nothing may be required by way of remediation unless the enforcing authority, acting in accordance with guidance issued by the

---

[69] *ibid.,* s.78M(4).
[70] *ibid.,* s.78M(7).
[71] *ibid.,* s.78M(5).
[72] *ibid.,* s.78A(7).
[73] *Draft Guidance on Identifying Contaminated Land,* para. 48–52.
[74] EPA 1990, s.78B(1).
[75] *ibid.,* s.78J.

Secretary of State, considers that the remediation is reasonable having regard to its likely cost in relation to the seriousness of the harm being caused or likely to be caused by the contamination.[76] However, if the enforcing authority decides that it cannot require the appropriate person to do a particular thing by way of remediation because this would entail unreasonable cost, it must prepare and publish a "remediation declaration".[77] This document must record the reasons why the authority would, were it not for the unreasonable cost, have required a particular thing to be done. It must also state the reasons why the authority has decided that it cannot require that thing to be done in a remediation notice. Thirdly, liability is restricted in respect of land to which contaminating substances have escaped from other land.

## Remediation where Substances Have Escaped from other Land

Many polluting substances are inherently mobile or can be displaced by natural forces from the land on which they were originally deposited. An owner or occupier of land may therefore find himself in possession of land which is polluted, through no fault of his own, by substances which have escaped there from other land. Where this is the case, the Act provides that a person who caused or knowingly permitted substances to be on any land (the original land), is to be treated as having also caused or knowingly permitted them to be on any other land to which they have escaped.[78] Where such a person can be found, therefore, he will be made the appropriate person in relation to that other land.

In cases where the original polluter cannot be found, it is possible, as has been said, for the owner or occupier of contaminated land to be made the "appropriate person". However, in cases where the land in question is contaminated because of substances which appear to the local authority to have escaped to that land from other land (as opposed to having been deposited there), the liability of an *owner or occupier* who becomes an "appropriate person" is limited: he cannot be required to do anything by way of remediation to any land or waters *other than those of which he is the owner or occupier*.[79] He is therefore in a different position from that of an owner or occupier of land which is contaminated because of substances which have been deposited there, whose liability may extend to remediation of the effects of those substances on another's land.

## The Effect of Remediation on Persons other than the Appropriate Person

The appropriate person may be required to do things by way of remediation even though normally he would not in law be entitled to do them.[80] For example, where the

[76] *ibid.*, s.78E(4).
[77] *ibid.*, s.78H(6).
[78] *ibid.*, s.78K(1).
[79] *ibid.*, ss.78K(3) and (4). The drafting of s.78K is somewhat obscure. Subs. 3 prevents remediation being required of a person in respect of "any land . . . other than land . . . of which he is the owner or occupier". For good measure, however, subs. 4 goes on to prevent remediation being required of a person in respect of "any further land . . . ('land B') . . . unless he is also the owner or occupier of land B". To make sense of the section as a whole, therefore, the expression "any land" must be given a restricted meaning, *viz.* the land *from which* the substances escaped, whilst "any further land" must refer to the land *to which* they have escaped. It is submitted, however, that the ordinary meaning of the expression "any land" is clearly wide enough to include the latter, and that subs. 4 is therefore otiose.
[80] EPA 1990, s.78G(1).

appropriate person is no longer the owner or occupier of the contaminated land, he may be required to enter on to that land even though this would normally constitute a trespass. Similarly, an owner may be required to enter on to adjacent land owned by another to assess how his land is affecting that land, or to remove contaminating substances from that land or from his own land where this necessitates access via adjacent land or the use of machinery positioned on it. Clearly, such activities would normally interfere with the property rights of owners, tenants and others who have an interest in the land affected.

The Act provides, however, that where the consent of any person is required before remediation can be carried out, that person: " . . . shall grant, or join in granting, such rights in relation to any of the relevant land or waters as will enable the appropriate person to comply with any requirements imposed by the remediation notice."[81]

The "relevant land or waters" are defined to include the contaminated land in question, any controlled waters affected by that land, and any land adjacent to the contaminated land or adjacent to the controlled waters affected by it.[82]

Before serving a remediation notice on the appropriate person, the enforcing authority is required reasonably to endeavour to consult any person who appears to be the owner or occupier of any relevant land or waters concerning the rights which he may be required to grant.[83] Moreover, the Act provides for regulations to be made under which a person who is affected by anything done by way of remediation may claim compensation from the appropriate person.[84]

The Environmental Protection Act 1990 does not specifically address the question of what powers an enforcing authority has in the event that a person whose property rights will be affected by remediation should refuse to co-operate. Such refusal is not a specific offence under the Act. However, under the Environment Act 1995, it is an offence to obstruct an "authorised person" in the exercise of his duties,[85] and any person may be made an "authorised person" for the purpose of carrying out the pollution control functions of an enforcing authority.[86] Although it is likely that the courts will construe the words "shall grant" so as simply to abrogate the property rights of an affected person, there remains the possibility of the enforcing authority making the appropriate person an "authorised person", so that the threat of criminal sanctions can be used to secure the co-operation of a recalcitrant affected person.

## Remediation by the Enforcing Authority

The enforcing authority has the power to enter into an agreement with the appropriate person, under which he bears the cost of remediation which has been required of him by a remediation notice, whilst the local authority carries out the work on his behalf.[87] It also has power to undertake remediation at its own expense in cases where it

---

[81] *ibid.*, s.78G(2).
[82] *ibid.*, s.78G(7).
[83] *ibid.*, s.78G(3) (Except in cases where there is an imminent danger of serious harm or serious pollution to controlled waters: s.78G(4)).
[84] *ibid.*, s.78G(5).
[85] EA 1995, s.110(1).
[86] *ibid.*, s.108.
[87] EPA 1990, s.78N(3)(b).

considers that, for reasons of likely hardship to the appropriate person, or in view of the Secretary of State's guidance, it will not seek to recover from him the full cost of remediation, or will seek to recover only a portion of that cost.[88] In addition, the authority can undertake remediation at its own expense where it is precluded from serving a remediation notice because, although pollution to controlled waters is being caused or is likely, no significant harm is being caused or is likely,[89] and in cases where, after reasonable enquiry, no appropriate person can be found.[90] In all of these cases, although the enforcing authority has the power to carry out remediation, it has no duty to do so.

Clearly, whether, and to what extent local authorities or the Environment Agency will be able to carry out remediation in respect of "orphan sites" for which no appropriate person has been found, or in cases where it is unreasonable to recover the costs of remediation, will depend on the financial resources advanced to them by central government for the purpose, and, in the case of local authorities, on the extent to which it is politically viable for them to secure resources through local taxation. The government has as yet given little indication of the precise extent of public resources which are to be made available for remediation of contaminated land.

## Recovery of the Cost of Remediation

In certain circumstances the enforcing authority is entitled to recover from the appropriate person the cost of remediation which it has undertaken itself in the absence of an agreement with the appropriate person.[91] It may do so where remediation has been necessary because of an imminent danger of serious harm or of serious pollution to controlled waters, and in cases where the person on whom a remediation notice has been served fails to comply with its requirements. It can also do so where it has carried out remediation to land in respect of which, after reasonable enquiry, no appropriate person was found, and such a person is subsequently found. In all these cases, however, in deciding whether and what proportion of the cost of remediation should be recovered, the enforcing authority must have regard to any hardship which might be caused to the appropriate person and to any guidance issued by the Secretary of State.[92]

## Charging Notices

Where the appropriate person from whom the enforcing authority decides to recover the cost of remediation is also both the person who caused or knowingly permitted the contamination and the owner of premises on the land in question, the authority may serve him with a "charging notice".[93] This has the effect of making the sum recoverable, together with interest, a charge on the premises, and for the purposes of

---

[88] *ibid.*, s.78N(3)(e).
[89] *ibid.*, s.78N(3)(d).
[90] *ibid.*, s.78N(3)(f).
[91] *ibid.*, s.78P(1).
[92] *ibid.*, s.78P(2).
[93] *ibid.*, s.78P(3).

enforcing the charge, the authority has the same powers and remedies as if it were a mortgagee by deed under the Law of Property Act 1925.[94] Moreover, the authority may require the sum recoverable, together with interest, to be repaid by instalments over a period of up to 30 years.

Where a charging notice is served on the owner of premises, a copy of the notice must also be served on any other persons who, to the knowledge of the local authority, have an interest in the premises capable of being affected by the charge.[95] The charge takes effect from the end of a period of 21 days beginning with the date on which the charging notice is served or, if an appeal is brought, from the date of the final determination or withdrawal of the appeal.[96] A person served with a charging notice has 21 days in which to appeal to a county court, which may confirm the notice, declare that it shall have no effect, or substitute a different amount from the amount specified as recoverable in the notice.

Charging notices will doubtless prove an effective tool in meeting the environmental costs of contaminated land. Their application, however, is limited: they cannot be used to recover the costs of remediation from an appropriate person unless he is both the owner of premises on the contaminated land *and* the person who has caused or knowingly permitted the contamination. This leaves a residual class of appropriate persons (*viz.* original polluters who are no longer owners of the contaminated land, and owners or occupiers who did not cause or permit the contamination) against whom the authority is entitled to recover the cost of remediation. The precise mechanism by which recovery of costs is to be enforced against these people is not prescribed by the Act, and, in the absence of guidance from the Secretary of State, remains unclear.

## Security for the Cost of Remediation

It is unclear whether the provision of the Act which entitles the enforcing authority to recover the costs of remediation will enable it to do so in respect of works which it considers necessary but has not yet carried out. The meaning of the provision will be especially important to local authorities which may lack the funds even to commence certain complex remediation operations. The relevant section (so far as is material) states: " Where . . . the enforcing authority does any particular thing by way of remediation, it shall be entitled . . . to recover the reasonable cost incurred in doing it from the appropriate person . . . "[97]

On the face of it, the wording of the section requires the authority at least to have commenced, and be in the process of "doing" the remediation, if not to have already done it, before costs can be recovered or a charging notice served. The marginal note to the section, however, reads: "Recovery of, and security for, the cost of remediation by the enforcing authority".

If the expression "security for cost" is to be construed in the sense in which it is generally understood by lawyers, it suggests that the scope of the section is wide

[94] *ibid.,* s.78P(11).
[95] *ibid.,* s.78P(6).
[96] *ibid.,* s.78P(7).
[97] *ibid.,* s.78P(1).

enough to allow the enforcing authority to serve a charging notice in respect of remediation costs which it has not yet fully incurred. If the issue is not clarified by forthcoming guidance, it may need to be settled by the courts, which may have regard to the wording of the marginal note. Although such notes are not, strictly speaking, part of the statute, because they have not received the scrutiny of Parliament, their use has been sanctioned by the courts as a guide to ascertaining the general purpose of the section to which they relate.[98]

## Public Registers

The Act requires the enforcing authorities to maintain public registers containing prescribed particulars of, *inter alia*, all remediation notices served and all special sites, as well as all notifications given to the authority by persons who have been served with a remediation notice of what they claim has been done by them by way of remediation. Authorities must also record particulars of convictions for breach of a remediation notice.[99] Registers may be kept in any form, for example as a computerised database, and must be available for public inspection at all reasonable times and free of charge. The enforcing authority is further required to provide facilities for members of the public to obtain copies of entries on the registers on payment of a reasonable charge.[1]

Significantly, the Act makes no specific mention of any requirement that a local authority maintain a register listing all the land in its area which it has identified as contaminated. This omission demonstrates the government's sensitivity to the fears of developers in relation to property blight, which shaped the ill-fated history of section 143 registers. However, such registers may eventually be required of local authorities by regulations, since, under the Act, the Secretary of State is empowered to require the keeping of registers in relation to "such other matters relating to contaminated land as may be prescribed".[2]

As is the case in relation to registers maintained under Part I of the Act, information will not be included in a register under Part IIA if it is commercially confidential or prejudicial to national security. As in Part I, information is commercially confidential if it would prejudice to an unreasonable degree the commercial interests of the person concerned,[3] and it is for the enforcing authority, or on appeal, the Secretary of State, to determine whether this is so.[4] In deciding the matter, however, any prejudice to the individual concerned must be disregarded so far as it relates only to the value of the land in question.[5] Where information is excluded from the register on grounds of commercial confidentiality, a statement must be entered on the register indicating the existence of such information.[6] Confidential information remains excluded for a period of four years, after which time the individual who furnished it may apply for it to remain excluded.[7]

---

[98] *Tudor Grange Holdings Ltd v. Citibank NA* [1991] 4 All E.R. 1, *per* Sir Nicolas Browne-Wilkinson V.-C. at 13.
[99] EPA 1990, s.78R.
[1] *ibid.*, s.78R(8).
[2] *ibid.*, s.78R(1).
[3] *ibid.*, s.78T(10).
[4] *ibid.*, s.78T(2).
[5] *ibid.*, s.78T(11).
[6] *ibid.*, s.78R(7).
[7] *ibid.*, s.78T(8).

## Planning and the Contaminated Land Regime

The statutory regime for dealing with contaminated land is seen by the Department of the Environment as supplementary to, rather than a replacement for, existing powers of local authorities to control the development of contaminated land through planning law.[8] It expressed this view in its policy document, "Framework for Contaminated Land",[9] in which it stated:

"The government believes that the normal process of development and redevelopment provides the best means of tackling much past contamination. Improvements to the condition of land can in most circumstances be created through voluntary, commercial activities of the private sector without the need for direct intervention by regulatory authorities."

Guidance on the relationship between planning and environmental protection is also provided in Planning Policy Guidance Note 23, "Planning and Pollution Control", which sets out the general requirements for dealing with contamination where a site is subject to a change of use. In particular, it may be made a condition of any planning permission for a change of use that the land in question is made suitable for the proposed use, and this may involve the removal of contaminants. Where this is the case, subsequent regulatory action is avoided.

[8] *Draft Guidance on Identifying Contaminated Land,* (DoE, May 5, 1995), para. 4 *et seq.*
[9] DoE, 1994.

# Chapter 8

# WASTE MANAGEMENT

*"Over the past twenty years the control of waste management in the United Kingdom has grown from relatively modest beginnings to become one of the most technically and legally complex areas of environmental litigation."*[1]

## Introduction

Most of the waste produced in the U.K is produced by industry. In 1989, for example, Britain produced approximately 2,500 million tonnes of waste, of which only 1.5 million tonnes was domestic and trade waste.[2] Industrial waste can take many forms. Much of it is produced in a semi-liquid state in the form of effluent or sludge. A great deal of this results from agricultural activities, from the chemical and oil refining industries, and from the activities of sewerage undertakers. Other forms of waste include solid industrial waste, waste from mines and quarries and waste from power stations. This chapter considers the statutory regime relating to the management of solid waste. The management of waste which is in liquid form is regulated by the water pollution regime, discussed in Chapter 9.

Solid waste can cause environmental problems not only when it is finally disposed of, but also when it is stored, transported or treated, either to reclaim useful substances within it or to change its form so that it can be disposed of more easily. The House of Commons Select Committee on the Environment, reporting in 1989, noted that waste disposal was the most significant cause of contaminated land in the U.K. and, in particular, identified the need to introduce controls to deal with the problem of gases emitted from landfill sites. Waste is regulated in the U.K. by statute alone. At common law, the concept of a substance being "waste" is unknown. Liability at common law is founded on harm to persons, or damage to property, it being irrelevant whether or not this results from substances known as "waste".

## THE POLICY BEHIND THE WASTE MANAGEMENT REGIME

### Methods of Waste Disposal

As has been said, most waste which the U.K. produces is disposed of by landfill, the problems associated with which were noted at the beginning of Chapter 7. This,

---

[1] Pocklington, "The Utility of the Concept of 'Waste' ", [1996] *Environmental Liability,* vol. 4(5), p. 94.
[2] House of Commons Environment Committee on Toxic Waste, Second Report.

however, is not the only method of disposal. Some waste is discharged to inland waterways, some is dumped at sea, and some is disposed of by incineration. All of these methods, of course, cause environmental problems. Waste disposal at sea, for example, poses a danger to marine life and is curtailed by international conventions, which have effectively put a stop to the dumping of industrial waste at sea by countries within the E.C.

The Royal Commission on Environmental Pollution, in its seventeenth report,[3] favoured greater use of incineration as a method of waste disposal. The incineration of waste, however, gives rise to problems of air pollution, and a recent report by the US Environmental Protection Agency into the harmful effects of dioxins in the atmosphere has led to increased concern about the viability of incineration as an alternative to landfill. The growing realisation that no method of waste disposal is without its environmental problems, coupled with the knowledge that existing landfill sites are reaching their full capacity and the availability of land for new sites is severely limited, prompted the E.C. to formulate policy in terms of reducing the amount of waste produced within the Community. This policy, with its emphasis on recycling, finds expression in the concept of a "waste hierarchy".

## The "Waste Hierarchy"

Within existing E.C. and U.K. waste policy there can be identified three distinct approaches to dealing with waste: minimisation, recycling and disposal. Each of these approaches is appropriate for a particular kind of waste. The concurrent implementation of these three approaches gives rise to the idea of a "waste hierarchy". In essence, waste can be divided into three categories:

(1)  Waste which need not be produced at all;

(2)  Waste which can be recycled;

(3)  Waste which must inevitably be produced but which cannot be recycled.

Needless to say, these categories are characterised by some degree of flexibility because there is no clear consensus on when waste arisings can be said to be economically preventable, or on which types of waste can be efficiently recycled. However, the distinctions are useful in that they enable policy to be directed towards an allocation of resources that is efficient in general terms.

In summary, the government's waste policy is that first, waste arisings should where possible be prevented or minimised at source; secondly, waste which *is* produced should be recycled where possible; and thirdly, that where waste is unsuitable for recycling, it should be disposed of by the method which causes least harm to the environment.

A consultation paper issued in January 1995, and likely to form the basis of the National Waste Strategy,[4] sets targets for the identification and management of

---

[3] RCEP (1993) Seventeenth Report: *Incineration of Waste,* Cmnd. 2181 (1993).
[4] The National Waste Strategy is to be drawn up by the Secretary of State in accordance with EPA 1990, s.44A, which was inserted by s.92 of the Environment Act 1995.

different types of waste. The implementation of U.K. waste policy, however, has not yet entailed the statutory classification of waste arisings in terms of the three categories described above. Rather, under the existing statutory regime, waste is variously classified as non-controlled waste, controlled waste, hazardous waste and special waste. These classifications evolved at a time when the principal method of dealing with waste was by disposal, and whilst they adequately serve the purposes of a *waste disposal* regime, they are, perhaps, not wholly appropriate for achieving the objectives of a statutory regime geared towards *waste management*.

The practical problem in implementing the concept of a "waste hierarchy" is the separation of recyclable waste from waste destined for final disposal. Minor initiatives such as "bottle banks" provide an inadequate solution because they do nothing to tackle the much larger problem of industrial waste. In the long term, it may be that the only effective way to prevent industry from disposing of recyclable waste is to incorporate into the waste management regime an extensive (and inevitably controversial) reclassification of waste according to its potential for recycling, with appropriate fiscal penalties for its wrongful disposal. The seeds of such a radical approach are to be found in existing policy and to a limited extent in the legislation which is examined below, but it remains to be seen whether they will germinate.

## THE INFLUENCE OF THE E.C. ON THE U.K.'S WASTE REGIME

E.C. policy on waste, as outlined in the Environmental Action Programmes, has remained constant. It is re-stated in the Fifth Action Programme in the following terms:

- The prevention of waste production: this is to be achieved by the increased use of clean technologies and by effecting changes in patterns of product consumption throughout the Community by such initiatives as eco-labelling;

- The recovery of waste products: this is to be achieved through sorting and segregation of waste material and subsequent recycling;

- The safe disposal of waste: this is to be ensured by a reduction in the volume of waste disposed of and by implementing stricter standards for the disposal of waste.

The European Commission has recently published its waste strategy.[5] This emphasises the concept of "producer responsibility", *i.e* that manufacturers must take responsibility for the waste which they create. The document has been criticised by Greenpeace, however, who have expressed the view that the Commission is hoping to conceal a limited number of concrete proposals behind a concept that is not in fact new, but is merely a restatement of the "polluter pays" principle.[6] Section 93 of the Environment Act 1995 gives effect to the concept of producer responsibility, by empowering the Secretary of State to make regulations.

---

[5] See COM (doc.) 96, 399.
[6] See ENDS 261, 36 1996.

The most significant influence of the E.C. on U.K. waste policy has been the Framework Directive on Waste, which was implemented by the Waste Management Licensing Regulations 1994. The Directive was originally adopted in 1975 and was substantially amended in 1991. It provides for a common definition of waste throughout the Community, and requires Member States to ensure that waste handling is licensed by a competent authority, and that waste is dealt with without environmental harm. In addition, the Directive provides that Member States must take appropriate measures to prevent or reduce the production of waste at source. In this regard, the Framework Directive is now supplemented by the Directive on Packaging and Packaging Waste. Besides the Framework Directive on Waste, there are a number of other Directives relevant to waste disposal. In particular, there are Directives on the incineration of waste.[7] These are implemented in U.K. law through the Integrated Pollution Control and Local Authority Air Pollution Control regimes contained in Part I of the Environmental Protection Act 1990.

Other moves by the E.C. in the field of waste, however, have run into difficulties. The proposed Landfill Directive, which aimed to harmonise the standards of landfill sites within the Community, was overwhelmingly rejected by the European Parliament (at the time of writing, the Commission has adopted a common position on its second attempt). During the debate, a major difference became apparent between the U.K. and the E.C. in relation to the treatment of waste before disposal. The E.C. favours the treatment of degradable waste before it is placed in a landfill site, in order to reduce emissions of methane gas, which not only causes landfill sites to explode, but also makes a significant contribution to the "greenhouse" effect, causing global warming. The E.C. also sees landfill sites as a method of waste disposal of last resort. In contrast, 85 per cent of waste in the U.K. is disposed of to landfill sites. Further, the U.K. is reluctant to treat waste before it is put into landfill sites, arguing that this will entail unnecessary expense. The U.K. is fortunate in having fewer problems with the emission of greenhouse gases than its continental partners because of its large resources of natural gas, which are displacing coal for use in power generation. The U.K. will therefore satisfy the timetable for the reduction of greenhouse gases set out in the Convention on Climate Change, without the need for pre-treatment of landfill waste.

Attempts by the E.C. to require producers of waste to compensate individuals suffering damage as a result of their activities have also run into difficulties. The Draft Directive on Civil Liability for Damage Caused by Waste is not to be proceeded with. The Commission has indicated that it is inappropriate to proceed with the concept of civil liability for waste while progress in the field of civil liability for environmental damage generally is so uncertain.

# THE WASTE MANAGEMENT REGIME IN THE U.K.

## The Regulatory Bodies

Prior to the Environment Act 1995, responsibility for waste was divided between three separate bodies: waste collection authorities (W.C.A.s); waste disposal authorities

[7] Dir. 89/369 [1989] O.J. L163/32 and 89/429 [1989] O.J. L203/50.

(W.D.A.s); and waste regulation authorities (W.R.A.s). These bodies were effectively departments of local authorities. The Environment Act 1995 transferred the functions of waste disposal authorities and waste regulation authorities to the Environment Agency with effect from April 1996.

Under the Environmental Protection Act 1990, local authorities were required to make administrative arrangements to ensure that their functions as waste disposal authorities did not conflict with their duties as waste regulation authorities.[8] In particular, they were required to form local authority waste disposal *companies* which carried out waste disposal operations at arm's length from both waste collection authorities and waste regulation authorities.[9] This separation of functions is still required even though the functions of W.D.A.s and W.R.A.s have been taken over by the Agency.

## Waste Collection Authorities

District councils, or in Greater London, London borough councils or the Common Council of the City of London, are waste collection authorities (W.C.A.s).[10] Each authority has a duty to make arrangements for the collection of all household waste from premises within its area. However, the authority need not arrange to collect waste which, in its opinion, is situated in so isolated or inaccessible a place that the cost of collecting it would be unreasonably high, provided that the authority is satisfied in such a case that adequate disposal arrangements can be made by the person who controls the waste.[11] In addition, W.C.A.s have a duty, if requested to do so by the occupier, to make arrangements for the collection of commercial waste from any premises.[12] They may also, if requested, arrange to collect industrial waste.[13] W.C.A.s are entitled to make a reasonable charge for the collection of commercial and industrial waste. Indeed, it is their duty to recover the cost of collecting industrial waste and (except in cases where they consider it inappropriate) to recover the cost of collecting commercial waste.[14] No charge, however, may be made by the authority for the collection of household waste, except where the householder has specifically requested the collection of certain types of household waste not normally collected by the authority.[15]

W.C.A.s also have a vital function to perform in respect of the recycling of household and commercial waste. They have a duty to make waste recycling plans for their area.[16] In addition, they may buy or otherwise acquire waste for recycling (*e.g.* by keeping it once they have collected it) and may then sell on the recycled products.[17] W.C.A.s also have a very important power to facilitate the recycling of waste by ensuring that when waste is left for collection, it is not mixed with other waste of a

[8] EPA 1990, s.30(7).
[9] *ibid.*, s.32.
[10] *ibid.*, s.30(3).
[11] *ibid.*, s.45(1) (a).
[12] *ibid.*, s.45(1) (b).
[13] *ibid.*, s.45(2).
[14] EPA 1990, s.45(4).
[15] Those types of household waste for which a reasonable collection charge can be made are set out in the Controlled Waste Regulations 1992 (S.I. 1992 No. 588).
[16] EPA 1990, s.49.
[17] *ibid.*, s.55(3).

non-recyclable type: a W.C.A. may, by serving a notice on the occupier of premises, require him to place his waste for collection in receptacles of a specified number and type. The notice may include a requirement that waste of different types must be placed in different receptacles.[18] In relation to household waste, this power is exercisable absolutely, provided that the requirements are reasonable. In relation to industrial and commercial waste, however, the power to require that waste be stored for collection in receptacles of a particular kind is exercisable only if it appears to the W.C.A. that the waste would cause a nuisance or be detrimental to the amenities of the locality if it were not so stored.[19]

In relation to commercial and industrial waste, then, there is no explicit statutory provision enabling the W.C.A. to require that waste destined for recycling be placed in separate receptacles. However, W.C.A.s have a general power to specify, in relation to such waste, what can and cannot be put into receptacles.[20] In relation to commercial waste, it is submitted that this power is capable of being exercised to ensure the separation of waste for recycling, given that the W.C.A. has the power to retain commercial waste for recycling unless the Environment Agency objects.[21] In relation to industrial waste, however, the W.C.A. has no power to retain such waste for recycling, and no duty to make recycling plans. Recycling plans for industrial waste are the responsibility of the Secretary of State in consultation with the Environment Agency.[22] It is submitted that if, in relation to industrial waste, a W.C.A. were to serve a notice requiring that certain types of waste be put into certain types of receptacles with a view to facilitating recycling, rather than for the prevention of a nuisance or detriment to the locality, the notice would be *ultra vires* and liable to be quashed on judicial review. Whether this result derives from legislative design or legislative accident is unclear. What is clear, however, is that if a W.C.A. cannot legitimately require the separation of industrial waste for recycling purposes, its waste recycling functions are severely curtailed.

## The Environment Agency

The Environment Agency is responsible for the disposal of controlled waste both by local authority waste disposal companies and by other persons (known as "waste disposal contractors"[23]) who keep, treat or dispose of controlled waste as part of a business. The Agency is responsible for granting waste management licences to such persons and for supervising their activities.

## The Removal of Controlled Waste

Both the Environment Agency and waste collection authorities may require the removal of controlled waste that has been unlawfully deposited.[24] They may serve a

---

[18] *ibid.*, s.46(2).
[19] *ibid.*, s.47(2).
[20] *ibid.*, s.47(3)(d).
[21] *ibid.*, s.48.
[22] *ibid.*, s.44A (inserted by EA 1995, s.92).
[23] *ibid.*, s.30(5).
[24] *ibid.*, s.59.

notice on the occupier of land requiring him, within a specified period of not less than 21 days, to remove the waste or to take specified steps to eliminate or reduce the consequences of the deposit. Failure to comply with the notice is an offence. The occupier may appeal against the notice to a magistrates' court which may quash the notice if it is satisfied that the occupier neither deposited nor knowingly caused, nor knowingly permitted the deposit of the waste. In addition, where waste is deposited on land but either the occupier of the land was not at fault, or the land is not in occupation, the Agency or the W.C.A. may remove the waste itself and charge the cost of so doing to the person who deposited the waste if and when he is subsequently found. It should be remembered that the deposit of waste on land may also give rise to the commission of a nuisance at common law or a statutory nuisance.

## The Old Statutory Regime

Prior to the Environmental Protection Act 1990, waste had been regulated by the Control of Pollution Act 1974, which provided that waste could be disposed of only in accordance with a "Waste Disposal Licence". This regime, however, had a number of significant failings. In particular, the offences which the Act created were narrowly directed towards the unlawful *deposit* of waste. The regime focused on the *final disposal* of waste and did little to ensure that waste did not cause problems prior to this. Moreover, little provision was made for the aftercare of waste disposal sites. The operator of a waste disposal facility could effectively abdicate responsibility for a site by surrendering his licence after he had completed his activities, even where they had resulted in contaminated land which was a continuing source of pollution. The ability to surrender licences effectively undermined any attempt to impose, through planning law, a proper system of monitoring of waste sites once operations had ceased.[25]

Another serious deficiency of the old regime was that local authorities, who were responsible for granting Waste Disposal Licences, very often carried out waste disposal operations themselves, so that they were in effect self-regulating. This did little to engender public confidence in the operation of the regime. The failings of the old regime were noted by the House of Commons Environment Committee on Toxic Waste, whose second report stated:

> "Never, in any of our enquiries into environmental problems, have we experienced such consistent and universal criticism of existing legislation and of central and local government as we have done during the course of this inquiry."

## The New Statutory Regime

The current waste management licensing regime seeks to remedy many of the defects of its predecessor. It eventually came into force in May 1994 after much bureaucratic delay and amidst a good deal of sharp criticism from the waste management industry, who felt that they had been ill-informed and under-prepared for its introduction by the Department of the Environment. Part II of the Environmental Protection Act 1990

---

[25] Ball and Bell, *Environmental Law* (3rd ed., 1995), p. 361.

provides the basic foundations of the regime. The provisions of the Act, however, are supplemented by the Waste Management Licensing Regulations 1994.[26] These regulations implement the E.C. Framework Directive on Waste.[27] In addition, there is guidance from the Department of the Environment in the form of Waste Management Papers[28] and a Circular.[29]

The fact that the law on waste derives from all of these sources together inevitably means that it is fairly difficult to understand. In general terms, however, Part II takes what may be referred to as a "cradle to grave" approach to waste. That is to say it ensures that legal control is exercised over waste from the moment it originates to the moment when it is finally disposed of. The regime therefore regulates waste when it is being kept, treated, deposited, and when it is being transported. In summary, Part II makes it a criminal offence to deposit, keep, treat or dispose of "controlled waste" otherwise than in accordance with the conditions of a Waste Management Licence.[30] Licences are issued to the operators of waste disposal facilities by the Environment Agency. This ensures that the Agency maintains control over all aspects of waste management. Central to the operation of the regime is the requirement that no-one is entitled to hold a Waste Management Licence unless that person is a "fit and proper person" to do so.[31]

Waste Management Licences are issued only to those persons who are in occupation of land, or who are operating a mobile plant for the management of waste. To secure control over wider aspects of waste management, such as the transportation of it, the Act imposes a "duty of care" (similar to that found in the tort of negligence) on anyone who imports, produces, carries, keeps, treats or disposes of waste. Such persons are required to take all measures which are reasonably necessary to prevent the waste from escaping, to ensure that waste is transferred only to an authorised person, and to prevent others from treating, keeping or disposing of waste without a licence. It is a criminal offence to fail to comply with the duty.

## THE MEANING OF "WASTE" AND "CONTROLLED WASTE"

### The Statutory Definition of "Waste"

The original definition of "waste" contained in the Environmental Protection Act 1990 was amended by the Environment Act 1995, which substituted a new statutory definition of "waste"[32] which is similar to that found in the E.C. Framework Directive on Waste. The Environmental Protection Act 1990 now therefore defines waste as: " . . . any substance or object in the categories set out in Schedule 2B to this Act which the holder discards or intends or is required to discard . . . "

---

[26] S.I. 1994 No. 1056.
[27] Dir. 75/442/EEC; [1975] O.J. L194/39 (as amended by Dir. 91/156/EEC); [1991] O.J. L78/32.
[28] *e.g. Waste Management Paper No. 4 (Licensing of Waste Management Facilities)* (DoE 1988).
[29] Circular 11/94 on Waste Management Licensing and the Framework Directive on Waste.
[30] EPA 1990, s.33.
[31] *ibid.,* s.36(3).
[32] EA 1995, Sched. 22, para. 88.

The categories of waste set out in Schedule 2B are the same as those contained in the Framework Directive. Although these categories are useful in providing a definition of waste by example, they fail to provide a comprehensive definition of waste for the simple reason that the last of them is a "catch-all" category, which defines as waste: "Any materials, substances or products which are not contained in the above categories."[33]

Therefore, in the absence of an exhaustive statutory definition of "waste", the question of whether a particular thing is or is not waste depends on the actions and intentions of the "holder" of the waste and is ultimately a matter for the courts, whose views on the question are examined below.

## The Concept of "Waste"

One of the most fundamental problems posed by the existing legislation is that of arriving at a practical definition of the concept of "waste". As has been said, according to the statutory definition of "waste", anything which the holder discards, intends to discard, or is required to discard will be treated as waste. A "holder" of waste for these purposes is defined as: " . . . the producer of the waste or the person who is in possession of it . . ."

A "producer" of waste is defined as: " . . . any person whose activities produce waste or any person who carries out pre-processing, mixing or other operations resulting in a change in the nature or composition of this waste."[34]

The fundamental question, however, is what is meant by "discarding" waste. The problem is that one person's waste may be another person's raw material. As greater emphasis is placed on recycling, the distinction becomes increasingly difficult to draw in practical situations where materials are transferred from one person, who does not want them, to another person, who wants them as a raw material for recycling. The Department of the Environment has suggested in a Circular[35] that the purpose of the Directive is to treat as waste: " . . . those substances or objects which fall out of the commercial cycle or out of the chain of utility."

On the face of it, therefore, where a material is destined to be subject to a recovery or recycling procedure, even if this involves the holder "discarding" the material by passing it on to another, that material is not waste because it has not fallen out of the commercial cycle or chain of utility.

The picture is complicated, however, by the distinction which the Circular draws between "waste recovery operations" and "specialist waste recovery operations". Substances destined for the former are not normally to be treated as waste, whilst those destined for the latter are. "Waste recovery operations" are listed in the Waste Management Licensing Regulations 1994, and include the recycling of materials such as oils and solvents. Such recycling will often take place as an integral part of a production process where the by-product of one part of the process forms the raw material for another part. On the other hand, a material which is destined for *specialist* waste recovery operations will be treated as having been discarded and as having

---

[33] EPA 1990 (as amended), Sched. 2B, para. 16.
[34] *ibid.*, s.75(2) (as amended by EA 1995, Sched. 22, para. 88).
[35] Circular 11/94 (DoE).

(albeit temporarily) fallen out of the commercial cycle or chain of utility. Such material will therefore be waste unless and until it has emerged from the specialist recovery process as a useful product.

The distinction between "waste recovery operations" and "specialist waste recovery operations" is a fine one and is not assisted by the fact that the Circular contains no clear definition of the latter. It is submitted, however, that the purport of the Circular is that where a substance is *heavily* contaminated, so that it has no useful purpose until the contaminants are removed at substantial cost, it will be waste, whilst where only *light* contamination is involved, the substance may be seen as having an immediate use (albeit that this involves some prior treatment at cost) and will not, therefore, be waste.

## The Approach of the Courts

Although the statutory definition of waste and the guidance contained in the Circular focus in general terms on the use to which a particular material is to be put (the "utility" of the material), this general approach does not wholly reflect the approach which was adopted by the courts in determining the meaning of "waste", as that word appeared in the Control of Pollution Act 1974. The relevant case law on the meaning of waste, which was decided on the basis of the definition of waste contained in that Act (substances which were broken, worn out, contaminated or otherwise spoiled), indicates that the sole consideration for the courts has been whether the producer of a material has, in common sense terms, discarded it. The courts have drawn a distinction between the producer of the material and a person who subsequently takes possession of it. In deciding whether a material is waste, the intentions of the former have been held to be relevant, whilst the intentions of the latter have not. In other words, under the Control of Pollution Act 1974, if the producer of a material had a use for it, that material would not normally be waste, but if a person was in possession of material which he had not produced, that material was capable of being waste even though he had a use for it.

In *Meston Technical Services Ltd* and *Wright v. Warwickshire County Council*,[36] the defendants were prosecuted under the Control of Pollution Act 1974 for breach of the conditions of their waste disposal licence. They carried on the business of purchasing liquid waste and processing it into materials which they then sold. After the liquid waste had been collected but before it had been processed, it had to be stored in drums. The defendants argued that because they had a use for the liquid material within the drums, it was not, once it had come into their possession, waste. Accordingly, they argued that the conditions of their waste disposal licence did not apply to the storage of the drums. The Divisional Court rejected the defendants' argument that if they themselves did not regard the material as waste, but regarded it as something of value, it could not be waste. Instead, the court held that the value of the material and the intention of the holder of it were not relevant. Once a material had been discarded by its producer, it remained waste until it had been changed into a different material by the recovery process for which it was destined.

---

[36] [1995] Env. L.R. D. 36.

This decision is in keeping with the approach adopted by the European Court of Justice in the linked cases of *Vessoso* and *Zanetti*,[37] in which two Italians were charged with transporting waste without an authorisation under Italian law. They argued that because the material in question was destined for recycling, it could not be waste. However, the court held that the definition of waste contained in the Framework Directive was concerned with the pollution and health hazards posed by the material and that a material could be waste notwithstanding its potential for recycling.

In *Cheshire County Council v. Armstrong's Transport (Wigan) Ltd*,[38] the defendants were prosecuted under the Control of Pollution Act 1974 for carrying out waste disposal operations without a licence. They collected rubble from a building site and subjected it to a crushing process. They then returned the crushed rubble to the site where it was re-used as a building material. The Divisional Court upheld the defendants' argument that their contractual obligation to return the material to the site in a crushed state meant that the original producers of the material (the builders) had not intended to discard it. This was sufficient to show that the rubble was not waste. The defendants' operations were not, therefore, waste disposal operations and accordingly did not require a waste disposal licence.

The facts of the *Armstrong's Transport* case may be contrasted with those in the earlier case of *Kent County Council v. Queenborough Rolling Mill Co. Ltd*,[39] where the court took the view that the building materials in question were waste because they had been discarded by their producer, even though they were put to a useful purpose by their subsequent recipient: The defendants were prosecuted under the Control of Pollution Act 1974 for depositing waste on land without a waste disposal licence. They collected china, china clay and broken pottery from a disused site and used it to infill an area of land which had subsided. The defendants argued that because the materials concerned were being put to a legitimate building use, they were not waste. However, the Divisional Court held that the use to which the materials were put was not a relevant factor in determining whether or not they were waste. What was important was the nature of the material when it was discarded by the person who had originally produced it.

Looked at purely in terms of the utility of the materials, it is not easy to reconcile the *Armstrong's Transport* case with the earlier decision in *Queenborough Rolling Mill*. In both cases the scrap materials in question were put to use as part of a construction process and, on the face of it, would not seem to have fallen out of the commercial cycle or chain of utility. The distinction between the cases rests on the difference of intention on the part of the people who originally produced the materials. In *Armstrong's Transport*, the builders did not intend to discard the materials, but intended to have them returned to them. In *Queenborough Rolling Mill*, however, the producer of the materials had intended to abandon them.

The problem with the courts' approach, then, is that it has depended on making a clear distinction between the producer of a material on the one hand and the non-producer in subsequent possession of a material on the other. This distinction, whilst acceptable for defining waste under the Control of Pollution Act 1974, may be

---

[37] Joined cases C–206/88 and C–207/88; [1990] I E.C.R. 1461.
[38] [1995] Env. L.R. 62.
[39] 89 L.G.R. 306.

inappropriate for defining waste under the new legislation. The distinction developed by the courts does not sit comfortably with the new statutory definition of waste, which explicitly provides that waste is to be defined by reference to the activities of the "holder" of a material, rather than by reference to the activities of the producer alone, and goes on to provide that the "holder" can be either the producer of the material or simply the person in possession of it. Thus it would seem that the courts, in developing a test for the definition of waste which depends on the intentions of the producer of a material, but excludes consideration of the intentions of its subsequent possessor, have been to some extent at odds with the policy of the Department of the Environment, which would allow waste to be defined simply by reference to the intentions of the person in possession of it.

## Definition of "Controlled Waste"

In general terms, the Environmental Protection Act 1990 regulates activities concerned with "controlled" waste only. Therefore, once it is decided whether or not a material is "waste", it is necessary to go on to consider whether or not it is "controlled waste". The expression "controlled waste" as it originally appeared in the Environmental Protection Act 1990, has, like the statutory term "waste", suffered a change in meaning by a convoluted route. "Controlled waste" was defined widely by the Environmental Protection Act 1990 as: " . . . household, industrial or commercial waste or any such waste."[40]

However, the Waste Management Licensing Regulations 1994 (by amending the Controlled Waste Regulations 1992[41]) implement the E.C. Framework Directive on Waste and provide that waste which is not "Directive waste" shall not be treated as household, commercial or industrial waste. In effect, therefore, the three categories of waste referred to in the Act are now subsumed under a single general category of "Directive waste", with which the statutory term "controlled waste" is synonymous. The old distinction between household, commercial and industrial waste, however, remains of limited importance in relation to the powers of waste collection authorities.[42]

## Waste which is not "Controlled Waste"

The 1994 Regulations provide that certain types of waste which are, by the Directive, excluded from its scope, are similarly excluded from the definition of "Directive waste" in the regulations (and are therefore excluded from the definition of "controlled waste").

The types of waste which the Directive excludes from its scope are:

(a) Gaseous effluents emitted into the atmosphere; and

---

[40] EPA 1990, s.75(4).
[41] S.I. 1992 No. 588.
[42] See p. 174 above. The distinction between the three types of waste is largely self-evident, and derives from the type of premises on which the waste is generated. For a thorough analysis of the distinction, however, see The Controlled Waste Regulations 1992 (S.I. 1992 No. 588) and Bates, *U.K. Waste Law* (1992).

# Diagram 4: The Meaning of "Waste"

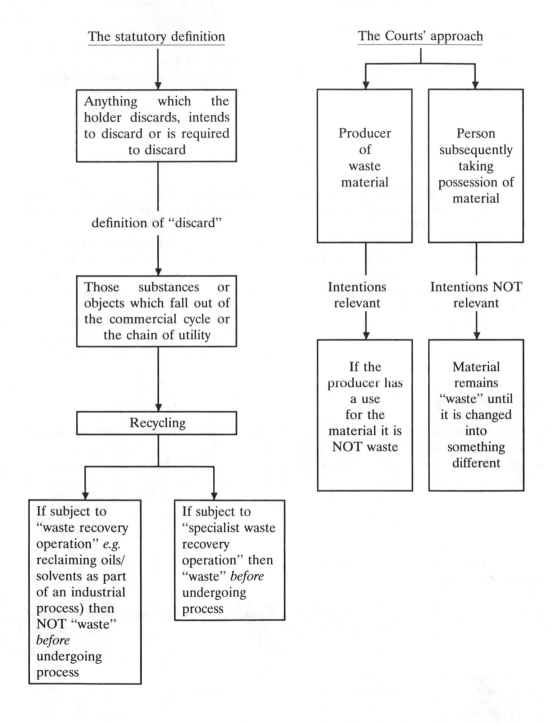

The statutory definition

Anything which the holder discards, intends to discard or is required to discard

definition of "discard"

Those substances or objects which fall out of the commercial cycle or the chain of utility

Recycling

If subject to "waste recovery operation" *e.g.* reclaiming oils/ solvents as part of an industrial process) then NOT "waste" *before* undergoing process

If subject to "specialist waste recovery operation" then "waste" *before* undergoing process

The Courts' approach

Producer of waste material

Person subsequently taking possession of material

Intentions relevant

Intentions NOT relevant

If the producer has a use for the material it is NOT waste

Material remains "waste" until it is changed into something different

(b) *In so far as they are covered by existing legislation within Member States*, the following types of waste:

   (i) Radioactive waste;

   (ii) Waste resulting from prospecting, extraction, treatment and storage of mineral resources and from the working of quarries;

   (iii) Faecal agricultural waste, animal carcases and other natural, non-dangerous substances used in farming;

   (iv) Waste water, with the exception of waste in liquid form;

   (v) Decommissioned explosives.

The policy of the E.C. is that Directives should address these waste issues on an individual basis. Some of them, for example the disposal of animal carcases, are covered by existing Directives,[43] and most are already specifically addressed by other U.K. legislation and consequently are exempt from control under the Environmental Protection Act 1990.[44]

Gaseous emissions and waste water have their own statutory regimes and are dealt with elsewhere in this book, whilst the complex and stringent controls relating to the handling of radioactive waste are beyond its scope. The deposit of mining and quarrying waste is controlled only by planning legislation. Explosive waste is regulated by the Explosives Act 1875.

In summary, then, all waste which is not excluded by virtue of one of the categories above is "Directive waste" (*i.e.* "controlled waste") and is subject to the requirements of the statutory regime contained in Part II of the Environmental Protection Act 1990.

## Special Waste

"Special waste" is defined by reference to the Control of Pollution (Special Waste) Regulations 1980,[45] which were made under the Control of Pollution Act 1974. Although the Environmental Protection Act 1990 empowers the Secretary of State to make regulations in respect of "dangerous or intractable waste" by designating it "special waste",[46] at the time of writing the relevant section of that Act is not in force and no such regulations have been made. The purpose of the section is to allow for the eventual implementation of the E.C. Directive on Hazardous Waste[47] by providing stricter controls than those already in existence under the Control of Pollution (Special Waste) Regulations 1980. These regulations define "special waste" as controlled waste that either:

   (i) Consists of or contains certain substances listed in the regulations and is for that reason dangerous to life; or

---

[43] Dir. 90/667/EEC; [1990] O.J. L365/51.
[44] On non-controlled waste see Bates, *U.K. Waste Law* (1992), p. 32 *et seq.*
[45] S.I. 1980 No. 1709.
[46] EPA 1990, s.62.
[47] Dir. 91/689/EEC; [1991] O.J. L377/20.

(ii)  Which has a flashpoint of 21 degrees Celsius or less; or

(iii)  Is a medicinal product available only on prescription.

## THE MECHANICS OF THE WASTE MANAGEMENT REGIME

### The Primary Offences

The Environmental Protection Act 1990 creates a number of offences in relation to waste:

It is an offence to *deposit* controlled waste on land or to *knowingly cause* or *knowingly permit* controlled waste to be deposited, unless a waste management licence authorising the deposit is in force and the deposit is in accordance with the conditions of that licence.[48]

It is also an offence to *keep, treat or dispose of controlled waste* either on land or by means of mobile plant *except in accordance with a licence.*[49]

The effect of the Waste Management Licensing Regulations 1994 has been to limit the meaning of the words "keep, treat or dispose of waste" to the waste management operations listed in the regulations.[50] These are known as "Directive disposal" and "Directive recovery" operations and are identical to the operations listed in the E.C. Framework Directive on Waste. They include all of the common methods of disposing of waste such as landfill and incineration, as well as the reclamation of certain substances such as acids, solvents and metals.

### The Residual Offence

For good measure, the Act also provides that it is an offence to deal with controlled waste in any manner which is likely to cause pollution of the environment or harm to human health.[51] Effectively, this means that whilst the conditions of a Waste Management Licence provide guidance to operators of waste disposal facilities, they can never provide an excuse for dealing with waste in an unacceptable way. Obviously, licence conditions cannot be imposed to cover every eventuality. The "residual" offence therefore ensures that environmentally acceptable standards are maintained in respect of any aspect of a waste handling operation not regulated by a specific condition. The "residual" offence is therefore similar to the "residual" duty, within the IPC regime, to use BATNEEC to render harmless all substances before they are released to the environment.

The Waste Management Licensing Regulations 1994 list a great many activities which are exempt from the requirement of a Waste Management Licence, for example, the storage of controlled waste at the place where it has been produced pending its collection and the deposit of certain organic controlled waste on land as a fertiliser.

[48] EPA 1990, s.33(a).
[49] *ibid.*, s.33(b).
[50] S.I. 1994 No. 1056, Sched. 4.
[51] EPA 1990, s.33(c).

However, any "establishment or undertaking" (as opposed to a private individual) which carries on an activity in respect of controlled waste which is exempt under the regulations must register that activity with the Environment Agency by giving notification of the activity and stating the specific exemption relied on.[52] Moreover, although the activities listed are exempt from the need for a licence, they may still fall foul of the "residual" offence. On the other hand, where household waste is dealt with within the curtilage of a dwelling with the permission of the occupier, not only is no Waste Management Licence required, but such activities can never form the basis of a prosecution for the "residual" offence.[53] In addition, the Secretary of State may prescribe that certain deposits, for example those which are small and of a temporary nature, should be entirely exempt from the provisions of the Act which govern controlled waste.[54]

## Depositing Dangerous Non-Controlled Waste

The Act also provides for a further offence which relates to the deposit of non-controlled waste, although the provision which creates it has not yet been brought into force.[55] The provision makes it an offence to deposit or knowingly cause or knowingly permit the deposit of *any* waste where, if the waste in question were "special waste", an offence would be committed. The drafting of this provision is somewhat obscure. In essence, however, it is designed to make it an offence to deposit, by fly-tipping or otherwise, any non-controlled waste which has the noxious or dangerous characteristics of "special waste" but has not actually been prescribed as "special waste" by the Secretary of State in regulations.[56]

## The Meaning of "Knowingly Cause"

Under the Control of Pollution Act 1974, it was an offence to "cause or knowingly permit" the deposit of waste. Causing the deposit of waste was an offence of strict liability which did not require proof of *mens rea*. In other words, once it had been shown that the defendant had caused the deposit, either by physically depositing the waste or by giving instructions for this to be done, it was not necessary to show that the defendant knew that the deposit was illegal.[57] The expression used in the Environmental Protection Act 1990, however, is "knowingly cause". According to one commentator, this implies that the prosecution must prove that the defendant not only caused the deposit of the waste, but also knew that the waste was controlled waste and that the deposit was not authorised by a waste management licence.[58] However, where waste is deposited from a vehicle, the Act provides that the person who controls the vehicle, or is in a position to control the vehicle, shall be treated as knowingly causing

---

[52] S.I. 1994 No. 1056, reg. 18(1).
[53] EPA 1990, s.33(2).
[54] *ibid.*, s.33(3).
[55] *ibid.*, s.63.
[56] Bates, *U.K. Waste Law* (1992), p. 39.
[57] See *Alphacell Ltd v. Woodward* [1972] 2 All E.R. 475, and Chapter 9, below.
[58] Bates, *U.K. Waste Law* (1992), p. 171.

the deposit of the waste whether or not he gave instructions for this to be done.[59] The effect of this provision is to make employers vicariously liable for unauthorised acts of "fly-tipping" perpetrated by their employees.

## The Meaning of "Knowingly Permit"

A person will "permit" the deposit, keeping or treating of waste if he has knowledge of the circumstances in which this is being done and, although he has some control over the operations, he fails to prevent them.[60] What precisely is meant by "knowingly" permitting under the Environmental Protection Act 1990 is unclear. This is because the courts, in interpreting this phrase as it appeared in the Control of Pollution Act 1974, gave to the word "knowingly" a restricted meaning. For example, in *Ashcroft v. Cambro Waste Products Ltd,*[61] it was held that the offence of "knowingly permitting" was made out if the prosecution could show that the defendant knew of the deposit; they did not have to go on to show that he knew that this was in contravention of a waste disposal licence. The restricted meaning given to the word "knowingly" in the phrase "knowingly permit" now appears to be inconsistent with the intention of Parliament as evidenced by the addition of the word "knowingly" to the word "cause" in the new legislation (see above). If such an old-style restricted interpretation is given to the words "knowingly permitting" as they now appear in Part II of the Environmental Protection Act 1990, it may produce the strange result that the degree of knowledge required to establish the offence of "knowingly permitting" may be lower than is required to establish the offence of "knowingly causing". It has been rightly suggested that since the offence of "knowingly permitting" is a penal provision, the correct approach for the courts should be to apply the same test as for "knowingly causing", and to require that the prosecution show not only knowledge of the operations but also knowledge that an offence was being committed.[62]

## Defences

It is a defence for a person charged with any of the offences described above to show that he took all reasonable precautions and exercised all due diligence to avoid the commission of an offence.[63] This defence is valuable in cases where, despite his making adequate enquiries, the receiver of a consignment of material has been misled by the person delivering it as to the nature of the material. However, in such a situation the defendant must show that his system of work is such that very thorough enquiries are made of the deliverer of the material in order to satisfy himself that it may properly be dealt with without a waste management licence.

The scope of an analogous defence, contained in the Control of Pollution Act 1974, was considered in *Durham County Council v. Peter Connors Industrial Services Ltd.*[64]

[59] EPA 1990, s.33(5).
[60] *Berton v. Alliance Economic Investment Co.* [1922] 1 K.B. 742; *Rochford R.C. v. Port of London* [1914] 2 K.B. 916.
[61] [1981] 3 All E.R. 703.
[62] Bates, *U.K. Waste Law* (1992), p. 172.
[63] EPA 1990, s.33(7).
[64] [1993] Env. L.R. 197.

The defendants in that case sought to show that they had a proper and adequate system for the regular collection of materials from a skip. They had been told at the start of their operations what the skip was to contain, but had proceeded to collect materials from the skip without checking its contents on every occasion. The court held that the defence required a separate enquiry to be made of a person who knew the nature of the contents of the skip on each occasion that its contents were collected.

It is a defence for an employee charged with an offence to show that he acted under instructions from his employer and that he neither knew, nor had reason to suppose, that his actions constituted an offence. It is also a defence to show that the acts alleged to constitute an offence were done in an emergency in order to avoid danger to the public, and that as soon as reasonably practicable after they were done, particulars of the acts were furnished to the Environment Agency.

## Penalties

The maximum penalty for the offences described above is a £20,000 fine and six months' imprisonment if the offence is tried in the magistrates' court, or an unlimited fine and two years' imprisonment where the offence is tried in the Crown Court. However, if the waste in question is special waste, the Crown Court may impose a maximum of five years' imprisonment.[65]

## Application for a Licence

As has been said, except in the case of activities which are exempted under the Waste Management Licensing Regulations 1994, a Waste Management Licence is required for the carrying on of operations which amount to "Directive disposal" or "Directive recovery" of "Directive waste" (controlled waste). Where the operations are carried out on land, the licence is known as a "site licence". Applications for site licences are made to the Environment Agency by the occupier of the land on which the operations are to be carried on. In the case of a licence relating to operations carried on by means of a mobile plant, the application is made by the person who operates the plant.[66] The application for a licence is made in writing, and it is an offence for an applicant to make a statement in an application (or in an application for modification, surrender or transfer of a licence) which he knows to be false in any material particular, or recklessly to make any statement which is false. The maximum penalty for the offence is a £5,000 fine in the magistrates' court or an unlimited fine and two years' imprisonment in the Crown Court.[67] Applications are made on a standard form provided by the Agency and must be accompanied by a fee and such information as the Agency reasonably requires of the applicant.[68] If the applicant fails to furnish this information, the Agency may either refuse to proceed with the application altogether, or refuse to proceed until the information is provided.[69]

[65] EPA 1990, s.33(8) and (9).
[66] *ibid.,* s.35.
[67] *ibid.,* s.44.
[68] *ibid.,* s.36(1) (as amended by EA 1995, Sched. 22).
[69] *ibid.,* s.36(1A) (inserted by EA 1995).

## Grant of a Licence

Before granting a licence, the Environment Agency must consult the local planning authority in the area of the proposed site (or, in the case of a licence for a mobile plant, the local planning authority in the area where the operator has his principal place of business).[70] The Agency must also consult the Health and Safety Executive in all cases and, where the site consists of land which has been designated a Site of Special Scientific Interest, the Agency must consult English Nature.[71] The Agency must grant or reject the application within four months of its receipt of the application form (or within such longer period as it may agree with the applicant), after which time, if the Agency has not granted the application, it is deemed to have been rejected.[72]

## Grounds for Rejecting an Application[73]

First, in cases where the proposed operation requires planning permission, no application for a Waste Management Licence can be granted unless that permission has been granted. Broadly speaking, planning permission will be required in relation to the deposit of waste on land where this involves extending the height of the land beyond its original ground level. It will also be required where the surface area of an original waste deposit is enlarged by a new deposit,[74] and where buildings or machinery are erected on a site for dealing with waste. Moreover, in some circumstances the mere act of depositing the waste can amount to an engineering operation which constitutes a material change of use of the land and requires planning permission.

Secondly, the Agency may reject an application if it is satisfied that the rejection is necessary for the purpose of preventing pollution of the environment or harm to human health. It may also do so in order to prevent serious detriment to the amenities of the locality of the site, except in cases where the operation requires planning permission and this has been granted. Thirdly, the Agency must refuse an application for a licence unless it is satisfied that the applicant is a "fit and proper person".

## The Meaning of "Fit and Proper Person"[75]

The Environmental Protection Act 1990 provides that a person will not be a "fit and proper person" to hold a waste management licence if it appears to the Environment Agency that:

(i) He or another "relevant person" has been convicted of a "relevant offence"; or

(ii) The management of the waste handling operations will not be in the hands of a "technically competent person"; or

---

[70] *ibid.,* s.36(4) (as amended by EA 1995).
[71] *ibid.,* s.36(7).
[72] *ibid.,* s.36(9).
[73] *ibid.,* s.36.
[74] Town and Country Planning Act 1990, s.55(3)(b).
[75] EPA 1990, s.74.

(iii) The person who is to hold the licence either has not made, or has no intention of making or is not in a position to make, financial provision adequate to discharge the obligations arising from the licence.

A "relevant person" may be an employee or partner of the proposed licence holder or a company of which the proposed holder was a director, manager, secretary, or similar officer. Where the proposed licence holder is itself a company, the licence may be refused if a director, manager, secretary or similar officer has been convicted of a "relevant offence", or if such a person was an officer of another company at the time when that other company was convicted of a relevant offence. The "relevant offences" are the environmental offences listed in the Waste Management Licensing Regulations 1994.[76] However, conviction of a relevant offence is not an absolute bar to obtaining a licence. The Agency may ignore relevant convictions if it considers this appropriate,[77] which it may do, for example, after a detailed consideration of the particular circumstances of an offence.

Under the regulations, a person is a "Technically Competent Person" if, and only if, he holds a "certificate of technical competence" granted by the Waste Management Industry Training and Advisory Board (WAMITAB).

The requirement that the proposed licence holder make adequate financial provision for obligations arising out of his activities has proved to be a controversial aspect of the waste management regime. The Department of the Environment has suggested in guidance[78] that financial provision for the aftercare of a site should generally be provided by the licence holder taking out insurance from a third party, or where that is not possible, by "self-insurance". There is, however, considerable uncertainty about what form this "self-insurance" should take. Originally, the Department of the Environment had taken the view that it should be in the form of a bond or pledge given by the licence holder, but this does not appear to be the position in practice. The position was succinctly considered by Lord Lucas during the passage of the Environment Bill in 1994:

" . . . waste management companies have to demonstrate that they are able to meet unquantified financial obligations for an indefinite period into the future. In some cases that date could be 50 or even 100 years away. The insurance market is not interested. So individual companies are required by the current regulatory authorities to put up, in some cases, as much as £1 million in cash — not in bonds or in promises but in hard cash — in order to meet undefined and unquantified problems."[79]

His Lordship went on to propose that, as a solution to this problem, a central fund be established for the aftercare of landfill sites, financed by a levy on the waste management industry as a whole and administered by the Environment Agency. Such a fund has not materialised, and in practice the Environment Agency continues to grant

---

[76] S.I. 1994 No. 1056, reg. 3.
[77] EPA 1990, s.74(4).
[78] *Waste Management Paper No. 4* (DoE, 1988).
[79] *per* Lord Lucas of Chilworth, *Hansard,* H.L., 1995, col. 1432.

licences on the basis of a pragmatic appraisal of the financial worth of a proposed operator, in some cases requiring no more than a business plan which deals with financial provision for aftercare of the site, and in others requiring sums of money by way of security.

## Licence Conditions

The Environment Agency may attach any conditions to a waste management licence which it considers are appropriate.[80] In particular, conditions may require things to be done in relation to a site both before the site is in operation and after it has been closed down. Such conditions may, for example, require insurance to be in place before a site is opened, or may require that a site be landscaped and monitored for gas emissions and leachate once operations have ceased.

The Agency's power to impose conditions, however, is not entirely unfettered. The Secretary of State may by regulations require that certain conditions are or are not to be included in licences.[81] He has, for example, stipulated in the Waste Management Licensing Regulations 1994, that no condition may be attached solely for the purpose of ensuring health and safety at work. Moreover, in accordance with the general principles of administrative law, conditions which do not reasonably relate to the purpose of the legislation, or which are not reasonably specific and of a kind which can reasonably be complied with by the site operator, are liable to be quashed on judicial review.

Under the Control of Pollution Act 1974, the power to impose conditions was limited to preventing the pollution of water, to ensuring that there was no danger to public health, and to preventing serious detriment to local amenities. In *Attorney-General's Reference (No.2 of 1988)*[82] it was held that the scope of this power did not allow for the imposition of a general condition prohibiting the creation of nuisances of any kind. Although the power to impose conditions is wider under the 1990 Act, it has been suggested that such a condition would still be too wide to be permissible.[83] Guidance from the Department of the Environment[84] states that in order to be reasonable, conditions should be necessary, comprehensive, unambiguous and enforceable and should enable operators to know precisely what they need to do in order to comply with them. The guidance also provides a checklist of matters which should be covered by conditions and states that conditions should not be imposed which overlap with conditions attached to planning permission for the site.

Conditions may require a licence holder to do things which, but for the condition, he would not in law be entitled to do.[85] He may, for example be required to enter on another's land to drill boreholes to monitor gases and leachate escaping from his site. The Act provides that where the consent of any person is required for such works to be undertaken, that person shall grant such rights in relation to his land as will enable the licence holder to fulfil the requirements of the condition. Before granting any licence

[80] EPA 1990, s.35(3).
[81] *ibid.*, s.35(6).
[82] [1989] 3 W.L.R. 397.
[83] Bates, *U.K. Waste Law* (1992), p. 201.
[84] *Waste Management Paper No. 4* (DoE, 1988).
[85] EPA 1990, s.35(4).

which is subject to a condition which may affect the rights of an owner, lessee or occupier of any land other than the proposed site, the Agency must give notice to and entertain representations from such persons.[86] Although the Act makes no specific provision for notice of entry to be given or for compensation to be paid to an affected landowner, it is likely that the courts will interpret the Act so as to require the landowner to grant rights on reasonable terms, which would, of course, include such matters.[87]

An operator who is aggrieved by the imposition of a condition may appeal to the Secretary of State[88] who will decide, on the basis of the criteria set out in the guidance, whether or not the condition is reasonable. In a decision concerning the conditions of a waste disposal licence granted under the Control of Pollution Act 1974, the Secretary of State stated that he will also have regard to whether conditions reflect the nature and scale of the proposed operations and the particular circumstances of the particular site. He stated that conditions should provide appropriate protection to local amenities, but should not impose an unreasonable burden on the operator of a site.[89]

## Variation of Licence Conditions

The conditions of a licence may be altered either on the initiative of the Environment Agency or on the application of the licence holder. However, where the Agency considers that it is *desirable* to vary the conditions, it can do so only to the extent that this is unlikely to require unreasonable expense on the part of the licence holder.[90] On the other hand, where the Agency considers that it is *necessary* to vary the conditions of a licence in order to prevent pollution of the environment or harm to human health, to ensure that the operations do not become seriously detrimental to the amenities of the locality, or to comply with new regulations made by the Secretary of State, it has a duty to modify the licence. In this event the authority can require modification of the licence irrespective of the cost to the operator. Alternatively it can revoke the licence entirely.[91]

Variation of the conditions of a licence is effected by serving a notice on the holder of the licence which states the time at which the modification of the licence is to take effect.[92] Where the Agency considers that the statutory consultees will be affected by the proposed modification it must, as is the case when a licence is originally issued, consult the local planning authority, the Health and Safety Executive and (where SSSIs are affected) English Nature before varying the conditions of a licence. In addition, where the varied licence contains a new condition which may require the licence holder to undertake work or do anything on another's land which he would not otherwise be entitled to do, the Agency must notify and consult the parties likely to be affected before modifying the licence.[93] In cases of emergency, however, the Agency may postpone all of these consultations.[94]

[86] *ibid.,* s.36A (inserted by EA 1995).
[87] Bates, *U.K. Waste Law* (1992), p. 202.
[88] EPA 1990, s.43(1)(b).
[89] DoE Appeal Decision, *Shakespeare Road, Herne Hill*, November 29, 1985, Ref. LW/APP/HE/195; cited by Bates, *U.K. Waste Law* (1992), p. 203.
[90] EPA 1990, s.37(1).
[91] *ibid.,* s.37(2).
[92] *ibid.,* s.37(4).
[93] *ibid.,* s.37A (inserted by EA 1995).
[94] *ibid.,* s.37(5) and s.37A(9).

## Supervision of a Licence

The Environment Agency is under a duty to supervise the activities of an operator to whom it has granted a Waste Management Licence.[95]

It has a specific duty to ensure that the conditions of the licence are being complied with, in addition to a more general duty to ensure that the licensed activities do not cause pollution to the environment, harm to human health, or serious detriment to the amenities of the locality. In cases of emergency, any person authorised in writing may carry out work on the land or the mobile plant to which the licence relates and the Agency may recover the cost of this from the licence holder.

If it appears to the Agency either that the conditions of a licence are not being complied with or that they are not likely to be complied with, it may serve a notice on the licence holder specifying what must be done to rectify matters and the time within which those things are to be done. If the licence holder fails to take the specified steps within that time, the Agency may revoke or suspend the licence. The Agency may seek an injunction where it considers that revocation or suspension of a licence would prove an ineffectual remedy.[96]

## Revocation of a Licence[97]

In certain circumstances the Agency has the power to revoke a licence either entirely or in part. The difficulty with revoking a licence entirely, however, is that all of its conditions, including those which relate to aftercare of the site, cease to have effect.[98] It will often be appropriate, therefore, to revoke a licence only in so far as it authorises waste handling operations whilst allowing aftercare requirements to remain in force. Besides non-compliance with the requirements of a supervision notice (above) there are two general grounds which entitle the Agency to revoke a licence entirely. These are, first, that the licence holder has ceased to be a fit and proper person *because he has been convicted of a relevant offence,* and secondly that the continuation of the authorised activities would cause pollution of the environment or harm to human health or would be seriously detrimental to the amenities of the locality *and* that harm or detriment cannot be avoided by varying the conditions of the licence. In addition, where it appears to the Agency that the licensed activities are no longer under the management of a technically competent person, it may revoke the licence in so far as it authorises the carrying out of those activities, but it may not revoke the licence entirely. The same power of partial revocation applies where the licence holder has failed to pay the prescribed fees for the subsistence of his licence.[99]

## Suspension of a Licence

Complete suspension of the licence has the effect of prohibiting all of the licensed activities during the period of suspension, whilst partial suspension prohibits the

---

[95] *ibid.,* s.42 (as amended by EA 1995).
[96] *ibid.,* s.42(6A) (inserted by EA 1995).
[97] *ibid.,* s.38.
[98] *ibid.,* s.35(11).
[99] *ibid.,* s.41(7).

activities specified by the Agency in suspending the licence. As with revocation, besides failure to comply with the requirements of a supervision notice (above) there are two general grounds on which the Agency may suspend the operation of a licence, but these are slightly different from the grounds for complete revocation. They are, first, that the licence holder has ceased to be a fit and proper person because management of the activities on that site is not in the hands of a technically competent person, and secondly that serious pollution or serious harm to human health has resulted from, or is about to be caused by, the activities and that continuing the activities would cause that harm or pollution to continue.

Where a licence is suspended, the Agency may require the licence holder to take such steps as it considers necessary to remedy or avert pollution or harm to human health. The steps stipulated for by the Agency may require the licence holder to do things which he would otherwise in law not be entitled to do. Where this is the case, the Act makes provision for the prior notification and consultation of affected parties, save in cases of emergency.[1] Failure to take the specified steps is an offence, the maximum penalty for which is a £5,000 fine in the magistrates' court or an unlimited fine and two years' imprisonment in the Crown Court. Where the waste in question is special waste, the magistrates have an additional power to imprison for six months and the maximum term of imprisonment in the Crown Court is five years. The Agency may also seek an injunction where it considers that prosecution would afford an inadequate remedy.

## Transfer and Surrender of a Licence

Central to the operation of the waste management regime is the idea that a licence cannot be transferred or given up without the approval of the Environment Agency. A licence may be transferred only where the holder and the proposed transferee make a joint application to the Environment Agency, and the Agency may only transfer the licence if it is satisfied that the transferee is a fit and proper person.[2] A licence for the operation of mobile plant can be surrendered by the holder at will. A site licence, however, can be surrendered only if the surrender is accepted by the Agency.[3] The holder of a site licence must apply to surrender it in writing.

The application is made on a prescribed form and must be accompanied by a fee, together with such information as the Agency reasonably requires. Before agreeing to the surrender, the Agency must inspect the land to which the licence relates and determine whether it is likely that the condition of the land, in so far as it is due to the licensed activities, is likely to cause pollution of the environment or harm to human health. Only where it is satisfied that this is unlikely can the Agency accept surrender of the licence. Before accepting the surrender, the Agency must also consult and consider representations from the local planning authority.[4]

Where the Agency accepts the surrender of a licence it will issue a "certificate of completion" which states that it is satisfied that pollution or harm to human health is

---

[1] *ibid.*, s.38(9A), (9B) and (9C).
[2] *ibid.*, s.40.
[3] *ibid.*, s.39.
[4] *ibid.*, s.39(7) (as amended).

unlikely. On the issue of the certificate, the licence, including any conditions relating to aftercare of the site, ceases to have effect, although any conditions of planning permission which relate to such matters as the restoration and landscaping of a site will continue to bind the former licence holder.

## Appeals[5]

An aggrieved person may appeal to the Secretary of State in relation to all of the Agency's decisions relating to Waste Management Licences. An appeal therefore lies against decisions relating to the rejection of an application, the conditions attached to a licence and the suspension, revocation, surrender and transfer of a licence. The Waste Management Licensing Regulations 1994 state that an appeal must be brought within six months of the relevant decision. The Secretary of State may determine the appeal himself, but will usually refer it to an inspector or other person for determination.[6]

Decisions relating to the revocation of a licence or the modification of its conditions are normally stayed until the outcome of the appeal, whilst a decision to suspend a licence remains in force pending the determination of an appeal. When revoking or modifying a licence, however, the Agency may stipulate that the decision is to remain in force notwithstanding an appeal if it considers that this is necessary to prevent or minimise pollution or harm to human health. As has been said, where a licence is suspended, the suspension remains effective even where an appeal is brought. This may cause hardship to an innocent licence holder. Therefore, where, on appeal, the Secretary of State finds that the suspension of a licence was unreasonable, the licence holder is entitled to compensation for losses consequent on the suspension.[7] This entitlement also applies in cases where, to prevent pollution or harm to human health, a decision is made to make a revocation or a modification of a licence effective throughout the period of an appeal and that decision is subsequently found to be unreasonable.

## Fees and Charges

The Agency is empowered to draw up, with the approval of the Secretary of State, a charging scheme in relation to Waste Management Licences. At the time of writing, charges for licences are calculated in accordance with the Waste Management (Fees and Charges) Scheme 1994 which was drawn up by the Secretary of State under the Environmental Protection Act 1990,[8] although this is to be replaced by a new but similar scheme drawn up by the Environment Agency which will apply to all environmental licences.[9] The government's policy in relation to charges is that they should reflect the true costs of administering the waste management regime and in particular of supervising licensed activities. The annual fee for holding a waste management licence therefore differs according to the type and quantity of waste

---

[5] *ibid.,* s.43.
[6] EA 1995, s.114.
[7] EPA 1990, s.43(7).
[8] *ibid.,* s.41.
[9] EA 1995, s.41.

handled by a particular operation, although it will normally run into thousands of pounds.

## Public Registers

The Environment Agency is under a duty to maintain registers in relation to the operation of the waste management regime.[10] Among the matters which must appear on the registers are details of all current applications for licences and of all applications made within the preceding 12 months, together with details of all licences granted in the preceding 12 months. Details of suspension, revocation and modification of licences must be included, as must monitoring information in relation to sites. Details of convictions of licence holders for offences under Part II of the Environmental Protection Act 1990 must also be included, together with matters relating to applications for the surrender of licences.

The Secretary of State can make provision for the exclusion of certain information on the basis of national security.[11] In addition, the licence holder can apply to the Environment Agency for the exclusion of matters which are commercially confidential and an appeal lies to the Secretary of State where the Agency refuses to do so.[12] Where such information is excluded, the register will nevertheless indicate the existence of commercially confidential information. Like other environmental registers, the waste management registers are available for public inspection and copies of entries may be obtained on payment of a reasonable charge. The registers fulfil an important function in providing information to handlers of waste who are required to comply with the statutory duty of care in relation to waste.

## THE STATUTORY DUTY OF CARE

The Royal Commission on Environmental Pollution, in its Eleventh Report[13] emphasised the need to adopt a "cradle to grave" approach in relation to waste which ensured that the producer of a waste material could not abdicate responsibility for it entirely by passing it on to another party. The Commission concluded that producers of waste owed a duty of care to society and that this duty of care should be enshrined in legislation. The outcome of the Commission's recommendations was the implementation, in April 1992, of the statutory duty of care as respects waste.

In essence this imposes on any person who deals with waste (whether he is a waste management licence holder or not) a set of specific and general requirements in relation to the handling of that waste.[14] Breach of the statutory duty of care is a criminal offence, the maximum penalty for which is a £5,000 fine in the magistrates' court or an unlimited fine in the Crown Court. The duty applies only to controlled

---

[10] EPA 1990, s.64 and S.I. 1994 No. 1056.
[11] EPA 1990, s.65.
[12] *ibid.*, s.66.
[13] RCEP (1985) Eleventh Report: *Managing Waste,* Cmnd. 9675 (1985).
[14] EPA 1990, s.34 and Environmental Protection (Duty of Care) Regulations 1991 (S.I. 1991 No. 2839).

waste, and is owed by any person who imports, produces, carries, keeps, treats or disposes of controlled waste or, as a broker who arranges for another to deal with such waste, has control of it.

There are three elements to the duty of care, each of which is examined below. First, the persons mentioned above must take all such measures that are reasonable in the circumstances to ensure that no *other* person commits an offence under Part II of the Act by carrying out Directive recovery or Directive disposal operations without a licence or in a manner likely to cause harm to human health or pollution of the environment (*i.e.* commits one of the "primary" offences or the "residual" offence described above). Secondly, such persons must prevent the escape of waste from their control or the control of any other person. Thirdly, such persons must, on the transfer of waste, ensure that the transfer is to an authorised person and that there accompanies the waste a description of it which will enable the person who takes control of it to avoid the commission of a waste·management offence and to avoid a breach of the statutory duty of care. The scope of the duty of care is principally defined by reference to three sources: The Environmental Protection Act 1990, the Environmental Protection (Duty of Care) Regulations 1991[15] and the Code of Practice on the Duty of Care issued by the Secretary of State. The latter is admissible in evidence and although its provisions are not binding on the courts, the Act provides that the Code of Practice must be taken into account by the courts in deciding whether there has been a breach of the duty of care.[16]

## Duty to Prevent the Commission of an Offence

In practice, this branch of the duty relates mainly to the transfer of waste. It requires the holder of waste to satisfy himself that it is being dealt with responsibly by persons further down the waste disposal chain to whom it is passed on. For example, where a producer of waste uses the services of a waste carrier to take away his controlled waste, he must take reasonable steps to ensure that the waste will be deposited in a lawful place. The Code of Practice suggests that this should involve the transferor of waste in checking the credentials of the operator of the site where the waste is to be deposited by inspecting the site operator's licence and asking whether it covers the waste in question.

## Duty to Prevent the Escape of Controlled Waste

This branch of the duty relates mainly to the storage of waste. The Code of Practice advises, for example, that waste should be left for collection in containers which are secure enough to resist bad weather and disturbance by animals. Different types of waste will require different types of packaging. Inflammable waste, for example, should be put into fire resistant containers. Waste which is left in skips and is liable to be disturbed by the wind should be adequately covered. Drums or closed containers should be clearly labelled to indicate their contents.

---

[15] S.I. 1991 No. 2839. See also Circular 25/91 (the Duty of Care) (DoE).
[16] EPA 1990, s.34(10).

## Duties on the Transfer of Waste

There are two "limbs" to this branch of the duty of care. The first requires the transferor of waste to take reasonable measures to ensure that the waste is transferred to a person who is authorised either to dispose of the waste or to transport it. In this context, a person will be authorised to transport the waste only if he is a registered carrier under the Control of Pollution (Amendment) Act 1989 or is exempt from registration by regulations made under that Act.

The second "limb" of the duty requires the transferor to ensure that the waste transferred is accompanied by a description of it which is adequate to enable the person to whom it is passed on to avoid the commission of an offence. The Code of Practice indicates that the amount of detail required in a description may differ according to the circumstances. In relation to chemical waste, for example, a full analysis of its composition may be required to enable it to be disposed of properly without its being mixed with other waste with which it may react.

## The Transport of Waste

The transport of controlled waste is governed by the Control of Pollution (Amendment) Act 1989, which makes it a criminal offence for any person to transport controlled waste in the course of a business or otherwise for profit unless he is a registered carrier of controlled waste.[17] The Act is supplemented by the Controlled Waste (Registration of Carriers and Seizure of Vehicles) Regulations 1991.[18] Under the regulations, charities and local authorities are exempt from the provisions of the Act, as are producers carrying their own waste, provided that it is not demolition or construction waste. A prospective carrier of waste must apply to the Environment Agency for registration, which can be refused only if:

(i) The applicant has been convicted of a relevant environmental offence, *and*

(ii) The Environment Agency considers that it is undesirable to authorise the applicant to carry waste.

Registration may be revoked by the Agency at any time on identical grounds. Unless it is revoked, a registration lasts for three years, after which time the carrier must apply for it to be renewed.

A police constable or an authorised officer of the Environment Agency may stop and search any vehicle in which he reasonably suspects that controlled waste is being or has been unlawfully transported and may require the driver to produce his (or his employer's) authority for transporting the waste. In addition, in cases where the Environment Agency has reasonable grounds for suspecting that a vehicle has been used for the illegal transport of waste but is unable to obtain proper information about the ownership and control of the vehicle at the time of the suspected offence, the Agency may seize the vehicle and if, after the Agency has publicised the seizure, the vehicle remains unclaimed, it may dispose of it.

---

[17] Control of Pollution (Amendment) Act 1989, s.1.
[18] S.I. 1991 No. 1624.

## Waste Brokers

Waste brokers are people who arrange for the transport of waste. They do not necessarily require a Waste Management Licence because they may not actually handle the waste themselves. Under the Waste Management Licensing Regulations 1994, however, any person who, as a dealer or broker, arranges for the disposal of waste must be registered with the Environment Agency. The requirements for registration are essentially the same as those for holding a Waste Management Licence, in that the Agency may refuse registration if relevant environmental offences have been committed by the applicant. Registration as a waste broker lasts for three years, after which time it must be renewed.

# WASTE RECYCLING

Apart from the powers given to Waste Collection Authorities under Part II of the Environmental Protection Act 1990, which were noted at the beginning of this chapter, there is very little legislation in the U.K. directed specifically at the recycling of waste. The E.C. Directive on Packaging and Packaging Waste, however, which was adopted in 1994, requires Member States to meet certain recycling targets in relation to waste packaging.

The Directive requires that by 2001, between 25 per cent and 45 per cent by weight of all materials used as product packaging are to be recovered and recycled. The Environment Act 1995 lays the foundations for the Secretary of State to give effect to the U.K. obligations under the Directive by making regulations imposing certain obligations on the producers of waste.[19]

The Producer Responsibility Obligations (Packaging Waste) Regulations 1997[19a] came into force on March 6, 1997. They give effect to the Directive's recovery and recycling obligations. The scheme of the regulations is to impose "Producer Responsibility Obligations" on those businesses and industries defined by the regulations as "producers". The obligations include:

- Registering with the Environment Agency;

- Making reasonable efforts to recover and recycle certain amounts (determined by a formula in the regulations) of packaging waste;

- Providing a certificate of compliance with the regulations to the Environment Agency.

The regulations are part of the U.K. government's initiative on producer responsibility for waste. In the consultation paper which preceded the regulations, the government stated that: "more of the real environmental costs of waste production and disposal should be borne directly by the producers of waste and made visible to the consumer."

---

[19] EA 1995, ss.93–95.
[19a] S.I. 1997 No. 648.

## Economic Instruments

Under existing legislation, economic instruments are used to control waste management in two ways. First, under Part II of the Environmental Protection Act 1990, Waste Collection Authorities are entitled to claim "recycling credits" from the Environment Agency. The idea is that where waste is removed from the environment, the Agency (or, formerly, the Waste Disposal Authority) no longer has a duty to dispose of it, and therefore makes a financial saving. The money which is saved in this way is paid to the Waste Collection Authority, and operates as an incentive for them to put their recycling powers into practice.

The second way in which economic instruments are used is to encourage the minimisation of waste disposal by making it more expensive to dispose of waste in landfill sites. This is done by means of a landfill tax. The Finance Act 1996 made provision for the introduction of the landfill tax, which is implemented by regulations.[20] Under these regulations, the levy on waste deposited in landfill sites is £7 per tonne. For inert waste such as building rubble, which does not decompose to produce methane gas, a reduced levy of £2 per tonne is imposed.

The consultation paper which was issued in March 1995, prior to the introduction of the tax, had suggested that the tax should be levied on an *ad valorem* basis in much the same way as VAT. The paper put forward the idea that a price-related tax would reflect the true environmental cost of each tonne of waste dumped because the disposal cost of waste usually depended on how hazardous it was. Waste which was particularly hazardous would therefore command a higher disposal price and would be subject to a higher rate of taxation. In addition, the consultation paper suggested that a higher price for disposal would usually be paid in areas where landfill sites were scarce and reasoned that since these areas were the most susceptible to environmental damage from increased dumping, a higher rate of taxation would be appropriate.

The proposals, however, met with sharp criticism from environmentalists. It was pointed out that waste producers were likely simply to choose the cheapest sites for disposal and that this might lead to a significant increase in the practice of transporting waste over long distances. Moreover, it was felt that a value added tax would provide a disincentive to landfill site operators to improve the environmental standards of their sites because this would mean making them more expensive to use. In the light of these criticisms, the landfill tax was implemented as a straightforward two band tax, which is expected to raise some £450 million per year for the Treasury. The consultation paper envisaged that the measures would give effect to the "polluter pays" principle by reflecting the full environmental cost of waste disposal. The tax, however, has been criticised by environmentalists such as Friends of the Earth as being far too low to do this and for failing to provide any real incentive for industry to reduce its waste output.[21]

[20] S.I. 1996 No. 1527.
[21] *Financial Times*, November 29, 1995.

# Diagram 5: An Overview of the Waste Management Regime

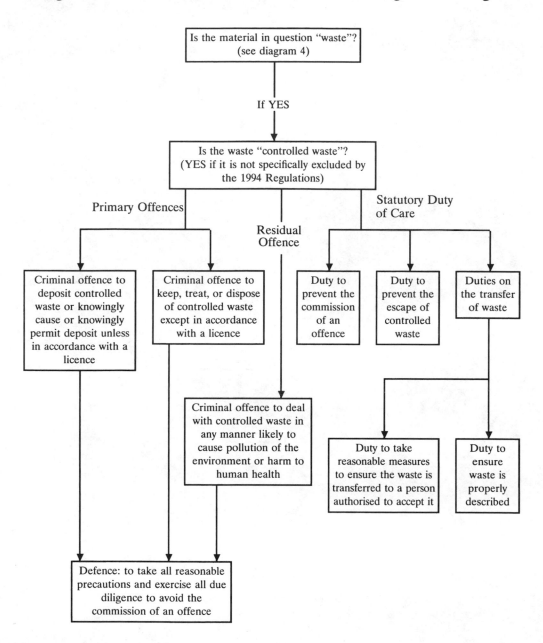

# Chapter 9

# WATER POLLUTION

---

*"Human health and development are threatened in many places because of insufficient or poor quality water . . . [I]ncreased water use, discharge of wastes, excessive application of fertilisers and pesticides and accidental spills of harmful substances have led to increasing pollution of many European waterbodies."*[1]

## Introduction

Water is vital. We drink it to stay alive, we wash in it. It is neeeded in agriculture for irrigating land and for rearing livestock. Industry uses it as a raw material and as a coolant. It provides a habitat for fish and aquatic animals. It has an important psychological function in that it provides recreational areas of natural beauty. In addition, it is the most important medium for processing and disposing of liquid waste. Estimates by the Water Research Centre suggest that about 80 per cent by weight of all waste arisings in England and Wales are liquid effluent. This is disposed of partly to seas and estuaries, but mainly to rivers.[2]

Water pollution can occur in a number of ways. Substances such as sewage, agricultural slurry, chemical effluents and detergents are commonly released into water both accidentally and deliberately. Acidification of waterways by acid rain, which results from the emission of pollutants to the air, is an increasing problem.

Combatting water pollution is made difficult by the fact that different types of waters (canals, ponds, lakes, tidal waters, for example) have different capacities for absorbing and dispersing pollution. River water, for example, has to some extent a natural purifying capacity by virtue of the micro-organisms present in it and the effects of sunlight and aeration. Because of this, discharges to rivers may safely be permitted up to a certain limit before pollution occurs. This makes river water a useful and effective medium for waste disposal. The problem for legislators, therefore, has been to impose sufficient controls to ensure that water does not become polluted, whilst avoiding needless over-regulation which would amount to the squandering of a valuable natural waste removal facility. Failure accurately to strike this balance has led to a decline in

---

[1] *Europe's Environment: The Dobris Assessment* (eds Stanners and Bourdeau) (1995), The European Environment Agency.
[2] Royal Commission on Environmental Pollution (1992) Sixteenth Report: *Freshwater Quality*, Cm. 1966 (1992).

the standard of waters in the U.K. in the last few years. A survey of the quality of rivers, canals and estuaries in England and Wales was carried out in 1990 by the National Rivers Authority. Although nearly 90 per cent of the length of freshwater rivers and canals was found to be of good or fair quality, the Authority concluded that there had been a deterioration in quality since a similar survey in 1985.

It should be remembered that the environment may suffer damage not only from the *pollution* of water, which is the focus of this chapter, but also from the way in which water resources are *managed*. In times of drought, for example, an increased demand for water may, if improperly managed, lead to rivers drying up with a consequent loss of flora and fauna, or to the intentional flooding and destruction of natural valleys to build reservoirs.

## Types of Water Pollution Control

As in other areas of pollution control, controls over water pollution may be either *preventive* or *remedial*. Preventive controls aim to stop water pollution before it happens, for example by setting limits on the concentrations of particular pollutants which are permitted to enter certain waters, or by curtailing certain industrial activities and uses of land which have the potential to cause water pollution. Remedial controls, on the other hand, are aimed at cleaning up pollution after it has occurred, punishing the polluter, ensuring that he pays the costs of clean-up, and compensating people who have suffered as a result of the pollution. Such controls are, of course, preventive in so far as they serve as a deterrent to potential polluters.

Where an activity is found to give rise to a pollution problem, an injunction or similar statutory device may be used to restrict the activity in question so that it ceases to pollute. This type of control contains an element of both prevention and cure, and may therefore be seen as a hybrid of preventive and remedial forms of control. Remedial and preventive forms of control are both found to varying degrees within the U.K.'s water pollution regime. The bulk of this chapter concentrates on the controls to be found in legislation relating to water pollution, and goes on to address those which exist in the common law and under planning law. Finally, the contribution of E.C. water law is considered. This chapter is concerned with the law relating to pollution of inland and coastal waters. Pollution of the high seas is regulated by a separate legal regime and is beyond the scope of this work.

## Definition of "Water Pollution"

The relevant U.K. legislation does not define pollution of water. An appropriate definition, however, is to be found in the E.C. Directive on Groundwater,[3] which describes water pollution as:

> "The discharge by man, directly or indirectly, of substances or energy into waters, the results of which are such as to endanger human health or water supplies, harm living resources and the aquatic ecosystem or interfere with the other legitimate uses of water."

[3] Dir. 86/68/EEC; [1980] O.J. L20/43 (Art. 1.2d).

It is to be noted that the Directive defines water pollution by reference to the *effect* of a substance in water rather than by reference to its presence there. This is the approach which has generally been adopted by U.K. courts in the relevant case law, although, following the decision in the unreported case of *National Rivers Authority v. Egger Ltd*,[4] which is more fully discussed below, it appears that it is inappropriate to consider the effect of a substance on the specific stretch of water into which it is released. Rather, what is considered is the likely effect of the substance on a hypothetical unpolluted stretch of water.

So far as the common law is concerned, the definition of water pollution has traditionally depended upon how the rights of others to use the water are affected. For example, if the temperature of water in a stream is altered so that a person downstream is unable to use the water as before, the common law will look upon the water as "polluted",[5] even though it may be free from harmful substances. This accords with the definition set out in the Groundwater Directive (above) under which pollution of water may be caused by the discharge of "energy".

## THE STATUTORY REGIME

Modern water legislation may be divided into two distinct strands. First, there is legislation which regulates the conduct of the water industry, the activities of which are an important potential source of pollution. Secondly, there is legislation which is specifically concerned with pollution control.

### The Water Industry

The water industry is concerned with the supply of water and with the disposal of waste water and waste in liquid form, particularly sewage. The Water Act 1973 established the basic framework of the modern water industry by creating *Water Authorities* to supply water and arrange for the disposal of sewage. The Water Authorities had a number of general regulatory functions including the conservation of water resources, the maintenance of fisheries and the supervision of land drainage. They were also responsible for controlling pollution by granting consents for the discharge of substances into water.

The Public Utility Transfers and Water Charges Act 1988 paved the way for privatisation of the water industry by enabling Water Authorities to separate their functions into two divisions. The first of these was concerned with the exercise of the Authorities' regulatory functions, whilst the second division was responsible for the practical business of water supply and sewage disposal. This move was welcomed by environmentalists, who had come to see the Water Authorities, with their overarching responsibility for the water cycle, as both poacher and gamekeeper in relation to water pollution. Indeed, one of the stated aims of the government's policy of water

---

[4] Newcastle Upon Tyne Crown Court, June 15–17, 1992, unreported. See Burnett-Hall, *Environmental Law* (1995), p. 351.
[5] *John Young & Co. v. Bankier Distillery Co.* [1893] A.C. 691.

privatisation was the achievement of greater "accountability", although, as has been noted, it is far from clear whether this means accountability to the public, to government, or to the companies' shareholders.[6]

The Water Act 1989 divided the functions of the Water Authorities between the newly established National Rivers Authority and the newly formed private companies which were the successors to the Water Authorities. The National Rivers Authority inherited the main regulatory and water management functions of the Water Authorities, whilst the functions of water supply and sewage treatment were privatised. Ten limited companies were created to provide these services. In 1991, the legislation was consolidated by five statutes: The Water Resources Act 1991; the Water Industry Act 1991; the Land Drainage Act 1991; the Statutory Water Companies Act 1991; and the Water Consolidation (Consequential Provisions) Act 1991. Of these, the two most important statutes are the Water Industry Act 1991 and the Water Resources Act 1991. The Water Industry Act 1991 regulates the privatised aspects of the water industry, whilst the Water Resources Act 1991 is concerned with pollution control.

## Pollution Control

The statutory regime in relation to water pollution exerts control in two main ways. First, it serves as a deterrent by imposing criminal sanctions on polluters. Secondly, it seeks to prevent pollution by creating protection zones where potentially polluting activities are curtailed and by regulating the amounts of substances released into water through a system of discharge consents.

Water pollution can derive from easily identifiable "point" sources, such as effluent pipes from industrial sites or sewage treatment works, or from "diffuse" sources such as acid rain or surface water "run-off" from agricultural land on which fertilisers and pesticides are present. The pollution control legislation is primarily concerned with discharges from point sources. Pollution from diffuse sources is very difficult to control, because it arises from a diverse range of activities which have proved difficult to restrict or prohibit. Moreover, the particular contribution of each of the many diffuse pollution sources to the overall picture of water pollution is difficult to identify. Nevertheless, under the Water Resources Act 1991,[7] certain areas may be designated as Water Protection Zones or Nitrate Sensitive Areas. The idea is that agricultural and industrial activities within these areas may be restricted so as to prevent pollution from diffuse sources. At the time of writing, however, no such areas or zones have been designated.

## History of the Pollution Control Regime

Legislation to control water pollution began in the fourteenth century with the passing of the Act for Punishing Nuisances which Cause Corruption of the Air near Cities and Great Towns 1388. This made it a criminal offence to throw garbage and entrails into rivers and other waters:

[6] Ball and Bell, *Environmental Law* (3rd ed., 1995).
[7] WRA 1991, ss.93 and 94.

" For that so much Dung and Filth of the Garbage and Intrails as well of Beasts
killed . . . be put in Rivers and other Waters . . . the Air there is greatly corrupt
. . . and if any do he shall be called before the Chancellor . . . and shall be
punished after the discretion of the Chancellor."

In the nineteenth century, with the passing of the Rivers Pollution Prevention Act
1876, it became a criminal offence to "cause or knowingly permit" the pollution of any
British river, and it is this phraseology which appears today in the Water Resources
Act 1991. The problem with the Rivers Pollution Prevention Act 1876, however, was
that it sought to impose an absolute prohibition on all discharges to rivers, which
proved impossible to enforce in practice. Moreover, such a prohibition was inappropriate given the ability of rivers to absorb a limited amount of pollution without harmful
effect.

The Rivers (Prevention of Pollution) Act 1951 laid the foundations for the modern
approach to pollution control. The River Boards, which were at that time the relevant
regulatory bodies, were placed under a general duty to maintain or restore the
wholesomeness of inland waters. To this end they were granted two important powers.
First, the River Boards had the power to grant consents for the discharge of trade and
sewage effluent. Secondly, they had the power to make byelaws prescribing the
amounts of particular substances which could be discharged. Effectively, this allowed
for the imposition of uniform emission standards, which until very recently formed the
basis of the approach to pollution control favoured by the E.C. (discussed below). The
River Boards' powers to set emission standards were little used, however, and were
repealed in 1961.

The Control of Pollution Act 1974 consolidated the discharge consent provisions of
the 1951 Act and extended them to cover underground, tidal and coastal waters. It also
provided for public participation in decisions relating to water pollution and introduced measures for the provision to the public of information about discharges. The
Water Act 1989 created the National Rivers Authority as a unified regulatory body
with responsibility for pollution control. It also improved the range of controls
available to curb pollution by giving the Secretary of State the power to establish
"water quality objectives" for particular stretches of water. The Water Resources Act
1991 consolidated these provisions. Under the Environment Act 1995, the functions
and duties of the National Rivers Authority have now passed to the Environment
Agency.

## Regulating Discharges to Water

The prevention of water pollution and the control of water resources are regulated by
Part III of the Water Resources Act 1991. Under the Act, the Secretary of State has a
duty to set targets for the quality of certain stretches of water.[8] These targets are
known as "water quality objectives" and indicate the environmental standards to which
water within specific designated areas is expected to conform. Once the water quality
objectives have been set, the Environment Agency and the Secretary of State are under

[8] WRA 1991, s.83.

a duty to ensure that the objectives are met so far as is practicable.[9] This is done by means of discharge consents. In general terms, no-one may discharge polluting substances to water without holding a discharge consent granted by the Agency. The Agency is thereby able to control the quality of a particular stretch of water by placing limits on the number of consents issued and by attaching conditions to those consents. Enforcement of the regime is provided for by a series of criminal offences which prohibit discharges to controlled waters without a consent.

## Water Quality Objectives

Since the late 1970s, waterways have been the subject of non-statutory quality objectives. These were set by the Water Authorities in purported compliance with the E.C. Directive of 1976 on Dangerous Substances in Water,[10] and were used by the Authorities as a basis for setting discharge consents and for targeting investments in river improvements. The non-statutory guidance, however, was insufficient to comply with E.C. law, which required the objectives to have a statutory basis. Water quality objectives were eventually placed on a statutory footing by the Water Act 1989, the provisions of which are reproduced in the Water Resources Act 1991. Under this Act, the Secretary of State has the power to prescribe water quality objectives in regulations. At the time of writing, however, U.K. water law is in a period of transition from the use of non-statutory water quality objectives to the use of quality objectives prescribed under regulations. In order to comply with E.C. law whilst this transition is taking place, the Secretary of State has issued two sets of "blanket" regulations which set *general* water quality objectives for all inland waters.[11] These regulations specify the maximum permitted concentrations of certain dangerous substances in water. The government's intention is that over the next few years additional regulations will be made under which the Secretary of State may prescribe *specific*, and in some cases more stringent water quality objectives in relation to particular stretches of water. These specific statutory objectives will eventually replace the specific non-statutory objectives currently in use.

## Classification and Water Quality Objectives

Under the Water Resources Act 1991, the setting of water quality objectives will involve a two-stage approach. First, water in the U.K. will be *classified* according to a particular proposed use. Water may be classified as bathing water or drinking water, for example. These two classifications have already been made by regulations.[12] The classification regulations will set out the environmental standards to which waters must conform if they are to fall within a particular classification and so be deemed suitable for a particular use. The second stage in the process will be the actual designation, by

---

[9] *ibid.,* s.84.
[10] Dir. 76/464/EEC.
[11] Surface Waters (Dangerous Substances) (Classification) Regulations 1989 (S.I. 1989 No. 2286) and Surface Waters (Dangerous Substances) (Classifications) Regulations 1992 (S.I. 1992 No. 337).
[12] Bathing Waters (Classification) Regulations 1991 (S.I. 1991 No. 1597) and Surface Waters (Classification) Regulations 1989 (S.I. 1989 No. 1148).

the Secretary of State, of particular stretches of water. The water quality objective set for each stretch of water so designated will then be for it to achieve a certain type of classification within a certain time. The water quality objective for designated stretch of water A, for example, might be for it to come within the bathing water classification within the next two years, whilst the objective for stretch of water B might be for it to achieve classification as water suitable for abstraction as drinking water.

At the time of writing, classification regulations have been made only in respect of rivers[13] and are awaited in respect of other waters such as lakes, canals, coastal waters and groundwater. Since the classification of waters is not yet complete, no individual statutory quality objectives have been set in relation to particular stretches of water. The informal non-statutory quality objectives therefore continue to apply in relation to specific waterways, alongside the statutory "blanket" quality objectives contained in the two existing sets of regulations which prohibit the presence of certain dangerous substances in any waters, whatever their classification. An informal classification scheme developed in 1978 by the National Water Council forms the basis for setting the informal non-statutory water quality objectives. Indications from the Department of the Environment are that the formal classification process will take a considerable number of years to complete, particularly because of scientific work yet to be done in establishing the precise environmental requirements for each classification. After that, the setting of individual quality objectives for particular stretches of water will take a further time, not only because of the sheer size of the administrative task, but also because of the government's understandable reluctance to come to terms with the political implications of burdening industry, and ultimately the consumer, with the costs of bringing certain waters within their appropriate classification.

## The Administrative Process

The Water Resources Act 1991 sets out the procedure to be followed in establishing water quality objectives. Under the Act, the Secretary of State may serve on the Environment Agency a notice which specifies a particular stretch of water and, as a quality objective for that water, the particular classification to which it must conform, together with the date from which that classification must be achieved.[14] The proposed quality objective must be brought to the attention of those likely to be affected by it, and the Secretary of State must give at least three months' notice of the proposed objective to enable representations and objections to be made. The Secretary of State has a duty to consider all such representations and objections and, in the light of them, may modify the proposed objective. He may hold a local inquiry to consider the matter if he considers it appropriate. Once a water quality objective has been set, the Secretary of State may decide to change it. He must then notify the Environment Agency and allow three months for representations and objections to be made. If, after hearing the objections, the Secretary of State decides to leave the water quality objective unchanged, he must serve on the Environment Agency a notice to this effect. Information about water quality objectives must be placed on a register,[15] to which the

[13] Surface Waters (River Ecosystem) (Classification) Regulations 1994 (S.I. 1994 No. 1057).
[14] WRA 1991 s.83.
[15] *ibid.*, s.190.

public has access. The details which must be placed on the register include, *inter alia*, the dates on which notices have been served by the Secretary of State, the waters to which those notices relate, the classification of the waters in question and the dates from which those waters must comply with the classification.[16]

Once a stretch of water has been made the subject of a statutory water quality objective and a date set from which it must conform to the objective (*i.e* fall within a particular classification), both the Secretary of State and the Environment Agency are under a duty to ensure that, so far as is practicable, from that date the quality objectives for the classification are met at all times.[17] It is conceivable that this duty might be enforced by way of judicial review undertaken by individuals and environmental pressure groups, who might challenge the Environment Agency's decisions relating to the grant of discharge consents, but the statutory wording: "so far as is practicable" makes the success of such an action unlikely. The Secretary of State, however, has a general power to direct the Environment Agency in the exercise of its functions,[18] and it has been suggested that a more appropriate way of achieving compliance with water quality objectives might be for interested parties to apply to the Secretary of State, seeking a direction from him in relation to the stretch of water in question.[19]

## Discharge Consents

As has been said, the method by which statutory water quality objectives are to be met, and indeed by which the existing non-statutory objectives are currently being met, is through the regulation of discharges to water. Under the Water Resources Act 1991, it is an offence to *cause or knowingly permit the discharge of certain substances into "controlled waters"*. It is also an offence to *cause or knowingly permit the entry into controlled waters of "poisonous, noxious or polluting matter"*. The possession of a discharge consent from the Environment Agency, however, provides a *defence* to prosecution. The details of the various water pollution offences, which are quite complex, are examined in the appropriate section below, after consideration has been given to the procedure for obtaining a discharge consent.

## Applications for Discharge Consents

The grant, modification and revocation of discharge consents is governed by Schedule 10 of the Water Resources Act 1991. At the time of writing, however, this schedule is due to be replaced (in accordance with Schedule 22 of the Environment Act 1995) by a new Schedule 10. The new schedule, which is not yet in force, gives the Secretary of State the power to make regulations covering many of the matters which are explicitly set out in the existing schedule. The current provisions call for a higher degree of public participation than is usual for the grant of environmental licences and it is

---

[16] Control of Pollution (Registers) Regulations 1989 (S.I. 1989 No. 1160).
[17] WRA 1991, s.84.
[18] EA 1995, s.40.
[19] *Encyclopedia of Environmental Law* (Sweet & Maxwell), vol. 3, D1048.

anticipated that, in keeping with the government's policy of deregulation, regulations made under the new Schedule 10 may involve some dilution of the publicity requirements set out in the existing Schedule.[20] The main requirements of the existing schedule, however, are set out below.

Application for a discharge consent is made to the Environment Agency. The Agency must publish a notice of the application at least once in each of two successive weeks in a newspaper circulating in the locality of the proposed discharge and in a newspaper circulating in the vicinity of any controlled waters which the Agency considers are likely to be affected by the proposed discharge. Thereafter the Agency must publish the notice in *The London Gazette* and must send a copy of the application to every water undertaker in the area of the proposed discharge. The Agency is entitled to recover the costs of meeting these publicity requirements from the applicant.

## Exemption from Publicity Requirements

Under the existing schedule, the Environment Agency is not required to publicise an application if it considers that the proposed discharge will have "no appreciable effect" on the receiving waters. The Department of the Environment[21] has suggested that this will be the case where there is less than a 10 per cent increase in pollution, as measured by the relevant quality objective parameters. Clearly, the danger of such an approach is that, without the public's knowledge, pollution may be allowed to increase considerably, albeit incrementally. The existing power to dispense with publicity has been translated in wider terms in the new schedule, which provides simply that the Agency is not required to advertise an application in any case where it considers that such advertising may be dispensed with.[22]

In addition, any person making an application for a discharge consent may apply to the Secretary of State for a determination that certain details relating to the application are contrary to the public interest or would prejudice to an unreasonable degree some private interest by disclosing information about a trade secret. If the Secretary of State is satisfied that this is the case, he may issue a certificate which exempts the application from the requirements of publicity both in relation to the advertising of the application and in relation to the appearance of details of the consent on the public register. Moreover, the Secretary of State has a general power to give directions to the Agency that certain types of information, or information relating to certain types of application, should not be placed on the register.[23] Exclusion from the register on grounds of commercial confidentiality lasts for four years, after which time an application may be made for the information to remain excluded.

## Determination of Applications

The Environment Agency must consider written representations and objections which are made to it within six weeks from the publication of the notice of application in *The*

---

[20] Ball and Bell, *Environmental Law* (3rd ed., 1995).
[21] Circular 17/84.
[22] WRA 1991, Sched. 10 (as substituted by EA 1995, Sched. 22), para. 1(2).
[23] WRA 1991 (as amended by EA 1995), s.191A.

*London Gazette*. The Agency will then consider whether to grant the consent unconditionally or subject to conditions. If the applicant has not heard from the Environment Agency within four months of the receipt of his application, the application will be deemed to have been refused unless the Agency and the applicant have agreed a longer period for its determination. Where the Agency decides to grant a consent in a case where there have been written objections, it must notify all those parties who objected. It must then wait a further 21 days before granting the consent. This gives the objectors time to request the Secretary of State to order that the application be determined by an inspector at a public inquiry. Once granted, a consent attaches to the particular discharge to which it relates rather than to the holder of the consent. It follows, therefore, that the new owner of premises in respect of which a consent is in force can take advantage of that consent, and in contrast with the position in relation to waste management there is no requirement that he should be a fit and proper person to do so.

## Consents without Applications

Under the existing schedule, in cases where discharges are already occurring which require authorisation by a discharge consent, but no consent has been applied for, the Agency has the power to give its consent in writing. Such a consent is not retrospective, and will not, therefore, be a defence to prosecution for pollution incidents which occurred prior to its having been given. Rather, the purpose of such consents is to enable the Agency to clarify the legal position in respect of a particular discharge and to attach conditions to the discharge so as to prevent it from being a source of pollution in the future. Where a consent is given in this way, a notice of the consent must be published as soon as practicable after it has been given and objections and representations made following its publication must be considered. In the light of these, the Agency may revoke or modify the consent.

## Consent Conditions

The Agency's power to attach conditions to a discharge consent is virtually unfettered. Under the schedule, it may impose such conditions as it thinks fit. This gives the Agency a wide discretion to include conditions relating, for example, to the places of the discharges, the temperature, volume and rate of the discharges and the times at which the discharges may be made. The schedule sets out, by way of example only, some of the types of condition which may be appropriate. These include conditions relating to the provision of facilities for taking samples (by means of boreholes and inspection chambers, for example) and the keeping of records in respect of discharges.

The power to impose conditions is, of course, subject to the normal constraints imposed by administrative law. Thus it has been suggested that,[24] since the power to impose consent conditions is the same type of power that is exercised where conditions are imposed for planning purposes, the criteria for the validity of planning conditions, established in *Newbury B.C. v. Secretary of State for the Environment*,[25] applies to

---

[24] Bates, *Water and Drainage Law* (1990).
[25] [1980] 1 All E.R. 731.

conditions imposed under Schedule 10, *i.e.* a condition may only be imposed for a purpose to which it fairly and reasonably relates and not for an ulterior purpose. Although this argument may well succeed in an appeal against, or an application for judicial review of a consent condition, the case law suggests that it will fail if pleaded as a defence to a prosecution. In *R. v. Etterick Trout Company Ltd and William Baxter*[26] the appellants argued, by way of a defence to a prosecution for breach of a consent condition, that the condition, which related to the volume of effluent which could be discharged, was invalid because it had not been imposed for a pollution control purpose but for an ulterior purpose, namely to limit the *volume* of water the appellants were permitted to discharge. Although the Court of Appeal accepted the point in principle, it took the view that, on the facts of the particular case, it was not permissible to challenge the validity of the condition by way of a defence to prosecution, since to do so was an attempt to bypass both the normal judicial review procedure and the procedure for statutory appeals. The court stated, however, that it was unable to say that in no circumstances could such a challenge provide a defence to prosecution. The position therefore remains unclear, although it is submitted that a challenge in criminal proceedings of a condition which is blatantly irrational may very well succeed.

## Revocation and Modification of Consents

Under the schedule, the Environment Agency has a duty to review from time to time the discharge consents which it has granted and the conditions to which they are subject. On review, the Agency may revoke the consent, modify any of its conditions, or make an unconditional consent subject to conditions. It does this by serving a notice on the person who is making the discharge. The wide nature of this power to vary consents reflects the need to accommodate changes in the circumstances under which the consent was originally granted. It may, for example, be used to prohibit the discharge of a newly-discovered pollutant. More controversially, perhaps, it may be used to accommodate the discharge requirements of newcomers to a particular stretch of water by reducing the amount of a substance that may be discharged by existing consent holders so as to preserve the overall quality objective for the water in question. Apart from the two year prohibition on revocation and variation, which is discussed below, there is nothing in the legislation which protects the right to hold a consent, or which indicates that in developing areas consents are to be held on a first come first served basis.

## Exemption from Revocation and Modification

Under the schedule, when the Agency grants a discharge consent, it will stipulate a period of time during which the consent is to be exempt from revocation and modification. This period cannot be less than two years from the date on which the consent was granted, but it may be a longer period. This enables those who apply for discharge consents to operate with a degree of commercial certainty. The new

---

[26] [1994] Env. L.R. 165.

Schedule 10 increases the minimum period before revocation or modification to four years.[27] If, however, it appears to the Agency when conducting a review of a consent that no discharge has been made in pursuance of that consent for the preceding 12 months, the Agency may revoke the consent even though the revocation occurs within the stipulated period of exemption.[28] In addition, the Secretary of State may direct the Agency to revoke a consent, modify the conditions to which it is subject, or make an unconditional consent subject to conditions if this is necessary in order to give effect to any European Community or international obligation, or for the protection of public health and flora and fauna which are dependent on the aquatic environment. In the latter cases only, compensation is payable to any person who suffers loss as a result of the Secretary of State's direction if the direction is made within the period during which the consent is exempt from variation, *unless* the Secretary of State can show that the direction was necessary in the light of circumstances which could not reasonably be foreseen at the time when the consent was given, or that he is now in possession of material information about the discharge which was not reasonably available to the Agency when the consent was given.[29] Where a consent is revoked or modified within the period of exemption in order to give effect to E.C. or international obligations, no compensation is payable. In practice, however, this is unlikely to happen, because, save in an emergency, the Agency will be aware well in advance of any forthcoming E.C. or international obligations, since negotiating these usually takes a number of years.

## Enforcement Notices

Where the Agency is of the opinion that the holder of a discharge consent is contravening the conditions of his consent, or that such a contravention is likely, it may serve on him an enforcement notice specifying the matters constituting the contravention (or likely contravention), the steps which must be taken to avoid it, and the time within which such steps must be taken.[30] Failure to comply with an enforcement notice is an offence the maximum penalty for which is three months' imprisonment and a £20,000 fine in the magistrates' court or two years' imprisonment and an unlimited fine in the Crown Court. Enforcement notices, which were introduced by the Environment Act 1995, provide an alternative means to immediate prosecution by which the Agency can ensure compliance with the conditions of a discharge consent. Their use may be appropriate, for example in cases where the Agency suspects that the person in breach of his consent conditions does not realise that this is the case.

## Appeals[31]

An appeal to the Secretary of State lies where the Agency refuses to grant a consent, where it attaches conditions which are unreasonable, or where it unreasonably varies or revokes a consent. The discharger may also appeal against the service of an

[27] WRA 1991, Sched. 10 (as substituted by EA 1995, Sched. 22), para. 8(3).
[28] *ibid.*, para. 7(3).
[29] *ibid.* para. 7(5).
[30] WRA 1991, s.90B (inserted by EA 1995).
[31] WRA 1991, s.91(as amended by EA 1995, Sched. 22).

enforcement notice. An enforcement notice remains in force pending the outcome of an appeal, but an appeal against revocation or modification of a consent has the effect of suspending the Agency's decision until the appeal is determined or withdrawn. Where the Agency is of the opinion that an immediate revocation or modification is necessary to minimise or prevent the entry of polluting matter into water or to prevent harm to human health, however, it may specify that the revocation or modification is to remain effective during the period of an appeal. Where the Agency decides to do this and that decision is, on appeal, found to have been unreasonable, the person affected is entitled to compensation.

## The Offences[32]

The Water Resources Act 1991 makes it a criminal offence, under section 85, to commit certain acts in relation to "controlled waters", but provides, in section 88, that acting in accordance with a discharge consent is a *defence* to prosecution for these offences. The Act sets out a number of inter-related water pollution offences. Under the Act, it is an offence to "cause or knowingly permit" any of the following:

(i) Any poisonous, noxious or polluting matter or any solid waste matter to enter any controlled waters (s.85(1));

(ii) Any matter, other than trade or sewage effluent, to enter controlled waters by being discharged from a drain or sewer in contravention of a prohibition imposed under section 86 (see below) (s.85(2));

(iii) Any trade effluent or sewage effluent to be discharged:

    (a) into any controlled waters, or

    (b) from land in England and Wales, through a pipe, into the sea outside the seaward limits of controlled waters (s.85(3));

(iv) Any trade effluent or sewage effluent to be discharged, in contravention of any prohibition imposed by section 86 (see below), from a building or fixed plant:

    (a) on to or into any land, or

    (b) into any waters of a lake or pond which are not inland freshwaters (s.85(4));

(v) Any matter whatever to enter any inland freshwaters so as to tend (either directly or in combination with other matter . . .) to impede the proper flow of the waters in a manner leading, or likely to lead, to a substantial aggravation of:

    (a) pollution due to other causes, or

    (b) the consequences of such pollution (s.85(5)).

The Act also makes it a specific offence to contravene the conditions of a discharge consent (s.85(6)).

---

[32] *ibid.*, s.85.

The penalty is the same for all of the offences, namely a maximum £20,000 fine and three months' imprisonment in the magistrates' court, or two years' imprisonment and an unlimited fine in the Crown Court.

## Prohibitions[33]

Under section 86 of the Water Resources Act 1991, the Environment Agency may prohibit, or restrict by conditions, the discharge of substances into water. Prohibitions, which were first introduced by the Water Act 1989, are designed to cover situations where a universally applicable statutory offence is not appropriate because the matter being discharged is not of its nature harmful, but where, in certain circumstances, its discharge may pose a risk of pollution. Selective use of prohibitions enables the Environment Agency to exercise control over many different forms of discharge in only those circumstances where control is needed and without the need to make reference to an endless list of specific statutory offences prohibiting the discharge of specific substances in specific circumstances. The prohibition may be used, for example, in relation to discharges from a drain or sewer of substances other than trade or sewage effluent (chemicals or surface water run-off, for example), or in relation to discharges of trade or sewage effluent into waters other than controlled waters or the sea. A prohibition is effected by a notice served on the holder of a consent by the Environment Agency, and, save in cases of emergency, comes into force three months after the notice has been served. In addition, however, there is a standing prohibition on the discharge of certain dangerous substances prescribed by regulations, so that a discharge containing these substances gives rise to the commission of an offence automatically, without the need for the Agency to notify the discharger.

## The General Offence

The first of the offences listed above, that of causing or knowingly permitting the entry of poisonous, noxious or polluting matter, may be termed the general pollution offence and is by far the most important in practice. It is widely drafted and prohibits the *entry* of polluting matter rather than simply its *discharge*. The offence of permitting the *entry* of matter may be committed where the offender is entirely passive, whilst permitting the *discharge* of matter may be seen as requiring acquiesence in a state of affairs which has previously been created by some positive act, *e.g.* allowing the matter to flow into the waters through a pipe. The general offence is not exclusive of the more specific offences. In other words, where an offence of discharging is committed, an offence of entry will invariably be committed as well. Thus, where the circumstances of an offence are unclear, it is common for the prosecution to charge the general offence alongside one or more of the specific offences.

## The Other Offences

The other offences are more narrowly defined. The offences in sections 85(2) and (4) are only committed where there is a prohibition in force under section 86. Where no

---

[33] *ibid.*, s.86.

prohibition is in force, the discharge from a drain or sewer of matter other than trade or sewage effluent (surface water run-off, for example) into controlled waters, and the discharge of trade or sewage effluent on to or into any land or into any lake or pond other than inland freshwaters will not necessarily be an offence. Such discharges, however, may give rise to the commission of an offence under section 85(1) (the general offence) if, for example, the surface water in question carries with it poisonous, noxious or polluting matter, or if trade or sewage effluent discharged on to land runs off from that land and enters controlled waters. The offence of aggravating pollution under section 85(5) is largely self-explanatory, whilst the reference to a pipe in section 85(3), may, as has been suggested, reasonably be seen as distinguishing the offence from one of discharging from a ship, which is subject to control under the Food and Environment Protection Act 1985.[34]

## Definition of "Trade or Sewage Effluent"[35]

"Effluent" is simply defined by the Water Resources Act 1991 to mean "any liquid". "Trade effluent" includes any effluent from trade premises (including agricultural, fish farming and research establishments), other than domestic sewage or surface water, whilst "sewage effluent" includes any effluent, other than surface water, from a sewerage works.

## Definition of "Controlled Waters"[36]

Controlled waters are defined by the Act so as to include almost all inland and coastal waters, as well as all territorial sea waters out to a distance of three miles. The act identifies four separate categories of controlled waters:

(i) "Relevant territorial waters". The territorial sea is measured outwards from a set of internationally agreed geographical baselines which link certain points on the U.K.'s coastline (in much the same way as a "join the dots" picture). The U.K.'s territorial waters extend outwards for 12 miles from these baselines. Controlled waters, however, do not extend this far; they extend only to a distance of three miles.

(ii) "Coastal waters". These are estuaries and other waters landwards of the territorial sea baselines as far as the limits of the highest tides.

(iii) "Inland freshwaters". These are the waters of any lake, pond or reservoir and of rivers and watercourses (including those underground) whether natural or artificial.

(iv) "Groundwaters". These are waters which run in underground strata, including, for example, waters which serve wells and boreholes.

---

[34] Burnett-Hall, *U.K. Environmental Law* (1995).
[35] WRA 1991, s.221.
[36] *ibid.*, s.104.

The definition of controlled waters also includes watercourses which have dried up. In *R v. Dovermoss Ltd*,[37] Stuart Smith L.J. held that a watercourse did not cease to be a watercourse simply because it was dry at a particular time. If, however, the watercourse was dry at the time when the poisonous, noxious or polluting matter was put into it, no offence could be committed under the Act unless and until water ran again in the watercourse. Moreover, since the Act defines inland freshwaters as "waters *of* any watercourse", rather than "waters *in* any watercourse", the fact that the stream in question had deviated from its normal course did not preclude it from being controlled waters.

## Definition of "Poisonous, Noxious or Polluting Matter"

The offence under section 85(1) requires "poisonous, noxious or polluting matter" to enter controlled waters. These words are not defined in the Water Resources Act 1991 and have been the subject of comparatively little judicial consideration. As has been noted, what is poisonous is necessarily a matter of degree. Paracelsus, who died in 1541, stated: "All substances are poisons. There is none which is not a poison. The right dose differentiates a poison and a remedy".[38] The Act contains no suggestion that "poisonous matter" should be construed merely by reference to its effect on humans. Indeed, protection of the quality of water used for rearing livestock and for fishing is of great importance. The Act refers to the nature of the matter which enters controlled waters and not to whether the waters themselves are thereafter rendered poisonous. It is, however, difficult to define "poisonous" in the abstract, and in most cases the word will only have meaning when considered in relation to the organisms on which a substance, ingested in a particular quantity, may have an impact. The best solution to this conundrum may be to regard as poisonous anything that may act as a poison on any organism with which it comes into contact, subject to a *de minimis* exception in cases where the amount of matter which enters the waters is so trivial as not to be a poison to anything.[39] "Noxious" is arguably somewhat broader than "poisonous" in that noxious may cover effects which are physically unpleasant without necessarily being dangerous in any respect.[40]

The term "polluting" has been the subject of judicial consideration, notably in *National Rivers Authority v. Egger U.K. Ltd*.[41] The case concerned a visible brown stain which extended for a length of 100 metres into the river adjoining the defendants' premises. There was no evidence that anything in the water had been harmed by the discharge, and the question arose whether mere discolouration of the river amounted to the offence of causing or knowingly permitting "polluting matter" to enter the water. Matter which merely caused discolouration of water had been expressly excluded from the definition of "poisonous, noxious or polluting matter" which had appeared in the Rivers Pollution Prevention Act 1876, and this provision had been repeated in the Rivers (Prevention of Pollution) Act 1951. No such exclusion, however,

---

[37] *The Times,* February 3, 1995.
[38] Burnett-Hall, *U.K. Environmental Law* (1995).
[39] *ibid.*
[40] *ibid.*
[41] Newcastle upon Tyne Crown Court, June 15–17, 1992, unreported. See Burnett-Hall, *ibid.* pp. 351–354.

appears in the Water Resources Act 1991. The judge in *Egger* held that, in the light of this omission, mere discolouration of water could indeed amount to "pollution" under the Act. He also dealt with the more general question of whether or not matter was "polluting" was to be decided by reference simply to the nature of the matter itself, or by reference to whether its entry worsened the quality of the receiving water. Whilst the judge accepted that the word "polluting" clearly has a relationship to what is polluted, he held that it did not necessarily follow that matter could only be "polluting matter" once it had been shown that some harm had been caused by it. He went on to say that what the statute is concerned with is the nature of the material which enters the water. Therefore, the question whether matter is "polluting" should be regarded objectively in relation to a natural, unpolluted river. Thus:

> "One looks at the nature of the discharge and one says, 'is that discharge capable of causing harm to a river, in the sense of causing damage to uses to which a river might be put; damage to animal, vegetable or other — if there is such other life which might live in a river, or damaging that river aesthetically?' "

If the statute is concerned only with the *potential* effect of a substance which enters controlled waters and not with its *actual* effect, it follows that it is unnecessary to show that actual damage has been caused to the waters for an offence under section 85(1) to be made out. It also follows that adding any potentially polluting matter to water amounts to an offence, even where the water is already so heavily polluted and the added matter is in so diluted a form, that the quality of the receiving water is in fact improved. Such a conclusion is entirely consistent with a policy of maintaining and improving the quality of waterways, even though it may appear anomalous in cases where only slightly contaminated water is discharged into a heavily polluted stream.

The meaning of "polluting" was again considered in *R. v. Dovermoss Ltd.*[42] Dovermoss argued that to establish that polluting matter had entered controlled waters, it was necessary for the National Rivers Authority to show that harm had resulted to animals or plant life in those waters. The Court of Appeal, however, rejected this argument, basing its decision on the dictionary definition of "pollute", *viz.* "to make physically impure, foul or filthy; to dirty, stain, taint, befoul". The court held that actual harm need not be shown. It was sufficient to establish the offence under section 85(1) if it could be shown that the matter in question gave rise to the likelihood, or simply had the capability of causing harm.

## Definition of "Causing or Knowingly Permitting"

Common to all of the offences under the Water Resources Act 1991 is the requirement that the offender must "cause or knowingly permit" the entry or discharge of pollutants to water. This wording involves two separate offences. First, that of "causing" and secondly that of "knowingly permitting".

---

[42] *The Times,* February 3, 1995.

## "Causing" Pollution

Causing polluted matter to enter or to be discharged into controlled waters is an offence of strict liability, that is to say it is not necessary for the prosecution to prove *mens rea*. In other words, so long as a causal link can be shown between the defendant's activities and the entry or discharge of the matter (the *actus reus*), liability will follow without the need to show that the defendant intended or was negligent as to the entry or discharge in question. The leading judicial decision on the matter is that of the House of Lords in *Alphacell v. Woodward*.[43] Alphacell, a paper-making company, were prosecuted under the Rivers (Prevention of Pollution) Act 1951 for causing polluting matter to enter controlled waters when polluted water overflowed from their settling tanks into a river. This occurred because, without the company's knowledge, leaves and debris had prevented a pump from working. Their Lordships pointed out that the word "knowingly" applies only to the second offence of "knowingly permitting" and held that Alphacell had caused the discharge. Lord Wilberforce stated that:

> "The whole complex process which might lead to this result was an operation deliberately conducted by the appellants and I fail to see how a defect in one stage of it, even if we must assume that this happened without their negligence, can enable them to say that they did not cause the pollution. In my opinion, complication of this case by the infusion of the concept of *mens rea*, and its exceptions, is unnecessary and undesirable."

Lord Salmon, in *Alphacell*, expressed the view that an offence of strict liability was justified on grounds of public policy:

> "If . . . no conviction could be obtained under the Act of 1951 unless the prosecution could discharge the often impossible onus of proving that the pollution was caused intentionally or negligently, a great deal of pollution would go unpunished and undeterred . . . As a result, many rivers which are now filthy would become filthier still and many rivers which are now clean would lose their cleanliness. The legislature no doubt recognised that as a matter of public policy this would be most unfortunate."

Thus, Alphacell were found to have caused the pollution simply by having carried on the activity which gave rise to it. According to Lord Cross and Lord Wilberforce in *Alphacell*, the offence of "causing" is established only by active participation in the operation or chain of operations which result in the pollution. It therefore requires that the pollution must be the consequence (albeit unintentional or unforeseen) of a positive act on the part of the defendant, rather than of a mere passive looking on, although pollution which occurs in the latter circumstances may form the basis of a charge of "knowingly permitting".

The imposition of strict liability, of course, can lead to some harsh decisions. In *CPC (UK) Limited v. National Rivers Authority*,[44] for example, a defectively installed pipe at

---

[43] [1972] A.C. 824.
[44] *The Times*, August 4, 1994; ENDS 235, p. 41, 1994.

a factory caused leakage into a river. The pipe had been installed about nine months before the appellants had bought the factory and a full survey at the time of purchase had not revealed the defect. Despite this, the company were held to have caused the pollution. The Court of Appeal stated that the only relevant question was whether the factory was under the control of the appellants when the leakage occurred. It was accepted, however, that the company had behaved impeccably at all times. It was therefore given an absolute discharge by way of sentence and was not required to pay the costs of cleaning up the river. Although the sentiments behind the decision can be understood, the giving of an absolute discharge in these circumstances fails to respect the "polluter pays" principle and is, perhaps, an indication that U.K. courts are still wedded to the idea of fault-based liability for the costs of environmental damage.

It is possible for two or more individuals to be found guilty of "causing" a pollution incident. In *Attorney-General's Reference (No. 1 of 1994)*,[45] for example, the first respondent ran a business for the disposal of toxic industrial waste under a licence granted by the second respondents, who were sewerage undertakers. The third respondent, a local authority, performed, for a profit, the day to day business of the second respondents. The first respondent deposited polluting matter into the second respondents' sewerage system. The matter then flowed into controlled waters because of a failure at a pumping station run by the third respondent. The Recorder at first instance acquitted all three respondents, directing the jury that the offence of "causing" an entry of polluting matter could only be committed by one person. The Court of Appeal, however, held that this had been a misdirection and that the offence could be committed by two or more defendants, not only in the obvious case of defendants engaged in a joint enterprise, but also where each had performed different and separate acts which had contributed to the entry. Lord Taylor C.J. said that the facts of the case illustrated the impracticability of confining causation to one party, since a jury faced with concurrent causative conduct by more than one party would experience difficulty and reluctance in choosing one culprit.

## The Chain of Causation

In order for an offence of "causing" to be made out, a direct causal link must exist between the conduct of the defendant and the occurrence of the pollution. Therefore, where the chain of causation is broken either by the intervening act of a third party, or by an Act of God, the defendant may escape liability. In *Impress (Worcester) Ltd v. Rees*,[46] for example, an unknown person opened a valve in an oil storage tank which caused fuel oil to escape into the river. The Divisional Court held that this was an intervening cause of so powerful a nature that the conduct of the defendants was not a cause of the pollution at all but merely part of its surrounding circumstances. Commenting on the *Impress* case in *Alphacell*, Lord Wilberforce said:

> "I do not desire to question this conclusion, but it should not be regarded as a decision that in every case the act of a third person necessarily interrupts the

---

[45] *The Independent,* January 31, 1995.
[46] [1971] 2 All E.R. 357.

chain of causation . . . The answer to such questions is one of degree and depends on a proper attribution of responsibility for the flow of polluting matter."

In *National Rivers Authority v. Wright Engineering Co. Ltd*,[47] where a vandalised oil storage tank leaked oil into a brook, the Divisional Court upheld the acquittal of the defendants. Although there was evidence that minor acts of vandalism had occurred on the defendants' premises in the past, the acts were on a smaller scale and of a different type. They had not been seen as a problem and no action had been taken to prevent them. In these circumstances, the Divisional Court held that it was permissible for the magistrates to decide that the pollution had been caused by the vandals rather than the company and that the different nature of the previous acts of vandalism had not been such as to mean that the company had caused the pollution by failing to take adequate preventive measures.

Where the nature of an intervening act of a third party is clearly foreseeable, however, the position may be different. Thus, in *National Rivers Authority v. Yorkshire Water Service Ltd*[48] the defendants were responsible for a sewer into which an unidentified industrial customer of theirs had discharged solvents. The House of Lords held that there was sufficient evidence on which a court could conclude that the defendants were *prima facie* guilty of causing the pollution, although, in the event, Yorkshire Water Services were able to escape liability by relying on a statutory defence.

## "Knowingly Permitting" Pollution

The offence of "knowingly permitting" an entry or discharge has been subject to less judicial consideration than has that of "causing" pollution. In essence, however, the offence is designed to catch the offender who knows that pollution is occurring, has the power to do something about it, and yet does nothing.

In *Price v. Cromack*[49] the appellant was a farmer who, by the terms of a contract, had bound himself to accept on to his land effluent from a neighbouring animal by-products company of which he was the director. The effluent escaped through the defective wall of a lagoon constructed on his land and flowed into a stream. Price was convicted of having "caused" the entry of poisonous, noxious or polluting matter to enter controlled waters. On appeal, the prosecution argued, following *Alphacell*, that the defendant had undertaken a positive act by entering into an arrangement whereby effluent was received on to his land.

Lord Widgery, however, did not accept that the nature of the arrangement was sufficient to maintain a conviction for "causing" pollution. Whilst he accepted in principle the proposition that there should be no substantive difference between the case of a man who generates pollution on his own land and that of one who agrees to accept pollution generated by another, his Lordship made the point that it was not so much a question of distinguishing between the culpability of those individuals, but of

---

[47] [1994] 4 All E.R. 281.
[48] [1995] 1 All E.R. 225.
[49] [1975] 1 W.L.R. 988.

ascertaining the precise nature of the offence committed. His Lordship could not accept that there was a "causing" of the entry of polluting matter "merely because the landowner stands by and watches the polluting matter cross his land into the stream, even if he has committed himself by contract to allowing the adjoining owner so to act." Lord Widgery implied what Ashworth J. had stated explicitly in the same case, that if the defendant had been charged instead with "knowingly permitting" the pollution, "I do not see what answer the present appellant could conceivably have had in the circumstances of this case."

The decision in *Price v. Cromack* was followed in *Wychavon D.C. v. National Rivers Authority*.[50] In that case, raw sewage escaped into the River Avon from a sewer which was operated and maintained by the district council, as agents of the water company. The council failed to remedy the situation for some hours, despite its being aware of the discharge. Quashing the conviction for "causing" the discharge, the Divisional Court held that the council should have been charged instead with "knowingly permitting", because it had not done anything positive to encourage the discharge, but had merely remained inactive.

It has been suggested,[51] and it is submitted rightly, that the decisions in both *Price v. Cromack* and *Wychavon D.C. v. National Rivers Authority* should now be treated with caution in the light of the reaffirmation, in *National Rivers Authority v. Yorkshire Water Services Ltd* and in *Attorney General's Reference (No. 1 of 1994)*, of the principles enunciated in *Alphacell*. As those authors point out, both of the decisions seem to ignore the fact that it is made clear in *Alphacell* that it is not the *immediate* cause of the pollution which must be the result of some positive act on the part of the defendant, rather, in the words of Lord Wilberforce, it is the "operation or chain of operations" underlying that cause which must be "active". Thus, in *Alphacell*, the establishment and management of a paper-making factory with an adjacent effluent treatment plant meant that it was inevitable that if something went wrong with the plant, polluted water would be discharged into the river. It is difficult to see how this situation differs from that in *Price v. Cromack*, where the defendant established a system for accepting effluent on to his land for treatment. In *Price v. Cromack*, however, Lord Widgery appears to distinguish *Alphacell* on the somewhat tenuous basis that the defendant, Price, had engaged in no physical act conducive to the flow of effluent on to his land. Rather, it had found its way there by gravity. It is respectfully submitted that this distinction ignores the fundamental principle, expounded by Lord Wilberforce in *Alphacell*, that liability for "causing" pollution should follow where the defendant, prior to the pollution incident, has actively put in place a system for the management of pollution, from which, in the event of its failure, the escape of pollution is the inevitable result.

## "Knowingly"

Knowledge that the matter in question was entering or being discharged into the water is, of course, a necessary element of a charge of "knowingly permitting". In the absence of a confession, however, it is notoriously difficult to prove the state of a man's mind. Therefore, if the prosecution are able to establish all of the relevant surrounding

[50] [1993] 1 W.L.R. 125.
[51] Ball and Bell, *Environmental Law* (3rd ed., 1995), p. 433.

facts, they are entitled to ask the magistrates or jury to infer that the accused acted with knowledge of those facts unless there is some convincing evidence from him to the contrary.[52] Thus in *Schulmans Incorporated Ltd v. National Rivers Authority*,[53] it was held that a defendant could be fixed with constructive knowledge of facts of which he ought to have been aware in circumstances where he had deliberately turned a blind eye to the obvious or had refrained from inquiry because he did not wish his suspicions to be confirmed.

On the question of whether or not the prosecution must establish that the defendant knows that the entry in question is poisonous, noxious or polluting, the case of *Ashcroft v. Cambro Waste Products*,[54] which concerned "knowingly permitting" the deposit of controlled waste, suggests that this may not be necessary and that it is sufficient for the prosecution to show only knowledge of the entry.[55]

*"Permitting"*

"Permitting" may mean either giving leave for an act which, without that leave, could not legally be done, or to abstain from taking reasonable steps to prevent an act, where it is within a man's power to do so.[56] It follows from this that a person cannot "permit" an occurrence of pollution which he is powerless to prevent. Thus, in *Schulmans Incorporated Ltd v. National Rivers Authority* convictions for "knowingly permitting" matter to enter controlled waters as a result of an oil spillage which flowed into a brook were overturned on appeal on the basis that there was no evidence that the appellants could have prevented the escape of fuel oil into the brook sooner than they did.

## Breach of Consent Conditions

As has been said, section 85(6) of the Water Resources Act 1991 makes it a specific offence to breach the conditions of a discharge consent. Two cases here are worthy of note, both of which illustrate that the courts have been prepared to adopt a tough approach and to impose strict liability in relation to this offence. In *Taylor Woodrow Property Management Ltd v. National Rivers Authority*[57] the defendants held a discharge consent relating to the outflow from an industrial estate of which they were no longer the occupiers. A third party discharged oil from the outfall pipe in breach of the conditions of the consent. The defendants were convicted of an offence under section 85(6) even though they themselves had not made the discharge. Similarly, in *National Rivers Authority v. Alfred McAlpine Homes (East) Ltd*[58] strict vicarious liability was imposed on the defendant company for the acts of its employees in causing a breach of the conditions of a consent, even though the employees in question could not be said to have been exercising the "controlling mind" of the company. Morland J stated that to hold otherwise "would render important environmental legislation almost entirely nugatory".

[52] *per* Lord Diplock in *Sweet v. Parsley* [1970] A.C. 132 at 164.
[53] [1993] Env L.R.D. 1.
[54] [1981] 1 W.L.R. 1349.
[55] But see Chapter 8, [waste] p. 185 above and Bates, *U.K. Waste Law* (1992), p. 172.
[56] *per* Atkin L.J. in *Berton v. Alliance Economic Investment Co. Ltd* [1922] 1 K.B. 742 at 759.
[57] [1995] J.E.L. 55.
[58] [1995] J.E.L. 60.

## Defences

In contrast with the position in relation to breaches of a Waste Management Licence, in relation to water pollution there is *no* general defence of taking all reasonable precautions and exercising all due diligence to avoid the commission of an offence. There are, however, a number of specific statutory defences to a prosecution under section 85 of the Water Resources Act 1991.[59] The most obvious, of course, is that the discharge in question was made in accordance with the conditions of a consent given under the Act. In addition, a discharge made in accordance with an authorisation granted under the IPC regime or in accordance with a waste management licence will be immune from prosecution, as will discharges made for works purposes under the Water Industry Act 1991 and those made in pursuance of a statute or statutory order. A licence for dumping effluent at sea granted under the Food and Environment Protection Act 1985 also provides a defence. Certain other kinds of defence are also afforded by the Act,[60] which provides that a person will not be guilty of an offence under section 85 in any of the following situations:

(i) Where the entry or discharge is made to avoid danger to life or health *provided that*:

   (a) such steps as are reasonably practicable in the circumstances are taken to minimise the extent of the discharge or to mitigate its effect *and*

   (b) details of the discharge or entry are furnished to the Environment Agency as soon as is reasonably practicable;

(ii) Where the discharge is of trade or sewerage effluent from a vessel. (This is regulated by byelaws);

(iii) Where a person permits (as opposed to causes) an entry of matter from an abandoned mine. (Note, however, that section 60 of the Environment Act 1995 provides that this defence will no longer apply after December 31, 1999 in relation to mines abandoned after that date);

(iv) Where a deposit on land of solid refuse from a mine or quarry is made with the consent of the Environment Agency and that waste falls into inland freshwaters *provided that* all reasonable steps have been taken to prevent this;

(v) Where a highway authority or other person entitled to open a drain causes or permits a discharge from that drain *unless* that discharge contravenes a prohibition made under section 86 of the Act.

In addition, as has been said, it may in very exceptional circumstances be possible to plead the irrationality of a condition as a defence to prosecution, notwithstanding the failure of this defence in *R v. Ettrick Trout Company Ltd and William Baxter* (above).

---

[59] WRA 1991, s.88.
[60] *ibid.,* s.89.

## Recovery of Clean-up Costs[61]

Where the Environment Agency considers that polluting matter is likely to enter controlled waters, or where such matter has already entered controlled waters, it may take action to prevent the matter from entering the waters or, in the latter case, to remedy pollution which has occurred. The power to take preventive measures enables the Agency, for example, to divert the course of a spillage away from controlled waters in the aftermath of a road or rail accident, whilst the power to remedy the effects of pollution extends, for example, to the restocking of a river with fish. In both types of case, the Agency may recover the costs of its operations from the person who caused or knowingly permitted the matter to be where it was likely to enter the waters or, as the case may be, to enter the waters. For some time it was unclear whether the Agency's power to take preventive steps enabled it to carry out mere investigations and to charge the cost of these to the suspected polluter. The question is now answered by the Environment Act 1995, however, which provides that such costs may be recovered only where the investigations result in the subsequent service of a "works notice" on the polluter.[62]

## Works Notices[63]

The Environment Act 1995 establishes a new procedure for the exercise of the powers described above by inserting into the Water Resources Act 1991 a number of provisions which, at the time of writing, have not yet come into force. Under these provisions, the Agency will be entitled to carry out preventive or remedial works *only* where it considers either that these are necessary "forthwith" (in the aftermath of a spillage, for example) or where, after reasonable inquiry, the person who caused or knowingly permitted the pollution (or accumulation of polluting matter) cannot be found. In all other cases, instead of carrying out the works itself, the Agency will be entitled to serve a "works notice" on the polluter, requiring him to take specified steps to prevent the matter in question from entering controlled waters or, as the case may be, to remedy the effects of pollution which has occurred. Such remediation may include the removal and disposal of the polluting matter and, so far as is reasonably practicable, the restoration of the waters in question to their former state of cleanliness.

The procedure for the service of works notices is broadly similar to that which obtains in relation to remediation notices served under the contaminated land regime. Thus, before serving the notice, the Agency is required to endeavour to consult the person on whom it is to be served, together with others whose rights may be affected by the proposed works. Where third parties are required to grant rights to the person on whom a works notice is served to enable him to comply with it, they are entitled to recover compensation from him. In addition, where the person on whom a works notice is served fails to carry out the specified works within the specified time, the Environment Agency may carry out those works itself and recover the costs of so doing

---

[61] *ibid.,* s.161.
[62] *ibid.,* s.161A(11)(b) (inserted by EA 1995, Sched. 22, para. 162).
[63] WRA 1991, s.161A (inserted by EA 1995, Sched. 22, para. 162).

from the defaulter. Failure to comply with the requirements of a works notice is an offence punishable in the magistrates' court by three months' imprisonment and a maximum fine of £20,000 and in the Crown Court by imprisonment for two years and an unlimited fine.

The provisions relating to works notices are an important new weapon in the Environment Agency's pollution control armoury, which had long been requested by their predecessors, the National Rivers Authority. Although works notices cannot be used to prevent the making of a discharge in pursuance of a consent,[64] they may be used to prevent the occurrence of illegal discharges and, where consent conditions have been breached, to secure remediation of pollution. Whilst this was, of course, possible under the old procedure, this required the National Rivers Authority to incur the initial expense of remediation in the hope that this could subsequently be recovered from the polluter. Under the new procedure, however, the initial costs of remediation are to be met directly by the polluter, thus preventing a drain on the financial resources of the Agency. The prospect of meeting the cost of cleaning-up pollution, which will usually be very much higher than any fine resulting from a conviction under section 85, acts as a powerful deterrent for industrial polluters.

## Precautionary Measures

Cleaning up waterways which have become polluted can be very costly. Pollution of the estuary of the Mersey Basin and its tributaries, for example, is necessitating works expected to last for 25 years and will cost an estimated £2.5 billion.[65] The growing realisation that such *ex post facto* measures are enormously expensive has led the U.K., in keeping with the policy of the E.C., to develop a system of controls which aims to prevent the occurrence of pollution.

To this end, the Water Resources Act 1991 gives the Secretary of State the power to make regulations prohibiting any person from having custody or control of any poisonous, noxious or polluting matter unless certain prescribed works are carried out to prevent that matter from entering controlled waters.[66] The regulations may also provide that persons already in custody or control of such matter should carry out similar works. Such regulations may create new criminal offences for breach of their provisions, provided that the maximum penalty is not greater than could be imposed for an offence under section 85.

To date, the only regulations which have been made under this provision are the Control of Pollution (Silage, Slurry and Agricultural Fuel Oil) Regulations 1991.[67] These impose a number of controls over silage making operations and the design and use of stores for slurry and agricultural fuel oil.

---

[64] WRA 1991, s.161A(7).
[65] Royal Commission on Environmental Pollution (1992) Sixteenth Report: *Freshwater Quality* (1992) (Cmnd. 1966).
[66] WRA 1991, s.92.
[67] S.I. 1991 No. 324.

## Water Protection Zones[68]

Under the Water Resources Act, the Secretary of State may create Water Protection Zones with a view to preventing or restricting the entry of poisonous, noxious or polluting matter into controlled waters. The zones are designated areas within which certain activities likely to have this result are curtailed or prohibited. The wording of the provisions gives the Secretary of State a large measure of discretion to control agricultural and other activities. Alternatively, the Secretary of State may, by the regulations, give the Environment Agency the power to determine which activities should be prohibited or restricted and the manner in which this should be done. It is not possible, however, for either the Secretary of State or the Agency to require the carrying out of positive works. The regulations may provide a procedure for obtaining consents from the Environment Agency to carry out the restricted activities and may create new criminal offences for breach of those consents punishable on the same scale as those under section 85.

The procedure for designating a Water Protection Zone is set out in Schedule 11 to the Water Resources Act 1991. In summary, where the Environment Agency proposes to create a Water Protection Zone, it must apply to the Secretary of State, submitting a draft of the order which it seeks and must comply with quite extensive publicity requirements involving publication of its proposals in two local newspapers and thereafter in *The London Gazette*. The Secretary of State must consult with the Minister of Agriculture, Fisheries and Food before designating a Water Protection Zone and *may* hold a public inquiry, although he has no duty to do so.

Water Protection Zones, by establishing specific regimes appropriate to the needs of particular areas, provide a useful means of controlling diffuse sources of pollution such as agricultural surface run-off containing pesticides. Although there is no specific provision in the Act for paying compensation to those affected by the creation of a Water Protection Zone, the Act provides that the Secretary of State may include in regulations such consequential and supplemental provisions as he considers appropriate. It is conceivable that such provisions might include compensation payable to farmers, who have so far opposed the use of Water Protection Zones for fear of the costs which their creation might entail. To date, no zones have been designated under the provisions, although one is proposed for the catchment of the River Dee.

## Nitrate Sensitive Areas[69]

Nitrates, which are contained in agricultural fertilisers, act as a plant nutrient. On entering waters they increase the numbers of some plants but cause a decline in the growth of those plants and species which flourish in nutrient poor waters. This leads to a deterioration in the quality of the waters in terms of biodiversity. Nitrates can enter water by one of three main routes: surface water run-off from agricultural land; discharge of effluent containing sewage or animal waste, and rain. The increased use of fertilisers has significantly increased nitrate levels in water over the last 50 years.

[68] WRA 1991, s.93.
[69] *ibid.*, s.94.

Therefore, to prevent further increases, the Act provides for agricultural activities to be restricted on land designated as a Nitrate Sensitive Area.

Although nitrates might adequately have been dealt with by means of Water Protection Zones, it was felt necessary to incorporate provisions specifically relating to nitrates into the legislation largely to allay public concern over levels of nitrate in water after action had been brought against the U.K. in the European Court of Justice for failure to comply with Directive 80/778 on Drinking Water. The provisions relating to Nitrate Sensitive Areas differ from those relating to Water Protection Zones in a number of respects. Nitrate Sensitive Areas are, in general, designated in England by the Minister of Agriculture Fisheries and Food, whereas Water Protection Zones are designated by the Secretary of State for the Environment, acting in consultation with the Minister, and in Wales by the Secretary of State for Wales acting alone. The order designating a Nitrate Sensitive Area may stipulate for either a mandatory or a voluntary system of control.

A mandatory order is similar to an order establishing a Water Protection Zone in that it imposes prohibitions and restrictions on certain activities with which failure to comply is an offence. In contrast with the position in relation to Water Protection Zones, however, in a Nitrate Sensitive Area the polluter may be required to undertake specific positive works such as the digging of ditches and construction of holding tanks. Also in contrast with Water Protection Zones, the Act explicitly provides that the order establishing a Nitrate Sensitive Area may provide for compensation to be payable to those affected by it. Unlike a voluntary designation order, a mandatory order can only be made where it has been requested by the Environment Agency and provided that the consent of the Treasury is obtained. The Agency may only request such an order where it considers that its other powers are insufficient to control pollution of water by nitrates, and it must comply with publicity requirements which are similar to those relating to Water Protection Zones. The relevant Ministers may hold a public inquiry before making a mandatory order, but have no duty to do so.

At the time of writing, no mandatory orders have been made and the government has indicated its preference for the use, at least initially, of a voluntary system of control. To this end, the Nitrate Sensitive Areas (Designation) Order 1990[70] designates 10 areas and provides for two types of scheme under which farmers within designated areas can enter into management agreements with the Environment Agency under which they agree to abide by certain agricultural practices for five years in return for an annual payment. The order provides for a "basic scheme" and a "premium scheme", the latter imposing more stringent restrictions than the former but in return for a higher level of compensation. These schemes have been well received by the agricultural industry and in the light of their success the government, by new regulations, has designated a further 12 areas.[71] The new regulations, which provide for a basic scheme as well as for two other schemes relating to arable land and grass land respectively, have been made under section 2(2) of the European Communities Act 1972 in order to give effect to E.C. Agri-Environment Regulation 2078/92, which concerns the de-intensification of agriculture. In relation to E.C. Directive 91/676 on Nitrates, however, it is clear that the present system of voluntary agreements,

[70] S.I. 1990 No. 1013.
[71] Nitrate Sensitive Areas Regulations 1994 (S.I. 1994 No. 1729).

underpinned by guidance contained in the *Code of Good Agricultural Practice for the Protection of Water* issued by the Ministry of Agriculture, Fisheries and Food, is not sufficient to comply with the requirements of the Directive. It is therefore likely that a system of mandatory control will be put into effect in the near future and that this will involve a reduction in the present amounts of compensation payable to farmers, since these appear to conflict with the "polluter pays" principle. It has been suggested, however, that it may be possible to justify the continuation of such payments as part of the E.C.'s policy of agricultural de-intensification as represented by Regulation 2078/92.[72]

## WATER POLLUTION AT COMMON LAW

Whilst the statutory regime is primarily concerned with punishing the polluter, the common law provides the principal means by which those whose private rights have been interfered with may claim compensation from him.

The main causes of action for water pollution are nuisance and the rule in *Rylands v. Fletcher*, together with a number of miscellaneous ancient rights attaching to the ownership of land, infringement of which is now generally regarded by the courts as the commission of a form of private nuisance. These property rights include, for example, the right to abstract water which flows through or under land and the right, known as a "riparian" right, to use water adjacent to one's land. It is a general principle of common law that a person over or under whose land water flows is entitled to receive that water in an unpolluted state.

### Riparian Rights

A person who owns land adjoining a river or a stream (*i.e* any watercourse which flows in a defined channel) is known as the riparian owner. He normally owns the bed of the river (or owns it to a point equidistant from his neighbour on the opposite side) but he does not own the water itself. The riparian owner has, as an incident of his ownership of the land, the right to receive waters in their natural state. This means that not only has the riparian owner the right to receive his water free from impurities, but that he is also entitled to receive water in the same *quantity* and of the same *natural character* as he has come to expect. The nature of the latter right is neatly illustrated by the decision in *Young & Co. v. Bankier Distillery Co.*,[73] where discharges from a mine upstream of the plaintiffs altered the character of the water downstream from soft to hard. This in turn caused changes to the quality of the plaintiff distillers' whisky. They were able to obtain an injunction to stop the defendants' activities even though the defendants had not made the water impure.

As has been said, riparian rights are an incident of land ownership. In other words they are a form of property right. It might be thought, then, that such rights are unqualified and absolute, and that liability for their infringement would be strict as is

---

[72] Ball and Bell, *Environmental Law* (3rd ed., 1995), p. 454.
[73] [1893] A.C. 691.

the case, for example, in relation to interference with an easement. The courts, however, have consistently tended to see riparian rights as related to the plaintiff's reasonable enjoyment of his land and have treated the infringement of riparian rights as analogous to the commission of a nuisance. It follows from this that such rights are not absolute, but are subject to the reasonable land use requirements of others. Thus it has been said that riparian owners upstream of the plaintiff may make "ordinary use"[74] of a watercourse in the exercise of their own riparian rights. As in an ordinary nuisance action, the courts engage in a "balancing act" to decide what is reasonable as between two riparian owners' conflicting uses of the water in question. That having been said, the courts have to some extent recognised the essentially proprietary character of riparian rights, in that they have been prepared to treat the interference with riparian rights as causing damage to property rather than a mere loss of enjoyment of that property,[75] thereby circumventing the doctrine of locality which so often stands in the way of the plaintiff in a traditional nuisance action.

Although the courts most commonly adopt a nuisance-based approach, liability for the infringement of riparian rights has sometimes been held to arise in trespass, which again reflects a recognition of their proprietary nature. In *Jones v. Llanwrst Urban District Council*,[76] for example, the plaintiff successfully brought an action in trespass against the defendant council, which had deposited solid waste in a river so that it came to rest on the river bed of which he was the riparian owner.

Additionally, liability in public nuisance may arise where the nuisance affects a "class of Her Majesty's subjects" one of whom can show that he has suffered special damage. This was the case, for example, in *R v. Bradford Navigation Co.*,[77] where a polluted watercourse was held to be a public nuisance when its smell affected residents living nearby.

## Rights in Respect of Groundwater

Water which percolates through or under land, as opposed to flowing in a defined channel above or beneath it, is known as "groundwater". Pollution of this is also an actionable nuisance. Thus, in *Ballard v. Tomlinson*,[78] the plaintiff brewery was successful when the defendant deposited sewage in a well on his land which polluted water percolating through the plaintiffs' land with the result that they were unable to draw fresh water from their own well.

The decision in *Ballard v. Tomlinson* was considered in *Cambridge Water Company Ltd v. Eastern Counties Leather plc*.[79] The plaintiff water company abstracted water from a borehole which had become contaminated when solvents had seeped into the watercourse beneath the defendant's tannery and had percolated towards the borehole. The water company brought an action in negligence, nuisance and under the rule in

---

[74] *per* Lord Macnaughten in *Young & Co. v. Bankier Distillery Co.* [1893] A.C. 691 at 698.
[75] *ibid.*
[76] [1911] 1 Ch. 393.
[77] [1865] 6 B. & S. 631.
[78] [1885] 29 Ch.D. 115. Note that whilst a defendant may not *pollute* groundwater to the detriment of his neighbours, he may *abstract* it without committing a nuisance: *Bradford Corporation v. Pickles* [1895] A.C. 587.
[79] [1994] 2 A.C. 264.

*Rylands v. Fletcher*. The Court of Appeal, following *Ballard v. Tomlinson*, held that the right to abstract unpolluted groundwater was a proprietary one and that accordingly, once the water company had shown causation, liability would follow. The House of Lords, however, reversed this decision, holding that the action was properly to be categorised as an action in nuisance, of which the rule in *Rylands v. Fletcher* was merely an offshoot, and that, following the dicta of Lord Reid in *The Wagon Mound (No.2)*[80] foreseeability of the type of harm was a necessary ingredient in the tort of nuisance. Therefore, because the tannery had permitted the solvents to be spilled at a time when their harmful effects were not known, they were able to avoid liability. *Ballard v. Tomlinson*, in which the issue of foreseeability of harm did not arise, was distinguished.

## PLANNING CONTROLS

Development has the potential to affect water quality by increasing surface run-off and, more significantly, by leading to the pollution of groundwater. The extent to which the environment is taken into account in planning decisions is considered in Chapter 5. Under the Planning and Compensation Act 1991, planning authorities are required to take account of environmental considerations, such as potential water pollution, in preparing their development plans, and must consult with, *inter alia*, English Nature and the Environment Agency in so doing. In addition, water pollution will be a material consideration in individual planning decisions.

## ECONOMIC INSTRUMENTS

The use of economic instruments to control water pollution is relatively undeveloped, although the issue was considered by the Royal Commission on Environmental Pollution in its sixteenth report. The Royal Commission concluded that the use of economic instruments was an essential component of effective polices to reduce pollution. Those economic instruments which the Royal Commission considered included tradeable permits to discharge which might be bought and sold on the open market and a tax on the discharge of effluent. At the time of writing, the Department of the Environment is preparing a discussion paper on tradeable discharge permits for certain stretches of water. A tax on effluent might take one of two forms. First, the tax might be imposed at a level which simply reflects the environmental cost of the discharge in question. Secondly, the tax might be set at a higher level than this in order to provide a stronger disincentive to pollute.

[80] [1967] 1 A.C. 617.

# EUROPEAN COMMUNITY WATER LAW

The U.K.'s statutory regime in relation to water has been heavily influenced by European Community law. Water pollution was the focus of the earliest environmental policies developed by the European Community and is now the most developed area of E.C. environmental law with more than 25 Directives and judicial decisions. E.C. legislation has been successful in improving water quality throughout the Community.

E.C. policy on water, however, is currently undergoing important changes. The European Council and the European Parliament called for a fundamental review of water policy in June 1995. In response, the European Commission published a Communication to the Council and to Parliament which outlines certain fundamental changes in the direction of water policy. These changes, which are discussed below, reflect the growing importance of the principle of subsidiarity[81] and accord with the views expressed by the European Council, which, meeting in Edinburgh in 1992, issued a statement in the following terms:

> "On the environment the Commission intends to simplify, consolidate and update existing texts, particularly those on air and water to take new knowledge and technical progress into account . . . on water quality the Commission intends, in line with subsidiarity, to reorientate the rules and regulations towards compliance with essential quality and health parameters, leaving Member States free to add secondary parameters if necessary."

## Current E.C. Policy

European Directives on water tend to be drafted in one of two ways. They are either concerned with prescribing *fixed emission limits* in relation to particular substances, which are applicable to all waters, or they are concerned with establishing *environmental quality standards* (objectives) for particular stretches of water according to the uses to which that water is put.

More recent Community legislation takes the emission limit value approach, which is often linked with the use of BAT (Best Available Technique).[82] Under this approach, an estimate is made of the maximum level of reduction in pollutants which can reasonably be expected, given the costs of current technology. Limits on discharges are then set to implement this reduction. The approach is a pragmatic one in that it strives to reduce pollution on the basis of what can actually be achieved, rather than on the basis of how much harm is being caused.

The U.K. has traditionally favoured the use of quality objectives, rather than fixed emission limits, and has purported to comply with E.C. water law by setting environmental quality objectives for particular stretches of water which are high enough to accommodate the E.C.'s universally applicable fixed emission limits. This approach, however, has occasionally brought U.K. water law into conflict with E.C. law, and although E.C. policy has exerted a strong influence on U.K. water pollution

[81] See Chapter 3, above.
[82] See Chapter 6, above.

law, the water pollution regime in the U.K. retains a distinctly national flavour because of its use of water quality objectives as the mechanism for ensuring compliance with emission limits.

The Commission has recently recognised that the use of fixed emission limits sometimes requires Member States to make unnecessary reductions in the discharge of substances and therefore to incur unnecessary costs. A new approach is apparent in the Directive on Urban Waste Water Treatment. The Directive makes a distinction between receiving waters which are "sensitive" and those which are "less sensitive", requiring higher levels of treatment for urban waste water discharged to the former than to the latter. The Commission has stated that approaches based on fixed emission limits and on quality objectives are complementary and that both should be used.

## Current E.C. Legislation on Water

There are a number of Directives on water, the most important of which are as follows:

- The Directive on Dangerous Substances in Water[83];
- The Drinking Water Directive[84];
- The Bathing Water Directive[85];
- The Groundwater Directive[86];
- The Nitrates Directive[87];
- The Urban Waste Water Treatment Directive.[88]

### The Directive on Dangerous Substances in Water

This Directive aims to control pollution of surface water by dangerous substances and requires Member States to control the discharge of certain listed substances by issuing permits. The Directive sets out two lists of dangerous substances: List I, or "black list" substances, are those which are highly toxic or which do not decompose easily and are therefore likely to persist in the environment. These are to be eliminated entirely from discharges into water. List II, or "grey list" substances, are those the effects of which depend upon the characteristics and location of the water into which they are discharged, so that it may be permissible to discharge them in certain circumstances.

The Directive on Dangerous Substances is a "framework" Directive. This means that it depends for its full implementation on the creation of "daughter" Directives which set the relevant emission limits for the substances in question. The procedure for establishing daughter Directives is slow and cumbersome. Moreover, the Directive has

---

[83] 76/464/EEC [1976] O.J. L129/23.
[84] 80/778/EEC [1989] O.J. L229/11.
[85] 76/160/EEC [1976] O.J. L31/1.
[86] 86/68/EEC.
[87] 91/676/EEC [1991] O.J. L375/1.
[88] 92/271/EEC.

been criticised because it does not address the issue of cumulative toxic effects caused by a large number of small discharges and because it fails to deal with certain newly discovered pollutants. Both of these criticisms are answered by the creation of the Directive on Integrated Pollution Prevention and Control.[89]

Despite its failings, the Directive on Dangerous Substances in Water has had a significant influence on U.K. water pollution policy. This has been evidenced less by a change in practice than by a refinement in thinking. In order to comply with the Directive, policy makers in the U.K. have been stimulated into developing previously imprecise ideas on the use of environmental quality objectives and have been forced to put them on a statutory, rather than simply an administrative basis. U.K. policy has now moved towards a combined system of water pollution control under which *both* environmental quality objectives and fixed emission limits are to be enforced. In order to comply with the Directive, the U.K. has drawn up its own "red list" of dangerous substances[90] which are subject to control by the Environment Agency. Major discharges of "red list" substances are required by the Agency to meet both the relevant environmental quality objective for the stretch of water concerned *and* a relevant emission limit.

## The Drinking Water Directive

The objective of this Directive is to safeguard human health by requiring Member States to establish strict standards for the quality of water intended for human consumption. The Directive sets out 62 parameters for the quality of water provided for human consumption and for the manufacture of food. It was this Directive which led to the government's setting statutory standards for the quality of drinking water for the first time.[91] There was considerable delay in implementing this Directive and its implementation in the U.K. proved problematic. This was because Article 9 of the Directive allows Member States to derogate from the parameters contained in the Directive where it is necessary to do so because of local geological conditions. The U.K. government interpreted this provision as allowing them to grant derogations in respect of levels of nitrate in water. The Commission, however, took the view that Article 9 cannot be used to grant derogations where, as in the case of nitrates resulting from agricultural activity, the geological conditions in question are self-induced. The U.K. government was therefore found by the European Court of Justice to be in breach of the Directive.[92]

The high costs of complying with the Directive are to be borne by the privatised water utilities, which have in many cases been unable to make the necessary changes to the water supply system within the required time frame. It appears from the decision in *R. v. Secretary of State for the Environment ex p. Friends of the Earth*,[93] however, that the Secretary of State may comply with E.C. law simply by accepting undertakings from the water companies to remedy breaches of the Directive.

---

[89] See Chapter 6, above.
[90] Trade Effluents (Prescribed Processes and Substances) Regulations 1989 (S.I. 1989 No. 1156) (as amended by S.I. 1990 No. 1629).
[91] Water Supply (Water Quality) Regulations 1989 (S.I. 1989 No. 1147).
[92] *Commission v. United Kingdom* [1993] *Water Law* 59.
[93] ENDS 245, p.44, 1995.

## Other Directives

The Bathing Water Directive aims to safeguard the health of bathers by maintaining the quality of bathing water. It lays down 19 parameters with which traditional bathing waters must comply and covers both costal and inland waters.

The Groundwater Directive requires Member States to control direct and indirect discharges of certain substances into groundwater through a consent system. Under the current proposals from the E.C., this Directive would be repealed.

The Nitrates Directive complements the Urban Waste Water Treatment Directive (below) by dealing with nitrate pollution from agricultural sources. It requires Member States to produce Codes of Good Agricultural Practice in order to reduce the level of nitrate loss from farming to surface waters and groundwater. Although such codes have been produced in the U.K., it is too early to assess the full impact of the Directive, since it is still in the process of implementation by Member States. It appears that to date there has been a general failure to implement this Directive.

The Urban Waste Water Treatment Directive aims to reduce pollution of surface waters by certain plant nutrients and by phosphates from urban waste water. It establishes certain conditions for the discharge, collection and treatment of waste water in industrial areas. Again, since the Directive is in the process of being implemented, it is too early to tell whether the standards required of Member States will be adequate to tackle the problem.

## The Proposed Policy Changes

The proposed changes in E.C. water policy are based on the recognition of a number of factors:

- Existing E.C. legislation appears to be patchy and piecemeal. This is because water policy is an area of mixed competence in which both the E.C. and Member States take action. The Community takes action only where it is better placed to do so;

- More effective Community controls are necessary in some areas, particularly for the protection of the natural ecological state of the aquatic environment;

- Much of the existing Community legislation on water is outdated;

- There is a clear need for greater integration between the many different issues which arise in water policy, namely the quality and quantity of water consumption in the Community, the extent to which water is polluted, whether pollution is best reduced by fixed emission limits or by the use of quality objectives, and the relationship between water use and other areas of environmental protection.

To this end, the Commission has put forward what it refers to as a "sustainable" water policy. This is far broader in its considerations than the prevention of water pollution and consolidates the water protection elements of the Fifth Action Programme.[94] The objectives of the sustainable water policy are:

[94] See COM(92)23 Final.

- To provide a secure supply of drinking water throughout the Community which is safe in quality and sufficient in quantity;

- To provide a supply of water which is of sufficient quality and quantity to meet the needs of industry and agriculture;

- To maintain and enhance the ecological state of the aquatic environment;

- To manage the water supply so as to prevent or reduce floods and drought.

The main vehicle by which these objectives are to be achieved is the proposed Framework Directive on water resources.[95] Under this Directive, designated stretches of water would be monitored and assessed for water and air quality. An assessment would also be made of the water needs of the surrounding community and of the impact of that community on water resources. Appropriate objectives would then be set in relation to the stretch of water in question. The proposed Directive would provide for public participation in the monitoring and assessment processes and in decisions about objectives. The aim, which reflects the principle of subsidiarity, is to leave much of the detail of implementation to Member States. In contrast with previous Directives, which set out common Community limit values to be adhered to by all Member States, the new approach now is to set common criteria to be used by Member States in establishing limit values at a local and national level. The Commission takes the view that this will provide the flexibility which is necessary to accommodate the diverse range of environmental conditions found in different parts of the Community. It has been questioned, however, whether environmental standards overall may decline if direct Community involvement in pollution control is lessened.[96]

[95] Proposed Council Directive establishing a Framework for Community Action in the field of Water Policy, COM(97) 0049 Final.
[96] See, for example, [1995] *Water Law,* vol. 6(4) (editorial).

# Chapter 10

# AIR POLLUTION

*"Air quality has a continuous and pervasive impact on human well-being and on our environment. As individuals we have little opportunity to pick and choose the air we breathe, still less to contract out, and the invisibility of many of our most significant contemporary air pollutants only further emphasises our dependence."*[1]

## Introduction

Each year, air pollution in the U.K. is responsible for several thousands of early deaths and for between ten and twenty thousand hospital admissions.[2] The U.K.'s emissions of sulphur dioxide and other substances from industrial processes, in particular the generation of electricity, combine with water in the atmosphere to produce acid rain. This rain is "exported" to other European countries, especially those in Scandinavia. Air pollution also causes the international problems of global warming and of ozone depletion. Vehicle emissions are becoming a significant cause of air pollution. Since 1980, vehicle use in the U.K. has doubled. The distances which people are travelling in private cars are also increasing.

The pollutants of primary concern are sulphur dioxide, carbon dioxide, carbon monoxide and nitrogen dioxide, as well as particulate matter emitted as smoke. An increasing concern is that air pollutants in combination can form "cocktails" (ammonium sulphate, for example, particles of which are deposited on crops) which pose a greater environmental threat than do their constituent parts alone.

## Definition of Air Pollution

None of the major environmental statutes defines air pollution in specific terms, so that its definition must be derived from the general definitions in Part I of the Environmental Protection Act 1990. The definition of the "environment" includes "the air", and "pollution of the environment" includes pollution due to the release into air of substances capable of causing harm to man or to any other living organisms supported by the environment.

---

[1] *Improving Air Quality: A Discussion Paper on Air Quality Standards and Management*, (DoE, 1994).
[2] See *The National Air Quality Strategy (Consultation Draft)*, (DoE, August 1996).

## The U.K.'s Air Pollution Regime

Air pollution is regulated in the U.K. by a number of different methods. Many industrial processes with the potential to cause air pollution are controlled by Part I of the Environmental Protection Act 1990, which requires that they cannot be undertaken without an authorisation, either from the Environment Agency (in the case of processes prescribed for IPC), or from a local authority (in the case of processes prescribed for Local Authority Air Pollution Control alone). Other industrial processes, whilst not subject to the regime in Part I of the Act, may be controlled on an *ex post facto* basis under the statutory nuisance provisions of Part III of the Act, as may the polluting activities of private individuals.

Emissions of smoke, grit and dust are controlled by the Clean Air Act 1993, which also regulates the content of fuels used in furnaces and motor vehicles, aiming to reduce the polluting emissions to which these fuels give rise. Vehicle emissions are further controlled by a miscellaneous collection of statutory instruments. The problems of global warming and ozone depletion are the subject of international conventions. At present, the U.K. regime of control is somewhat fragmented. A more coherent approach to regulation is gradually emerging, however, and this is evidenced by the duty of the Secretary of State, under the Environment Act 1995, to prepare and publish a National Air Quality Management Strategy.[3]

## The History of Air Pollution Control in the U.K.

Control of air pollution has a long history. Indeed, smoke from the burning of sea coal was the first pollutant ever to be regulated in the UK, by Royal Proclamations issued in 1272 and in 1306.[4] It was not until the Public Health Act of 1875, however, that the first general legislation to control smoke emissions was passed. The provisions on smoke abatement which that Act contained have formed the basis of modern legislation. The 1875 Act, however, was unsuccessful in securing major changes in air quality, so that Victorian cities were characterised by soot-blackened buildings and heavy smogs.

In December 1952, a very severe smog in London, caused by a combination of fog and smoke particles, which inhibited the dispersion of air pollution, resulted in the death of an estimated 4,000 people. The government appointed a Committee to look into its causes. Its recommendations led to the passing of the Clean Air Act 1956. This legislation produced a dramatic reduction in smog by imposing a prohibition on "dark smoke" from chimneys and by the creation of "smoke control areas" in which it became an offence to emit any smoke from domestic and industrial chimneys. The Clean Air Acts of 1956 and 1968 were consolidated by the Clean Air Act 1993. During the 1970s, the increased use of smokeless fuels, such as coke and gas, in preference to coal, coupled with the adoption by the electricity generating industry of taller chimney stacks aimed at dispersing air pollutants over greater distances, led to a reduction in air pollution by particulates. Particulates in the atmosphere are of special concern, because their presence can severely inhibit the dispersal of other air pollutants.

---

[3] EA 1995, s.80.
[4] See Chapter 1, above.

These measures, however, did little to reduce the problem of acidity in the air which, though invisible, causes considerable damage to crops and to waterways which support life. Acidity first became a real problem during the industrial revolution. "Alkali works", set up to produce soda, emitted large volumes of foul-smelling hydrogen chloride gas. This combined with atmospheric moisture to form acid rain which stripped the leaves from trees and shrubs. The recommendations of a Royal Commission, appointed to consider the problem, led to the passing of the Alkali Act 1863 and later the Alkali Act 1874. The latter Act required industry to use the "best practicable means" to minimise the emission of noxious and offensive gases. The implementation of the "best practicable means" test (the ancestor of BATNEEC) led to the adoption of the first emission standards in the UK, which detailed the amounts of specified substances which were permissible in given amounts of gas. The legislation also led to the establishment of the Alkali Inspectorate, the predecessor to HMIP and latterly to the Environment Agency. Both of the Alkali Acts were consolidated by the Alkali etc. Works Regulation Act 1906.

Whilst the Alkali Acts exerted control over much industrial activity, problems were emerging in relation to other industrial activities such as ferrous metal foundries, plants manufacturing asbestos based products, and plants producing glass and ceramics. Pollution was also arising from such sources as hospital incinerators. Control over these forms of pollution was not exercised by the Alkali Inspectorate. Rather, it rested with local authorities, in the exercise of their statutory nuisance powers under the Public Health Acts. Unlike the Alkali Inspectorate, local authorities could take action only after a nuisance had occurred and could not require plants to operate using the "best practicable means" to reduce pollution. The increasing volume of pollution produced by these activities, however, made it clear that some form of preventive control was necessary.

In 1976, the Royal Commission on Environmental Pollution recommended new and more comprehensive legislation to cover all aspects of industrial air pollution, which would give local authorities the power to exercise preventive control by making their prior consent necessary for the carrying out of certain processes.[5] The Commission also recommended that a new unified pollution inspectorate be established to supervise activities which discharged pollution into more than one environmental medium. In the light of these recommendations, the government embarked on a prolonged period of review, eventually outlining its proposals in a consultation paper issued in December 1986.[6] This document stressed the necessity of conforming to E.C. legislation, in particular the E.C. Framework Directive on combatting air pollution from industrial plants.[7] The Directive required, amongst other things, that particular categories of industrial operation should be authorised before they commenced and that emissions from existing operations should be gradually improved. A few of the processes which the Directive identified as requiring prior authorisation were, in the UK, under the control of local authorities, whose powers at the time were insufficient to exert the sort

[5] *Air Pollution Control: An Integrated Approach,* RCEP, Cmnd. 6371 (1976).
[6] *Air Pollution Control in Great Britain: Review and Proposals, A Consultation Paper* (DoE, December 1986).
[7] Council Directive, [1984] O.J. L188/20.

of preventive controls demanded by the Directive. Therefore, the power to supervise certain industrial processes by granting or withholding licences was eventually conferred on local authorities by Part I of the Environmental Protection Act 1990.

# THE ENVIRONMENTAL PROTECTION ACT 1990

## Local Authority Air Pollution Control

As has been said, historically, control of industrial air pollution in the U.K. was divided between central and local agencies. The Alkali Inspectorate supervised the more difficult air pollution problems, whilst local authorities controlled emissions from other industrial activities. This division of control is continued in the Environmental Protection Act 1990. Part I of the Act provides for two distinct regulatory regimes: the Integrated Pollution Control regime, which is administered by the Environment Agency (and is examined in Chapter 6) and the Local Authority Air Pollution Control regime. By regulations made under Part I, the Secretary of State may prescribe particular industrial processes for control under one of these regimes or the other, but not both. The IPC regime is beginning to result in significant reductions in industrial emissions to the air. In particular, marked reductions have been achieved in the amount of sulphur dioxide emitted by power stations.[8]

Under the Local Authority Air Pollution Control regime, local authorities have the same powers in relation to processes prescribed for their control as does the Environment Agency in relation to processes prescribed for IPC. Thus, local authorities are responsible for granting authorisations, without which it is an offence to operate a prescribed process. Authorisations must be made subject to conditions which regulate the process in question so as to ensure that BATNEEC is used, and into every authorisation there is implied a condition that the process operator must use BATNEEC to minimise the release of prescribed substances and to render harmless the release of all other substances. Local authorities can issue enforcement, prohibition and revocation notices and may appoint inspectors who have the same powers of entry, search and seizure as do those appointed by the Environment Agency.[9] They are also required to maintain public registers relating to their administration of the regime. All of these powers are examined, in the context of the IPC regime, in Chapter 6. The key differences between the IPC regime and the Local Authority Air Pollution Control regime are simply that the latter is administered at a local rather than a central level and that it controls only releases of substances into the air and not releases into other environmental media.

Those processes prescribed for Local Authority Air Pollution Control include metal-decontamination processes, the use of cement in bulk, the use of spray paints in garages and light industry, and the operation of crematoria and hospital incinerators. At the commencement of the new regime, the government predicted that some 25,000 processes would be subject to local authority control, ensuring that local authorities

---

[8] See: *National Air Quality Strategy* (DoE).
[9] EA 1995, s.108.

would play a much greater rôle in industrial pollution control than they had done hitherto. Guidance notes, issued by the Department of the Environment, are available to cover all the main categories of processes coming under local authority control. These make recommendations as to the techniques most appropriate to ensure the implementation of BATNEEC. In exercising their functions, local authorities must also have regard to the Secretary of State's National Air Quality Strategy (below).[10]

The first three years of the regime's operation saw 44 prosecutions undertaken by local authorities, with one appeal being heard in the High Court. In *Tantridge District Council v. P&S Civil Engineering Limited and Others*,[11] the respondents, in the absence of an authorisation, operated a process which involved coating road stone with tar — a prescribed process under Part I of the Act. On appeal, they sought to take advantage of the exemption from authorisation provided in regulation 4 of the Environmental Protection (Prescribed Processes and Substances) Regulations 1991, which provides that no authorisation is required where the process in question will result in the release of prescribed substances in such trivial quantities as to be incapable of causing harm. The court held that the burden of proof lay with the respondents to show that the exemption was applicable, and that since they had adduced no evidence to support their claim, the magistrates should be directed to convict. The fines for causing air pollution can be high. Coalite Chemicals, for example, was recently ordered to pay a record £450,000 in fines and costs for emitting dioxins from an incinerator at its site in Bolsover, Derbyshire.[12]

## The Statutory Nuisance Regime

Air pollution is controlled both by the common law of nuisance and by the law relating to statutory nuisances contained in Part III of the Environmental Protection Act 1990. Both of these topics are examined in Chapter 4. The operation of the statutory nuisance regime is also considered in Chapter 11, which deals with noise pollution. Statutory nuisances will not, therefore, be dealt with here in any detail. It should be remembered, however, that under section 79 of the Act, the following are statutory nuisances:

- Smoke emitted from premises so as to be prejudicial to health or a nuisance;

- Fumes or gases emitted from premises so as to be prejudicial to health or a nuisance;

- Any dust, steam, smell or other effluvia arising on industrial, trade or business premises and being prejudicial to health or a nuisance.

---

[10] EPA 1990, s.4(4A) (inserted by EA 1995, Sched. 22).
[11] [1995] Env. L.R. 67.
[12] ENDS 253, February 1996. (The prosecution was actually brought under Health and Safety at Work etc. Act 1974).

## THE CONTROL OF SMOKE

The Clean Air Act 1993 controls the emission of smoke and the emission of grit and dust. It also allows the Secretary of State to make regulations with respect to fuels. Under the Act, it is a criminal offence to emit "dark smoke" from the chimney of any building[13] or from the chimney of a furnace serving any fixed boiler or industrial plant,[14] although the Secretary of State, by regulations, may exempt the emission of certain forms of smoke, during certain periods, from control under the Act.[15] "Dark smoke" is defined by the Act as smoke which is darker than shade two on the Ringlemann Chart.[16]

There are a number of defences to prosecution,[17] namely;

- That the emission in question was due solely to the lighting of a furnace which was cold and that all practicable steps had been taken to prevent the emission;

- That the emission was due to the failure of a furnace, or of apparatus used in connection with it, where that failure could not be reasonably foreseen and provided against, and where the emission could not reasonably have been prevented by action taken after the failure;

- That the emission was due solely to the use of an unsuitable fuel, provided that suitable fuel was not obtainable, that the least unsuitable available fuel was used, and that all practicable steps were taken to prevent or minimise the emission resulting from the use of that fuel.

For industrial polluters, a "catch-all" section is provided in the Act, which makes it an offence to cause or permit the emission of dark smoke from industrial or trade premises (*i.e.* otherwise than by way of a chimney).[18] The Act further provides that in proceedings for an offence there shall be taken to have been an emission of dark smoke unless the defendant proves that no dark smoke was emitted. In *Sheffield City Council v. ADH Demolition Ltd*,[19] the court was prepared to attach a wide meaning to the phrase "trade or industrial premises", holding that it covered a demolition site. Under the "catch-all" provision, it is a defence for the accused to show that the emission in question was caused inadvertently and that all practicable steps were taken to minimise the emission.[20] The Act defines "practicable" so as to mean reasonably practicable, having regard, *inter alia*, to local conditions, the current state of technical knowledge, and to the financial implications for the defendant.[21]

In *O'Fee v. Copeland Borough Council*,[22] the defendant appealed against a conviction for emitting dark smoke, arguing that there was no evidence that the smoke went

[13] CAA 1993, s.1(1).
[14] *ibid.*, s.1(2).
[15] See: Dark Smoke (Permitted Periods) Regulations 1958 (S.I. 1958 No. 498).
[16] CAA 1993, s.3(1).
[17] *ibid.*, s.1(4).
[18] *ibid.*, s.2.
[19] (1983) 82 L.G.R. 177.
[20] CAA 1993, s.2(4).
[21] *ibid.*, s.64(4).
[22] *The Times*, April 22, 1995.

beyond the boundaries of his premises. Whilst the court was prepared to accept that an "emission" must mean a movement of the smoke above the surface of the ground within the boundaries of premises, it held that the prosecution need not prove that the smoke had travelled beyond the premises from which it had been emitted.

## The Installation of Furnaces

A furnace which has been properly built and installed should not emit smoke. Therefore, the Act provides that no furnace may be installed in any building, or in any fixed boiler or industrial plant, unless it is, so far as is reasonably practicable, capable of being operated continuously without emitting smoke,[23] and unless notice of the proposal to install it has been given to the local authority.[24] Installing a furnace in contravention of these provisions is an offence. The provisions do not apply to domestic furnaces.

## Grit and Dust

The Act provides that the Secretary of State may, by regulations, prescribe limits for the emission of grit and dust from industrial furnaces.[25] Under the regulations, where no limits have been prescribed, the occupier of the building in which the furnace is operated is placed under a general duty to minimise the emission of grit and dust. The Act also provides that industrial furnaces which burn certain types of fuel, or which operate at certain capacities, are to be fitted with grit arrestment plant.[26] In relation to domestic furnaces, it is an offence to burn pulverised fuel without local authority approved grit arrestment plant fitted, and to burn any other form of solid fuel, or solid waste, at a rate of 1.02 tonnes an hour or more without such plant.[27]

## The Height of Chimneys

The height of furnace chimneys has a direct effect on the rate at which pollutants are dispersed. The Clean Air Act 1993 therefore provides that it is an offence for the occupier of any building in which a furnace is situated knowingly to cause or permit the burning of pulverised fuel, or the burning of other fuels at certain rates, without prior approval of the furnace's chimney height by the local authority.[28] Under the Act, the local authority may not approve the height of a chimney unless it is satisfied that it is sufficient to prevent, so far as is reasonably practicable, the emission of smoke, grit, dust, gases or fumes from becoming prejudicial to health or a nuisance, having regard, *inter alia*, to the chimney's purpose, the position and description of buildings near it, and the level of neighbouring ground.[29]

---

[23] CAA 1993, s.4(2).
[24] *ibid.,* s.4(1).
[25] See Clean Air (Emission of Grit and Dust From Furnaces) Regulations 1971, (S.I. 1971 No. 162).
[26] CAA 1993, s.6(1) See also Clean Air (Arrestment Plant) (Exemption) Regulations 1969 (S.I. 1969 No. 1262).
[27] CAA 1993, s.8.
[28] *ibid.,* s.14. See also Clean Air (Height of Chimneys) (Exemption) Regulations 1969, (S.I. 1969 No. 411).
[29] CAA 1993, s.15.

## Smoke Control Areas

The Beaver Committee, which was set up to investigate the causes of the London smog disaster in 1952, found that half of the smoke in the U.K. came from domestic chimneys. It therefore recommended the establishment of "smoke control areas". This recommendation was implemented by the Clean Air Act 1956, which was consolidated by the Clean Air Act 1993. Under this Act, local authorities have the power to make an order declaring that either the whole or part of its area shall be a smoke control area.[30] The emission of any smoke from a chimney within such an area is an offence.[31] It is a defence to prosecution, however, for the defendant to show that the emission was not caused by the use of any fuel other than an "authorised fuel"[32] The local authority, or the Secretary of State, may limit the scope of the order so that certain types of buildings, or smoke emitted from certain types of fireplaces, are exempt from the order.[33] In addition, the local authority can compel the occupier of premises to adapt an existing fireplace so as to comply with the order (for example, by replacing a metal grate with a thicker one which can withstand the extra heat generated by the burning of smokeless fuel).[34] The local authority has a duty to make a financial grant to the occupier of any "old private dwelling" (built before August 15, 1964) to cover at least 70 per cent of the costs of such an adaptation.[35] It may also reimburse the occupiers of certain buildings used for the advancement of religion, education or social welfare for the costs of adaptation.[36] Whilst the provisions relating to smoke control areas apply to both industrial and domestic premises, they do not apply to industrial processes which have been prescribed for control under Part I of the Environmental Protection Act 1990.[37]

## The Composition of Fuels

Under the Act, the Secretary of State may make regulations prescribing the content of any kind of motor fuel for the purpose of reducing air pollution. Such regulations have been made prescribing limits for the content of sulphur and of lead in petrol.[38] For the same purpose, the Secretary of State can impose limits on the sulphur content of oil fuel which is used in furnaces or engines.[39]

---

[30] *ibid.*, s.18.
[31] *ibid.*, s.20.
[32] *ibid.*, s.20(4).
[33] *ibid.*, s.18(2); Smoke Control Areas (Exempted Fireplaces) Order 1991 (S.I. 1991 No. 2892).
[34] *ibid.*, s.24.
[35] *ibid.*, s.25.
[36] *ibid.*, s.26.
[37] *ibid.*, s.41.
[38] *ibid.*, s.30 ; Motor Fuel (Sulphur Content of Gas Oil) Regulations 1976 (S.I. 1976 No. 1989) (as amended by S.I. 1990 No. 1097), and Motor Fuel (Lead Content of Petrol) Regulations 1981 (S.I. 1981 No. 1523) (as amended by S.I. 1985 No. 1728).
[39] CAA 1993, s.31; Oil Fuel (Sulphur Content of Gas Oil) Regulations 1990 (S.I. 1990 No. 1096).

## OTHER FORMS OF AIR POLLUTION

### Straw and Stubble Burning

The burning of agricultural crop residues causes environmental problems not only for residents in agricultural areas, but also for motorists using roads in those areas. Therefore, under the Environmental Protection Act 1990, the Secretary of State may make regulations prohibiting or restricting the practice.[40] The Crop Residues (Restriction on Burning) Regulations 1991[41] have been made under this provision.

### Odour Pollution

In June 1996, The Environmental Data Service reported: *"East London 'dog food' smell ended by new process."*[42]

The problems associated with odour pollution are illustrated by the story to which this headline refers. A company in east London was involved in the production of glucose and other sugar syrup products. The fumes emitted by this process were described by residents as having a smell similar to dog food. Numerous complaints were made, including some from a local school whose pupils were unable to work when they became nauseated by the smell. The local council served an abatement notice on the company, under the statutory nuisance provisions of the Environmental Protection Act 1990, ordering the company to modify its process so as to prevent the smell. The company eventually put an end to the problem by adopting a new industrial process, but at a cost of £25 million.

Odour pollution is regulated both by the statutory nuisance regime in Part III of the Environmental Protection Act 1990 and by the IPC and Local Authority Air Pollution Control regimes in Part I. There are various applicable heads of statutory nuisance:

- Any premises in such a state as to be prejudicial to health or a nuisance;

- Smoke emitted from premises so as to be prejudicial to health or a nuisance;

- Fumes or gases emitted from premises so as to be prejudicial to health or a nuisance;

- Any dust, steam, smell or other effluvia arising on industrial, trade or business premises and being prejudicial to health or a nuisance;

---

[40] EPA 1990, s.152.
[41] S.I. 1991 No. 1399 (as amended by S.I. 1991 No. 1590).
[42] ENDS 257 p.8, June 1996.

- Any accumulation or deposit which is prejudicial to health or a nuisance;

- Any animal kept in such a place or manner as to be prejudicial to health or a nuisance.

Under the air pollution control regime in Part I, the first case to come before the courts concerning the proper application of section 6(4) of the Act was one concerned with pollution by smell. Section 6(4) of the Act states:

> "An application [for a process authorisation] shall not be granted unless the enforcing authority considers that the applicant will be able to carry on the process so as to comply with the conditions which would be included in the authorisation."

In *R. v. Secretary of State for the Environment and R. J. Compton & Sons, ex p. West Wiltshire District Council*,[43] R. J. Compton & Sons ran a piggery and operated a prescribed process involving animal by-products. There were numerous complaints about the smell. The local authority, relying on section 6(4), refused the company's application for an authorisation under the Local Authority Air Pollution Control regime. The company appealed to the Secretary of State, whose inspector allowed the appeal and granted the authorisation, subject to numerous conditions. On appeal by the local authority to the High Court, however, it was held that the inspector had failed properly to apply section 6(4) of the Act. The inspector had found that the company did not have the necessary management ability to be able to carry out the process properly, and the court held that this lack of ability could not be "cured" by the imposition of stringent conditions. The inspector had therefore failed to justify his conclusion that an authorisation should be granted.

Under the IPC regime in Part I, Mobil Oil was prosecuted by HMIP for the emission of odorous gas from its Croydon refinery, in breach of the conditions of its process authorisation, after the district council had received a 3,000 signature petition complaining of odour problems on the weekend of the incident. The company entered a plea of guilty and were fined £16,000.

## Vehicle Emissions

The law on vehicle emissions, which implements emission standards set largely by the E.C., is subject to continual review. In addition to the regulations prescribing the content of motor fuel made under the Clean Air Act 1993, the Secretary of State has also made certain regulations relating to the emissions of newly produced vehicles.[44] The various Road Vehicle (Construction and Use) Regulations, made under road traffic legislation, prescribe certain emission limits for different categories of vehicles currently in use. They also regulate the use of catalytic convertors and of unleaded petrol by certain vehicles. Older vehicles, subject to annual MOT testing, must comply with emission standards in relation to smoke and carbon monoxide.

[43] [1996] J.P.L. 115.
[44] Motor Vehicles (Type Approval) (Great Britain) Regulations 1994, (S.I. 1994 No. 981).

# THE FUTURE OF U.K. AIR POLLUTION CONTROL

## The National Air Quality Management Strategy

As will now be apparent, the U.K.'s air pollution regime is currently somewhat lacking in coherence, with a number of different legal regimes responding to various manifestations of air pollution such as smoke, industrial and vehicle emissions, in the absence of any full analysis of overall air quality in particular geographical areas. The introduction of the National Air Quality Management Strategy aims to remedy this situation and reflects a move towards a more holistic and sophisticated policy of control. The reasons for this change in policy are various:

- The need to implement the concept of sustainable development: urban air quality was cited as a priority area for improvement in the government's policy on sustainable development, published in January 1994.

- An improvement in scientific knowledge about the origins and effects of air pollution, which has enabled regulation to be more specific.

- A marked increase in the incidence of asthma and other respiratory diseases: the publication of the draft National Air Quality Strategy, in August 1996, has been described as the clearest official acceptance yet of air pollution's impact on public health.[45]

- The recognition that E.C. and U.K. legislation was fragmented and had introduced a wide range of different control mechanisms whose application and relation to each other was not clear or readily understood.

The Environment Act 1995 requires the Secretary of State to prepare and publish a National Air Quality Management Strategy.[46] Both the Environment Agency and local authorities are required to have regard to this strategy in exercising their pollution control functions.[47] In August 1996, a consultation draft of the strategy was published. The ultimate objective of the strategy is that polluting emissions to the air should be rendered harmless, but, as a medium-term objective, the strategy states that citizens should have access to public places without risk to their health. This is to be achieved by focusing on eight particular pollutants and by establishing air quality standards for those pollutants. The standards will specify acceptable concentrations of each pollutant in the atmosphere and are to be set solely on the basis of scientific assessment.

Once the standards have been set, "air quality objectives" will then be set for particular areas.[48] These will be based on an analysis of costs and benefits in the light of current technology. The strategy adopts an "effects-based" approach to substance control, so that the scientific analysis, on the basis of which the standards are to be set,

---

[45] ENDS 256 (June 1996), p. 15.
[46] EA 1995, s.80(1).
[47] *ibid.,* s.81(1).
[48] For an understanding of the relationship between "quality standards" and "quality objectives", see the operation of the water pollution regime, discussed in Chapter 9.

will concentrate on the effects of each pollutant on human health. Protection of human health is at the heart of the new regime. The draft strategy makes it clear that the government is not, for the time being, proposing to define air pollution standards by reference to the effects of air pollutants on the ecosystem as a whole.

The mechanism by which the strategy is to be implemented is set out in Part IV of the Environment Act 1995. Under the Act, local authorities are required to conduct a periodic review of air quality within their areas.[49] If the standards and objectives of the strategy (which are to be prescribed by regulations accompanying the strategy[50]) are not being achieved, or are not likely to be achieved within a particular area, the local authority must make an order designating that area as an "air quality management area",[51] Once an area has been so designated, the local authority is under a duty to make a formal assessment of the air quality in the area, noting the respects in which the relevant standards and objectives are not being met. The authority must, within twelve months, prepare a report outlining the results of this assessment and thereafter must prepare an "action plan" to assist it in exercising its air pollution control powers.[52] The Secretary of State has reserve powers to direct the local authority in the exercise of these functions.[53]

There is considerable uncertainty about the resources which will be made available to local authorities for implementing their obligations under the strategy. The draft strategy has also been criticised by environmentalists for not addressing the growth of traffic, which is a significant cause of air pollution today. The strategy puts forward few new measures to tackle this problem other than requiring a closer integration of air quality considerations with transport and planning policy.[54]

## E.C. AIR POLLUTION LAW

Air pollution has formed a significant part of E.C. environmental policy since the mid 1980s, when a growing awareness of the dangers posed by acid rain prompted the development of European "air quality standards". These prescribe the maximum concentrations of particular substances permitted to be present in the atmosphere at ground level at given times. A number of Directives set mandatory standards for sulphur dioxide and smoke,[55] and for lead[56] and nitrogen dioxide.[57] They are implemented in the U.K. by the Air Quality Standards Regulations 1989,[58] under which the Secretary of State is required to ensure that atmospheric concentrations of these pollutants do not exceed the limits prescribed by the Directives, and to establish sampling stations to monitor air quality. (A Directive on ozone[59] is implemented in a similar way by the Ozone Monitoring and Information Regulations 1994.[60])

[49] EA 1995, s.82.
[50] *ibid.,* s.87.
[51] *ibid.,* s.83.
[52] *ibid.,* s.84.
[53] *ibid.,* s.85.
[54] ENDS 257, p. 17.
[55] Dir. 80/779/EEC [1980] O.J. L229/30.
[56] Dir. 82/884/EEC [1982] O.J. L378/15.
[57] Dir. 85/203/EEC [1985] O.J. L87/1.
[58] S.I. 1989 No. 317.
[59] Dir. 92/72/EEC [1992] O.J. L297/1.
[60] S.I. 1994 No. 440.

The fundamental aim of the E.C.'s Fourth Environmental Action Programme was to reduce emission levels at source, and this philosophy was implemented in the Directive on emissions from large combustion plants,[61] Rather than impose specific fixed emission limits for the release of particular substances from particular processes, the Directive imposes a general overall limit on the amount of substances which may be released from power stations and other large combustion plants within each Member State. Member States are thereby given some flexibility in ensuring that these limits are complied with, since they may permit greater releases for certain processes, or in certain areas, and less in others. This Directive is implemented by Part I of the Environmental Protection Act 1990.

In 1994, a review of the effectiveness of the E.C.'s air quality Directives, undertaken by the Commission, identified a number of problems:

- Member States were taking too long to comply with the air quality standards required by the Directives. (The U.K., for example, had made maximum use of the derogation provisions provided in the 1980 Directive on smoke and sulphur dioxide, so that the standards were not complied with until 1993.);

- There were large differences between Member States in the extent to which air quality was monitored. (In 1992, the U.K. was criticised by the Commission for having just seven nitrogen dioxide monitoring sites, some of which were situated well away from traffic.);

- The existing Directives had failed to achieve full harmonisation of air quality measurement methods in Member States.

As a result of these findings, the Council adopted the Air Quality Framework Directive in September 1996.[61a] This Directive has three main goals:

- To maintain the quality of air where it is good and to improve it where it is poor;

- To establish objectives for ambient air pollution control throughout the Community;

- To move closer towards harmonisation of national air quality measurement programmes and provide monitoring information to the public.

The extent to which these broad objectives will be fulfilled depends very much on the content of the "daughter" Directives, which will establish specific requirements on air sampling and quality measurement techniques as well as prescribing new air quality standards. Daughter Directives are to be drawn up in relation to twenty different substances, including those already covered by existing Directives, which the new Directives will replace.

---

[61] Dir. 88/609/EEC [1988] O.J. L336/1.
[61a] Council Directive 96/62/EC of September 27, 1996 on ambient air quality assessment and management.

## INTERNATIONAL AIR POLLUTION LAW

The movement of air does not, of course, confine itself to within national borders. More than 75 per cent of the U.K. emissions of sulphur dioxide, and as much as 90 per cent of its nitrogen dioxide emissions, are deposited in other countries or in the sea. Air masses from the United States also travel eastward across the Atlantic over the British Isles and continental Europe.[62] Given the mobile nature of air pollution, the problems of acid rain, depletion of the ozone layer and global warming which it causes require an international response.

### Acid Rain

Acid rain is caused mainly when nitrogen dioxide and sulphur dioxide, produced by the burning of fossil fuels in power stations and in car engines, combine with atmospheric water vapour. This vapour can often be blown thousands of miles before it falls as rain. Acid rain has caused the decline of forests in central and eastern Europe, and many lakes in Scandinavia and Canada are now incapable of supporting life because of acidification.[63]

The 1979 Convention on Long Range Transboundary Air Pollution[64] imposes a widely-phrased obligation on contracting States to develop policies and strategies to combat air pollution "by means of exchanges of information, consultation, research and monitoring". Four protocols establish the substance of these obligations. The first is concerned with the financing of air pollution reduction programmes, whilst the other three are concerned with reduction programmes in respect of particular pollutants. The second protocol requires parties to the convention to reduce annual sulphur dioxide emissions by at least 30 per cent as soon as possible, and in any event no later than 1993 (using 1980 levels as a basis for the reduction). The third protocol, adopted in 1988, requires a reduction in annual emissions of nitrogen oxides. It adopts a more flexible approach than the second protocol, which required a blanket reduction by all States, in that it makes provision for individual difficulties faced by contracting States. The 1991 Protocol on Volatile Organic Compounds is concerned with organic compounds emitted through incomplete combustion of fossil fuels, particularly in car engines. It is a more sophisticated instrument than the previous protocols and establishes specific targets and timetables for the reduction of emissions, whilst allowing contracting States to do so by methods of their own choosing.

### Depletion of the Ozone Layer

The ozone layer, which is defined as "the layer of atmospheric ozone above the planetary boundary layer",[65] filters sunlight and protects the earth from ultra-violet

---

[62] *The National Air Quality Management Strategy,* (DoE).
[63] *Europe's Environment: The Dobris Assessment* (eds David Stanners and Philippe Bourdeau) (European Environment Agency, 1995).
[64] 18 I.L.M. 1442 (1979).
[65] Convention on the Protection of the Ozone Layer, March 22, 1985, Vienna, 26 I.L.M. 1529 (1987), Art. 1.

radiation. Excessive exposure to ultra-violet radiation is dangerous to all forms of life. In humans, it increases the likelihood of skin cancer, cataracts and tumours. It can also suppress the immune system, increasing the likelihood of epidemic disease. In plant and animal life, mutations may occur, reducing crop yields and altering the ecosystem. In terms of secondary effects, depletion of the ozone layer is likely to cause an increase in acid rain and in levels of urban ozone (smog). It will also contribute to global warming.[66]

The ozone layer is depleted by the presence in the atmosphere of chlorofluorocarbons (CFCs), carbons, and other chlorine based substances. Evidence of ozone depletion in this way emerged in the 1980s. A "hole" in the ozone layer was identified above Antarctica and losses in ozone were also recorded in the Arctic. Unusually high levels of ultra-violet radiation have been recorded in Antarctica, Australia and in mountainous parts of Europe.

The 1985 Convention for the Protection of the Ozone Layer[67] required contracting States to formulate agreed standards with respect to ozone-depleting substances. This Convention was essentially an empty framework which provided scope for further action by States. The substantive obligations of States are set out in the Montreal Protocol on Substances that Deplete the Ozone Layer, which entered into force in January 1989. This establishes a timetable for reducing emissions of substances such as CFCs and halons and sets deadlines by which the consumption and production of these substances within States must be reduced to specified levels.

In what has been described as a novel development for international law,[68] the protocol recognises the special difficulties which developing countries face in complying with its requirements. It pledges that States will provide financial aid for alternative technology and in some circumstances gives developing countries an additional 10 years to meet the reduction goals. Subsequent protocols brought forward the deadline for a complete prohibition on the production and consumption of ozone-depleting substances to January 1996.[69] Because the substances in question persist in the environment for a very long time, however, ozone depletion is expected to continue well into the next century and beyond.

## Climate Change

Climate change, or "global warming", is mainly caused by the presence in the atmosphere of carbon dioxide, CFCs, methane and nitrogen oxides. These pollutants trap long wave radiation emitted by the earth's surface and prevent it from escaping, causing the earth to warm up (the "greenhouse effect"). The effects of global warming will not be uniform across the world. The Department of the Environment's Climate

---

[66] See Margaret E. Somerset, "An Attempt to Stop the Sky from Falling: The Montreal Protocol to Protect Against Atmospheric Ozone Reduction", (1988-1989) *Syracuse Journal of International Law and Commerce,* vol. 15, p. 391.

[67] 26 I.L.M. 1529 (1987).

[68] Sands, "International Law in the Field of Sustainable Development", *British Yearbook of International Law,* 1994, p. 303.

[69] Adjustment to the Montreal Protocol on Substances that Deplete the Ozone Layer, June 29, 1990, London. Adjustment to the Montreal Protocol on Substances that Deplete the Ozone Layer, November 25, 1992, Copenhagen.

Change Impacts Review Group, which, in July 1996, reported on the potential effects of climate change in the U.K., predicted that very warm seasons would become more frequent, and that rainfall would increase and become more intense. Wind speeds would also increase, with gales becoming 30 per cent more frequent by the middle of the next century. Infectious diseases would increase, as would heat-induced deaths.

In other parts of the world, the effects of global warming will be far more severe, with a predicted rise in sea level of approximately 65 centimetres in the next 100 years causing the disappearance of many low level islands. Climate change will also lead to increased numbers of hurricanes and cyclones, drought and desertification.

Whilst a consensus exists that there will be some form of climate change if polluting emissions are not reduced, there remains considerable scientific uncertainty about the precise nature and extent of its effects, and this presents a problem for policy makers. At an international level, and at arm's length from hard and fast domestic political commitments, the world community appears to take the view that the consequences of stronger storms, higher seas and less water in rivers are so far reaching that an application of the "precautionary principle" is worthwhile. Regardless of what happens to the climate, there will be benefits deriving from a reduction in greenhouse gas emissions, such as the longer availability of fossil fuels through more rational and efficient energy use, and the development of cleaner technologies.

The UN Framework Convention on Climate Change[70] entered into force in March 1992. Its ultimate objective is stated as achieving the stabilisation of greenhouse gas concentrations in the atmosphere at such a level as to prevent "dangerous anthropogenic interference with the climate system". To achieve this objective, contracting parties must publish reports, establish programmes, and develop processes to control emissions of greenhouse gases not covered by the Montreal Protocol. In its introduction, the Convention notes that the largest amounts of greenhouse gases are produced in developed countries, but recognises that emissions in developing countries will increase in line with their developmental needs.

The Convention has been described as marking an important new phase in the development of international environmental law[71] for a number of reasons: it is the first international environmental instrument to have been negotiated by nearly the entire international community (143 States) and it is unique because of the breadth of its consequences — it is difficult to identify any type of human activity which falls beyond its scope.

Although the eventual form of the Convention reflected a compromise between those States which were seeking specific targets and timetables for emissions reduction and those which wanted only a bare framework for achieving this, the Convention is important because it may provide the mechanism for developing international policy aimed specifically at integrating environmental and economic considerations.

The most important provisions of the Convention are as follows:

- Contracting States should protect the climate system for the benefit of present and future generations of mankind, on the basis of equity and in accordance with their common but differentiated responsibilities and respective capabilities, so that developed countries should take the lead in combatting both the causes and the adverse effects of climate change;

[70] 31 I.L.M. 849 (1992).
[71] Sands, "The UN Framework Convention on Climate Change", (1992) RECIEL, vol. 1(3) p. 270.

- Consideration should be given to the special needs of developing nations, especially those which are particularly vulnerable to the effects of climate change;

- States should take precautionary measures to anticipate and to prevent or minimise the causes of climate change, and to mitigate its adverse effects. Where there are threats of serious or irreversible damage, lack of full scientific certainty should not be used as a reason for postponing such measures, although measures to deal with climate change should be cost effective, so as to ensure global benefits at the lowest possible cost;

- Developing States should have the right to derive information and funds from industrialised nations to assist them in combatting global warming.

The convention itself obliged developed nations to stabilise greenhouse gas emissions at 1990 levels by 2000. Until very recently, scientific uncertainty about the reality of global warming had prevented States from undertaking further commitments. The Intergovernmental Panel on Climate Change, however, in its second five yearly assessment of climate change, concluded that: " . . . the balance of evidence suggests a discernible human influence on the global climate."

The Panel was able to draw this conclusion much sooner than it had originally forecast. The result has been that at the second conference of the parties to the Convention, held in July 1996, it was agreed that a legally binding instrument, containing targets and timetables for the reduction of greenhouse gas emissions, should be negotiated. This is expected to be accomplished in December 1997 in Japan.[72]

---

[72] ENDS 258 p.13, July 1996.

# Chapter 11

## POLLUTION BY NOISE

*"Increasingly throughout the world noise is seen by the public as a significant problem. Recent opinion polls in France and Japan showed that noise appeared a more serious object of concern than air pollution. According to an O.E.C.D. report in 1981 some recent opinion polls have ranked noise as the most annoying single environmental problem."*[1]

### Introduction

Noise pollution is one of the fastest growing environmental concerns. Although, in contrast with other pollutants, noise does not persist in the environment and seldom leaves physical scars, its consequences can be catastrophic. In September 1994, for example, a fire bomb was thrown into the home of a noisy neighbour, causing his death. Noise related suicides have also risen in recent years. Noise levels have greatly increased with the growth of industry and urban development. The growth of rail, road and air traffic has increased noise levels throughout the country, as has the increased use of domestic appliances such as lawnmowers, power tools, televisions and hi-fi.[2] Between 1992 and 1993 there were 111,515 complaints about noise nuisance in England and Wales, a rise of over 30 per cent from the previous year, and as compared with just over 31,000 complaints in 1980.[3]

### Definition of Noise

Noise has been variously defined as: " . . . sound which is undesired by the recipient",[4] and as: " . . . a number of tonal components disagreeable to man and more or less intolerable to him because of the discomfort, fatigue, disturbance and, in some cases, pain it causes."[5]

---

[1] Evidence given to the House of Lords Select Committee on the Environment (Session 1981–1982), Thirteenth Report: *Noise in the Environment,* para. 60.
[2] See The E.C.'s Second Action Programme on the Environment (1977-1981), O.J. C139, para. 64.
[3] *Neighbour Noise Working Party Review of the Effectiveness of Neighbour Noise Controls: Conclusions and Recommendations* (DoE).
[4] Final Report of the Parliamentary Committee on the Problem of Noise, 1963.
[5] Second European Community Action Programme on the Environment (1977–1981), above.

Both of these definitions illustrate the subjectivity of noise pollution. A sound that may be acceptable in an industrial area may become "noise" if it is present in a residential area. What may be an acceptable sound during the day may become a noise at night. Music in a nightclub may exhilarate the individual who then finds it unbearable when he is trying to sleep in the house next door. A sound of small intensity, such as that from a dripping tap, may become unbearable simply by its repetition. The subjectivity of noise pollution, then, makes it very difficult to tackle by traditional legal mechanisms, which usually set objective criteria as to when and at what level pollutants should be controlled.

## Legal Control of Noise

Legal controls have traditionally divided noise into various categories, such as neighbourhood noise, noise on construction sites and transport noise. In its report entitled "Noise in the Next Ten Years", for example, the Noise Advisory Council conveniently classified noise under four headings:

- Road traffic noise;
- Aircraft noise;
- Neighbourhood noise;
- Occupational noise.

Noise may be controlled in a number of ways: at the point of its generation, during its transmission, or at the point of its reception by the hearer. The prevention of noise at source, rather than subsequently trying to counteract its effects, is acknowledged as the best answer to the problem, but this, for technical or financial reasons, is often not possible.[6] Preventive controls can be implemented by designating geographical zones where noise cannot go above a certain level. Noise may be controlled during its transmission by sound-proofing buildings and by enclosing noisy machinery. Control of noise at the point of its reception by the hearer may be exercised through development plans designed to keep noise away from residential areas, as well as through transport policy, for example by the control of aircraft flight paths.

Legal regulation of noise in the U.K. is somewhat disparate. It is achieved through the common law of nuisance and by a number of statutes including the Control of Pollution Act 1974, the Civil Aviation Act 1978, the Road Traffic Act 1988, the Environmental Protection Act 1990, the Noise and Statutory Nuisance Act 1993 and the Noise Act 1996. Despite relatively recent statutory intervention in the field of noise, the opportunity has not been taken to create a comprehensive regime of noise control. Unlike other pollutants, noise does not affect areas remote from its source. For this reason, local authorities, who have knowledge of local conditions, are the main agencies involved in combatting noise pollution. The traditional legal response to noise has been to employ the concept of nuisance, first in the common law, and later through the development of a simpler "statutory nuisance" procedure. Whilst nuisance

---

[6] See the First European Community Action Programme on the Environment, [1973] O.J. C112.

remains at the heart of the legal framework, a number of preventive controls have been devised which do not rely on the concept. This chapter concentrates on *ex post facto* control of neighbourhood noise through the statutory nuisance procedure, but also examines the rôle of preventive measures used to control such things as construction and transport noise, and the operation of "noise abatement zones". The policy of the European Community will also be considered.

## NEIGHBOURHOOD NOISE

"Neighbourhood noise" has been defined as: " . . . the great variety of sources of noise which may cause disturbance and annoyance to the general public not including road traffic and aircraft noise and industrial noise affecting workers."[7]

Examples of neighbourhood noise, then, include the playing of sound systems or watching of television at high volumes, the noise of refrigeration plant emanating from butchers' shops and supermarkets, the noise caused by roadworks and the activities of local industry, such as use of drop hammers, riveting machines and extractor fans. Neighbourhood noise is the greatest source of noise nuisance complaints in England and Wales. A survey, conducted by the Building Research Establishment in 1986, provided the following analysis of the source of complaints:[8]

- Amplified music: 34 per cent;
- Dogs: 33 per cent;
- Domestic activities: 9 per cent;
- Voices: 6 per cent;
- DIY activities: 5 per cent;
- Car repairs: 3 per cent;
- Other sources: 10 per cent.

The main way of controlling these problems is by securing abatement of the noise once it has exceeded nuisance levels. This can be achieved either through a common law action or through the statutory nuisance procedure under Part III of the Environmental Protection Act 1990. In exceptional circumstances, prevention of noise can also be achieved through these mechanisms, as where a *quia timet* injunction is sought at common law, or where an abatement order is issued under Part III to prohibit an anticipated nuisance. In practice, the law on statutory nuisances is one of the most important legal tools for combatting noise nuisance.

[7] Report of the Noise Advisory Council, 1972, p. 11, paras. 54 and 55.
[8] See *Neighbourhood Noise Working Party Review of the Effectiveness of Neighbour Noise Control (Conclusions and Recommendations)* (DoE, March 1995).

## Noise as a Statutory Nuisance

Under Part III of the Environmental Protection Act 1990, the regime of control is activated by the occurrence, or by the likely occurrence, of a statutory nuisance. The Act sets out various heads of statutory nuisance.[9] In relation to noise, the following heads are relevant:

- Noise emitted from premises so as to be prejudicial to health or a nuisance[10];
- Any other matter declared by any enactment to be a statutory nuisance.[11]

The Noise Review Working Party considered that one of the main drawbacks of existing legislation was that local authorities could not control noise in the street. Therefore, by the Noise and Statutory Nuisance Act 1993, the Environmental Protection Act 1990 was amended so as to include a new category of statutory nuisance, namely noise that is prejudicial to health or a nuisance and is emitted from or caused by a vehicle, machinery or equipment in the street.[12]

## Statutory Definition of "Noise"

The Environmental Protection Act 1990 does not define noise, except to say that it includes vibration.[13] The Act also provides an example of noise when it states that the statutory nuisance provisions do not apply to noise caused by aircraft other than model aircraft.[14]

## The Meaning of "Statutory Nuisance"

The word "nuisance" is not defined by the Act, but is traditionally thought to bear the same meaning as it has at common law.[15] There may be some minor differences, however, between statutory and common law nuisances. In particular, in contrast to the position at common law, it may not be necessary for a statutory nuisance to emanate from premises *other than* those occupied and enjoyed by the person who is affected by the nuisance. In *Carr v. Hackney Borough Council,*[16] it was argued that a statutory nuisance had been created by the local council when its tenants found damp and mould in their house. Although, on the facts, the council were not liable for the damp, the court proceeded on the basis that the matters complained of could constitute a "nuisance", and failed to address the question of whether this could properly be the case even though the damp could not be said to have resulted from one person's activity on his own land which interfered with enjoyment of land by

---

[9] EPA 1990, s.79(1); see also Chapter 4, above.
[10] EPA 1990, s.79(1)(g).
[11] *ibid.,* s.79(1)(h).
[12] *ibid.,* s.79(1)(g)(a)) (inserted by the Noise and Statutory Nuisance Act 1993).
[13] EPA 1990, s.79(7).
[14] *ibid.,* s.79(6).
[15] *National Coal Board v. Thorne* [1976] 1 W.L.R. 543.
[16] [1995] 93 L.G.R. 606.

another. The approach adopted in *Carr*, then, may be an indication that the courts are now prepared to attach a different, wider, meaning to the word "nuisance" as it appears in the Part III of the Environmental Protection Act 1990.

## "Prejudicial to Health"

Under the Act, proceedings may be brought where the act complained of is "prejudicial to health *or* a nuisance". It is not, therefore, necessary for the complainant to make out in every case that the act complained of is prejudicial to his health, but there will be many circumstances in which he will be able to do this. The Act defines "prejudicial to health" as "injurious or likely to cause injury, to health".[17]

In broad terms, noise might be said to be prejudicial to health when it prevents sleep, induces stress, disturbs concentration, or interferes with communication so as to affect personal safety, for example by making it impossible for cries for help to be heard. Studies in Germany, Japan and the Netherlands suggest that the growth of the foetus may be inhibited, and the birth weight of babies reduced, by exposure to high levels of aircraft noise during pregnancy.[18] The various government working parties on noise have been of the view that there is no evidence to suggest that moderate noise levels, associated with domestic and social situations, can produce any direct and measurable physiological effects, so that the effects on health of such noise are psychological rather than physical. The courts, however, appear to have accepted that these psychological effects can be "prejudicial to health" within the meaning of the Act. Thus, in *London Borough of Lewisham v. Fenner,*[19] where noise emanating from equipment used to heat and ventilate a swimming pool had caused the complainant to lose sleep and to visit his doctor for depression, the court accepted that the noise was prejudicial to the complainant's health.

## "Premises"

"Premises" are defined by the Act to include land and any vessel,[20] except one which is powered by steam reciprocating machinery.[21] Since "premises" include "land", noise from a "rave" in a field, for example, will constitute noise from premises, as will noise from roads and railways.

## "Street"

"Street" is defined as meaning a highway and any other road, footway, square or court that is for the time being open to the public.[22] Because "equipment" used in the street includes musical instruments, the noise made by buskers can constitute a statutory

---

[17] EPA 1990, s.79(7).
[18] Royal Commission on Environmental Pollution, Eighteenth Report: *Transport and the Environment* (Cmnd. 2674), p. 48.
[19] Unreported, Knightsbridge Crown Court, June 14, 1996.
[20] EPA 1990, s.79(7).
[21] *ibid.,* s.79(12).
[22] *ibid.,* s.79(4)(c) (inserted by the Noise and Statutory Nuisance Act 1993).

nuisance. Other examples of street noise regulated by the Act include noise from vehicles (including car alarms) and from vehicle repairs carried out in the road, as well as noise from machinery used in road building, such as generators and air compressors.

## The Duties of Local Authorities

Every local authority is under a duty periodically to inspect its area for the presence of statutory nuisances, and if a complaint is made to the authority by a person living within its area, the authority must take reasonably practicable steps to investigate that complaint.[23] If the local authority fails to do this, the Secretary of State may make an order declaring the local authority to be in default, and may direct the authority to carry out its duty in a specified manner.[24] If the local authority fails to comply with the order, the Secretary of State may transfer the relevant functions of the authority to himself, or he may seek an order of mandamus (a public law remedy which compels a public body to perform its functions) from the High Court.[25]

Where the local authority is "satisfied" that a statutory nuisance exists, or is likely to occur or recur in its area, it is under a duty to serve an abatement notice. The appropriate standard for the authority to apply in determining whether the nuisance exists is the civil standard, namely the balance of probabilities, because although the criminal law may be used eventually to enforce the abatement notice, at the time of its service the proceedings are civil.

The decision in *R v. Carrick District Council, ex p. Shelley and Another*[26] has made it clear that once the authority has discovered the existence of a statutory nuisance, it has no discretion as to whether or not to serve a notice. The court held that the local authority had failed in its statutory duty when, in the light of complaints about pollution on its beaches, it resolved not to take any action, but merely to monitor the situation. In granting an application for judicial review of the authority's lack of action, the court held that the authority's inaction had not been based on a decision that there was no statutory nuisance (a judgment of fact which it would have been entitled to make); rather, it had been based on a decision that serving a notice was not appropriate (a judgment based on the exercise of discretion, which it did not possess.) It is to be noted that the wording of the section allows a local authority to serve an abatement notice even before the nuisance has commenced, in order to prevent it from occurring.

## The Abatement Notice

The local authority must serve the abatement notice on the relevant person by delivering it to him personally, by leaving it at his proper address, or by sending it to him by post at that address.[27] The notice must inform the recipient that he has the right to appeal against it to a magistrates' court within 21 days.[28] The abatement notice

---

[23] EPA 1990, s.79(1).
[24] *ibid.,* Sched. 3, para. 4.
[25] *ibid.,* Sched. 3, para. 4(3).
[26] *The Times*, June 15, 1996.
[27] Local Government Act 1972, s.233.
[28] EPA 1990, Sched. 3, para. 6.

may require the abatement of the nuisance by imposing a complete prohibition on the activity in question, or by restricting the occurrence of the activity. It may also require the execution of works necessary to abate the nuisance, such as soundproofing in the case of noise. The notice must also specify a time limit within which its requirements are to be carried out.[29]

There are no other statutory provisions specifying what the notice must contain. In accordance with general principles of administrative law, however, the notice must tell its recipient clearly what he has done wrong and what is required of him to remedy that wrong. Just how detailed may be the steps which a local authority requires the recipient to take has been considered by the courts. In *Wivenhoe Port v. Colchester Borough Council,*[30] an abatement order, served under similar legislation which predated the Environmental Protection Act 1990, directed the company in question to use a specifically described cargo-handling system at all times. The court held that although the wording of the relevant legislation enabled a court to require the recipient of the order to undertake positive works to abate the nuisance (as does the current legislation), what was being asked for in this case went beyond "works", and that the legislation did not empower the court to direct the company as to how it should carry out its day to day operations.

Similarly, in *Network Housing Association Ltd v. Westminster City Council,*[31] an abatement notice was held to be invalid when it stated that noise levels had to be reduced to a certain level of decibels, but did not say how it was to be achieved. The court held that although in some obvious cases a notice requiring little more than a reduction in noise levels might suffice, in the circumstances of this particular case, Westminster City Council should have made up their minds about the nature and extent of the works required and should have identified these in the notice. The court's decision was influenced by the fact that, whatever work was carried out, it would be practically impossible to measure or guarantee the results of that work in advance. Bearing in mind the risk of exposure to penal sanctions for non-compliance with the notice, it is essential that the appellant should be told clearly exactly what works he is required to undertake.

The notice must be served on the "person responsible for the nuisance", except in cases where he cannot be found, when it may be served on the owner or occupier of the premises on which the nuisance arises. In cases where the nuisance is attributable to structural defects in premises, the notice should be served on the owner of those premises.[32] The "person responsible" for a statutory nuisance is defined by the Act as "the person to whose act, default or sufferance the nuisance is attributable".[33] Thus, the person responsible for inadequate soundproofing in a block of flats, so that tenants can hear the day to day living noises of their neighbours, is either the landlord (on the basis that the nuisance can be attributed to his default or sufferance) or the person who originally converted the building into flats (on the same basis).[34] The landlord may also receive an abatement notice simply because the nuisance arises from a structural

---

[29] *ibid.,* s.80.
[30] [1985] J.P.L. 175.
[31] [1995] 93 L.G.R. 280.
[32] EPA 1990, s.80(2).
[33] *ibid.,* s.79(7).
[34] *Network Housing Association Ltd v. Westminster City Council* (1995) 93 L.G.R. 280.

defect in premises of which he is the owner. Where the person responsible cannot be found, the notice may be served on the owner or occupier of the premises, reflecting the traditional rule that such persons are responsible for abating nuisances arising on their property.

## Unattended Vehicles, etc.

Establishing the ownership of, or the identity of the person responsible for vehicles, machinery and equipment left unattended in the street can be difficult and time-consuming. The Noise and Statutory Nuisance Act 1993 therefore introduces an expedited procedure for the service of abatement notices in these circumstances, which, according to the Department of the Environment, is:

> " . . . designed to balance the rights of an owner not to have his vehicle broken into, or his machinery interfered with, against the needs of those who live or work in the vicinity and who are suffering a noise nuisance."[35]

If the noise reaches nuisance levels from a vehicle, or from machinery or equipment, which has been left unattended in the street, the abatement notice should be served on the person responsible for that vehicle, machinery or equipment. This will include the person in whose name a vehicle is for the time being registered and any other person who is for the time being the driver of the vehicle (or, where machinery or equipment are concerned, its operator).[36] The environmental health officer must spend one hour trying to trace the person responsible for the unattended vehicle, etc. so that he may be served with an abatement notice. If, after an hour, this person cannot be found, the officer may affix the notice to the vehicle, etc. itself, and may then take whatever action he considers appropriate to abate the noise nuisance.[37] The environmental health officer has the power to open and enter, if necessary by force, any vehicle, machinery or equipment on the street, and to remove it to safe place if that is necessary to abate the noise.[38]

## Appeal against the Notice

The recipient of the notice has 21 days from the date the notice was served in which to appeal against it to a magistrates' court.[39] The grounds on which an appeal can be made to the magistrates' court include the following[40]:

- That the notice is not justified (*i.e.* that there is no nuisance);

---

[35] *Guidance on the Noise and Statutory Nuisance Act 1993* (DoE, December 1993).
[36] Noise and Statutory Nuisance Act 1993, s.2(4)(b).
[37] EPA 1990, s.80A (inserted by the Noise and Statutory Nuisance Act 1993).
[38] EPA 1990, Sched. 3, para. 2A (inserted by Noise and Statutory Nuisance Act 1993).
[39] EPA 1990, s.80(3).
[40] See the Environmental Protection (Statutory Nuisance) (Appeals) Regulations 1990, as amended by the Statutory Nuisance (Appeals) Regulations 1995 (S.I. 1995 No. 2644).

- That there is some informality, defect or error in the notice;

- That the authority has unreasonably refused to accept an offer to comply with alternative requirements in abating the nuisance, or that the requirements set out in the abatement notice are unreasonable or unnecessary;

- That the time limit for completion of works specified in the notice is unreasonably short;

- Where the nuisance consists of noise from construction works, that those works are the subject of a consent or notice issued under the Control of Pollution Act 1974;

- That the notice has been served on the wrong person.

The magistrates may either dismiss the appeal or may quash or vary the abatement notice.

## Failure to Comply with the Notice

A person on whom an abatement notice has been served commits a criminal offence if he fails to comply with its requirements *without reasonable excuse*.[41] The offence is triable only in a magistrates' court, where the maximum penalty is a £5,000 fine, together with further fines of £500 in respect of each day on which the defendant remains in default after conviction.[42] Although the defendant may be able to avail himself of the defence of "best practicable means" (below), it has been held that lack of finance is not a reasonable excuse for failing to comply with an abatement notice,[43] nor is the fact the nuisance constitutes music at a birthday celebration to which the neighbours have all been invited![44]

The local authority has a discretion whether or not to bring a prosecution for failure to comply with an abatement notice. Whether or not it chooses to do so, however, the local authority may itself take action to abate the nuisance and may recover the cost of so doing from the person responsible for the nuisance (or from the person who owns or occupies the premises on which the nuisance arose).[45]

## The "Best Practicable Means" Defence

If the noise which constitutes a statutory nuisance is made on industrial, trade or business premises (or, if it is a noise in the street, is the result of a business, trade or local industry), it is a defence for the accused to show that the "best practicable means" were used to prevent or to counteract the effects of the nuisance.[46]

---

[41] EPA 1990, s.80(4).
[42] *ibid.*, s.80(5).
[43] *Saddleworth Urban District Council v. Aggregate and Sand* (1970) 114 Sol. Jo. 931.
[44] *Wellingborough Borough Council v. Gordon, The Times*, November 9, 1990.
[45] EPA 1990, s.81(4).
[46] For the applicability of the defence to other forms of statutory nuisance, see EPA 1990, ss.80(8) and 82(10).

"Practicable" means reasonably practicable having regard, amongst other things, to local conditions and circumstances, to the current state of technical knowledge, and to the financial implications of the means employed.[47] The "means" which may be employed to abate the nuisance include the design, installation, maintenance of plant and machinery, as well as the manner and the length of time for which it is operated. They also include the design, construction and maintenance of buildings and structures.[48] In practice, the defendant's raising the defence of best practicable means has posed serious problems for local authorities, who lack the information and investigative resources to refute the defendant's claims.

## Proceedings in the High Court

If the local authority is of the view that summary conviction in the magistrates' court is an inadequate remedy, it can seek an injunction in the High Court to abate, prohibit or restrict the statutory nuisance.[49] The idea behind this provision is to stop companies from treating a fine in the magistrates' court simply as an overhead, which they pass on to consumers in the price of their goods and services.

In *City of London Corporation v. Bovis Construction Ltd,*[50] the Court of Appeal noted that the test for the court to apply in exercising its discretion whether or not to grant an injunction was whether it could be inferred that the defendant's unlawful operations would continue unless and until they were effectively restrained by the law, and that nothing short of an injunction would be effective to restrain those operations. The court held that, in contrast with cases concerning injunctions in planning matters, the criminal law need not have been broken for an injunction to lie. Planning cases were to be distinguished from statutory nuisance cases, where the local authority, albeit through public law, was enforcing private rather than public rights.

## Action by a "Person Aggrieved"

An individual who suffers from a statutory nuisance can take proceedings against the person responsible for the nuisance (or, where he cannot be found, against the owner or occupier of the premises on which the nuisance has arisen) by making a complaint to a magistrates' court.[51] Before he does so, however, he must inform the person responsible of his intention to bring proceedings.[52] If the magistrates are satisfied that a nuisance exists (or, although abated at present, is likely to recur in the same premises or street) they may make an order requiring the defendant to abate the nuisance or prohibiting its recurrence and may, in that order, require the defendant to take certain specified steps to facilitate this. The magistrates can also, at the time the order is made, impose a fine up to a maximum of £5,000. Because the magistrates are imposing sanctions under the criminal law in such cases, the standard to which they must be

---

[47] EPA s.79(9)(a).
[48] *ibid.,* s.79(9)(b).
[49] *ibid.,* s.81(5).
[50] [1992] 3 All E.R. 697.
[51] EPA 1990, s.82.
[52] *ibid.,* s.82(6).

"satisfied" of the existence of the statutory nuisance is the criminal standard, namely, beyond reasonable doubt.[53]

If at the magistrates hearing it is proved that the alleged nuisance existed at the date on which the complaint was made, then, even if it does not exist at the time of the hearing, or by that time is not likely to recur (so that the magistrates have no power to make an abatement order), the magistrates may nevertheless order the defendant to pay the reasonable costs of the complainant in bringing the proceedings.[54] In addition, where neither the person responsible for the nuisance, nor the owner or occupier of the premises can be found, the magistrates, after giving the local authority the chance to make representations, can direct the local authority to abate the nuisance or take action to prevent it from recurring.[55]

The meaning of "person aggrieved" was examined in a general context by Lord Denning MR in *Attorney-General of the Gambia v. N'Jie,*[56] who held that the phrase was of wide import and should not be subjected to a restricted interpretation. "Persons aggrieved" will not, of course, include mere "busybodies" interfering with matters which do not concern them, but the phrase is wide enough to cover practically anyone who has a genuine grievance.[57] Thus, in *Sandwell Metropolitan Borough Council v. Bujok*[58] it was held that anyone whose health, or the health of whose family, is affected is a person aggrieved, whilst in *Birmingham District Council v. McMahon*[59] it was held that a council tenant in a block of flats, who complained of a nuisance affecting the block in general but not his flat in particular, was not a person aggrieved.

Failure to comply with the requirements of an abatement or prohibition order is a criminal offence for which the maximum penalty is an initial fine of £5,000, together with additional fines of £500 a day for each day on which the contravention continues after conviction. The defence of "best practicable means" is available.

It will be apparent, then, that there are certain differences between proceedings taken by a local authority and proceedings taken by a "person aggrieved". When a local authority wishes to take action to abate a statutory nuisance, it serves an abatement notice. The procedure is at this point civil. Therefore, if the recipient of the notice appeals to the magistrates, the standard of proof in any matter requiring to be proved is "the balance of probabilities". However, once the requirements of the abatement notice are disobeyed, the matter becomes criminal. By contrast, where a person aggrieved takes action by making a complaint to the magistrates, the proceedings are criminal from the outset, because the magistrates have power to fine the defendant. Accordingly, the standard of proof is "beyond reasonable doubt".

There is some authority for the proposition that criminalising the defendant's actions by imposing a fine will immediately give the magistrates an additional power to make a compensation order in favour of anyone suffering personal injury or property damage as a result of the nuisance.[60] This is on the basis that a finding against a person

---

[53] *London Borough of Lewisham v. Fenner,* unreported, Knightsbridge Crown Court, June 14, 1996.
[54] EPA 1990, s.82(12).
[55] *ibid.,* s.82(13).
[56] [1961] A.C. 617.
[57] Wade and Forsyth, *Administrative Law* (7th ed., 1994), p. 752.
[58] [1990] 3 All E.R. 385.
[59] (1987) 151 J.P. 709.
[60] *Botross v. Hammersmith and Fulham London Borough Council* (1994) 27 H.L.R. 179.

responsible for a nuisance means that they are a person "convicted" of an offence within the meaning of section 35 of the Powers of Criminal Courts Act 1973, which grants the court a general power to make compensation orders. It seems, however, that compensation orders are rarely made in this context and that civil proceedings therefore remain the primary means for an aggrieved person to obtain compensation for the effects of a nuisance.

## The Regime in Practice

The inadequacies of a statutory nuisance action for problems of noise are numerous. They include the difficulties experienced by complainants and by local authorities in establishing that a noise nuisance has occurred in the first place. Because of the degree of subjectivity involved in the concept of "noise" (and indeed in the concept of "nuisance"), it is often not easy to predict in advance whether the magistrates, on appeal against a notice, will decide that the barrier between reasonable noise and noise nuisance has been crossed. The difficulties of proving noise nuisance mean that statutory nuisance proceedings are more likely to be successful in cases of long and continuous noise emissions, as opposed to short, intermittent noise emissions. Although, in theory, proceedings can be taken to abate noise nuisances before they occur, in practice this is difficult.

Local authorities scarcely have the resources to fulfil their statutory duty of inspecting their areas for the existence of nuisances already occurring, let alone to inspect for likely sources of future noise pollution. The right of the aggrieved individual to bring proceedings in a magistrates' court is not well publicised and is under-used. Most individuals will perceive litigation on their own as involving expense and as daunting in its complexity, and will therefore complain to the local authority in the first instance. Local authorities, however, often respond to domestic noise complaints too slowly for the complaint to be dealt with effectively. Between 1993 and 1994 there were 131,153 complaints about noise from domestic premises alone. Abatement notices, however, were served only in a few thousand cases. 0.3 per cent of the 131,153 complaints resulted in a conviction. In the light of these statistics, the government considered that a more immediate response, and one which removed the administrative burden on noise sufferers, was needed for the problem of domestic noise.

## The Noise Act 1996

The government's response was the Noise Act 1996. This puts in place a summary procedure for dealing with noise at night. The powers under the Act apply only to the local authority's area if either the local authority or the Secretary of State have so resolved. This enables local authorities to exercise their discretion in deciding whether or not noise is a priority problem in their area which they have sufficient financial resources to tackle, and allows for the Secretary of State to supervise the exercise of that discretion. One of the primary concerns before the Act was passed, however, was that noise control varied from area to area. This problem has not been resolved by the Act, because the application of the regime it creates is voluntary.

The requirement of a complaint is fundamental to the operation of the regime. The aim of the regime is not that local authorities should secure the abatement of *all* night-time noise. Rather, it is to secure the abatement of noise which causes annoyance. Therefore a local authority only has power to act following receipt of a complaint. Under the Act, where a local authority receives a complaint from an individual who is present in a dwelling during the night that excessive noise is being emitted from another dwelling, it must ensure that an officer of the authority takes reasonable steps to investigate the complaint. If an officer is satisfied that noise exceeding the permitted level is being emitted from the offending dwelling during night hours (11 p.m.–7 a.m.), he may serve a "warning notice" on that dwelling. The officer need not actually measure the level of noise being emitted in order to be "satisfied" that a notice should be served. The officer of the authority has a discretion whether or not to serve a warning notice. Therefore, if the noise complained of results from a "one-off" event, such as a birthday party, the officer may decide simply to ask that the noise level be reduced.

The warning notice served by the officer must state that an officer of the authority considers that noise is being emitted from the dwelling in night hours, that the noise exceeds the permitted level, and that the person responsible for the noise may be guilty of an offence if he continues to make the noise in the period beginning 10 minutes after the time when the notice is served and ending the following morning at 7 a.m. A "person responsible" for the noise is a person to whose act, default or sufferance the emission of noise is wholly or partly attributable. It will be appreciated that this is a very wide definition which could, conceivably, cover every guest at a party. The precise scope of the term, however, awaits judicial determination.

Where a warning notice has been served in respect of noise emitted from a dwelling, any person who is responsible for noise emitted in the period specified in the notice which exceeds the permitted level, as measured from within the complainant's dwelling, is guilty of an offence, although it is a defence for the accused to show that he had a reasonable excuse for making the noise. The defendant is liable to a fine on conviction by the magistrates, but may pay a fixed penalty instead if the officer decides it is appropriate.[61] As to the meaning of "reasonable excuse", in *A. Lambert Flat Management Ltd v. Lomas*,[62] Ackner L.J., considering the matter *obiter* in the context of the Control of Pollution Act 1974, regarded reasonable excuses as: " . . . special reasons such as illness and non-receipt of the notice".

The permitted level of noise in a given area is determined by the Secretary of State on an area by area basis, in order to cater for the particular needs and characteristics of different areas. Parliament has suggested a base level of 35dB, reflecting World Health Organisation guidelines which, in 1980, stated that "a level of less than 35dB is necessary to preserve the restorative process of sleep." It is extremely difficult, however, to measure noise levels accurately. Walls and structures may absorb and deflect noise so that the precise angle or location at which the measurement is taken proves vital. Moreover, the variance of noise levels caused by absorbtion and deflection can mean, for example, that a party in house A may be very much quieter than a party in house B, but cause greater annoyance. If the person responsible for the quieter

---

[61] NA 1996, s.8.
[62] [1981] 1 W.L.R. 898.

party in house A is found guilty of a criminal offence, whilst his noisier neighbour escapes prosecution, a sense of unfairness may be promoted. If the law is seen to be unfair in its application, it is unlikely to be complied with. The Act may also be criticised because it fails to deal with the problem of "cumulative noise". In many of the most serious noise pollution cases, the annoyance is caused by a repetition of incidents involving relatively small levels of noise which cannot be dealt with under the Act because they do not exceed the prescribed level, but which nevertheless cause great annoyance.

## NOISE FROM SPECIFIC SOURCES

### Raves

The Criminal Justice Act 1994 contains provisions enabling the police to deal with raves which are in progress and to prevent them from being held. During the passage of the legislation, Earl Ferrers, opening the debate for the government in the House of Lords, said that raves had caused "appalling misery" to local residents and had "ripped apart the peaceful lives of rural societies."[63] Under the Act, a "rave" is defined as a gathering of 100 or more people on land in the open air which includes the playing of amplified music. Where the music, by reason of its loudness and duration and the time at which it is played, is such that it is likely to cause serious distress to the inhabitants of the locality, the police may take steps to secure that it ceases.[64] Moreover, a constable who has reasonable grounds for believing that a person is on a way to a rave may stop him and prevent him from going.[65]

### Intruder Alarms

Intruder alarms which are set off accidentally and sound for a considerable time have become a blight in many neighbourhoods. Therefore, the Noise and Statutory Nuisance Act 1993 provides that local authorities may, if they choose, apply the following regime to their area. Anyone installing an alarm must ensure it complies with prescribed requirements. The police must hold a list of the names and addresses of certain key alarm users. The local authority must be notified within 48 hours that an audible alarm has been installed. Failure to comply with these requirements without reasonable excuse will constitute a criminal offence. The regime also provides that where an alarm has been sounding for an hour after it was activated and the audible operation of the alarm is giving people living or working in the vicinity reasonable cause for annoyance, the local authority may enter premises to turn it off.

---

[63] *Hansard,* H.L. 1993, Vol. 554, no. 71, col. 384–5.
[64] CJA 1994, s.63.
[65] *ibid.,* s.65.

## Loudspeakers

Loudspeakers cannot be used in the street between the hours of 9 p.m. and 8 a.m. for any purpose, or at any time to advertise entertainments, trade or business.[66] If a person wishes to use loudspeakers in the street at night, he must apply to the local authority for consent.[67] The police and the fire brigade are exempt from these provisions, as are loudspeakers used in public transport systems for making announcements to passengers.

## Construction Noise

Construction and demolition works pose special noise problems compared with most other types of industrial activity. They are mainly carried on in the open air, they are of temporary duration, and the noise involved emanates from a wide variety of different activities such as the use of pneumatic concrete breakers and the operation of excavators. The intensity and character of construction noise may vary greatly depending on the phase of the work which is being undertaken. Unlike other sources of noise pollution, construction sites cannot be kept away from areas which are sensitive to noise through the operation of planning law. The statutory nuisance procedure is often too slow to abate construction noise, which may last only for a few weeks before a contractor moves elsewhere.

Control over construction noise is exercised by local authorities under the provisions of Part III of the Control of Pollution Act 1974, in particular, sections 60, 61 and 59A.[68] The emphasis is on preventive action rather than on action to secure abatement. Construction noise is widely defined under the Act as noise resulting from the "erection, construction, alteration, repair or maintenance of buildings, structures and roads, or from breaking up, opening or boring under any road or adjacent land in connection with the construction, inspection, maintenance or removal of works, demolition or dredging work and any work of engineering construction."

Where such works are in progress or are to be carried out in the future, the local authority has a discretion to serve a notice imposing requirements in relation to the way in which the works are carried out.[69] The conditions which a local authority may specify include those governing the type of plant and machinery which can be used, the hours during which the works may be carried out, and the level of noise that may be emitted.[70] In practice, most notices served under section 60 prohibit work outside specified hours where that work is audible beyond the boundary of the construction site. In this way, the local authority exercises stringent control over construction operations.

It is a criminal offence to contravene a requirement of the notice without reasonable excuse, but it is a defence to prosecution that the works are carried out in accordance with a consent issued under section 61.[71] In *City of London Corporation v. Bovis*

---

[66] Control of Pollution Act 1974, s.62(1).
[67] Noise and Statutory Nuisance Act 1993.
[68] Inserted by the Noise and Statutory Nuisance Act 1993, with effect from January 5, 1994.
[69] COPA 1974, s.60(2).
[70] *ibid.*, s.60(3).
[71] *ibid.*, s.61 (8).

*Construction Ltd,*[72] Bovis Construction were prosecuted when they breached a notice served under section 60 of the Control of Pollution Act 1974 requiring them to restrict operations which caused noise outside the boundaries of the site to the hours between 8 a.m. and 6 p.m. on weekdays, between 8 a.m. and 1 p.m. on Saturdays, and entirely on Sundays and bank holidays.

## Prior Consent for Construction Work

If a developer wishes to carry out construction work, he may apply in advance to the local authority for a consent to allow the works to be carried out at the particular noise level which he proposes. The advantage of applying for a consent in advance, of course, is that the contractor obviates the risk that a local authority will serve a notice under section 60 requiring a change in working methods and hours of work which might cause the developer expense. Once a consent is granted, it becomes a criminal offence knowingly to carry out works or knowingly to permit works to be carried out in contravention of the conditions of a consent.[73]

The consent procedure under section 61 of the Act is rarely used. It has been suggested that industry may well be reluctant to seek prior consent for noise levels because of a fear that the local authority will impose too many restrictions on working practices,[74] the implication being that many contractors prefer to "take their chances" with a local authority and see what level of noise they can get away with. However, where discussions have been held between local authorities and representatives from industry, there have been few concerns over the conditions of consents or the contents of notices.

## Transport Noise

In its eighteenth report on transport and the environment, the Royal Commission on Environmental Pollution concluded that present levels of exposure to noise from transport are causing serious damage to people's quality of life and are therefore incompatible with the notion of sustainable development. Over the last 25 years, the average distance travelled per person in Britain each day has risen by almost 75 per cent to nearly 18 miles. For the majority of people in the U.K., transport is the most pervasive source of noise in the environment. In a survey carried out over a 24 hour period in 1990, noise from roads was recorded outside 92 per cent of a sample of dwellings in England and Wales. This section focuses on the two main problems: road traffic noise and aircraft noise.

### Road Traffic Noise

In terms of the number of people affected, road traffic noise is the most serious of all transport noise problems. Roads are everywhere and there are few restrictions on the

---

[72] [1992] 3 All E.R. 697.
[73] COPA 1974 s.61(5).
[74] See Report of the Noise Review Working Party 1990.

vehicles which may use them. Noise is emitted from vehicles because of bad maintenance, accidental damage or, occasionally, because of deliberate interference to silencing systems. Certain types of silencers deteriorate in use before finally failing with the result that the vehicle may emit more noise than when it was new. A significant proportion of noise from road traffic is produced by tyres and can therefore be influenced by the nature of the road surface.[75]

Preventive control over road noise is exercised through secondary legislation which governs the construction of vehicles and the way in which they may be driven.[76] For example, horns must not be sounded between 11.30 at night and 7 o'clock in the morning.[77] It is a criminal offence to contravene these regulations.[78] A more long sighted preventive approach can be taken through the planning system. Vehicles produce their maximum noise when they are accelerating in low gear. Traffic noise can therefore be substantially reduced by minimising the number of occasions on which vehicles start and stop. This can be achieved by constructing by-passes and outer ring-roads so as to reduce through traffic in town centres.[79] Noise from roads can also be reduced by using earth banks or barriers made of timber, metal, or plastic. These are much less widely used in the U.K. than in France, Germany and Japan, partly because of their cost, but also because they are considered unsightly.[80]

## Aircraft Noise

The International Civil Aviation organisation has noted:

> "The ability to travel safely, comfortably and quickly across vast distances has given human beings greater access to distant places and a heightened awareness of their own cultural and social diversity. However it must be recognised that — like many other human activities — civil aviation can sometimes have adverse environmental consequences."[81]

Air transport is the most rapidly growing mode of transport, both in the U.K. and globally. Between 1982 and 1992 the number of passengers on international scheduled services to and from U.K. airports more than doubled.[82] Because of its geographical position and historical links with other nations, the U.K. has a disproportionately large share of international air traffic. The Department of Transport forecast that the number of passengers passing through U.K. airports will increase by between 73 per

---

[75] Royal Commission on Environmental Pollution, Eighteenth Report: *Transport and the Environment*.
[76] See The Road Vehicles (Construction and Use) Regulations 1986 (S.I. 1986 No. 1078). The Secretary of State has made regulations in relation to the use and construction of vehicles with respect to noise, in particular to ensure that silencers are efficient and kept in proper working order. Various E.C. Directives are relied on to set noise levels and methods of measurement. The Directives referred to include Directives 77/212, 81/334, 84/372, 84/424 and 78/1015. A more recent Directive (Dir. 92/97), which lowers noise limits further, will need to be implemented by new regulations.
[77] Reg. 99.
[78] Road Traffic Act 1988, s.42.
[79] RCEP, Eighteenth Report (above).
[80] *ibid.*
[81] *International Civil Aviation Organisation Environmental Technical Manual on the Use of Procedures in the Noise Certification of Aircraft* (2nd ed., 1995).
[82] RCEP Eighteenth Report, p. 63.

cent and 163 per cent between 1992 and 2010. Aircraft noise arouses a good deal of anger in local communities. Current plans to build a second runway at Manchester Airport, for example, have fiercely divided local opinion.

Aircraft noise is regulated by the Civil Aviation Act 1982, under which the Secretary of State has set maximum noise levels for aircraft serving Heathrow, Gatwick and Stansted. By section 78 of the Act, the Secretary of State has the power, if he considers it necessary to reduce or avoid noise, to specify the maximum number of occasions on which aircraft may be permitted to take off or land at an airport, or even to prohibit take-off during a specified period. Under section 79 of the Act, schemes may be established which require designated aerodromes to make grants towards the cost of insulating certain buildings in the vicinity which require protection from noise.

## PREVENTIVE CONTROL OF NOISE

### Noise Abatement Zones

The concept of nuisance provides limited control over noise. The law of nuisance comes into play when an unjustified noise is emanating from an identifiable "point" source, but it is of little use where the general level of noise in an area, from often unidentifiable and arguably justifiable sources, gradually rises over time. Moreover, nuisance procedures are concerned largely with abating excessive noise once it has occurred. Even though a local authority may serve an abatement notice where a nuisance is *likely* to occur, in order for the problem to have come to the authority's attention, there must have been some indication that a nuisance was likely. Thus, the nuisance procedure is not truly a form of preventive control, because it does not allow for controls to be instigated before noise has caused at least some problems.[83]

General noise from "diffuse" sources, which is known as "ambient" noise, may be controlled by a local authority, which may designate certain areas or the whole of its area as a "noise abatement zone". Within such zones, target levels are set for noise emissions in order to reduce (or prevent an increase in) the ambient noise level. The statutory framework for noise abatement zones is to be found in Part III of the Control of Pollution Act 1974.

### *Noise Reduction Notices*

If, having set target noise levels in a noise abatement zone, the local authority decides that in order to hold steady or to reduce ambient noise levels there should be a reduction in the level of noise from certain sources, it may issue a noise reduction notice on the person responsible for the noise. The notice may require any reduction which is reasonably practicable and would secure public benefit. It may specify particular times or days during which the noise level is to be reduced and may require noise to be reduced to different levels at different times or on different days.[84]

[83] See *Neighbourhood Noise* (The Noise Advisory Council, 1971.)
[84] COPA 1974, s.66(4).

Very few noise abatement zones have been designated. This has been ascribed to the laborious procedures that have to be followed to designate a zone, maintain the necessary public registers and to carry out noise measurements. It has been suggested that noise abatement zones, whilst suitable for commercial and industrial areas, are not well suited to dealing with neighbourhood noise in residential areas created by the residents themselves and their visitors.[85]

## Building Regulations

Building Regulations are designed to ensure that buildings are constructed to an adequate standard. Part E of Schedule 1 to the Building Regulations 1991 is designed to prevent undue noise being transmitted between separately occupied units of the same building (*e.g.* blocks of flats) or between individual buildings in a group of contiguous buildings (*e.g.* terraced or semi-detached houses). Carrying out work in contravention of the building regulations is an offence. Moreover, the local authority may require the removal or alteration of the offending work. These controls, however, are often inadequate in practice because compliance with the regulations does not always produce an acceptable reduction in noise.

## Highways

Highway authorities must either carry out noise insulation works or provide grants to insulate certain buildings against the effects of traffic noise where those effects increase as a result of the construction or alteration of highway.

## Protecting Workers

The Noise at Work Regulations 1989 directly regulated for the first time what had become a well established risk to workers' health and safety. Under Regulation 6, every employer (with certain limited exceptions) is required to reduce the risk of damage to the hearing of employees and others to the lowest level reasonably practicable.

## Planning and Noise Pollution

The planning system can be very effective in preventing or reducing noise pollution. Noise levels are a material consideration for planning authorities in determining planning applications. Because noise decreases with distance, noise from local industry can sometimes be reduced by the imposition of planning conditions which require the noisiest parts of factories to be located in the middle of sites, as far as possible from the site boundary.

Government guidance makes the somewhat obvious point that noise sensitive developments (such as housing, hospitals and schools) should be separated from major

---

[85] See Report of the Noise Review Working Party 1990.

sources of noise (road, rail and air transport, and certain types of industrial development). It suggests that development plans should give developers and local communities a degree of certainty about the areas in which particular types of development would be acceptable and those in which special measures may be required in order to mitigate the impact of noise.

## EUROPEAN COMMUNITY POLICY ON NOISE

Noise pollution is one of the least developed areas of Community policy. Such action as has been taken has been concerned to eliminate noise emitted from specific products rather than to secure an overall reduction in noise pollution. As has been noted, unlike other pollutants, noise does not persist in the environment and does not affect areas remote from its source. The European Commission takes the view that, in general, the transfrontier effects of noise are minimal and localised, so that they cannot readily be called upon to justify Community legislation to control noise pollution.

Nevertheless, Community thinking on noise has produced some interesting ideas. The Second Environmental Action Programme put forward the idea of a Community-wide anti-noise plan. The basic elements of the plan included the concept of zoning in areas where particular activities predominated, so that designated rest zones, residential areas, leisure areas, industrial estates, roads, railways, airports and waterways would be subject to different levels of noise control. The idea was that the Community would set up the framework of such a system by establishing quality objectives, whilst leaving the details to be worked out at a national level.

The Fourth Environmental Action Programme contained a section on noise[86] which referred to the anti-noise programme suggested by the Second Action Programme as "ambitious" and accepted that, because of limitations on staff resources, the Commission had not yet been able to progress beyond a product-orientated approach to noise control. The Commission's approach, therefore, would be to continue to establish noise emission limits for specific products and to consider the setting of quality objectives in relation to ambient noise levels. In addition the Commission would consider the use of economic instruments aimed at discouraging noisy products.

The regime outlined in the Directive on Integrated Pollution Prevention and Control, which broadly follows the U.K.'s Integrated Pollution Control regime, differs from the U.K.'s IPC regime in that it includes noise as a reason for registering an industrial process.

European legislation with respect to air transport noise has been a comparatively recent development. Four Directives have placed duties on Member States to ensure that subsonic aircraft registered in Member States comply with certain requirements set by international standards.[87]

---

[86] Chapter 4; see also the Commission's Green Paper on Noise, COM(96) 0540.
[87] Dir. 80/51/EEC [1980] O.J. L18/26; Dir. 83/206/EEC [1983] O.J. L117/15; Dir. 89/629/EEC [1989] O.J. L363/27; Dir. 92/14/EEC [1992] O.J. L76/21.

# Chapter 12

# NATURE CONSERVATION

*"Halfway through this century nature went into rapid retreat as intensive farming —
driven first by Government and then by European Union subsidies — took off.
Ancient pastures were ploughed up and doused with pesticides and fertiliser.
Countryside was gobbled up by suburbs and new roads. Survey after survey showed
plant and animal species in decline and some becoming extinct at the hand of
man."*[1]

## Introduction

Concern to protect animals and plants and the habitats in which they live originated in
Victorian times. It was evidenced by public reaction against such practices as cock-
fighting and bear baiting and by the establishment of parks and zoological gardens.
Today the main threat to flora and fauna is from intensive modern farming methods.
Between 1932 and 1984, for example, 97 per cent of traditional hay meadows and
pastures disappeared from the U.K.[2]

Contrary to the romantic notion that landscapes are formed solely by natural forces,
which can be left to their own devices, what is sometimes perceived as nature in a
"wild" state is often in reality the result of human activity. Downs, for example, would
become covered with shrubs and trees were it not for the grazing activities of animals
brought there by man. The task of nature conservation, then, is more complex than it
might at first appear. It involves balancing the interests of plants and animals against
mankind's interests — not only in the aesthetic characteristics of the environment as
he has come to love it — but in the uses to which the environment can be put for non-
aesthetic purposes. Of these uses, the most significant is land development, which,
every five years, causes the U.K. to lose an area of countryside at least the size of
Leicestershire.[3]

The interests of wildlife are not endangered principally by people acting with
destructive intent, but by those who are largely unaware of the effects of their actions.
The destruction of natural plant-covering and hedgerows in the interests of agriculture,

---

[1] Nicholas Schoon, "To save the world, start here", *The Independent*, November 22, 1996.
[2] Schoon, "Going, Going Gone: The Story of Britain's Vanishing Natural History", *Bookman Projects* (1996).
[3] *Hansard,* H.C., 1980–81, Vol. 3 col. 548.

the substitution of one species of farm animal for another, and the introduction of new plant and animal species, can often cause changes in nature which far exceed the results of human activity levelled deliberately against particular species or landscapes. For this reason, nature conservation has emerged as perhaps one of the most politically controversial areas of environmental regulation, in which the interests of landowners have clashed dramatically with those of conservationists and animal rights campaigners. The focus of the debate is the extent to which the rights of a landowner to use his land as he wishes, as the common law has traditionally allowed, should be compromised in the name of ecology. The pattern of legal regulation in the U.K. is one of statutory restriction of landowners' rights to undertake certain activities such as the cutting of wild flowers or the collection of birds' eggs. Wild animals, which belong to no-one, are also protected by statute.

Nature conservation and conservation of the landscape are logically elements of the same topic. In the U.K., however, these tasks have traditionally been subject to the operation of two separate regimes. This chapter therefore considers each of these in turn before considering the position under E.C. law and international law.

## NATURE CONSERVATION

In 1947, a special committee of the House of Lords (the "Huxley Committee") reported on nature conservation,[4] and its recommendations still form the basis of nature conservation policy today. These recommendations were:

(i) That nature conservation should be the responsibility of central government;

(ii) That protection should be based on the designation of sites which are important examples of their type;

(iii) That conservation policy should be based on scientific research into the complex relationships between animals and plants and between plants and the soils and rocks upon which they depend.

The Huxley Committee's recommendations led to the passing of the National Parks and Access to Countryside Act 1949. This legislation introduced the practice of designating certain sites as worthy of protection and established "National Nature Reserves" (NNRs) and "Sites of Special Scientific Interest" (SSSIs). These are the two main forms of site designation currently in use.

The principal source of legislation on nature conservation is now the Wildlife and Countryside Act 1981. This strengthens the provisions relating to Sites of Special Scientific Interest contained in the 1949 Act and establishes a comprehensive scheme of protection for those sites. The Act provides for the protection of specified animals and plants and gives effect to the E.C. Directive on Birds.[5] The passage of the Act was

---

[4] Report of the Wildlife Conservation Special Committee: *Conservation of Nature in England and Wales* (1947), Cmd. 7122.
[5] Dir. 79/409/EEC [1979] O.J. L103/1.

controversial. Over 2,000 amendments were proposed, reflecting wide divisions between conservationists and landowners. In introducing the Bill to the House of Commons, the Secretary of State for the Environment accepted that it was a compromise between competing interests.[6]

## The Nature Conservation Bodies

Following the recommendations of the Huxley Committee, a central body known as the Nature Conservancy was established with responsibility for nature conservation matters throughout the U.K. This body was responsible for a number of matters ranging from education and research to the designation and management of National Nature Reserves. In 1973, it became the Nature Conservancy Council,[7] whose main functions were to establish, maintain and manage National Nature Reserves, to provide advice to Ministers, and to advise generally on nature conservation matters.

The Wildlife and Countryside Act 1981 gave the Nature Conservancy Council important new functions, including the power to select sites for designation as SSSIs and the power to enter into agreements with the owners and occupiers of those sites. The Act provided that the Council was to be consulted where decisions with the potential to affect nature conservation were taken, most importantly in relation to certain applications for planning permission.

In what was an extremely controversial move, the Environmental Protection Act 1990 reorganised the institutional framework of nature conservation in England, Scotland and Wales. The Nature Conservancy Council was split into three councils: the Nature Conservancy Council for England, the Nature Conservancy Council for Scotland, and the Countryside Council for Wales.[8] The three councils, which were to perform the same functions as had the Nature Conservancy Council, were to establish a joint committee to be called the Joint Nature Conservation Committee.[9] This was to be concerned with nature conservation in Great Britain as a whole as well as with nature conservation outside Great Britain.

Critics accused the government of trying to dilute the power of a national conservation agency to placate worried landowners. A House of Lords committee[10] rejected the government's view that the U.K. could be split ecologically into three distinct units, stating that the evidence clearly supported the view that the U.K. was a biological continuum and that scientific research into nature conservation was therefore best conducted on a national basis. The Committee, whilst accepting that nature conservation had to be delivered at a local level, also noted that dividing up the administration of nature conservation in the U.K. was contrary to international trends. The government's view, however, prevailed.

The law of nature conservation divides into two main topics: the preservation of species and the preservation of the habitats in which they thrive, each of which is considered below.

---

[6] *Hansard,* H.C., 1980-1981, Vol. 3, col. 525.
[7] Nature Conservancy Act 1973.
[8] EPA 1990, s.128(1).
[9] *ibid.,* s.128(4).
[10] House of Lords Select Committee on Science and Technology (1989–90).

## PRESERVATION OF SPECIES

The main provisions relating to the preservation of species are to be found in the Wildlife and Countryside Act 1981. As has been said, this Act was passed, *inter alia*, to give effect to the Birds Directive,[11] which was adopted by the European Community in response to the deliberate annual killing in southern Europe of migratory birds, and which aimed to protect all species of wild birds in Europe. In introducing the Wildlife and Countryside Bill to Parliament, however, the Secretary of State for the Environment was of the view that little new legislation was necessary to give effect to the provisions of the Birds Directive. It is certainly correct that at the time Britain had in place much greater protection for birds than any other European country.[12] Since 1880, there had been 14 statutes passed for the protection of birds, culminating in the Protection of Birds Act 1954. Indeed, the scheme of the Directive appears to have been influenced by U.K. legislative provisions on birds. General protection is provided for all wild birds with extra protection for some.

The Wildlife and Countryside Act 1981 uses the same methodology to protect plants, birds and other animals. Schedules identify different categories of species and different levels of protection are afforded to each category of species according to their needs. In this way, the legislation retains a simple central structure whilst catering for the needs of many species. It imposes general prohibitions on activities which endanger the species in question, such as killing, taking, selling or attempting to sell it. Breach of these prohibitions is normally a criminal offence, although, under a licensing scheme, the holder of a licence may be granted exemption from the Act's provisions.

The protection given to birds under the Act extends to their eggs. Indeed, birds have traditionally been afforded more legal protection than have other species (which is reflected by the fact that the Royal Society for the Protection of Birds was expected to recruit its millionth member in 1996). Thus it is an offence to kill, injure or take into captivity *any* wild bird, to damage a nest, or to be in possession of any wild bird or egg. It is not, however, an offence under the Act to kill, injure or take any other wild animal *unless* that animal is listed in the relevant schedule to the Act. This schedule affords protection to all bats, reptiles and amphibians, but only to the rarest mammals, insects and fish. The law relating to animals other than birds is more fragmented, with statutes such as the Protection of Badgers Act 1992 and the Conservation of Seals Act 1970 working alongside the Wildlife and Countryside Act 1981.

### Introduction of New Species

It is an offence under the Act to introduce into the wild certain species of animals and plants or any animal not normally found in Great Britain. The aim of this provision is to prevent a recurrence of such problems as those which have faced the red squirrel, which may become extinct in the U.K. because it is unable to compete with the larger and tougher grey squirrel introduced from North America.

[11] Dir. 79/409/EEC [1979] O.J. L103/1.
[12] Haigh, *Manual of Environmental Policy: the E.C. and Britain,* 1992.

## The Natural Habitats Directive

The 1992 European Directive on the Conservation of Natural Habitats and of Wild Fauna and Flora[13] ("The Natural Habitats Directive") extends the wildlife protection provisions of the 1981 Act. The Directive is implemented by the Conservation (Natural Habitats etc.) Regulations 1994.[14] These regulations effectively repeat large sections of the Directive — a form of drafting which doubtless owes itself to uncertainty over the meaning of some phrases in the Directive.

The regulations do not significantly alter the operation of the 1981 Act, but do create some further offences, for example by making it an offence to take or destroy the eggs of any animal that is protected under the Directive. (The 1981 Act extends protection only to the eggs of birds.) The regulations afford protection to plants and animals defined by the Directive as "European protected species". These include bats, the dormouse, the great crested newt, the otter and the large blue butterfly, all of which are already protected under the 1981 Act. Protected plants include the Lady's Slipper and the Fen Orchid, also protected under the Act. Under the regulations, it is an offence deliberately to capture, kill, disturb, take or destroy a protected species, its eggs or breeding site, or its resting place. The use of the word "deliberately", as opposed to "intentionally", which appears in the Wildlife and Countryside Act 1981 is noteworthy. However, the words bear the same dictionary meaning and there have as yet been no cases which suggest any difference of meaning in law.

## PRESERVATION OF HABITATS

Legal regulation is necessary to protect an animal's habitat as well as the animal itself because without an appropriate habitat which provides food and shelter an animal cannot survive. Indeed, the main threat to most species is the loss of its habitat rather than individual persecution.

Habitat protection in the U.K. is based upon provisions in planning law, and upon the designation of areas of land considered worthy of a higher level of protection than is afforded by normal methods of land-use control such as planning, anti-pollution legislation and the law of nuisance. Special statutory protection for habitats is necessary in the light of the inadequacies of the common law, which allow an owner to do as he wishes on his land. This was starkly illustrated by the fate of the RSPB's first nature reserve. The reserve, set up in 1930 at Romney Marshes in Kent, had to be abandoned when drainage activities on neighbouring land, permissible under the common law, destroyed the features that had made it worthy of protection.

### The Protection Afforded by Planning Law

In recent years consideration of the environment has assumed a far greater importance in planning decisions than previously. Nature conservation is a material consideration

[13] Dir. 92/43/EEC [1992] O.J. L206.
[14] S.I. 1994 No. 2716.

in decisions whether to grant planning permission. Moreover, where an SSSI may be affected, the planning authority must consult with the appropriate conservancy council before making a planning decision.[15] Planning Policy Guidance from the Department of the Environment states that where there is a risk of damage to a designated site, the planning authority should consider attaching conditions to planning permission which protect the site.[16] There are significant controls over development in sites designated under European legislation as Special Areas of Conservation (see below).

The protection provided by planning law, however, is limited. Agriculture is currently the biggest threat to habitats, but the use of land for agricultural purposes does not constitute "development" and does not therefore require planning permission.[17] Where planning permission *is* required, the decision whether to grant it is a discretionary one based on a balancing of *all* material factors in the public interest, of which ecological issues are one. Planning Policy Guidance states that local planning authorities should not withhold planning permission if other material considerations are sufficient to override considerations of nature conservation.[18]

The limitations of planning law in protecting ecological interests are illustrated by the decision in *R v. Poole Borough Council, ex p. Beebee.*[19] The council granted itself planning permission to build houses on an SSSI site which supported several rare breeds of snake and lizard. The Nature Conservancy Council had objected to the development proposal on the grounds that the area was of great conservation interest, containing an exceptionally wide range of plants. It had requested that the Secretary of State for the Environment call in the decision to decide it for himself. This was not done. An application for judicial review of the decision failed. The court, whilst holding that the approach of the local planning authority could be faulted in some respects, stated that the overall rôle of the court in an application for judicial review was to ask itself whether there was anything that vitiated the decision-making process. On the facts, it could not answer this question in the affirmative. Following this decision, the Secretary of State took the very unusual step of intervening to revoke the planning permission. The government then issued a consultation paper entitled "Planning Controls over Sites of Special Scientific Interest" which proposed further protection for SSSIs.

## Designation of Sites

There are now a number of different designations of land for nature conservation purposes, with varying objectives and legal effects. Moreover, there are many different methods of control which may be exercised over a designated site. A nature conservancy council may, for example, acquire ownership of the land in question, or may require the owner or occupier, in return for compensation, to undertake or forbear from certain activities with respect to the land to preserve its nature conservation value. A landowner may be required to notify the nature conservation

[15] The Town and Country Planning (General Development Procedure) Order 1995 (S.I. 1995 No. 419).
[16] PPG 9, (DoE October 1994).
[17] TCPA 1990, s.55(2)(e).
[18] PPG 9, above.
[19] [1991] J.P.L. 643.

body if he intends to undertake any activity potentially harmful to the land. In addition, byelaws may be made to control how the land is used. The main forms of site designation, established under the National Parks and Access to Countryside Act 1949 and consolidated by the Wildlife and Countryside Act 1981, are Sites of Special Scientific Interest (SSSIs) and National Nature Reserves (NNRs). Other designations include Local Nature Reserves, Marine Nature Reserves and areas designated under Limestone Pavement Orders.

## Sites of Special Scientific Interest[20]

The designation of SSSIs was introduced by the National Parks and Access to Countryside Act 1949. Under that Act, however, the provisions relating to SSSIs were relatively weak, so that designation of a site as a National Nature Reserve was seen as the better option. The 1981 Act, however, significantly extended the provisions relating to the management of SSSIs and the duties of owners and occupiers, which shifted the focus of attention to SSSIs as a primary means of nature conservation.

In essence, the difference between NNRs and SSSIs is that the former are a means of achieving "total" conservation, whilst the latter achieve only "partial" conservation. A National Nature Reserve is usually purchased by the appropriate nature conservancy council, which then takes complete control of it and actively manages it. In contrast, a Site of Special Scientific Interest continues to be controlled by the owner or occupier, subject to certain restrictions of use to which he may (or may not) agree.

Under the 1981 Act, where the appropriate conservancy council is of the opinion that an area of land, by reason of its flora, fauna or geological or physiographical features,[21] ought to be designated as a Site of Special Scientific Interest, it is under a duty[22] to issue a "notification" with respect to that land, specifying the features which make the land of special interest. The notification will specify any operations that are likely to damage those features.[23] Commonly cited operations include ploughing, reseeding, making changes to the grazing regime of animals on the land, and the application of fertilisers.

Once he has received the notification, the owner or occupier of the land may not carry out any of the specified operations unless he has notified the conservancy council and either the council has consented to the operation, or four months have elapsed from the date on which the conservancy council was notified of the proposed operation. The requirement of prior notification of proposed damaging operations was a major innovation, introduced by the Wildlife and Countryside Act 1981, which strengthened the Nature Conservancy Council's control over SSSIs. Prior to the 1981 Act, operations on vulnerable land which were not caught by planning controls could be carried out by owners and occupiers without any warning being given to the nature conservation authorities.

The Act makes it a criminal offence to carry out a specified operation without reasonable excuse unless the nature conservancy council has been notified and has

[20] WCA 1981, s.15.
[21] *ibid.,* s.28(1).
[22] The council has no discretion whether to notify: *R. v. Nature Conservancy Council, ex p. London Brick Property* [1995] E.L.M. 95.
[23] WCA 1981, s.28(4).

consented to the operation or four months have elapsed after the council has been notified.[24] Only the owner or occupier, however, can be prosecuted for carrying out an operation within the four month period without consent, and this significantly weakens the protection afforded to designated sites. In *Southern Water Authority v. N.C.C.*,[25] the water authority, which owned an SSSI, carried out drainage operations on adjacent land not belonging to them but which was also an SSSI. In the House of Lords, Lord Mustill described these operations as acts of "ecological vandalism". Their Lordships, however, concluded that Southern Water could not be prosecuted. They were not "occupiers" of the land because they were there only temporarily in order to carry out the works. Their Lordships took the view that an "occupier" was someone who had a stable and continuing relationship with the land. Lord Mustill, however, was highly critical of the statutory regime, which he described as "toothless".

It has been noted,[26] however, that the view expressed by Baroness Blatch, in the House of Lords debate on amendments to the Environmental Protection Act 1990, may be considered in interpreting the word "occupier". Rejecting an amendment to clarify the meaning of the word, her Ladyship stated: "It is our firm view that the construction of section 28 of the 1981 Act is such as to include those owners, lessees or occupiers with a lesser interest in the land such as commoners and crofters."

Although Baroness Blatch was speaking in a debate on the 1990 Act, her comments are addressed directly to the construction of the 1981 Act and are clear and unambiguous. If her Ladyship's comments in this context can be seen as "promoting" the 1981 legislation, then, according to the criteria set out in *Pepper v. Hart*,[27] regard may be had to them in judicial proceedings. Moreover, it appears the nature conservancy councils now treat Baroness Blatch's comments as an accurate statement of the law.

Under the 1981 Act, potentially damaging operations are not prohibited altogether. If the four month period after notification expires without the consent of the nature conservancy council being given, the owner or occupier may carry out the operation in question unhindered. The four month period, however, provides the conservancy council with an opportunity to consider the effect of the proposed operation. If the operation is unacceptable, the conservancy council will either negotiate a management agreement for the site or will apply for further legal controls to be imposed by means of a Nature Conservation Order.

## Management Agreements[28]

The principal means of protecting SSSIs is by management agreements. These are voluntary agreements made between the conservancy council and the owner or occupier of the land or of any adjacent land about how the land is to be managed. Under a management agreement, restrictions may be placed on how the land may be

[24] *ibid.*, s.28(7).
[25] [1992] 3 All E.R. 481.
[26] Withrington and Jones, "The Enforcement of Conservation Legislation" in *Agriculture, Conservation and Land Use* (eds Howarth and Rogers) (1992).
[27] [1993] 1 All E.R. 42.
[28] Countryside Act 1968, s.15.

used and substantial compensation may be awarded to the owner or occupier who forbears from the harmful activity in question.

## Nature Conservation Orders — "Super SSSIs"

If a site requires greater protection than can be achieved through designation as an SSSI, a Nature Conservation Order can be made. Where such an order is made, a wider range of people than owners and occupiers may be prosecuted for carrying out damaging operations without consent, and a wider range of sanctions are available. If, once an order has been made, the conservancy council offers a management agreement, damaging operations may be delayed for a period of 12 months. The purpose of this extra time is to enable the conservancy council to decide whether or not to compulsorily to acquire the site. Compulsory purchase, however, is an expensive option and is rarely used; current information suggests that it has been used only once in 10 years.

Sites protected by a Nature Conservation Order are known as "Super SSSIs". These are sites of particular interest and importance and are designated by the Secretary of State for the Environment, in consultation with the relevant nature conservancy council. The Secretary of State may decide to make a Nature Conservation Order where he is of the opinion that enhanced protection of the land is necessary for any of the following reasons[29]:

- To ensure the survival of a particular animal or plant;
- To conserve the flora, fauna, geological or physiological features of the site;
- To give effect to an international obligation.

A Nature Conservation Order comes into effect immediately it is made, for otherwise the owner of the land might destroy the features which make the land of special ecological value.[30] It lasts for nine months unless the Secretary of State decides that it shall continue.[31] After the order is made it must be publicised and, if objections are made to the order, the Secretary of State has a duty to hold a public inquiry. He may then amend or revoke the order in the light of the objections.[32]

It is clear from the decision in *Sweet v. Secretary of State for the Environment and the Nature Conservancy Council*[33] that the Secretary of State has a wide discretion in relation to the extent of the land classified under a Nature Conservation Order and also in relation to the operations he specifies as potentially damaging. The applicant, Mr Sweet, challenged a Nature Conservation Order made with respect to Westhay Moor in Somerset. The order included three fields owned by Mr Sweet and prohibited operations such as grazing, cultivation and burning. Mr Sweet challenged the order on the basis first that his fields were not themselves of national importance, which was the

[29] WCA 1981, s.29(1)(a)–(b).
[30] Sched. 11.
[31] *ibid.*
[32] *ibid.*
[33] (1989) J.E.L. vol. 2, p. 245.

criterion by reference to which the order had been made. Rather, they were designated so that they would be a "buffer area" for the purposes of conserving land of national importance. He also challenged the list of prohibited operations on the basis that "operations" should be construed as entailing physical alteration to the land. Most of the prohibited operations would not do so. The court refused to uphold either challenge, holding that the boundaries of an SSSI may be drawn widely so as to include "buffer areas" and that the concept of potentially damaging "operations" was to be given a broad interpretation.

As is the case in relation to a "normal" SSSI, the owner or occupier of a "Super SSSI" to which a Nature Conservation Order relates must notify the nature conservancy council if he proposes to carry out operations specified as likely to damage or destroy the ecological value of the site. It is an offence to carry out such operations without a reasonable excuse.[34] It appears, however, that statutory authority will provide a reasonable excuse. Thus, in *Ward v. Secretary of State for the Environment*,[35] a Nature Conservation Order prohibited works likely to damage certain vegetation on a bridleway. The highway authority, which was under a duty to maintain the bridleway under section 41 of the Highways Act 1980, needed to carry out certain engineering operations. The court was of the view that the authority could not be guilty of the offence of carrying out a potentially damaging operation.

The greater seriousness of breaching a Nature Conservation Order is reflected in the penalties available. The offence can be tried in the Crown Court as well as in the magistrates' court. The maximum fine in the magistrates' court is £5,000 but in the Crown Court the fine is unlimited.[36] The offence may be committed by persons other than the owner or occupier of the site, such as independent contractors or trespassers. Upon conviction, the court may order the offender to restore the land in question to its former condition.[37] The availability of such an order, however, is often of little use where the ecological value of the site has been irreparably destroyed.

## National Nature Reserves

There are approximately 250 National Nature Reserves in the U.K., compared with approximately 5,500 SSSIs. The provisions relating to National Nature Reserves (NNRs) have remained substantially the same since they were introduced by the National Parks and Access to Countryside Act 1949. Designation of a NNR performs two functions[38]:

- To preserve the flora, fauna or geological or physiographical features of the designated land;
- To ensure that the land is managed so as to provide suitable conditions for the study and research of matters relating to the fauna and flora of Great Britain and the physical conditions in which they live, or for the study of geological and physiographical features of special interest in the area.

[34] WCA 1981, s.29(8).
[35] [1994] E.L.M., vol. 7(4), p. 153.
[36] WCA 1981, s.29(8).
[37] *ibid.*, s.31.
[38] *ibid.*

In contrast with other designations, where importance is attached to the ability of the general public to appreciate the site, the primary objective in designating a NNR is to facilitate the study of nature. That this is so is reflected by the fact that, in order to protect a reserve, byelaws can be made excluding all visitors from the area. The relevant conservancy council may designate a site as a NNR if it is satisfied that this is expedient in the national interest. The designation of a NNR usually requires the agreement of the landowner either to sell or to lease the land to the conservancy council. Although the conservancy council has powers of compulsory purchase, they are rarely used. NNRs, however, are expensive to acquire and to run, with the result that the conservancy councils have tended to designate on an *ad hoc* basis as and when land becomes available, rather than on the basis that a site requires protection.

## Local Nature Reserves

Local authorities may establish nature reserves if they consider it expedient to do so.[39] By this means protection can be given to small sites which are not of national significance but which contain important habitats.

## Marine Nature Reserves

The U.K. has many coastal areas of important nature conservation status. Indeed, of the 30 estuaries in Europe and North Africa that provide a home for approximately 20,000 wintering wading birds, over half are in Britain.[40] The power to designate Marine Nature Reserves was first established in the Wildlife and Countryside Act 1981 in response to pressure from the House of Lords. As their Lordships made clear, international conventions such as the Berne Convention on the Conservation of European Wildlife and Natural Habitats and the Bonn Convention on the Protection of Migratory Species, to which the U.K. is a signatory, and which stimulated the passing of the 1981 Act, clearly placed a duty on the U.K. to protect the marine environment as well as habitats on land. Moreover, 40 other States, ranging from Indonesia to Ireland, already had provisions for marine reserves.[41]

The provisions relating to Marine Nature Reserves are similar to those relating to nature reserves on land. Under the Act, the Secretary of State may order that land and waters should be managed by the relevant conservancy council for the purposes of conserving marine flora or fauna or geological or physiographical features of special interest for research purposes.[42] Byelaws can then be made for the protection of the site.[43]

[39] NPACA 1949, s.21.
[40] *Hansard,* H.L., 1980-1981, Vol. 415, col. 990.
[41] *per* Lord Melchett, *Hansard,* H.L., 1980-1981 Vol. 415, col. 990.
[42] WCA 1981, s.36.
[43] *ibid.,* s.37.

## Limestone Pavements

Limestone pavements possess features of great natural beauty and of botanical and geological interest. They have, however, often been plundered to provide materials for garden rockeries. Their protection under the Wildlife and Countryside Act 1981 serves to prevent this. Where the conservancy council is of the opinion that any land in the countryside which comprises a limestone pavement is of special interest by reason of its flora, fauna, geological, physiographical or physiological features, it may notify the relevant local planning authority.[44] Where it appears either to the Secretary of State or to that authority that the character or appearance of any land in respect of which such notification has been given would be likely to be adversely affected by the removal of the limestone, or by its disturbance in any way, the authority or the Secretary of State may make a Limestone Pavement Order prohibiting the removal or disturbance of the limestone. Contravention of such an order without reasonable excuse is an offence punishable by a fine.

# THE U.K.'S APPROACH TO NATURE CONSERVATION

The approach underlying nature conservation legislation in the U.K. is that it should be based upon co-operation with landowners and upon voluntary agreements made with them. As the Department of the Environment has put it:

> " . . . The best guardians of nature are those who are closest to it. The government remains firmly committed to the voluntary principle; helping and encouraging those who live and work in the countryside, and those who visit it, to conserve our natural heritage. Much of our wildlife and important habitats readily co-exist with man's activities, indeed in many cases rely on it. A long history of sympathetic land management has shaped the character of landscape and habitat on which the diversity of species largely depends. The government wants to encourage management agreements with landholders which encourage positive conservation."

## The Failings of the Regime

The SSSI system forms the cornerstone of the habitat protection regime in the U.K. There has, however, been significant criticism of the system. In particular, it is felt that conservation interests are not sufficiently protected because the most that the regime can achieve is to delay potentially damaging operations for four months. The penalty for carrying out a potentially damaging operation in contravention of a notification is relatively low: it is fixed by statute at £2,500. Moreover, because the regime focuses on preventing particular damage caused by specified operations, it does nothing to protect the ecological value of a site which can be lost through simple neglect, for example

---

[44] *ibid.*, s.34.

where scrub is allowed to invade land. A further anomaly of the system is that management agreements and compensation will usually only be offered when an owner or occupier proposes to carry out damaging operations, so that those who voluntarily conserve their land may receive no recognition or reward. In addition, the system may encourage unscrupulous landowners to obtain compensation from the nature conservancy council by threatening to undertake unnecessary operations. Landowners complain that there is no right of appeal against designation of a site, and that the list of potentially damaging operations contained in the notification can be long and daunting and can involve a considerable administrative burden in terms of notifying the conservancy council of proposed operations. Although Nature Conservation Orders provide a higher level of protection than the SSSI regime, relatively few orders have been made. At the time of writing there were 17 Nature Conservation Orders in England, compared with 3,874 SSSI sites. Only 31 Nature Conservation Orders have been made since the passing of the 1981 Act.

Critics argue that under the present system of voluntary control too much weight is given to the private interests of landowners at the expense of the public interest in nature conservation. As has been noted, the voluntary approach was strongly criticised by Lord Mustill in *Southern Water Authority v. Nature Conservancy Council,*[45] where his Lordship said:

> "It needs only a moment to see that this regime is toothless, for it demands no more from the owner or occupier of an SSSI than a little patience . . . In truth the Act does no more in the great majority of cases than give the council a breathing space within which to apply moral pressure, with a view to persuading the owner or occupier to make a voluntary agreement."

In contrast with the Town and Country Planning regime, there is no equivalent of the enforcement notice or the stop notice. Moreover, the philosophies underlying each system are very different. Whilst both systems place restrictions on the use of land which are considered desirable in the public interest, the planning system (save in a few exceptional cases) offers no compensation to the landowner who finds he cannot develop his land as he wishes. In relation to nature conservation, however, it is only upon payment of compensation that development restrictions may be imposed.

The conservancy councils have suggested the introduction of "management notices" by which owners and occupiers might be required to carry out positive management works. If the person to whom the notice was addressed failed to carry out the specified works, the conservancy council would have the power to enter the land and to carry out the work themselves, charging the costs of so doing to the owner or occupier. An analogous situation already exists for listed buildings under section 54 of the Listed Buildings and Conservation Areas Act 1990, reflecting the idea that heritage can be effectively protected only by positive maintenance and not by protection from destruction and damage alone.

[45] [1992] 3 All E.R. 481.

## PROTECTION OF THE LANDSCAPE

As has been said, protection of the landscape is logically an aspect of nature conservation, yet has traditionally been treated separately by U.K. legislation, so that it has been the responsibility of different bodies. It has been said that the National Parks and Access to the Countryside Act 1949 created the "great divide" between nature and landscape conservation in Britain, which lasted until the restructuring of the agencies in 1991.[46]

The approach of the bodies responsible for landscape conservation has traditionally been very different from that of nature conservation bodies. The nature conservation bodies had a strongly scientific bias and were concerned with the *study* of nature, whilst the Countryside Commission, the agency responsible for protecting the landscape, approached its subject from the point of view of planning and the promotion of recreation, forging close links with local planning authorities. During the 1980s, however, it became clear that these two approaches overlapped because, as we have noted, conserving nature "in the wild" usually involves conserving landscapes and the traditional uses which man has made of them. The anomaly of a divided regime has now been resolved in Wales, where the Countryside Council for Wales is responsible both for nature conservation and landscape conservation matters, and in Scotland, where Scottish Natural Heritage has a similar dual function. The position in England, however, is unchanged, so that the Nature Conservancy Council for England (called "English Nature") has separate responsibilities from the Countryside Commission.

Protection of the landscape is achieved primarily through the planning system and by the designation of National Parks and Areas of Outstanding Natural Beauty.

### Planning and the Landscape

The Countryside Act 1968 imposed on every Minister, government department and public body a duty to have regard to the desirability of conserving the natural beauty and amenity of the countryside in the exercise of their functions relating to land. To this end, unitary development plans, structure plans and local plans are required to include policies in relation to these matters.[47] The effectiveness of landscape control through planning, however, is limited, principally because (with very few exceptions) the use of land for the purposes of agriculture or forestry does not constitute "development" and is therefore exempt from the need for planning permission.[48] These uses, however, are the very uses most likely to cause undesirable changes in the landscape.

In relation to those agricultural and forestry activities which do constitute development, but for which planning permission is granted in the General Development Order,[49] the order provides that 28 days' notification must be given to the planning

[46] Adams, "Places for Nature Protected Areas" in *British Nature Conservation in Progress* (eds Goldsmith and Warren) (1993).
[47] TCPA 1990, ss.12 and 31.
[48] *ibid.*, s.55.
[49] Town and Country Planning (General Permitted Development) Order 1995 (S.I. 1995 No. 418).

authority before such developments are commenced. This enables the authority to impose planning conditions relating to the siting and external appearance of these developments in the light of their impact on the surrounding landscape. A local planning authority may make a management agreement for land in the countryside in order to conserve or enhance its natural beauty and amenity.[50]

## Designated Sites

### National Parks

The National Parks and Access to Countryside Act 1949 provided for the designation of National Parks and Areas of Outstanding Natural Beauty. These were originally designated by the National Parks Commission, but are now designated by the Countryside Commission. The Countryside Commission makes a proposal of designation to the Secretary of State for the Environment which, after extensive publicity requirements have been met and a public inquiry held, he may confirm.

The 1949 Act set out two broad objectives for the designation of National Parks, namely the preservation and enhancement of the natural beauty of the area, and the promotion of public enjoyment of the area.[51]

The Environment Act 1995 amends these objectives so that the cultural heritage of the area may also be considered.[52] Accordingly, a National Park may now be designated for two reasons:

(a) To conserve and enhance the natural beauty, wildlife and cultural heritage of the area;

(b) To promote opportunities for the understanding and enjoyment of the special qualities of those areas by the public.

There is, of course, a potential for conflict between these two objectives, the second of which relates to the pursuit of leisure activities, especially in the light of modern forms of outdoor leisure activity such as war games, bungee-jumping and the use of off-road vehicles and microlight aircraft. These activities can often place considerable pressure on a fragile environment. Therefore, the Environment Act 1995 provides that where there is a conflict between the two purposes, greater weight should be attached to the former than to the latter.[53] Jurisdiction over development in National Parks is currently exercised by a national park authority which, in conjunction with the local planning authority, must exercise its functions having regard to the objectives set out above, although the Environment Act 1995 makes it possible for a national park authority to acquire exclusive jurisdiction over most planning matters.

[50] WCA 1981, s.39.
[51] NPACA 1949, s.5(2).
[52] EA 1995, s.61.
[53] NPACA 1949, s.11A (inserted by EA 1995, s.62).

## Areas of Outstanding Natural Beauty

The 1949 Act also makes provision for the designation of Areas of Outstanding Natural Beauty.[54] These are in very many respects similar to National Parks, although they may be designated only for the purposes of conserving the beauty of an area and not to promote public recreation. Jurisdiction over planning matters within these areas is retained by the local planning authority, although the authority must consult with the Countryside Commission in the making of development plans.

# E.C. Nature Conservation Law

The rationale for its policy on protecting flora and fauna has been identified by the E.C. in the following terms:

> "Wild fauna and flora are part of mankind's common heritage. The steady decline in the number of wild species is not only in itself an impoverishment of our natural heritage, but it lessens the diversity of non-renewable genetic resources whilst at the same time affecting the ecological balance with various degrees of severity."[55]

The main effect of European legislation has been to add another layer of site designations to those provided for in U.K. law. The Birds Directive[56] and the Habitats Directive[57] constitute the main legislative activity of the European Community on nature conservation.

The Birds Directive was adopted because of concern over the slaughter of birds for sport in certain southern European Member States and requires the designation of Special Protection Areas as "safe havens" for birds. The Natural Habitats Directive, adopted because of widespread concern about the loss and destruction of habitats, requires the designation of areas as Special Areas of Conservation. The provisions of these Directives must, of course, be given effect to in U.K. law, but it remains questionable whether this has been fully achieved.

## Special Protection Areas

The Birds Directive aims to stem the decline in population which is occurring in a large number of species of wild birds in Europe. It is concerned with the conservation of all species of wild birds in the European territory of the Member States to which the Treaty applies. It covers the protection, management and control of these species and lays down rules for their exploitation.

---

[54] NPACA 1949, s.87.
[55] Resolution of the Council and of the Representatives of the Governments of the Member States meeting within the Council of May 17, 1977, on the continuation and implementation of European Community policy and action on the environment [1977] O.J. C139/26.
[56] Dir. 79/409/EEC [1979] O.J. L103/1.
[57] Dir. 92/43/EEC [1992] O.J. L206.

Under the Directive, Member States must maintain the population of all birds naturally occurring in their territory. Certain species of bird, however, are singled out for particular protection. The schedule to the Directive lists 170 bird species which are to be the subject of special conservation measures because they are either in danger of extinction, vulnerable to changes in habitat, considered rare because of their small populations, or because they occur only in certain areas. In relation to these species, Member States are required to find the most suitable territories in number and size for the birds in question and to designate them as Special Protection Areas. Once an area has been so designated, Member States must take appropriate steps to avoid pollution, deterioration or disturbance of the habitats in question.

The Birds Directive has been implemented in the U.K. by the Wildlife and Countryside Act 1981 and by the designation as Special Protection Areas of sites which are already protected under U.K. law as SSSIs, NNRs, or as "Super SSSIs". However, the designation of sites that are already protected under U.K. law may not be sufficient to comply with the requirements of the Directive. For example, Article 3 of the Directive refers to the upkeep and maintenance of habitats, suggesting the imposition of positive obligations to preserve habitats. The existing system, with its focus on preventing particular damage, does not require positive maintenance. Moreover, where a Special Protection Area is an SSSI, it is still lawful for damaging operations to take place if there has been an express grant of planning permission.[58]

## Special Areas of Conservation

The Habitats Directive is the E.C.'s response to the continuing deterioration of natural habitats, and represents a significant advance in Community policy on nature conservation because it covers both animals and plants. Until recently protection of flora was not a prominent feature of E.C. environmental policy.

Under the scheme of the Directive habitats that are rare or are in danger of disappearing, and those which are outstanding examples of their type, are to be designated as Special Areas of Conservation. Examples of habitat types listed in the Directive include estuaries, reefs, dry heaths and lowland hay meadows. Habitats which are found mainly only on European territory, and which are in danger of disappearing, are given a higher level of protection on the basis that the European Community has a particular responsibility to preserve them. These are referred to as "priority habitats". Examples include limestone pavements and Caledonian pine forests.

Once a site has been designated as requiring protection, Member States are under a duty to avoid the deterioration of the site and disturbance of the species within it, and any plan or project which is likely to affect the site significantly must be assessed to determine whether it will cause ecological damage. A project which will cause such damage will be permitted only if there are overriding grounds of public interest to justify the project's proceeding. The obligations of Member States are phrased in wide terms and the precise nature of the duties which arise under the Directive are not yet apparent because the sites in question have not yet been designated.

Special Areas of Conservation will form part of a network of sites across Europe, to be known as "Natura 2000", which will include Special Protection Areas under the

[58] WCA 1981, s.28(8).

Birds Directive. The Habitats Directive sets out a timetable and methodology for establishing Special Areas of Conservation. In 1995 the government sent to the European Commission a preliminary list of appropriate sites. The Commission is in the process of establishing a draft list of sites of Community importance, drawn from the lists provided by Member States, which is to be completed by June 1998.

## Implementation of the Habitats Directive

The United Kingdom gave effect to its obligations under the Directive by the Conservation (Natural Habitats) Regulations 1994,[59] which came into force on October 30, 1994. The government has taken the view that the existing system of nature conservation provides a sound basis for implementation of the Directive and that all that is required is a number of minor additional measures to fill certain gaps in existing legislation. To this end, the Regulations impose a duty on Ministers and nature conservation bodies to exercise their functions under existing legislation in such a way as to comply with the requirements of the Directive. The government has made it clear that any sites designated as Special Areas of Conservation will already be Sites of Special Scientific Interest.

The Regulations extend the current practice of specifying potentially damaging operations to sites designated under the Habitats Directive and introduce the concept of a Special Nature Conservation Order. Under such an order, potentially damaging operations may be prohibited indefinitely in the absence of consent by the relevant nature conservancy council unless the operation is carried out in accordance with a management agreement. Because of the indefinite effect of a Special Nature Conservation Order, the Regulations introduce an appeal procedure. Thus, if the conservancy council refuses consent for an operation, the landowner may appeal to the Secretary of State, who may only consent to an operation if there are "imperative reasons of overriding pubic interest" for allowing the operation to proceed. Under the Regulations, where the site in question is a "priority site", these reasons must relate to public health or safety or beneficial consequences of primary importance to the environment.

The regulations introduce significant new controls over development in Special Areas of Conservation, integrating nature conservation issues into the planning system in three ways:

(1) Local authorities are required to assess all new planning proposals to determine whether they will have a significant impact on the ecology of a designated site. Planning permission will only be granted for ecologically damaging development if there are "imperative reasons of overriding public interest" for allowing the development to proceed. In the case of ordinary sites these reasons may include social and economic ones but in the case of priority sites only public health and safety or beneficial environmental consequences of primary importance may be considered;

(2) Local authorities are required to undertake a review of planning permission already granted and, where development has not yet been carried out in

[59] S.I. 1994 No. 2716.

accordance with those permissions, to modify or revoke them where appropriate;

(3) The regulations restrict existing permitted development rights in respect of designated sites by declaring that any deemed planning permission is invalid if it significantly affects a designated site. This effectively extinguishes certain permitted development rights in relation to the site.

These provisions, which apply only to Special Areas of Conservation, give those sites a far greater level of protection than is afforded to SSSIs.

It is difficult to assess whether the U.K. has successfully implemented the Directive because the approach of the Directive is to specify a particular level of protection and leave Member States to decide how best to achieve this level. The level of protection required by the Directive is left to be determined by interpretation of such vague phrases as "favourable conservation status", "adversely affecting the integrity of the site" and "overriding grounds of public interest". These broad concepts, however, provide little guidance as to the precise level of protection needed to comply with the Directive. In the circumstances, it is perhaps not surprising that the regulations tend to adopt the language of the Directive *verbatim* rather than risk defining its requirements in precise terms.


## THE E.C.'S APPROACH TO NATURE CONSERVATION

Case law from the European Court of Justice appears to indicate that the U.K.'s approach to the designation of sites may, by E.C. standards, be inadequate. The primary issue for consideration by the ECJ has been the scope of the discretion exercised by Member States when designating and protecting sites. In particular, the question has arisen whether a Member State can take into account economic considerations, such as the effects of designation on local jobs, when deciding upon action with respect to a site. Although the case law has arisen under the Birds Directive, it is suggested that the same principles would apply to Special Areas of Conservation designated under the Habitats Directive.

The issue first arose when a Member State proposed to reduce a Special Protection Area designated under the Birds Directive. In *Commission v. Germany*,[60] the ECJ held that economic and recreational reasons were not legitimate reasons for a Member State to reduce a Special Protection Area. This case having set a high standard of protection for designated sites, the focus of attention has now shifted to the classification of sites. If the obligations on Member States with respect to designated sites are onerous, there will inevitably be a reluctance to designate sites and attempts to avoid doing so. According to a spokesman for the Royal Society for the Protection of Birds, this has been especially true in the U.K. The RSPB has referred to: "a frustrating degree of secrecy surrounding the process of devising criteria for site selection."

[60] Case C–57/89 [1991] I E.C.R. 883.

The key question with respect to the classification of Special Protection Areas under the Birds Directive has been whether, once a site satisfies certain ornithological criteria, it should be designated automatically, or whether economic considerations may be taken into account at the designation stage. The ECJ has held Spain to be in breach of the Birds Directive by failing to designate an important wetland area, the Santona Marshes, as a Special Protection Area and has made it clear that designation should be on ornithological grounds alone.[61]

The philosophy of protection reflected by these decisions runs directly contrary to the approach adopted by the United Kingdom. The U.K.'s approach was summarised in evidence given by the Department of the Environment to a House of Lords select committee:

> "The British government has attached considerable importance to the need to strike a balance. That is at the cornerstone of our own method of site protection. Due consideration and weighing of factors cannot . . . imply any preconception of which way the balance must fall . . . That was one of the problems of the draft Directive. It was quite clear from the wording that in Special Protection Areas the interest of nature conservation would always override any other consideration. That . . . would cause considerable difficulty not just in this country but to most other Member States."[62]

The question of the relevance of economic considerations in designating a site arose recently in *R. v. Secretary of State for the Environment, ex p. Royal Society for the Protection of Birds.*[63] The case concerned a decision by the Secretary of State for the Environment to exclude an area known as Lappel Bank, in the Medway Estuary and Marshes, from land to be designated as a Special Protection Area. The Medway Estuary is a valuable ornithological habitat immediately adjoined by Lappel Bank. It is a wetland of international importance for a substantial number of wildfowl and water species, in particular avocets and little terns. The port of Sheerness, however, which is the fifth largest in the U.K. in terms of freight handling, also adjoins Lappel Bank. In order to remain competitive, the port must expand, and this can be done only by reclamation of Lappel Bank.

In deciding to exclude Lappel Bank from the Special Protection Area, the Secretary of State, whilst recognising the ecological importance of Lappel Bank, took the view that this was outweighed by economic and development considerations. His decision was judicially reviewed by the RSPB, which argued that at the designation stage only ornithological considerations were relevant. The matter was eventually referred to the European Court of Justice,[64] which held that, under the Birds Directive, a Member State was not authorised to take account of economic considerations when defining the boundaries of a Special Protection Area. In the light of this finding, it appears that the U.K. is in direct conflict with the European Community in its use of criteria for the designation of sites.

---

[61] *Commission v. Spain* Case C–355/90 [1993] I ECR 4221.
[62] House of Lords Select Committee on the European Communities (session 1988–1989), Fifteenth Report: *Habitat and Species Protection* (1989).
[63] *The Times*, August 2, 1996.
[64] Case C–44/95.

# PROTECTION OF THE WIDER COUNTRYSIDE

It is increasingly being recognised that a coherent scheme of nature conservation must afford protection to areas of countryside which are wider than designated sites. Many species are dependent upon components of the environment which are found outside designated sites, and species which thrive over wide areas, such as the golden eagle, clearly cannot be protected solely by the designation of sites unless those sites are impractically large.

To this end, there are a number of provisions relating to protection of the wider countryside. For example, as has been mentioned, a local planning authority may, for the purpose of conserving or enhancing the natural beauty or amenity of any countryside in its area, or to promote its enjoyment by the public, enter into a management agreement with any person who has an interest in land either for a limited or unlimited term.[65] Such an agreement may restrict, for example, the method of cultivation of the land, or may impose obligations to carry out positive works. In return, the affected party may receive a grant from the Countryside Commission. A local authority, however, has no power to compel a person to enter into a management agreement, so that conservation of the wider countryside in this way depends on the co-operation of its human inhabitants.

The Habitats Directive also contains a provision which relates to the wider countryside. Outside the Special Areas of Conservation, Member States are under a duty to endeavour in their land-use planning and development policies to encourage the management of features of the landscape which are of major importance for wild fauna and flora. This general duty, however, adds little to the regime which is already in place and has been described by the RSPB as a "pale vestige" of the stronger measures for which they had hoped.

Many landscapes and habitats in the U.K. have been shaped by agricultural practices and are now threatened by economic pressure on farmers to adopt more efficient but less environmentally sensitive production methods. Competition between farmers has resulted in an excess supply of certain agricultural produce, often to the detriment of the environment.

E.C. Regulation 797/85 (now repealed) on Improving the Efficiency of Agricultural Structures, which was given effect to by the Agriculture Act 1986, aimed to reduce agricultural overproduction by environmentally harmful means and provided for the designation of Environmentally Sensitive Areas. In these areas, farmers were encouraged to enter into voluntary agreements under which, in return for compensation paid by the Ministry of Agriculture, Fisheries and Food, they agreed to follow agricultural practices which are compatible with conserving landscape and wildlife. These provisions were closely related to the general operation of the E.C.'s Common Agricultural Policy.

In 1992, the Policy underwent considerable reform and it became a precondition for the receipt of a number of E.C. agricultural subsidies that producers should undertake not to follow environmentally damaging practices (allowing for the repeal of Regulation 797/85). The implementation of Agri-Environment Regulation 2078/92[66] in the

---

[65] WCA 1981, s.39.
[66] Regulation on agricultural production methods compatible with the requirements of the protection of the environment and maintenance of the countryside [1992] O.J. L215.

U.K. has involved the creation of a Habitat Improvement Scheme under which, specifically for environmental purposes, farmers may enter into agreements whereby, in return for payment, they undertake not to farm certain land.

Outside the agri-environment programme, the government has been developing policies to ensure that designated sites are not isolated. A range of measures have been introduced such as the Woodland Grant Scheme. Under this scheme the Forestry Commission provides an income for anyone planting trees until the trees have grown sufficiently to yield an income.

# INTERNATIONAL NATURE CONSERVATION

The diversity of species is being diminished on an international scale by an expanding human population requiring greater space in which to live and making greater use of environmental resources, particularly by the exploitation of species. Around 70 per cent of the world's fish stocks, for example, are being harvested at levels near or beyond sustainability. It has been estimated that the destruction of the tropical rainforests in South America is causing the extinction of two species every hour.[67] In response, international policy on conserving "the variety of life in all its forms" (biological diversity) has been embraced in a number of bilateral, regional and global conventions. In its approach to conserving biological diversity (or "biodiversity"), international law has only recently moved away from the idea of protecting individual species and habitats towards a more comprehensive and global approach.

## Protection of Individual Habitats and Species

The Convention on Wetlands of International Importance[68] (the Ramsar Convention) aims to protect wetlands, which accommodate an abundant source of animal and plant life. Signatory States are required to designate and monitor certain areas of marsh, fen or peat land. (The Medway Estuary — the subject of the Lappel Bank decision discussed above — is listed as a wetland of international importance.)

The 1976 Convention on the Conservation of Migratory Species of Wild Animals (the Bonn Convention) provides a framework for States to co-operate to preserve migratory species. Those migratory species to be protected are listed in appendices to the convention, which may be amended to take account of other species as they become in need of protection.

## Widening the Net of Protection

The E.C.'s Habitats Directive (E.C. law forms part of international law) reflects a move towards a more comprehensive approach to nature conservation by extending

---

[67] Schoon, "Going, Going Gone: The Story of Britain's Vanishing Natural History", (*Bookman Projects* 1996).
[68] February 2, 1971, Ramsar, 11 I.L.M. 963 (1972).

protection to *all* species and habitats within the E.C. But the problem with conserving living creatures, of course, is that they do not often confine themselves within man-made boundaries. Therefore region-based or habitat-based protection schemes can be of only limited effectiveness. A global protection scheme is needed.

The 1973 Convention on International Trade in Endangered Species of Wild Fauna and Flora (CITES)[69] exhorts governments to regulate, and in some cases prohibit, trade in species threatened by extinction. The Convention, to which a large number of States are party, has established a permit system to regulate international trade in endangered species.

## The Convention on Biological Diversity[70]

The most sophisticated and ambitious of the nature conservation treaties is the Convention on Biological Diversity. It was signed in Rio de Janeiro by representatives of 150 States in June 1992 and came into force on December 29, 1993. Its principal objectives are the conservation of biodiversity and the sustainable use of species. The Convention defines biodiversity as "the variety of life in all its forms" and recognises that the concept divides into three areas, namely the diversity of ecosystems, the diversity of species, and genetic diversity within each of those species.

Within the same species, each individual animal has unique genetic characteristics which are different from those of every other animal within that species. Protection of genetic diversity within individual species is necessary in order for species to adapt to new conditions and to develop resilience to disease. Some animals, because of their genetic make-up, will be resistant to diseases or changes in their environment which prove fatal to others of the same species. It follows, then, that the greater the number of individual animals which are conserved within a species, the greater are that species' chances of survival. It also follows that conservation of species in very small numbers, such as is occurring with pandas, for example, cannot necessarily ensure their survival.

Biological diversity is also important because it provides the raw material for the scientific application of biological organisms for the benefit of agriculture and medicine, known as "biotechnology". Little known plant species, such as the rosy periwinkle, which is used in treating some forms of cancer, have often proved invaluable in combatting disease. In agriculture, often the only way effectively to ensure that crops are resilient to blight is by cross-breeding them with naturally resistant wild strains. The consequences associated with allowing the pool of species from which biotechnology may draw its material to diminish, therefore, are incalculable and potentially enormous.

There is a tendency for developed countries to rely on the availability of bio-technological resources of Third World countries without compensating those countries for providing what, in effect, amounts to a valuable service. Unsurprisingly, it is the wealthy and industrialised countries of the world which develop, and largely benefit from, new medicines and agricultural practices. Many of these are protected by patents, so that the developing world cannot afford to exploit them even though in

---

[69] March 3, 1973, Washington, 12 I.L.M. 1085.
[70] June 5, 1992, Rio de Janeiro, 31 I.L.M. 822 (1992).

many cases it has provided the materials which have made the technology possible. At the Rio Conference, this parasitic approach was identified by Third World delegates, who sought a guarantee that their countries would be compensated for any commercially useful discoveries attributable to the conservation of biological diversity within their borders. The developed States, however, refused to agree to this.

The most important obligations deriving from the Convention on Biological Diversity are set out in Article 6, which provides that each contracting State, "in accordance with its particular conditions and capabilities", should:

(a)  Develop national strategies, plans or programmes for the conservation and sustainable use of biodiversity, or adapt existing strategies, and

(b)  Integrate, as far as is possible and appropriate, the conservation and sustainable use of biodiversity into relevant plans and programmes.

The wording of the Convention is heavily qualified throughout with such phrases as "as far as possible" and "where appropriate". It is therefore questionable whether, in real terms, the contracting States have committed themselves to substantial action. As yet, it remains unclear whether the Convention is of merely symbolic value or is to provide a framework for real change.

# INDEX